Skyblazers

Skyblazers

JACK PARSONS ED FORMAN

Gerard Denza

authorHOUSE®

AuthorHouse™
1663 Liberty Drive
Bloomington, IN 47403
www.authorhouse.com
Phone: 1 (800) 839-8640

Published by AuthorHouse 05/22/2015

ISBN: 978-1-5049-1305-8 (sc)
ISBN: 978-1-5049-1304-1 (e)

Library of Congress Control Number: 2015908041

Print information available on the last page.

TABLE OF CONTENTS:

PREFACE

This collection of plays is the sum total of my play writing efforts to date; five of which have been performed Off-Off Broadway. I've chosen for this edition the title of SKYBLAZERS in commemoration of Jack Parsons 100th birthday on Oct. 2, 2014. It was a little over 30 years ago when I first learned of Jack Parsons, but it wasn't until recently that I did research into his life and achievements. I was impressed by Jack Parsons and his best friend, Ed Forman. In part, I dedicate this book to their memory and legacy. I also dedicate this book to my business partner and best friend, Phil Strumolo, who came up with the title of SKYBLAZERS. And, a special thanks to Nova, Donovan, Rags, Giacomo, Merlin, Tristan, Parkway, Whiskey, Samuel "Sammie" Rogers, Wilkie, and Cinnamon.

Gerard Denza

May 2015

INTRODUCTION

ICARUS is a man searching for his destiny amidst two antagonists who want his mind and his body. MAHLER: The Man Who Was Never Born tells of a teenage boy who sells his soul for, literally, nothing. THE DYING GOD: A Vampire's Tale is about a cynical vampire who wants to see the world die about his as he remains its undying witness. In SHADOWS BEHIND THE FOOTLIGHTS, an opera singer is targeted for murder; but, he's a lot harder to kill that his would-be murderer had bargained for. THE HOUSEDRESS is about a killer trying to do in authoress, Sybil Schmidlap-Schwab. In EDMUND: The Likely, an amateur bodybuilder tries to stop terrorists from detonating an atomic bomb over New York City. MOON STRIKE is an occult mystery, pre-dating EDMUND: The Likely. SKYBLAZERS is the fictional biography of Jack Parsons and Ed Forman, the pioneers of modern day rocketry. LEFT, RIGHT, and NOWHERE is a science fiction tale about the end and the beginning of the universe. It was also the first version of ICARUS. VESTA and her friends are terrorized by a murderous alien. PRISON BOYS: Patrick and Marco tells of two young men in prison and how one of them got there. ELLIPSIS is about a magus who is trying to change the course of history for herself. And, in I, SYBIL SCHMIDLAP-SCHWAB, authoress, Sybil, is mistaken for Queen Nefertiti. DEATHDREAMER CAFÉ is a human drama of seven desperate people in search of a reason to live. TWO VAMPIRES is a conversation between a vampire and his physician.

Gerard Denza
May 2015

ICARUS

A Play in Two Acts

by

Gerard Denza

Copyright 2002

ICARUS was presented at the Pantheon Theatre in New York City on October. 2, 2002 with the following cast:

ICARUS	Vincent LoRusso
THE PRIEST	Phil Strumolo
THE PRIESTESS	Nora Drummond

ICARUS was revived at the Producer's Club in New York City on November 4, 2008 with the following cast:

ICARUS	Thane Floreth
THE PRIEST	Phil Strumolo
THE PRIESTESS	Susan Charette

Set by Phil Strumolo.
Directed by Gerard Denza.

PLACE
A dimension between lives.

TIME
It could be a moment just prior to dawn or a moment toward the infinity of night.

SCENES

Prologue

Act One
A place between Heaven and Earth.

Act Two
A place between Heaven and Earth.

CHARACTERS

ICARUS, a confused demi-god.
THE PRIEST, an immortal cynic.
THE PRIESTESS, a manipulator.

PROLOGUE

ICARUS enters center stage. He is wearing a white toga and on his back are golden wings. His arms are outstretched as he looks upward. For a moment, he is blinded by the light of the sun. He staggers and loses control of his flight through the sky. A strong wind can be heard in the background as ICARUS plummets towards the earth. He cries out.

ACT ONE

Drawn down stage left is a luminescent line that acts as a barrier separating ICARUS from THE PRIEST who is upon his throne. Two columns are placed on either side of the stage. At center stage, an ancient sun-dial stands ready to be rotated and next to this are ICARUS' melted wings.

ICARUS: It is once again occurring. (*Staggering to his feet and placing his hand to his chest.*) Dearest gods in the heavens, have pity on your son who calls out to you. Hear one who once stood in your presence in the great Hall of Truth and Light. Hear the disobedient son! (*Facing the audience.*) Why have I come to be in this forsaken place? Have I fallen into the vestibule of the lower world where there lies only the feeble hope and malice of faith and the evils of forgiveness? The light? Where has it gone? How long have I been here and toward what end does it signify? I need to take possession of my soul once more to form my being as a man, as a god, as a soul of creation…as an Atlas of the gods.

THE PRIEST (*sitting upon a throne with an air of power ready to be unleashed*): Oh, loosen up. There is no past, Greek. I think you lie to yourself. Liar. And, Fool. Maybe, you're caught in a segment of time. What do you say to that? Turn around. Look at me. That's a good boy. But, the truth has many variations and perspectives or so I'm told. Rather convenient that. One could call it pragmatism, as I believe Pontius Pilate once did;

and, we all know where that landed his name in the history books.

ICARUS: You are the stillness and the "eye" of the storm that greets the vessel with a treacherous calm. The flash of white lightning that blinds a man and destroys him…shatters him upon the rocks until the waves come to drag his lifeless body into its depths forever.

THE PRIEST: If you insist, Tarzan. Who am I to refute such a poetically inarticulate description?

ICARUS: This is your appearance: the storm that a warrior dreads. Or are you the uncertainty that distorts a man's perception of existence?

THE PRIEST (*leaning forward*): Well…

ICARUS (*moving toward THE PRIEST, he is stopped by an invisible barrier*): You are imprisoned in a temple. It is your refuge, but from whom do you cower?

THE PRIEST: It's your limited image of me, Greek. It's your rather distorted view of reality -- my reality, at any rate. I'll draw it out for you. You must understand that I rather like subjectivism: it's quite convenient when one happens to have need of it, for one can break all the rules and still remain in the game. You take yourself and life far too seriously. Learn to be a bit more practical; it will help. Trust me.

ICARUS (*backing away from the invisible barrier*): You are the unspoken agony of every man's fear that pierces his soul.

THE PRIEST: And, I'm always there and here. Happy to meet the thorn in your side, face-to-face? Careful, it may turn into a crown of thorns.

ICARUS: You speak as a priest of evil who rejoices in the sufferings of another man. And, yet, you are placed upon a throne.

THE PRIEST: Do you like that? I am the priest. Why don't I come over to you and, then, we can greet each other like the good friends we're not? We should be properly introduced. I insist upon observing the civilities. It helps maintain the façade.

ICARUS: If that is your wish.

THE PRIEST: You're not afraid of your old friend, are you? I mean where does it get you to be afraid?

ICARUS (*rushing toward the invisible barrier and slamming his fist upon it*): Here with you in this forsaken place! Scoundrel! By the gods, I have sinned! There is darkness all about me and, yet, I see the glimmer of light from the stars and constellations. Is there no moon on such a night as this?

THE PRIEST: None that I've noticed. Fearless man. Fearful man. Want to be good enemies?

ICARUS: I choose my enemies and defeat them.

THE PRIEST (*turning around*): I beg your pardon? We have another uninvited guest in our midst. (*THE PRIESTESS makes her entrance from center stage.*)

THE PRIESTESS: I see that you two gentlemen have met. Icarus, I welcome you to this place of anticipation...yes...a term that will do for now as a description for what is yet to unfold.

ICARUS (*staring incredulously*): I do not know you. Tell me who you are that I may address you properly.

THE PRIESTESS (*approaching ICARUS and placing her hand gently upon his chest*): Perhaps, it was I who attempted to break your fall? Your plummet from the sky was a dreadful thing to witness. In that moment, I was helpless!

ICARUS: Tell me how such a thing is possible?

THE PRIESTESS: It simply occurred. I would now enjoy this moment that will be over so quickly. Forgive me my indulgence. You're scarred. (*Seductively, she touches ICARUS' chest.*)

THE PRIEST (*jumping up from his throne*): Oh, hi kids! Remember me? Nobody's asked me my name. How insulting and ill-mannered. I'm offended. Truly.

THE PRIESTESS (*laughing and tossing her head back in genuine delight*): My intention wasn't to offend. However, neither do I ask your forgiveness: a worthless thing that would be.

ICARUS (*looking past THE PRIESTESS who is standing between him and THE PRIEST*): Tell me your name.

THE PRIEST: I'm not telling.

ICARUS: Foul mouth that seeks to mock. Speak your name so that I may remember it.

THE PRIEST (*placing his hand to his chin*): Ha! He knows more than he lets on, this one. He's a wit -- and, not so dim, either. He may actually have a few possibilities in him.

THE PRIESTESS: Always the inscrutable one. Some things simply never change with the passage of time, do they? When will you take that lovely and fatal step over the precipice? Plunge yourself into the heroism of a risk -- a challenge, if you would? Do you dare?

THE PRIEST: What about yourself, my dear? Eh? And, some of us do get older and a bit used over the course of time.

THE PRIESTESS (*smiling sweetly*): That may very well be true. How old are you? Or is that far too direct a question for your vanity to count the untold centuries? Does an egotist have his vanity? I dare say that he does and conceit, as well; but, others are required for the unfair comparison. Vanity and conceit aren't able to withstand the test of solitude very well for they crave the comparative standard. Well? Nothing to say for yourself?

THE PRIEST: Harlot!

THE PRIESTESS (*speaking in soft and mocking tones*): Poor Priest, always needful of jest; how truly pitiful for you. Well, one imagines that that would be the next best thing in lieu of the actual experience. It's what they tell me, but quite frankly, it rings rather hollow.

THE PRIEST: You should know, my dear. You should know.

THE PRIESTESS (*moving toward ICARUS*): Icarus, why don't you leave us? Why do you linger in this place? Save yourself and don't glance back.

ICARUS (*gesturing helplessly*): I do not know where I am or how I came to be here. This place contains a stillness that I find almost alluring. It is as if it beckons me to stay...to place myself at its mercy.

THE PRIESTESS: Pause for a moment and listen to that stillness. Hear it and envelope it...envelope your soul with the smooth velvet of night's caress. Don't fear it; and if it's fear that grips you, don't deny it, but conquer it!

THE PRIEST (*leaning on his throne*): Don't let her flatter you, Greek. She does that quite well and convincingly. It's an acquired habit of her profession.

ICARUS (*looking at THE PRIESTESS*): I am a man who does not resist the sweet words of a beautiful woman.

THE PRIEST: Oh? What else don't you mind?

THE PRIESTESS (*gesturing toward upstage-center at a glowing white light*): Attempt to capture it, Icarus. It belongs to you. Lay claim to your property.

ICARUS: I do not know what it is that you speak of.

THE PRIEST: You've been hanging around me too long. Simply tell the man what you want him to do.

THE PRIESTESS: That's truly a bruising insult. You seem to intimate that you exert a certain amount of influence here. You're mistaken of that, I can assure you.

THE PRIEST: To hell with you. And, I don't mean anything by it. It's just my discreet and wicked way.

THE PRIESTESS (*unaffected by the vulgarity and left-handed honesty*): I'm aware of your wicked ways. Your so-called discretion camouflages your cunning. It's an effective lure that you've developed. And, that's not a compliment.

ICARUS: Tell me what it is that belongs to me. I must know.

THE PRIESTESS: Beyond the furthest pillar and across the chasm...it's said that that's where the cornerstone of creation begins.

ICARUS (*laughing*): No! It is but a spectre of light. One cannot grasp what does not possess substance. It cannot be done.

THE PRIEST: He does have a sense of humor. Still want to be friends? Or do you fancy a look at a forbidden cornerstone?

ICARUS: What is it that is forbidden?

THE PRIESTESS (*annoyed at the diversion*): Why do you hesitate by listening to him? Won't you behold, once again, the light of the sun? The sun that you so recklessly sought to caress?

THE PRIEST: Not if he's smart. Don't let her trick you, boy. Careful with your intentions, they can kill you, even the good ones. Don't get too carried away with the game playing, my dear. Remember, it is game playing…all of it.

ICARUS: My games are war games of life and death and the test of a man's mettle.

THE PRIESTESS: I admired your bravery when you undertook your flight with your father, Daedalus, in a quest for freedom. However, your reason failed you when you placed a momentary whim above the value of life. Don't repeat that mistake.

ICARUS: Tell me your meaning! I beg thee!

THE PRIEST (*looking straight ahead*): The dear boy is confused! I knew it. And, how satisfying.

THE PRIESTESS: Icarus, lay claim to the light beyond. Find it and add it to your arsenal and tools of cognition. It's a weapon of light and perception and, as such, it's priceless!

THE PRIEST: Let's party!

THE PRIESTESS: Are all things under Heaven nothing more that an amusement for you? Aren't you able to at least make a pretense toward sobriety? Must you desecrate the sacred by the profanity of your sarcasm?

ICARUS (*crouching down near stage right*): I could do with a draught of good wine. My limbs are weary but, yet, I feel my strength returning.

THE PRIEST (*standing for dramatic effect*): A stiff drink, did we say? Would that satisfy your need?

ICARUS (*getting to his feet*): You are a swine!

THE PRIESTESS: What would you give me if I were to release you from this temple?

THE PRIEST: Could I ask for anything: say a head on a silver platter?

THE PRIESTESS: How trite. You do your own willful confining because it suit's the purpose of the moment. Now, answer my question, please.

THE PRIEST: You almost annoy me, bitch.

THE PRIESTESS: That's an admission I'd be very careful of making.

THE PRIEST: Yes. One must be careful, mustn't one? And, what do you mean it is not a prison? It is! It is! It is!

ICARUS (*exiting downstage center toward the phantom light*): The game will soon be won. The spectre of light will fuse itself to my being as the lamps of the heavens have done to the goddess of the night.

THE PRIEST (*waving to ICARUS*): See you soon. Idiot. (*Turning his attention back to THE PRIESTESS.*) A word of advice: don't overplay your hand, my dear. Be aware of how you shuffle the deck of cards…your card may just come to the top and, then, you would be exposed.

THE PRIESTESS: A nice play on words, that. I appreciate your wit when it's not laced by cunning. I believe that's when one passes over the border to cynicism.

THE PRIEST (*pointing upstage to where ICARUS cannot be seen*): What of it? And, do you think your friend will be able to see once he "claims" the light? Eh? And, see what, pray tell?

THE PRIESTESS: He's able to see now.

THE PRIEST: Then, what are you putting him through this for? Sport? Fun? Cruelty?

THE PRIESTESS (*carefully weighing her words*): I'm not "putting" him through anything. His vision needs a reality. It needs focus and the sphere of light will help him. One arm reaching toward the heavens while the other hand reaches into hell; the stance of the Magician: one of the dreaded cards of the deck.

THE PRIEST: Whatever you say. You should have placed the dreaded tree across the chasm, as well. That lovely Tree of Life which places immortality at one's feet. Tempting! And, what would they do with eternity? Waste it, as they do with each life they are given…with each day and passing hour and moment. Such a waste of time! To waste eternity on mortals? A ghastly thought! Now, the Tree of Wisdom…to recognize what one is bespeaks of purpose: an actual reason for one's mortality.

THE PRIESTESS: A raison d'etre? What a tantalizing thought. When may I take you up on it? But, the serpent… one would be needed and, of course, fruit to feast upon and to sicken one's stomach, as well. But, you're correct…purpose and, yet, a weapon is needed to procure that precious thing… vision and the reason of a man and, perhaps, integrity.

THE PRIEST: Integrity, did you say? I'm not for sale.

THE PRIESTESS: Not for sale, did you say? To what end?

THE PRIEST (*sitting on the arm of his throne*): To your end! To my end! To his end! Until-the-end! And, there is no end! It's eternal for what comes out of nothing? Nothing! Even I must admit that much.

THE PRIESTESS (*heaving a sigh*): The concept of "nothing" is a contradiction in terms. Heaven help us not to face a beginning. You are more original than that, I trust?

THE PRIEST: Worried? Breathe easy, I am more original than that. Perhaps, I'm the very root of originality...the sin of originality that started with the seed of this rather unique universe of ours. Yes. The originator. I like that. The energy chamber that spewed forth this unholy mess. But, that would put me on the feminine branch of things.

THE PRIESTESS: You just mentioned originality; a product of man's mind. Don't deny it.

THE PRIEST: I'm not denying anything. That's just the part that hurts...the beginnings...or the ends.

THE PRIESTESS: Dying? That's not where the punishment resides. It's the necessity of having to start once again as if recovering from a catastrophic stroke and grasping to regain one's faculties. Horrible! It's an unspeakable punishment to be held accountable for a crime that one hasn't even a memory of. The sins of the forefathers upon themselves: it reeks of primitivism, this theory of re-incarnation. How I loathe it!

THE PRIEST (*agreeing*): How do they ever manage to get through it at all?

THE PRIESTESS: They seek solace in religion. Religion doesn't offer solace, only dedicated ritual may give that and that's pretty dangerous. If they possessed any semblance of knowledge-

THE PRIEST (*interested*): You mean hindsight, don't you?

THE PRIESTESS: It's knowledge that I mean; consciousness that a mind possesses and that's arbitrarily referred to as the soul.

THE PRIEST (*changing the subject*): Why am I a prisoner here?

THE PRIESTESS: There's no jailer standing guard in violation of your freedom.

THE PRIEST: But, if no one knows it...why the possibilities are endless -- infinite, in fact. I could call myself anything and you only one thing.

THE PRIESTESS: I'm growing a little tired of your distortions.

THE PRIEST: Distortions, did you say?

THE PRIESTESS: When one lies, one distorts. One should adhere to reality. Honesty is simplicity itself.

THE PRIEST: But, I don't want to be honest. It's more challenging not to be because one has to remember the details of untruthfulness; the innuendos of the lie. It's difficult this lying. A petty art, granted.

THE PRIESTESS: What's the motive behind this pretense? What do you take me for?

THE PRIEST: I'd take you for real cheap. But, I bet lover boy over there wouldn't. Too much honor in him.

THE PRIESTESS: Are you jealous of him?

THE PRIEST: Jealousy is an artificial emotion, Madame. I have placed myself above such mundane things; and, it surprises me that you haven't. Doesn't that hamper you in your work...your profession? Aren't emotions, genuine emotions, that is, enemies of yours?

THE PRIESTES: How did you come to be here at this one fixed moment?

THE PRIEST: You really don't care how I came to be here. Besides, it's him you're interested in. Not me. You both belong in the shuffle: one card on top of the other, so to speak... pressing ever so firmly against one another.

THE PRIESTESS: How did you come to be here?

THE PRIEST: Chance?

THE PRIESTESS: I don't believe in chance. And, besides, you've already been caught.

THE PRIEST: Caught, did you say? And, by whom? I want some company in my little confinement. It was my intention to be caught...this time.

THE PRIESTESS: The captured cannot make demands, only pleas. And, begging is rather pathetic.

THE PRIEST: Keep me company. Or him? We'll make a threesome of it; what say?

THE PRIESTESS: Lonely, are we? You are thirsting for company because by yourself, you're nothing. You need to be surrounded on both sides for meaning of any kind. Admit it. You require others for definition.

THE PRIEST: Nothing of the kind. Want to keep me company?

THE PRIESTESS: I was under the impression that I was doing just that.

THE PRIEST: Why are you here? Did they let you out for a respite from your various and sordid pleasures?

THE PRIESTESS: How did you come to arrive in this temple? I'm a woman. I'm curious. Tell me!

THE PRIEST: Avoiding the question, are we? The middle-man put me in here. Want to keep me company? I won't ask again.

THE PRIESTESS: No one may keep me company for very long; and, I make no pretense to being a prisoner. A wanderer, perhaps. A woman who has lost sight of her desires. Yes.

THE PRIEST (*assuming the position of a monarch upon his throne*): You losing sight of anything? That is good for a laugh. Your sights are always set, harlot. Ha! You have all the company you need and seduce. You are surrounded by others pressed to your left and your right: by a Fool, a Hermit, a Priest… to corrupt…you've no want of company. They prostrate themselves at your feet and you love it! You revel in the carnal!

THE PRIESTESS: I understand your meaning completely.

ICARUS (*emerging from upstage center*): Do the two of you never cease your sport? So many words and to what avail? I do not enjoy mockery. (*Turning to THE PRIESTESS.*) The light… it eluded me.

THE PRIEST: I didn't figure you for a masochist. Although, that does bring up some delightful possibilities. Whom do you want? Me? Or her? Or both of us?

THE PRIESTESS (*approaching ICARUS*): Perhaps, I may assist you. Play your cards with precision and there may not be a next lifetime.

THE PRIEST: Talk about a play on words! It's the cards that play and deceive. They give the false leads. They look for slaves!

ICARUS: Speak to me.

THE PRIESTESS: Utilize your mind and that will tell you far more than I ever could.

THE PRIEST: That's enough! It's all she can tell you. Don't give yourself more credit than you deserve. Or is it? Does he know how to play the game? You're clever, woman. You live up to your reputation even fully clothed. I like your arrogance.

ICARUS (*moving away from THE PRIESTESS toward center stage*): I recall it as if...as if a long, forgotten dream had come back to my awareness.

THE PRIEST: You remember nothing, Greek. Nothing. Remember that: nothing.

ICARUS: I can see them, now. I can see my wings of glory and my flight across the sea. The white and gold wings that my father fashioned for us to span the arc of Heaven with and lift us toward the clouds.

THE PRIEST (*looking at the audience*): Uh-oh. I knew this was coming. A soliloquy: a precursor to the Bard, himself, no doubt.

ICARUS (*abruptly clasping his hands to his chest*): I can see them uplifting my human form toward the chariot of the sun...that vehicle which glides through the sky and brings with it day and warmth and the blue haze of the dawn.

THE PRIEST: You and everyone else.

ICARUS (*poised on the stage like a Greek statue*): Will my hand not touch upon that orb of radiant gold? Again, will I not soar like the Phoenix of that fabled legend?

THE PRIEST: Why not?

THE PRIESTESS (*standing stage right*): Please, keep silent. I wish to hear the beautiful one's discourse.

ICARUS: Will I see into the next awakening? Will I awaken within a new body that the gods have fashioned for my soul? My body…my pride…the prowess of my ability. Will my eyes pierce the veil that suspends itself atop the altar?

THE PRIEST: You may find her sitting there.

ICARUS: I reached for the sun and droppeth from the heavens. I plummeted like the stricken bird.

THE PRIEST: Do tell?

THE PRIESTESS: Your memory's returning to you.

ICARUS: The sun shimmered as a painted gold coin suspended above the heavenly sea. It radiated warmth and, then, death. It would not have me, a mortal, approach.

THE PRIEST: How quaint. You are a mortal. A curse or a blessing, pray tell?

ICARUS: And, then, I imagined that I saw the magnificent coin descend beneath the horizon and all the colors of the earth became clear and as beautiful as the robe upon a goddess.

THE PRIEST: He's babbling. And, this one usually discards the robe.

THE PRIESTESS: Would you please be still? You're worse than a malicious child.

THE PRIEST: I am a child.

ICARUS (*gazing out into the audience*): The stars appeared. The beautiful constellations of the night glittered like brilliant gem stones...so soft...and, yet, bright. But, how could I perceive this? The stars seemed to spread out before me as if reaching into the black velvet sky beyond infinity's edge. Did I glimpse what a mortal could not...but, no longer was I a mortal.

THE PRIEST: No. You were dead.

ICARUS: My flight through the heavens brought me to where a mortal should not trespass. The sky hovered over me as I swept through it like an eagle on a glorious flight. It was a moment of supreme triumph! A moment not to be held, for what is a moment? What is time, itself, but the thread to be cut by Death? Upon my wings were the specters of death... the heat and, then, the flame that robbed me of my wings. The moment was lost. I held it no longer! The radiant god driving his chariot of golden flame over the sacred pathway would not allow me entrance into his kingdom. And, then, I saw within the eternity of a moment, the shimmering blue glass of the water as it caught the reflection of the fire of heaven. The fiery pinpoints of light were caught upon the waves and hurled toward the shore. All of this wonder as my body was flung earthward.

THE PRIEST (*leaning on his throne*): He really is carrying this poetry a bit too far.

ICARUS (*like a lightning bolt, he reaches to grab THE PRIEST, but is stopped by the invisible barrier*): Have I? I disobeyed my father's command to steer the middle course that separates the waters from the heavens.

THE PRIEST: Yes. We know.

ICARUS: You are keeping watch over me. Why?

THE PRIEST: Paranoid?

THE PRIESTESS: He's incapable of performing any harm in this phantasmic realm. Did I phrase that correctly? I don't mean to intentionally offend, unlike another entity present.

THE PRIEST: I've known every plague and curse that has ever set foot upon the earth.

THE PRIESTESS: Is it necessary to lie?

THE PRIEST: I have known every pestilence, because this hand has forged and named it! I am the blackness and redness of annihilation.

ICARUS: He speaks with a severity in his voice. Perhaps, we should take heed.

THE PRIESTESS: He's a pragmatist. It's the moment's need that dictates his words and convictions -- or lack of them.

THE PRIEST (*clenching his fist*): If you hear me, you love me. The one who traversed the desert in abstinence for forty days and nights. He heard me! Do not say that it is not true; for now, I speak the truth and listen well when I do.

THE PRIESTESS: I didn't say a word.

THE PRIEST: My reign spans the shortness of eternity and the eternity of this moment: that laughable word that grips the throat of every man. They are all fools, because they always listen to me and for me. They need not look for me at all.

Servant upon master and master become servant. Civilization has yet to reach the damned planet. They are all dependent cretins who look for me!

THE PRIESTESS: Icarus, do you think that you'll be able to remember any of this?

THE PRIEST (*turning threateningly on her*): He won't. But, you will!

ICARUS: I shall speak for myself, Priest.

THE PRIEST: Then, speak, Philistine; but, don't interrupt me! Everyone's desolation is fed unto me. And, I, in turn, unleash it back upon them so as to fulfill their most dread hope of seeing it. I dare not even hope for any challenge, but a mere silence would do. A silence before my horse tramples upon the half-wit. A silence before my scimitar detaches the empty head from its pathetic body. Acknowledgement? Is there a glimmer of it here? Dare I hope to find the man who stands on his own? A worthy opponent whom I may respect with my pure hatred?

THE PRIESTESS (*nodding toward ICARUS*): He stands before you now. And, have you nothing else to look forward to?

THE PRIEST: I? Mere repetition. And, still more repetition. The simplicity of folly and so simple-mindedly predictable. The hollow mind that is incapable of thought: my feeding ground, actually. A hunger that is never quite satisfied.

ICARUS: He begins to sound like himself.

THE PRIESTESS: Full circle?

THE PRIEST (*startled*): I beg your pardon, harlot?

THE PRIESTESS: Full circle, Icarus?

ICARUS: A step further into delusion.

THE PRIESTESS: Into the abyss, perhaps?

ICARUS (*looking over at THE PRIEST*): Would it not be a step further?

THE PRIESTESS: Yes. Look at me.

THE PRIEST (*getting up from his throne*): I thought you were talking to me. How very disconcerting. Are you falling for this Greek? He is a beauty.

ICARUS: To soar once more.

THE PRIESTESS: Toward?

ICARUS: Heaven.

THE PRIEST: The perplexities of life and death. And, what is death, really? Nothingness? But, if matter never dies, then thought…energy…does it die?

THE PRIESTESS: Did I hear you make mention of death just now? What an odd thing to hear coming from you. Why does that spectre frighten me so?

THE PRIEST: I'm hearing a lot of frightening things myself, lately.

ICARUS: He is a nuisance, is he not? Priest? You are filth and an annoyance. Take to heart what I say to you. We exist here and, yet, there is a question that I am unable to formulate.

THE PRIEST: Perhaps, you're a high school drop-out?

ICARUS: My education rests upon the teachings of Aristotle. A man should teach himself the things of life and learn through the experience and pain. Yet, pain is not the natural course of life: beauty and fulfillment are its natural course, I think.

THE PRIESTESS (*in a burst of anger*): Why did you hesitate just then? With this bastard, there can be no hesitation. He delights in it. How I hate him for that.

THE PRIEST: Are we upset, my dear? Has lover boy said something to ruffle your pretty, little feathers? Chalk it up to his youth. (*He hears the sound of a desert wind.*) Does no one hear it, but little ole' me?

THE PRIESTESS: I shall regret asking this, but what is it that you hear?

THE PRIEST (*looking quite innocent*): Nothing at all. You heard something, you say?

THE PRIESTESS: How I detest glib answers.

ICARUS: He is a fabricator of deceit.

THE PRIEST: I don't know what you two are talking about.

ICARUS: Did you hear a sound like that of wind...a breeze upon the desert sands? Perhaps, life beckons to me?

THE PRIESTESS: Why not simply tell us what you heard?

THE PRIEST: I know hundreds of languages. Now, why did you make this difficult? The Greek hears it.

ICARUS: In the name of truth, what is that sound? It is as if the souls of Hades shore were calling out to me! What is its origin? All I see about me is the sky and its endless beacons.

THE PRIESTESS: It could have been anything. It won't be able to affect us here -- there's not very much that could, I'm afraid.

ICARUS: It has already intruded upon us: a vibration that one feels with every sense of his being. The vibration of a god's presence...or the vengeance of a god.

THE PRIEST: How very interesting and astute. It's called the touch of a god.

ICARUS: Silence, Priest! Your tongue is stained with lies.

THE PRIESTESS: It's very quiet all of a sudden.

THE PRIEST: Perhaps, there's a storm coming up.

THE PRIESTESS: There's something that Icarus must do.

ICARUS: What is that? Speak to me in words of truth. I do not know of anything other than truth.

THE PRIEST (*yawning*): We know.

ICARUS (*turning sharply to THE PRIEST*): Careful, Priest.

THE PRIEST: You're no fun at all.

THE PRIESTESS: Gentlemen, please behave as civilized men should.

THE PRIEST: Oh, please, baby him, if you will; but, not me. Have I told you about my latest consumption?

THE PRIESTESS: Why, no, you haven't. But, then, again, I don't recall asking.

THE PRIEST: I am not asking for permission to speak, Madame. I grant permission to my lessors. Remember that, my dear.

THE PRIESTESS: Wouldn't it be more polite if you did ask?

THE PRIEST: You offend me, almost. What does offend me is that there is no victory for there cannot be because there is no battle and, yet, the bodies mount up: so many corpses strewn upon the battlefield.

ICARUS: There are battles for brave men willing to fight and to die and, then, to be ferried across the river of death.

THE PRIEST: As I was saying, why is it so easy to rip one's throat out?

THE PRIESTESS (*laughing*): Your own throat? Or will anyone's throat do?

THE PRIEST: You really do know how to carry off a mocking question: a part of your trade?

THE PRIESTESS: What throat was cut out of whom?

THE PRIEST: Why the masses, of course. The doddering, stupid masses who share a singular and malleable mind: the collective, humanitarian mind. Pitiful. Even I loathe him: the man who turns to faith for hope and redemption -- redemption from whom?

THE PRIESTESS: I'm sure that makes you happy and superior to loathe someone?

THE PRIEST: Oh, it does! But, it's a trifle too easy. Why do the masses fall prey to silence? It still baffles me; although, it pleases me rather immensely. One enjoys winning, for defeating even an inferior carries with it a certain amount of satisfaction. Their silence defeats them and their egalitarian ways softens the throat. (*ICARUS is standing on the edge of stage right near a column -- his frustration is ready to erupt into anger.*)

THE PRIESTESS: They await a savior and worship him as a god. May the gods forgive me.

THE PRIEST: Does anyone know what they're actually doing or to what purpose it is? Can they conceive of the victory of acceptance and it's inevitable defeat?

ICARUS: I do not accept defeat for that would signal an end to life.

THE PRIEST: Not as stupid as he looks, is he? Yes, my boy, to conquer fear. But, how? Tell us. Or would you rather that I define it? The only task for me is to select a definition from the many incoherent and incorrect ones: a smorgasbord of such delicious chaos.

ICARUS: Tell me, Priest.

THE PRIEST: Does conquer mean to annihilate? That's what everyone thinks; and, that's why they fail every single time.

THE PRIESTESS: Not everyone and not every time.

THE PRIEST: What of it? A dozen, perhaps, if one is given to being generous.

THE PRIESTESS (*moving toward THE PRIEST*): You admit it! You admit that there have been exceptions. Perfect!

THE PRIEST: You make me laugh. Exceptions: a very few, but not the rule -- not my rule.

THE PRIESTESS: Enough so that you conveniently overlook them. The heroes who are hated for their god-like ability. Heroism: the mark of an individual who stands his ground and doesn't capitulate. He doesn't wait upon a savior or grovel at an altar.

THE PRIEST: Not good enough, Madame. There just haven't been enough.

THE PRIESTESS: One would be enough to cause you a great deal of anguish. You've been defeated by the courageous man; the hero who worships not any god. You loathe such a man. Say it, I dare you!

THE PRIEST: There haven't been enough to fill this habitat of mine.

THE PRIESTESS: Go on, please. Keep defending yourself.

THE PRIEST: As I was saying…all the marks of man's reliance upon man…a chain of fools. And I? I do rely upon them. I need to. Who else can I blame for anything? Who else could be held responsible? Not I, surely; for what do I know?

ICARUS: Does the Priest question himself? Does he question his own false words? You cannot stand on your own values because they are not yours. You are the worst of thieves. Your posture always changes. You do not remain consistent. I cannot grasp what you are.

THE PRIEST: Oh? Are you still here?

THE PRIESTESS: Still game playing?

THE PRIEST: I was talking to my Greek friend. And, do you know what?

THE PRIESTESS: I don't.

THE PRIEST: Liar. I think he's ready to incarnate, again and, again -- and still more!

ICARUS: You seek to confuse a man so that he will not recognize the truth when it is spoken. I shall become a mortal once more and come to realize the glory contained within my mortality. (*THE PRIESTESS rushes over to ICARUS.*)

THE PRIEST: How touching. How very, very touching. Why not disrobe and "pray" while you're at it? Show him what your brand of compassion really is...or, should I say your brand of passion? Eh? Eh?

THE PRIESTESS: Keep silent, please.

THE PRIEST: Madame, I must warn you-

THE PRIESTESS: Don't make me laugh my head off.

ICARUS (*walking toward THE PRIEST*): Perhaps, the Priest is lonely in his confinement? Perhaps, it is time that two enemies met face-to-face in the arena of the temple? Evil...the blackness of a man's sins...evil...to partake of a wrongdoing.

THE PRIEST: Our present arrangement will do splendidly, thank you.

ICARUS: I carry neither sword nor shield to protect me. (*In a supreme moment of strength, he breaks through the invisible barrier.*)

THE PRIEST (*placing his throne between himself and ICARUS*): I really don't believe any of this is happening.

ICARUS: I bid thee greeting, Priest.

THE PRIEST: I would have come out to you if you had asked politely like a civilized man. Are you, Greek? Are you civilized?

THE PRIESTESS: Gentlemen, take your time for time within that temple should be well spent.

ICARUS: Does time exist with neither the sun nor the moon to hold it in place? Movement is a measure of time spent, is it not?

THE PRIEST: Why not ask Galileo or Copernicus or Kepler or a Swiss cuckoo clock when their time comes? I'm sure they'd be quite precise about it. Did I mention Einstein?

ICARUS: Do not leave. A witness is needed.

THE PRIESTESS: Nothing that exists in the heavens or beyond could remove me.

THE PRIEST: Icarus! Come no closer! (*ICARUS places his hand upon the throne.*)

ACT TWO

THE PRIEST, THE PRIESTESS, and ICARUS are in the temple. They are circling about the throne.

ICARUS: Do you see me, Priest, standing before you? Or will you deny your own senses? Tell me!

THE PRIEST: Pray, do not shout at me, Greek.

ICARUS: I bare my soul to you now. The soul that yearned for the warmth of the sun now stands before you scarred, but not defeated.

THE PRIEST: Good God!

ICARUS: No! Not God! Does my presence cause you discomfort? Are we not both men? Or do you apologize for being a man?

THE PRIEST: That is precisely what is making me uneasy. And, I wouldn't bandy that three letter word about if I were you.

ICARUS (*shouting to the heavens*): You are the deceitful one of the intellect! And, I? I am an inventor's son: a man who passeth as a fallen demi-god -- but it is what I am!

THE PRIEST: Of course.

ICARUS: You are learned in the black arts of invocation that suit well your blackened heart and mind.

THE PRIEST: Who am I to argue with the truth?

ICARUS: You have cunning as do all priests of faith. Yours is neither beauty nor truth. You preach weakness.

THE PRIESTESS: You know your opponent well. The knowledge you've accumulated in so short a span of time is impressive. He's impressed.

THE PRIEST: Shut your filthy, treacherous mouth, harlot; it drips with admiration for this Greek.

THE PRIESTESS: Isn't this an open forum? Or, perhaps, we're as opponents on the battlefield?

THE PRIEST: Please stop prattling. I've no friends for they will never fail to disappoint you. Never.

THE PRIESTESS: Close the gap, Icarus. Close in upon your enemy. Quickly!

THE PRIEST: One more word from you…

THE PRIESTESS: Yes?

ICARUS: Let the woman speak. She is a Priestess of the temple and it becomes her to speak as she wishes.

THE PRIEST: What do I care of rights? The rights of the masses? The masses do not maintain the fragile structure of civilization much less its culture and religion. I do that and others like unto me! We are the apex atop the pyramid as the slaves labor beneath our feet. Listen to what I say, Greek. You're close enough to hear me, now.

ICARUS: Cowards are your slaves, but not I. As I live, I am no man's slave.

THE PRIEST: I am not a man. Dolt!

ICARUS: What would you be called, Priest? Give meaning to your wretched existence.

THE PRIESTESS: Answer that question, if you dare.

THE PRIEST: Exerting your "rights," again?

ICARUS: Priest, I command you to remain still!

THE PRIESTESS: Ask him why he dare not remain still for very long.

THE PRIEST: Again, Madame? Baiting me or him -- your would-be lover? Who is it?

ICARUS: I will not harm you, not yet. If you are my enemy, I will vanquish thee and show no mercy.

THE PRIESTESS: Icarus, you may now accomplish what countless other men have failed to do for lack of courage.

THE PRIEST: Madame, shut up! No one dies here; that feat, at least, has been accomplished.

THE PRIESTESS: Do you order me about? How amusing and distasteful.

ICARUS: You have nothing to fear, unless you fear a free man.

THE PRIESTESS: Why don't you stand still if we're reaching the end of this sordid, little drama?

THE PRIEST: Is that an order? I simply deplore orders; well, that kind, anyway.

ICARUS: You dislike orders, Priest?

THE PRIEST: The kind directed at me! Those are the orders that I despise. Understand? Savvy? Comprende? Verstehen sie?

THE PRIESTESS: Cease moving about! The both of you are going nowhere quite quickly.

ICARUS: He will not cease his movements and neither will I. Not until I strike his foul and slithery snake-like body!

THE PRIEST: The mind of a mad, stricken child: a gnat ready to be crushed! Give me your head!

THE PRIESTESS: No longer a child.

THE PRIEST: Stop throwing out hope to him. You've done that before and it's proven useless. Hope denotes purpose and I won't have any of that here. It's distracting to me.

ICARUS (*shouting at the top of his lungs*): Stop! I have inquiries and I demand answers!

THE PRIEST: Why, of course, dear boy. Speak up. Speak up. Get it all off that beautiful chest of yours.

ICARUS: Tell me where I am. This place is not Hades…it is not the earth.

THE PRIEST: Keep eliminating, you're doing quite well at it.

THE PRIESTSS (*moving slowly toward stage right*): What do you think it is, Icarus.?

ICARUS: My body feels as if it has passed through that golden orb of fire: it feels aflame, but my heart and mind seem touched by the moon's cool and calming ray.

THE PRIEST: Ho-hmm. Oh, did I interrupt? Were you stringing sentences together?

THE PRIESTESS: You're right, Icarus, this is no prison for it was meant to be entered. You don't propel a being into it, but someone does need a push to extricate oneself.

THE PRIEST: Why did you tell him that?

THE PRIESTESS: To annoy you, of course.

THE PRIEST: Should I pour the sand over his head about now?

ICARUS: By the gods, I will strike thee to the ground! What are you staring at?

THE PRIEST: You. Who else? (*Staring about the stage.*) Where's your girlfriend gone off to? (*An abrupt change occurs from an almost unbearable tension to a quiet stance between THE PRIEST and ICARUS.*)

ICARUS: She is gone. I did not see her leave, so subtle was the movement. Her destination?

THE PRIEST: I'm sure I don't know.

ICARUS: You hate me.

THE PRIEST: Let's just say I feel cold toward you. You might be one of the very few people I've met whom I actually don't hate. That's high praise coming from me, Greek.

ICARUS: Will you not ask me my disposition toward you?

THE PRIEST: The answer seems quite obvious.

ICARUS: I do not possess your cunning, compromiser's tongue.

THE PRIEST: Don't underestimate yourself. I can see the grains of intelligence shifting about in that skull of yours. Maybe next time around, you won't play with fire.

ICARUS: You seek that men alter their reasoning. To speak another's words? To feign his thoughts? To be another man's pawn? Never!

THE PRIEST: Continue, please. Do you find me appealing in a repulsive sort of way? Tell me, I won't mind. I'm quite used to flattery.

ICARUS: I think. I act...and my actions demonstrate my speech.

THE PRIEST: Oh, I'd say you've been holding up your end of this conversation. As you were saying? Speech? Thought?

ICARUS: I feel naked standing here before a priest. It is somehow improper. Before another athlete, it is accepted as common-place.

THE PRIEST: I'm sure. Then, why did you follow me in here?

ICARUS: I did not follow you in. That I would not do. I entered to confront you.

THE PRIEST: Phrase it anyway you like. I forget that I was in here already. Technically, you are correct. Now, you said there was something about me...

ICARUS (*moving away from THE PRIEST'S throne*): Do not mock me. Is not my fall from Heaven mockery enough?

THE PRIEST: It will do. And, I never make fun of people. I am merely forthright in my opinions and insults. I have something to say and I simply say it.

ICARUS: What do you say?

THE PRIEST: Never mind, athlete. By the way...how are you feeling about now? A bit pooped, are we?

ICARUS (*placing his hand to his forehead*): My body feels racked with pain. It is as if I were seeing through a sea's mist. My body is in turmoil.

THE PRIEST: Energy to cross over into nothingness. A contradiction in terms, granted; but, savor it, for now.

THE PRIESTESS (*entering from center stage*): Did I hear you mention something about nothingness just now?

THE PRIEST: Oh, we were just chatting away until your triumphant return. You are glorious, my dear. Glorious.

ICARUS: The Priest fears me.

THE PRIEST: You'd be consumed by now if I were. My enemies don't remain enemies for very long. They don't remain much of anything.

THE PRIESTESS: Are we dieting? How dreadful for you!

THE PRIEST: Oh, do be careful, Madame.

ICARUS: Cease your threats, coward.

THE PRIEST: Yes. Of course. By the way, you are not unique. I know that you think you are; but, you are not. They all think they're unique: these self-proclaimed heroes. How I adore them!

ICARUS: A hero…perhaps.

THE PRIEST: Perhaps.

ICARUS: Filthy Priest! Stand ready to fight. But, first, your tongue should be loosed from its accursed skull to poison the air no more! (*He leaps around THE PRIEST'S throne in one swift movement and grabs him, pinning his arms behind his back.*)

THE PRIESTESS: This is priceless! Icarus, don't release him! For the first time in all the eternities, I am begging for a pleasure not to end too quickly.

THE PRIEST: Idiot! You'll never- why you're hurting me! Stop! Immediately! And, that is part of your trade, woman: begging, pleading, simpering.

THE PRIESTESS: If you're so powerful then make him stop. He has the strength of an Olympian, hasn't he? I knew that he would. I knew it!

THE PRIEST: Wise after the fact, are we? You should lower yourself to your knees as you are so accustomed to.

THE PRIESTESS: Not too tight! Just enough to let him squirm and redden at the temples. We don't want to cut off his speech altogether. Not quite yet, anyway.

ICARUS: Would you have me bring him to you for some sport?

THE PRIESTESS: Would you?

THE PRIEST: How dare you!

ICARUS: Careful, lest my grip tightens about your throat. Do not tempt me beyond endurance.

THE PRIEST: To be bested by an inferior! An inferior, I tell you!

ICARUS: Silence! I do not utter idle threats.

THE PRIESTESS: Bested by an inferior, did you say? Quite an inferior by the look of it. He's wrested you from your throne -- your seat of power. And, he's caught you off guard. How very painful that must be.

THE PRIEST: Did I say that? It was said in haste, I assure you.

THE PRIESTESS: Now that you have him, why not force him to answer a few pertinent questions?

ICARUS: A splendid idea.

THE PRIEST: Brilliantly conceived by a fool and his whore-

ICARUS: Tell me: I will walk upon the earth as a man once more? Tell me!

THE PRIEST: You're choking me!

ICARUS: Answer me!

THE PRIEST: All right! Then, choose nothingness -- as if that were a choice. You've earned the right to cross-over; but, be careful to land on your feet this time. You made quite a mess of yourself the last flight out.

THE PRIESTESS: And? That answer was quite unsatisfactory. He mocks you still.

THE PRIEST: You miserable-

ICARUS: My patience with you is at an end. Speak!

THE PRIEST (*trying to make a jest of it*):
I-thought-we-were-friends?

ICARUS: For the last time, speak!

THE PRIEST: Nothingness is to start from nothing and end in nothing.

ICARUS: One cannot begin from nothing for that is a contradiction in terms. Life must come from life and know of itself. Now, continue and do not lie.

THE PRIEST: You'll progress to a new cycle. You'll know of yourself and the things you've done. You'll remember everything and can, therefore, judge yourself. I can't believe I told him that. It's your fault. Where's your cup of blood? You should be thirsty about now.

THE PRIESTESS: What is it that I've done? And, it's true, my throat does feel quite parched. How very kind of you to consider that. Have you a glass of wine?

THE PRIEST: If it takes me the rest of eternity-

ICARUS: How does one begin this new cycle? What manner of man shall I become?

THE PRIEST: Have you no mercy? At least, may we sit down for a bit?

ICARUS: No! Better to die as a man than as a slave! -- as an implement to be discarded among the rubbish once it has outlived its usefulness. Better to die than to exist as an amusement to the empty verses of decay!

THE PRIESTESS: If I were you, I would tell him all that I know.

THE PRIEST: I'll never tell. Never. Never! In the name of all that is sacred-

THE PRIESTESS: Did something sacred just leak from your lips? I'm pleased to be present at such a momentous occasion. Perhaps, I should hold on to this throne for support?

ICARUS: You have more to tell me.

THE PRIEST: Why not? It's not up to me to decide.

ICARUS: Then, by whom? and decide what?

THE PRIEST: Oh, he is an idiot- I didn't mean that!

THE PRIESTESS: Is it up to superior minds to decide a man's fate after life? Say it!

THE PRIEST: Yes! Now, get back on your horse and straddle it as you do all manner of man.

ICARUS: Where do I find these minds?

THE PRIEST: In the abyss. You've already been there. Careful of the plummet, it's a descent one never gets used to. The winged one with his wings clipped. And, for this I'm being mangled.

ICARUS: I will release him now.

THE PRIESTESS: I've savored the moment long enough. The embrace…it begins to bore me.

THE PRIEST: Impertinence! And, after all I've done to help you. The ingratitude of it all.

THE PRIESTESS: Ingratitude?

THE PRIEST: You agree. (*To ICARUS.*) Why didn't you try to kill me? Your type usually does.

ICARUS: Killing is of no great import. Men die every day; free men and slaves alike. But, to die without purpose is unforgivable.

THE PRIEST: There are those who would disagree with that rather cold observation. Brrr!

THE PRIESTESS: Would you, I wonder?

THE PRIEST: Must you always interject?

ICARUS: I will take leave of this beautiful place.

THE PRIEST: It was lovely. Let's do it, again, real soon.

ICARUS: I pray that he has not had an evil influence upon me.

THE PRIESTESS: He hasn't.

ICARUS: My body is intact. The was fall not crippling…merely fatal. I know what it is that I perceive and that perception is sculpted into existence.

THE PRIEST: I can see screamed the blind man plunging into the chasm. How poetic and obvious we've become.

THE PRIESESS: Ignore the rantings of this megalomaniac.

ICARUS: I have traveled a great distance and, yet, the odyssey has just begun. Do all men walk into this accursed place as beautiful as it appears? Do all men breach that temple?

THE PRIEST: Well, they should, Icarus. You call me a priest, but I disagree.

THE PRIESTESS: You really are administering the hints. Can it be that you like this man? Are you confirming my suspicions?

THE PRIEST: Well, kids, now what?

THE PRIESTESS: Why not give this sundial a rotation? A touch of the hand will trigger the mechanism. You may even set fire to it. Flame…it destroys the very vehicle that it utilizes for it cannot co-exist with it. It consumes its host for its very life: a lesser giving way to a superior and, yet, it too dies.

ICARUS: I shall depart.

THE PRIEST: Going so soon? Oh, do stay for some scones and tea. I'll pour!

THE PRIESTESS: Your humor is degrading to whomever it touches.

THE PRIEST: Party poop! (*On impulse, THE PRIESTESS touches the sundial.*) Now, that's not fair! He should've done that.

THE PRIESTESS: It's the blaze of light that men call creation. Marvelous! I had to indulge myself the pleasure of setting off the mechanism.

ICARUS: Are you both the phantoms of my own mind: a deception of my own making? Or are you the thoughts that I once pondered long ago in the darkness of the temple? Perhaps, what has not been told to me is of great import. Were the veiled answers as markers in a strange forest that a lost traveler finds in his wanderings? Shall I awaken from a dream or has the dream been discarded long ago? A priest…a man…a king, perhaps, or something that I cannot begin to imagine? A priestess…a woman. May we not leave this place together?

THE PRIESTESS: That's impossible. I must send you on your journey.

ICARUS: Perhaps, I will one day discover that race of gods that Man was once a part of. Life is not eternal nor should it be.

THE PRIESTESS: Farewell, Icarus.

THE PRIEST: We'll never see you, again. How sad.

ICARUS: Farewell! (*Exits center stage.*)

THE PRIESTESS (*leaning against the column*): He's escaped. So quickly did it end. One less soul for our collection.

THE PRIEST: You made it easy enough for him.

THE PRIESTESS: The game is over…and the victor? May a victor be crowned? Or have the two of us been defeated this time? His memories were coming back to him too quickly.

THE PRIEST: Is the game over, my dear? You violated the rules. But, no matter. I'm patient. I've all of eternity before me and so have you.

THE PRIESTESS: More sport? More game playing?

THE PRIEST (*turning to the audience*): Does the dear boy think he's escaped? A fallen angel taken flight? The hunt has just begun. I hope all of you now realize that there is no escape from us.

End of play.

MAHLER:

The Man Who Was Never Born

A Play in Three Acts

by

Gerard Denza

MAHLER: The Man Who Was Never Born premiered at the Producer's Club on November 20, 2003 with the following cast:

MAHLER	Justin Langin
AUNT KIT	Catherine Crawford
THE STRANGER	Phil Strumolo
MAGDALENA	Georgina Kess
CORINNE	Maureen Cohen
FRANCINE	Diane Ordelheide
ANNE	Harmony Goldstein

Set by Phil Strumolo.
Directed by Gerard Denza.

PLACE
The action takes place in Mahler's apartment in New York City, a cellar, Francine's bakery, and a bookstore.

TIME
The year is 1965.

SCENES

Act One
Scene One: Mahler's apartment in 1965. It is late night.
Scene Two: A few weeks later at the book shop.
Scene Three: The same day at Francine's bakery.
Scene Four: The same day in the cellar
of the apartment building.

Act Two
Scene One: In the book shop in 1947.
Scene Two: In the cellar of the apartment
building later that same day.

Act Three
Scene One: In the cellar of the apartment building: 1965.
Scene Two: Later that same day in the cellar.

CHARACTERS

MAHLER, an angry teenager.
KIT, Mahler's good natured aunt.
THE STRANGER, a being from another universe.
MAGDALENA, Kit's friend and business partner.
CORINNE, Mahler's mother.
FRANCINE, Mahler's friend and bakery owner.
ANNE, a colleague of the Stranger's.

ACT ONE
Scene One

MAHLER leaning forward on a stool. The stage is bare except for a few chairs and an old coffee table with a book of Shakespeare's plays, a pack of cigarettes, and a dagger on it.

MAHLER: When morning comes, my father will be buried alive. It must be close to midnight, but still I cannot sleep. So much anguish fills my heart and mind that sleep and dreams could not contain those emotions. There are no lights on in the apartment. There is a book on the coffee table: it is a collection of Shakespeare's plays; but, I do not have the ambition to pick it up and focus upon those inspired verses. (*He goes over to the window where a full moon is glowing like a milky pearl.*) Before I continue with this narrative, I must present myself. A narrator has that obligation. He is very much a slave to his narrative. (*Bowing to the audience.*) My name is Mahler Peri. I am with the lower middle classes and just touching on poverty. Poverty is hateful because it eats away at your mind and spirit. (*He places his hands to his face almost as if to re-orient himself to the flow of his thoughts.*) Where does my story begin? The precise beginning is not so precise; but, perhaps, the actions that began it are. Perhaps. I hear someone coming. (*He goes to open the door.*)

KIT (*laughing*): You just take a bath, Mahler?

MAHLER: What gave it away?

KIT: You look brand, spanking new, dear nephew. Were you planning on going to bed soon? It might be a good ides. You look tired.

MAHLER: Come in.

KIT (*accepting the invitation*): For a minute. I can't stay. I'm expecting company soon.

MAHLER: Just a minute? No chit-chat?

KIT: No chit-chat. Come with me downstairs. Don't stay all alone here by yourself, it's not good for you.

MAHLER: Why not? I'm not grieving, if that's what you're concerned about. Crying isn't my style at all.

KIT: You don't have to cry to grieve, Mahler. Come on. Please?

MAHLER: Have I been sent for?

KIT (*reprimanding him good-naturedly*): Stop grinning, that's not nice. And, no, you haven't been sent for. If anyone is "sending" for you, it's me; and, I'm doing it in person.

MAHLER: What is it that my aunt wants?

KIT: I wasn't aware that I wanted anything. Well…there is something that I'd like to discuss with you; and, it's a subject that I know you're interested in.

MAHLER: Yes?

KIT: I won't talk about it here. Come down and meet my guest. You'll like her.

MAHLER: I don't like many people. You know this. I'm the recluse of the family.

KIT: By your own choice, young man.

MAHLER: By my own choice.

KIT: Well, now that that's settled, can I expect you downstairs?

MAHLER: Yes.

KIT (*looking up at the ceiling*): Good...

MAHLER: Why are you looking up at the ceiling?

KIT: For some reason, I just thought about that new tenant of mine. You know, the man on the third floor right above you. He's strange, Mahler. I don't know that I like him. He frightens me.

MAHLER: Has he actually done anything? He does keep to himself. I can't find fault with that. I do pretty much the same.

KIT (*lowering her voice*): It's when he passes close by. Mahler, I know you're going to think I'm crazy or something, but-

MAHLER: Go on, Aunt Kit, complete the thought.

KIT: But, when he passes close by the air feels so cold! It's as if death were breathing down my neck. It's horrible! I try to walk the other way whenever I see him, which isn't that often, thank God!

MAHLER: Has he ever spoken to you?

KIT: Only in passing. He is very well mannered. I'll say that much about him. But, it's like he's being tolerant of an inferior. It's as if he'd prefer that I didn't exist.

MAHLER: I've never really gotten close to him, myself; that is to say, not physically.

KIT (*releasing her hand from his arm*): Lucky you! I don't know why he's even living here. It's not his kind of neighborhood at all. He doesn't really fit in; but, I can't hold that against him.

MAHLER (*admiring her perceptiveness*): You mean our working class neighborhood? But, he could be looking for work of some sort and he finds that his circumstances have changed for the worse.

KIT (*regaining her composure*): You mean to have to move into this dump? Yes! Anyway, come downstairs when you're up to it. Like I said, you'll like my guest. She's a bit of a scholar, like you, Mahler. She's a teacher of the classics -- or used to be, anyway. I think she's fed up with all the politics and low standards. See you later?

MAHLER: I'll be down soon.

KIT: Sure? Don't humor your aunt, and try not to be too long. (*She exits stage left.*)

MAHLER (*sitting back down on the stool*): That new tenant on the third floor…an interesting figure and clearly unsuitable for this dwelling. (*A knock at the door.*) Yes?

THE STRANGER: May I come in for a moment? I wish to express my condolences.

MAHLER: My mother is downstairs with my aunt. I'm sure she wouldn't mind it if you dropped in.

THE STRANGER: I would mind, Mr. Peri. Now, may I come in?

MAHLER: I'm sorry. I'm not used to visitors, except family.

THE STRANGER: A realization of one's limitations; you are to be commended for your honesty to a guest. May I be seated?

(*Before MAHLER can respond, he sits down.*) You do not intend to stand there for my entire visit, do you? (*MAHLER sits down rather stiffly on his stool.*) There are several matters that I wish to discuss with you.

MAHLER: With me?

THE STRANGER: Does that surprise you?

MAHLER (*leaning forward*): I don't know you. What could you want to say to me?

THE STRANGER: Perhaps, it is I who am acquainted with you?

MAHLER: I don't understand.

THE STRANGER: Understanding takes time, patience, and intelligence combined with wisdom.

MAHLER: I guess.

THE STRANGER: Don't use that pedestrian term when speaking with me. It has no meaning. If you are grieving, you disguise it quite admirably. I appreciate that and its significance.

MAHLER: I am grieving, but no one but myself can see it.

THE STRANGER: Good. A man should never expose himself.

MAHLER: What do you want to say to me, sir?

THE STRANGER: I will begin. A man is altered by darkness. One feels darkness, but does not actually see it manifesting within himself and turning his soul into blackness. A man must change himself from the primeval essence that is undeniably his starting point and begin the metamorphosis into his role of a civilized man, a human being, if you would. When a civilized man finds himself in the midst of a savage landscape, he cannot help but become affected. He knows that his countenance can be shattered. He realizes that he is not a being who is at the apex of human evolution. He discovers that the primeval instincts are still within him.

MAHLER: What are you talking about?

THE STRANGER: Don't you know? Haven't you guessed?

MAHLER: You're talking about yourself and my father?

THE STRANGER: Yes.

MAHLER: I don't see the point to what you're saying.

THE STRANGER: Don't you?

MAHLER: No.

THE STRANGER: I'm giving you a direction in which to position yourself, if you choose it. I'm offering you a wider range of life's choices that might otherwise have not been possible to a boy of your low social standing.

MAHLER: Let me get this straight. I can be like you, whatever that is, or like my father whom you thought of as some primeval?

THE STRANGER: Yes.

MAHLER: Maybe, I don't accept that. Maybe, there's even a third choice for me.

THE STRANGER: To do what?

MAHLER: To find my own path.

THE STRANGER: Tripe. Don't hide from the truth, young man. Make your decision to join us.

MAHLER: "Us?" You and who else and why me?

THE STRANGER: Become as I am and I will answer all your questions. If your answer is "no," then we will never again speak.

MAHLER: You mean that you'll leave?

THE STRANGER: Don't live with the regret of refusing me. A lifetime of regret is a difficult burden to bear.

MAHLER: There's truth in that. But, what's your purpose?

THE STRANGER: Our purpose lies within the cellar of the apartment building.

MAHLER: A good mystery: I love the sound of that.

THE STRANGER: Say "yes" to me and that reply will end our first conversation.

MAHLER: But, who are you?

THE STRANGER: I am a man who once lived here many years ago.

MAHLER: Lived here? In this building? When?

THE STRANGER: "Yes" to both questions.

MAHLER: Why have you come back?

THE STRANGER: I have come back for you.

MAHLER: Why?

THE STRANGER: You and I are one.

MAHLER: We're not related. We can't be.

THE STRANGER: We are most intimately related. Our bond does not consist of so vulgar a thing as blood ties. Our bond is that of a shared soul. Our "link" is neither limited nor bound up in the earth, proper. It extends itself to the infinite and to that which cannot be grasped by human consciousness.

MAHLER: But, you seem to understand it.

THE STRANGER: I am not human…not any longer. That is a thing which has been discarded along the tortuous path. Many years ago, this area was inhabited by a few of us who had come from beyond the wall which separates this universe from the other unknown. We found ourselves pre-dating even the ancients of your race. We were here and we remembered how we came to be here and also…we were able to answer the question "why?"

MAHLER: Why?

THE STRANGER: When one dies, one separates himself from the body of choice and then must re-establish himself into another form of choice -- a choice of dire necessity.

MAHLER: But, you haven't died.

THE STRANGER: It has been my refusal to rid my body of that spectre that lingers within and which longs for life. When my bodily senses had ceased to function, the flame of life within the spirit remained kindled by my greed to live and not to die…not to release the spectre that would have meant death and forgetfulness. Perhaps, that is my unforgivable sin.

MAHLER: Why are you telling me all this? You said there were others like yourself. Where are they? What's their part in all this?

THE STRANGER: I have distanced myself from most of them. You doubt what I say?

MAHLER: Yes. Does it matter, though?

THE STRANGER (*standing up*): It will matter a great deal. Think over all that I have told you and we will speak, again. For the moment, though, you know enough. (*He exits stage left.*)

MAHLER: Now, I am awake. (*He glances over at his Shakespeare book.*) My third reading of Hamlet and still it fascinates me with the introspective questioning of life and a wish for death. (*There is a knock on the door.*) Hello?

KIT: (*walking in and mussing MAHLER'S hair*): We've brought the party to you, Mahler. Do you mind so much? I wasn't sure whether or not you would come down; and, I don't like the idea of your being up here all by yourself.

MAHLER (*nodding curtly*): Good evening. My name is Mahler Peri.

MAGDALENA: Good evening. I am Magdalena. I'm so sorry to hear the news of your father's death. It's very difficult for a young man to lose his father. I extend my condolences to you.

MAHLER: Thank you.

MAGDALENA: You are a student? I am a teacher.

KIT: Magdalena was a Professor of Literature at university until last Spring.

MAHLER: Literature is sort of a passion with me, especially Shakespeare. "Hamlet's" my favorite play, but I love them all.

MAGDALENA: Have you memorized any of that great man's sonnets, yet? You should for their poetry and magic.

MAHLER: I've read them; but, I haven't put them down to memory.

MAGDALENA: Do. It's well worth the effort for they will remain in your memory for a lifetime.

CORINNE (*carefully smoothing out the folds of her dress*): You're putting an idea into my son's head. He'll start memorizing them tonight.

MAGDALENA: Mahler, how did your father die, if I may ask?

MAHLER: Some say that he had a heart attack.

MAGDALENA: And, what do you say? What is your feeling?

MAHLER: I don't know. I'm not certain. It was sudden and he was a relatively young man.

MAGDALENA: Even young men can be stricken by a heart attack. My own father died of a stroke.

MAHLER: Sorry to hear that, truly.

MAGDALENA: It was a tragedy, yes.

MAHLER: You're still grieving him.

MAGDALENA: I am. There are some shocks one never completely recovers from.

MAHLER: Are you a friend of my aunt's?

MAGDALENA: An acquaintance of hers. We met only a few months ago.

MAHLER: That would be long enough for a friendship with most people.

MAGDALENA: I am not like most people, Mahler; are you?

CORINNE: He certainly isn't like anyone I know; except, perhaps, his father.

MAHLER (*trying to ignore the insult*): No. At least, I'm told that I'm not.

MAGDALENA: You should say that with more satisfaction in your voice. An individual who possesses a mind of his own will always make his presence felt.

CORINNE: My son wants to go to college, someday. So he dreams.

MAGDALENA: Of course. Any intelligent young man would want to. That's very much to his credit.

MAHLER: How did you come to meet my Aunt Kit?

MAGDALENA: You're curious about my being here, aren't you?

MAHLER: Yes.

CORINNE: My son has an insatiable curiosity.

KIT: Good for him!

MAGDALENA: Would you believe me if I told you that I'm looking to solve a very old mystery?

MAHLER: Why wouldn't I believe that?

MAGDALENA: A man with an imagination would believe it. You have an imagination and the intelligence to use it.

MAHLER: Thank you for the compliment.

MAGDALENA: I will now tell you how I came to meet your Aunt Kit. May I, Kit?

KIT: Please.

MAGDALENA: We met on the train a few months ago. Neither one of us ventured to get up and come over to the other; but, when the train reached its last stop, the two of us exchanged greetings. As it turned out, we were traveling to the same book shop in the downtown business area.

MAHLER: I think I know the one you mean.

CORINNE (*in a condescending voice*): My son is acquainted with most book shops in the city.

MAGDALENA (*addressing MAHLER*): Yes. It's changed ownership several times over the years.

MAHLER: How did you know that?

CORINNE: Excuse my son, Miss Lima. He doesn't know enough to mind his own business.

MAGDALENA: It's quite all right. I had inquired and the reason for that is that I wish to purchase the store. Your Aunt Kit and I are entering into a joint venture. I wish to own and run my own shop and carry on a life within that sphere. And, there are other reasons, as well. The store had a certain "flavor" that appeals to me. It will contain the classics. We will cater to a specific type of clientele who will always be in the market to purchase good and durable books to be kept in one's personal library.

MAHLER: You mentioned other reasons.

MAGDALENA: I referred to a mystery before; didn't I?

MAHLER: You did.

MAGDALENA: This bookstore will be the means of solving that mystery, I hope.

MAHLER: What mystery?

MAGDALENA: I can't elaborate anymore, at the moment.

MAHLER: Just giving out enough hints to tantalize?

MAGDALENA: Do you mind?

MAHLER: But, why tell me any of this? Should I care?

MAGDALENA: You should. It involves someone you may know…and, it may even involve you.

MAHLER: Was the book shop for sale?

MAGDALENA: Fortunately, yes.

MAHLER: And, my Aunt Kit agreed to go in on this with you? That surprises me.

KIT: Why, Mahler?

MAHLER: I didn't know you liked the classics. Romance books, yes, by the dozen.

KIT (*laughing good-naturedly*): What makes you say that? I'm quite well read.

CORINNE: And, so am I, young man.

MAHLER: When does the holy alliance begin?

MAGDALENA: It will begin the first of the year. And, Mahler, your mother has decided to also be a part of our group.

MAHLER: Well, being that my mother and aunt are partners, do I get to work there and read the books?

CORINNE: Could we stop you?

KIT: Mahler, you'll be our first customer.

MAGDALENA: Would you like to?

MAHLER: You bet I would.

MAGDALENA: I also gamble.

MAHLER: What brings you here, tonight?

MAGDALENA: The night and early morning are special hours for me. The essence of time and space change. We are in the presence of the night sky and shielded from the ancient furnace of life. In ancient Egypt, the god, Ra, would ride his chariot across the sky giving light and heat and also merciless punishment to those violators of his laws. But, at night, Isis shields us from his fire. The moon watches over us with a calm and cold eye. She judges, but in a different manner from that of her sun god. (*Getting up.*) And, now, I must go. I enjoyed meeting you. Good night. Ladies? Good night. (*Exits stage left.*)

MAHLER: Aunt Kit? I'll see you at the funeral, tomorrow?

KIT: Of course. Will you be all right? Corinne? How about you?

CORINNE: I'm fine. Good night, Kit.

KIT: Tomorrow's going to be a long day for everybody. Get some sleep -- the two of you. (*Exits stage left.*)

CORINNE: Well, you certainly were the talkative one, tonight. Since when have you been so friendly?

MAHLER: I don't know how to answer that question.

CORINNE: You never utter more than two words to anyone and you avoid strangers like the plague. You've always been too sensitive and a bit of a snob.

MAHLER: Could you be accused of that, mother?

CORINNE (*laughing*): Your father isn't here anymore to protect you. You have to rely on me, now -- and, don't. He spoiled you. What did your father say about me? Tell me.

MAHLER: He never spoke about you.

CORINNE: You're not going to cry, are you? Weren't you doing that when you were hiding out here before?

MAHLER: I wasn't crying. And, I wasn't hiding

CORINNE: My how you went on tonight! Do you like Magdalena? Are you capable of liking a woman?

MAHLER (*catching the innuendo*): I'm capable of liking this one.

CORINNE: In the Platonic sense, I take it? Poor Mahler.

MAHLER: Why do you hate me?

CORINNE: It's you who hates me.

MAHLER: Did you hate my father?

CORINNE: How dare you ask me that? Who put you up to it? It was Kit, wasn't it? Or was it that bakery friend of yours. What's her name? She's so common.

MAHLER: Her name is Francine. And, she's not common. And, she did not put me up to anything. I have a mind of my own.

CORINNE: I'd like to know what goes on in that perverted mind.

MAHLER: You wouldn't.

CORINNE: You didn't know your father very well, did you? You knew the side of him that he wanted you to know. But, you didn't know the "man," shall we say? I did. I had to live with him and his son.

MAHLER: I'm my father's son.

CORINNE: Then, I do hate you. Lock up before you go to bed. (*She exits stage right. MAHLER reaches for the dagger on the coffee table and, with one thrust, he plunges it into the wood.*)

ACT ONE

Scene Two

MAGDALENA is finishing her second cup of coffee. Her cigarette is in the ashtray. Her pocketbook is on the counter. It's late Saturday afternoon and cold outside. Suddenly, there's a sharp tap on the door and the sound of retreating feet.

MAGDALENA: Who is there? Answer me, please. No? No one. How disappointing. Perhaps, someone is trying to frighten me? (*Taking out her compact, she touches up her face.*) Where are the others? (*The shop's door opens and KIT, CORINNE, and MAHLER enter.*)

MAHLER: Magdalena? Are you all right?

MAGDALENA: I'm fine. Thank you.

KIT: Well, ladies and Mahler? Shall we take inventory? These light bulbs have to go. I hate them. They're so garish and cheap looking.

MAGDALENA: Yes. Let's take inventory. And, then, we must also get some supplies for the kitchen: flour, coffee, cereal, tea: non-perishable items. And, by the first of the year, we'll be ready to open our doors to customers.

MAHLER (*moving slowly toward the back of the shop where he hears a scuffling sound*): Magdalena? Is there someone in back here? I hear footsteps- no, wait. They've stopped. That's strange. I don't hear anything now. But, whoever it is must still be there; mustn't they?

MAGDALENA: Yes. They must.

MAHLER: There was more than one person, I think. Do they have any business being in there?

MAGDALENA: None at all.

MAHLER: How did they get in? Magdalena, you don't seem too surprised. Was there any sign of a break-in when you opened up?

MAGDALENA: There was no break-in or any sign of forced entry.

MAHLER: Then, I can think of only two alternatives.

KIT (*smiling in anticipation*): Is my little nephew playing Sherlock Holmes? The game of deduction, isn't it? Oh, I used to love reading Conan Doyle. He's in our inventory, you know.

MAGDALENA: We're straying from the topic. Mahler, what are those two alternatives?

MAHLER: The first one would be that the person gained access through the building that's adjacent to this one: maybe, through some forgotten connecting passageway or door. Or, this intruder had a key. Isn't that the original lock on the door?

KIT: Why does that first alternative scare me?

MAHLER: The next question is: what are they looking for? Magdalena, were you in there before we arrived?

MAGDALENA: No. But, there was a sharp knock on the door just before you arrived; but, no one was there.

MAHLER: Maybe, they're playing some kind of macabre game with us.

MAGDALENA: I don't believe there's anyone in there now, do you?

MAHLER: No…not anymore.

CORINNE: Good. Can we bring this discussion to an end? Or does my son still have the floor?

KIT: Shouldn't we have a look around in there? All this guessing is getting us nowhere. And, it's just making me more nervous not to know.

MAGDALENA: I'm sure we wouldn't find anything.

KIT: Oh, you don't know that, Magdalena. It wouldn't hurt to look around, would it? I mean, we really should, you know.

MAGDALENA: It's all right. No one is there, now.

KIT (*not believing her*): Now? Which means there was somebody there before? Please, don't say that.

MAGDALENA: I'm afraid my imagination is as active as Mahler's. Ladies? Would you mind so much if I left? I'm afraid that I'm not feeling very well, today. Perhaps, we could postpone the inventory until tomorrow?

CORINNE: What's wrong?

MAGDALENA (*not liking the tone of the question*): Nothing is wrong except for my own frayed nerves. If you like, please feel free-

KIT: Oh, that would be no fun at all, Magdalena. Oh! (*Glancing out the window.*) Look how dark it's getting outside!

It's pitch black out there! I didn't hear anything over the radio about rain or I would have brought my umbrella with me.

MAGDALENA (*getting ready to leave*): It has gotten terribly dark. I must run for my bus. Tomorrow, then? Same time? I promise that I will be more accommodating.

KIT: Be careful going home. And, if you're feeling up to it, come over tonight for some dinner. Okay?

MAGDALENA: Not tonight. But, thank you for the invitation. (*Exits.*)

MAHLER: I think that's probably the storm that's making it so dark outside.

CORINNE: My son knows everything, didn't you know that? Everything except his own mind, isn't that right, Mahler?

MAHLER: Let's just say that I know how to think with a rational mind.

CORINNE: Just how many books do you read a year?

KIT: We could use you as a customer, Mahler. I'll put you on our official waiting list.

MAHLER: More than I can remember to count. And, I don't count them. And, why are we staying here?

KIT: Does one need a reason?

CORINNE: With my son, you need a reason for everything. He's not very impulsive. He's boring, like his father was.

MAHLER: My father wasn't boring.

KIT: I liked your dad. He didn't say much; but, what he said was always to the purpose. I miss him.

MAHLER: So do I. And, talk about counting, has anyone taken the trouble to count the number of books we have in our book shop?

CORINNE: Since when is it "our" book shop?

MAHLER: Sorry, mother, I didn't realize my place. I won't forget it in the future.

CORINNE: I won't let you.

KIT: Ignore her for pity's sake. She's a bitch!

MAHLER: May I ask why my mother decided to go into the book business? Were Magdalena's powers of persuasion so strong? Or do I already know the answer?

CORINNE: (*turning on MAHLER*) You know nothing, young man. Remember that: nothing! Do you hear me?

MAHLER: I hear you. I've been hearing you all afternoon.

ACT ONE
Scene Three

MAHLER enters the bakery. The proprietress is wearing her white, starched uniform with a blue trimmed apron over it. Her face is very expressive with "startled" brown eyes. And, when FRANCINE speaks it's with great eagerness.

FRANCINE: Why good evening, Mahler. Out on such an unholy night as this? And, how is mother in her time of sorrow? I'm offering up a novena for her.

MAHLER: I'll tell her that. But, to speak the truth-

FRANCINE: Of course!

MAHLER: I don't think she's sorry that my father's gone.

FRANCINE: Why didn't you say dead? You stopped yourself. I saw! And, your mother has no grief in her heart. How sad! She didn't love your father? However, she should respect his... being gone?

MAHLER: You know, Francine, I met this Jewish girl once-

FRANCINE: A Jewess?

MAHLER: Well...I met this girl and she started telling me her feelings about death and consciousness. She seemed to be afraid of dying because she felt that even a corpse lying buried is not really dead, but still capable of feeling and desperation.

FRANCINE: Was she desperate?

MAHLER: In a way, yes. She told me a little about herself and some of the paths that she's traveled and turned away from.

FRANCINE: Look how it storms outside! No one else will be coming here, tonight. I'll treat you to a cup of coffee. (*Pouring the coffee into two white cups.*) Now, let's talk, my friend and tell Francine about this Jewess. Did she have designs on you?

MAHLER: I wasn't aware of any.

FRANCINE: Ah! I'm certain she did. I remember a Rabbi once telling me -- my God, how it rains! -- that we must be careful of our dead. But, I stray from our topic. What did this girl reveal to you?

MAHLER: Not all that much really. She seemed a bit desperate as if torn between making decisions that she didn't really want to make.

FRANCINE: And, what were those decisions? I don't like her.

MAHLER: You don't know her.

FRANCINE: She had designs on you, didn't she?

MAHLER: Francine...

FRANCINE: Yes, dear?

MAHLER: :She was concerned about dying and wasn't sure what that actually meant. She was very much against cremation.

FRANCINE: It's against their faith, for the dead must rise again.

MAHLER: Something to do with a bone.

FRANCINE (*sipping her coffee, daintily*): Yes! I seem to recall my Rabbi friend telling me that -- a very learned man. But, what's become of this girl?

MAHLER: I don't know. Talk to me about the dead.

FRANCINE: Mourn them and do not mock them, lest they pull you into the grave with them. They watch us and they move within their confinement. And, at times, they come back.

MAHLER: What do you mean?

FRANCINE: They slip out and escape. It's happened before. Jesus helped Lazarus do it.

MAHLER: Whatever became of Lazarus? Surely, his mind was altered.

FRANCINE: It was! And, that was the dreadful thing! The Bible mentions it only in passing and dares not say more.

MAHLER: Does any other writer pick up the tale?

FRANCINE: Yes! But, those books are difficult to find.

MAHLER: Have you found any?

FRANCINE: Perhaps.

MAHLER: Now, you're being coy.

FRANCINE: No, not coy, simply secretive. Never reveal yourself to anyone! Play your cards close to your chest for your best friend is you most dangerous enemy.

MAHLER: How do the dead come back?

FRANCINE: They learn the craft because the Others teach them so cleverly and well.

MAHLER: Who are the Others? Do you spell it with a capital letter?

FRANCINE: Out of dread and respect. Let's not speak of them.

MAHLER: Where do the dead go?

FRANCINE: To another world and, then, sometimes they manage to get back to this one.

MAHLER: Why?

FRANCINE: Unfinished business. Hatred. Anger.

MAHLER: Why don't we ever hear of this?

FRANCINE: It's carefully hidden from us.

MAHLER: Have you known this to happen?

FRANCINE: I have known of it.

MAHLER: I think about my father...and something wasn't quite right with the manner of his death. I don't think he's really dead and, yet, by now he must be.

FRANCINE: Indeed.

MAHLER: Do you read the Tarot, Francine?

FRANCINE: You know I do. Why do you ask such a rhetorical question?

MAHLER: You must come over some night and tell my fortune. Tonight would be a perfect setting for it, wouldn't it?

FRANCINE: Too frenzied and chaotic. The elements must be at peace and willing to cooperate with us mere mortals.

MAHLER: Well, I better be going now. Thanks for the coffee. Oh! I forgot to mention him to you: our upstairs neighbor: the new tenant.

FRANCINE: I know of him.

MAHLER: And?

FRANCINE: He isn't human.

MAHLER: What is he, then?

FRANCINE: Why is he here, Mahler?

MAHLER: Don't ask that question.

FRANCINE: Do you have an answer for it?

MAHLER: Not one that satisfies me. Not yet. He talks in pretty well phrased riddles.

FRANCINE (*placing her hands to her head*): You've spoken to him? You've actually spoken to him? Alone? Be very careful, Mahler!

MAHLER: Do you think the man so dangerous?

FRANCINE: Yes!

MAHLER: Why?

FRANCINE: Why is he hiding?

MAHLER: What makes you think that? To tell the truth, that's my impression, too.

FRANCINE: Look around this area: it's like a deep side pocket hidden away in some forgotten pair of trousers. It's in the middle of a vibrant borough and, yet, so remote. And, we are living in the very bowels of a valley: a power center. (*Glancing out the window.*) Perhaps, we should have your reading tonight?

MAHLER: But, you said-

FRANCINE: Look outside! It's stopped raining. Tonight, then?

MAHLER: Why not? But, a guest might be coming over later.

FRANCINE: Your mother's and aunt's new business partner? She has made my acquaintance.

MAHLER: How is that?

FRANCINE: This morning.

MAHLER: Today? I didn't know that she was in the area.

FRANCINE: She dropped in for some coffee.

MAHLER: It makes no sense. Why didn't she just stop by our apartment house and go with us directly to the book shop?

FRANCINE: She had her reasons, I'm sure.

MAHLER: What did you think of her?

FRANCINE: I liked her. A very educated and refined woman. She plays her cards carefully and I wondered...

MAHLER: Yes?

FRANCINE: Who is using whom?

ACT ONE
Scene Four

MAHLER notices a light in the cellar window -- it flickers off.

THE STRANGER: Was my signal discreet enough?

MAHLER: Were you expecting me?

THE STRANGER: Yes. Tonight, Mahler, things will happen.

MAHLER: Things are happening now.

THE STRANGER: I am aware of them.

MAHLER: Are we talking about the same thing?

THE STRANGER: There is a séance soon to be in progress upstairs and we, my friend, are to be participants.

MAHLER: A séance?

THE STRANGER: I once mentioned to you that there was something hidden down here.

MAHLER: Is that why we're here now?

THE STRANGER: A séance is to be held and we must utilize its energy for our own needs.

MAHLER: What needs are those?

THE STRANGER: Those dear ladies are going to prove very useful...as foolish as all amateurs are. All female energy at a ritual? At best, it's futile. At worst, deadly. (*MAHLER pulls the string on an overhead light.*) We will need that rather ghastly light. Stay close to me. (*He takes MAHLER'S hand and guides it along the outline of the light bulb.*) The penetration should be in this quadrant.

MAHLER: Are we trying to listen in to the séance? Why?

THE STRANGER: Precisely. Why? To use its misguided energy for our own purposes.

MAHLER: To what purpose?

THE STRANGER: To raise the dead?

MAHLER: Was that a question?

THE STRANGER: Frightened?

MAHLER: Yes. I-

THE STRANGER: What? Whom do we seek to raise?

MAHLER: I don't know.

THE STRANGER: You do. Someone who is not really dead.

MAHLER: It feels like we're being watched...like our movements are needed to-

THE STRANGER: To do what?

MAHLER: Start something.

THE STRANGER: Go on.

MAHLER: We have to stay, don't we?

THE STRANGER: As scientists of an unknown art, we must stay. (*A moment's silence.*) They've begun. Already it has had an effect upon the structure of the air. You feel it. You must!

MAHLER: I feel it.

THE STRANGER: There is one amongst those fools with knowledge and skill.

MAHLER: Magdalena.

THE STRANGER: You chose her well. My congratulations to you.

MAHLER: Who are they contacting?

THE STRANGER: Your undead father. It was his money that made the purchase of the book shop possible. Your mother killed her husband. You are not surprised.

MAHLER: No. (*The women's voices are becoming distinct as a "split" stage is now seen.*)

MAGDALENA: We seek to know of a presence that stalks us. It is malevolent. Are we pawns in its game? Have we been deceived in our enthusiasm for our new business?

FRANCINE (*speaking in a trance-like state*): "My death came cheaply."

MAGDALENA: It was not brought about by your own hand?

FRANCINE: "By hers."

CORINNE: Stop it! Stop it at once!

MAGDALENA: Why were you killed? Was it for money?

FRANCINE: "Yes."

CORINNE: He's a liar! This bakery woman is a fraud. Don't listen to her!

FRANCINE: "But, I was not killed. He saved me."

MAGDALENA: Who was it that saved you, Mr. Peri?

FRANCINE: "Mahler. But, there will be more victims."

MAGDALENA: Who? And for what reason?

FRANCINE: "To be alone."

KIT: But, that doesn't make any sense.

MAGDALENA: To be alone; why?

FRANCINE: "She fears us."

MAGDALENA: Whom do you mean?

THE STRANGER: Don't run away, Mahler. It may be necessary to shift you back in time.

MAHLER: To go back in time? It's not possible.

THE STRANGER: But, you must first have some idea of what you will be facing.

MAHLER: Facing? Or what I've already faced? You see how it makes no sense. If I were able to transcend time, I would have a memory of it.

THE STRANGER: Your murdering mother cries out. She's attempting to break the circle; but, she won't be able to do it so easily.

MAHLER: Who's stopping her?

THE STRANGER: Your father.

MAHLER: My God!

THE STRANGER: Pray to Him.

MAHLER: For what? To be spared?

THE STRANGER: For the courage to accomplish what must be done.

MAHLER: What has to be accomplished?

CORINNE: You can't prove anything. What will you tell anybody? That you spoke to a ghost? I'll get even with all of you for this.

MAGDALENA: Who else has she killed?

CORINNE (*attempting to get up*): Why are you doing this to me?

KIT: We can't let you leave, Corinne.

CORINNE: You can't keep me here.

KIT: We can go to the police. We have a suspect for them now. But, why did you do it?

CORINNE: You're so stupid -- all of you!

KIT: We're stupid? Smart people don't get caught. And, I never thought of you as being very smart.

CORINNE: Maybe, just maybe, I murdered him. What of it? Was it a crime to kill someone who was inhuman? You think you're beginning to understand? You don't understand anything, because they won't let you. You don't have the courage to know what I know. Keep out of this, Magdalena and you, too, Kit. Recognize a warning when you hear it. You think I'm the enemy? I'm not. You hate me for hating my son? Fair enough. But, ask yourself why I hate him...because he's like them!

THE STRANGER: There will be a momentary fading of vision...close your eyes if you wish for it may be best for reasons of sanity. When you regain your senses, time will have refocused itself.

MAHLER: Then what?

THE STRANGER: Investigate all that you've heard tonight.

MAHLER: How do I get back to my own time?

THE STRANGER: Touch the light. Good luck! (*MAHLER cries out as the overhead light goes off.*)

ACT TWO
Scene One

The stage is almost in complete darkness except for the light of a blue shaded lamp. There is a liquor bottle on the floor and two glasses. MAHLER'S clothes are different. He is now wearing a two-piece, grey suit. His appearance is different. He is now a young man of twenty-five. Carelessly, but with an adept hand, he lights a cigarette. A young woman is standing behind him. The year is 1947.

ANNE: Mahler? I called your name several times, but you didn't answer. Why not?

MAHLER (*sitting on a crate opposite her*): I'd given up on you.

ANNE: When you didn't come, I decided to look for you. You seemed disoriented, so I brought you here to this book shop.

MAHLER (*offering her a cigarette which she refuses*): Do you know me?

ANNE: I know you now and, I know that one day I will meet you as the son of the man I now speak to.

MAHLER: That's very well put. You're a sensitive of some type.

ANNE: I'm simply stating facts. My name is Anne Terrell. It's the name that I'm now legally using to simplify my life as much as possible and to avoid standing out in the crowd. One shouldn't draw attention to oneself if it can be helped.

MAHLER: I'd agree with that; but, sometimes it can't be helped.

ANNE: That's very true.

MAHLER: What am I to do, now, Miss Terrell?

ANNE: Please call me Anne. There are some unpleasant things that we have to talk about. The reason for your being here is one of them.

MAHLER: The reason being?

ANNE (*evading his question*): We are in the book shop that will one day be purchased by your aunt and Magdalena.

MAHLER (*looking about the room*): I have no aunt. And, I know no one by the name of Magdalena.

ANNE: May I offer you a drink? You do drink?

MAHLER: Scotch, neat.

ANNE: That's my drink, too. Good. We do have something in common. (*She pours the drinks and hands MAHLER his.*) I think it might be raining outside. It could be important.

MAHLER: Important to whom?'

ANNE: They function when there's difficulty imposed on mortals.

MAHLER: Whom do you mean by "they?"

ANNE: The man who sent you back to this time…and the dead.

MAHLER (*pointing at her with his drink*): Who are you, Anne? Tell me your story and, then, we can talk about my friend and the so-called dead.

ANNE: And, you.

MAHLER: And, me -- or my father, if you will.

ANNE: Same difference, really.

MAHLER: What am I doing here in this time of 1947.

ANNE: That's not an easy question to answer.

MAHLER: Give it a try.

ANNE (*staring into her drink*): It began many years ago with the man you will one day meet. He and I and a few others came here and waited. We waited for our chance to encounter individuals open to our way of perception.

MAHLER: Such as life and death?

ANNE: Yes. May I freshen your drink?

MAHLER: Not yet. Continue. Where do you come from?

ANNE: From here. In a place that occupies the same boundaries as this world, but our concepts are quite different as are our limitations. We are finite beings but not in the sense that you define that term. Although our world is here it is a journey of billions of light years and, then, one must cross over the boundary that separates the borders of our universes.

MAHLER: Why did you and your kind come to this planet?

ANNE: To live and breathe and taste the sweet essence of immortality. Many were to cross over, but only a few of us actually survived.

MAHLER: How many of you are left?

ANNE: There are four of us.

MAHLER: Don't lie to me.

ANNE (*placing her drink on the floor*): I'm not lying to you. I've no reason to.

MAHLER: You're not telling me everything, though: that's called deception. What am I doing here?

ANNE: You're being used, but not by me.

MAHLER: To what end?

ANNE: To have you kill your mother, Corinne.

MAHLER: Why?

ANNE: She's a murderess.

MAHLER: She killed my father -- that is, she will kill me.

ANNE: Yes. She will kill you. Do you appreciate the import of what I'm telling you?

MAHLER: If I were to kill my future mother, which is not the most unpleasant thought, then Mahler Peri would never be born. Where does that leave me?

ANNE: In your present body. You and your father would remain as one entity. Is that prospect so unpleasant for you?

MAHLER: Not at all. Refill, please?

ANNE: I can use another one, myself.

MAHLER: Why am I being enlisted for murder?

ANNE (*hands him his drink*): The answer should be obvious: to save yourself. Here you go.

MAHLER: Thank you. When do I meet my "mother?"

ANNE: Then, you've decided to go through with it?

MAHLER: Yes. Not that I have much of a choice: kill or be killed. I'll be stuck here, won't I? I could turn myself into a very rich man. But, send me back, anyway.

ANNE: Wait until you've completed your task before deciding that.

MAHLER: When do I meet her?

ANNE: It's just past midnight. Soon, you will meet her and-

MAHLER: -kill her. (*He drains the last of his drink.*) When?

ANNE: Tonight. It will be the place where you entered this time: in the cellar of that building.

MAHLER: Won't that be awkward? How do I explain my returning there?

ANNE: You'll be visiting a friend.

MAHLER: The tenant who propelled me back in time?

ANNE: He's waiting for you. Be there at two o'clock.

MAHLER: I'd better go.

ANNE: It's stopped raining. Mahler, it's not too late to turn away from this. You can simply stay here or-

MAHLER: No. I've an appointment to keep: an appointment I'm looking forward to, rather.

ACT TWO
Scene Two

THE STRANGER is waiting for MAHLER to arrive. The only light in the cellar is from the overhead light bulb.

THE STRANGER: Good evening. You've seen Corinne enter the building, haven't you.? (*Looking toward the rear of the cellar.*) Take off your jacket. Listen. I hear her footsteps. Take your crude weapon. (*Placing a knife in MAHLER'S hand.*) Try not to get an erection. (*CORINNE moves into view. MAHLER plunges the knife straight into her heart.*)

CORINNE: You fool! You poor fool.

THE STRANGER: I knew that you had the cold-blooded murdering instinct in you. Throw the knife on the floor. We'll clean it up later and you can take it with you as a souvenir.

MAHLER: I don't want it.

THE STRANGER: I insist. Put your jacket back on. Anne will be here shortly and, then, the fun really begins. (*Looking down at the murdered woman.*) And, now, I must see to the body. (*He exits upstage dragging the corpse. ANNE enters from stage right and moves close to MAHLER.*)

MAHLER: The damned cellar! Another body instead of mine.

ANNE: He'll rejoin us soon.

MAHLER: Why?

ANNE: To send you forward to your time and also for safety.

MAHLER: Safety? For a while, I thought you might keep me here. Something's not being told to me.

ANNE: It will soon start.

MAHLER: What?

ANNE: The dead will rise once more. It's happened before in your past.

MAHLER: Where will these dead come from?

ANNE: I've said too much, Mahler…had it not been for the clouds, tonight, there would have been a new moon.

MAHLER: Is there some occult significance to that?

ANNE: That's a very dangerous time. I hear him returning.

THE STRANGER: Ready for a push forward in time? As it stands, you've done a commendable job. The most fitting executioner, Anne?

ANNE: Yes. He was. (*MAHLER and THE STRANGER are standing opposite each other with ANNE standing a few feet back and between them.*)

MAHLER: Anne just mentioned some danger.

THE STRANGER: No! No danger. My friend has her times confused.

MAHLER: When I get back, no one will know me.

THE STRANGER: You will come forward and I'll be standing next to you as I am now. It's not over, but it will be. Close your eyes.

MAHLER: Was I deceived?

THE STRANGER: Isn't one's existence a very clever deception?

MAHLER: That doesn't answer my question.

THE STRANGER: I've carefully avoided it. Do you mind? Enough! Soon you will be back in what is no longer your time to claim. Ready? (*MAHLER reaches for the light bulb. Black out.*)

ACT THREE
Scene One

The two men are standing in the cellar underneath the overhead light bulb. THE STRANGER has his hand on MAHLER'S shoulder.

THE STRANGER: It was a successful journey: a boy left and a man returns in his place. (*He removes his hand and appraises the young man.*) You're more suited to be a man than a youth. I know of the details of your journey. You may stay with me for the time being. Anne is not here, although she wanted to be. Are you all right, Mahler? Should I call you by that name?

MAHLER: It's a name that hasn't existed until now.

THE STRANGER: How do we explain you to the others?

MAHLER: A stranger who happens to resemble someone.

THE STRANGER: Yes. That will do. Not very original, but serviceable.

MAHLER: What's the secret buried here?

THE STRANGER: You'll have to find that out for yourself.

MAHLER: Have things changed very radically?

THE STRANGER: Your family never came into being; but, the other parts of the puzzle have come together. The séance is over, of course, but Corinne never took part in it.

MAHLER: Then, I know all these women?

THE STRANGER: But, they do not know you. Remember that.

MAHLER: No matter.

THE STRANGER: It matters a great deal.

MAHLER: The business is finished, no?

THE STRANGER: The business in not finished, no.

MAHLER: What remains to be completed?

THE STRANGER: Find the buried treasure.

MAHLER: Who lives in my former apartment?

THE STRANGER: Francine.

MAHLER: And, Magdalena? What of her?

THE STRANGER: You like her, don't you? Mahler, we've achieved what no one else has ever imagined. Today will be your first day upon the new world. And, by the way, your voice has taken on a hardness that you might want to conceal.

MAHLER: I'll go to the bakery and introduce myself. Is it morning?

THE STRANGER: It is and her bakery is open for business. She'll try to interrogate you so be careful. And, in your journeys, get back here by nightfall.

MAHLER: Why?

THE STRANGER (*evading the question*): When you return, I will have some proper identification for you.

MAHLER: Money? I'll need some money.

THE STRANGER: It's in your jacket pocket. You have done us a tremendous service and we are greatly in your debt. And, besides, assassins are usually paid quite handsomely. Now go… and be wary of those you know. (*The stage darkens and, then, he is seen standing outside of FRANCINE'S bakery.*)

MAHLER: Good morning.

FRANCINE: Good morning! May I help you?

MAHLER: Yes, please. May I have a coffee: black. And, may I drink it here?

FRANCINE: Of course! Would you like something to go with it?

MAHLER: Perhaps, later. (*He sits down and addresses KIT and MAGDALENA.*) Good morning, ladies.

KIT: Good morning.

MAGDALENA: Good morning.

KIT: Do I know you?

MAHLER: I'm afraid we've never met.

KIT: I don't mean to stare, but it's as if I've dreamt about you and can't quite remember the dream. Please forgive the familiarity, but it's such a disturbing feeling.

MAHLER: I find your comment most interesting; but, I don't quite know how to respond to it. (*FRANCINE brings over the coffee.*) Thank you.

FRANCINE (*sitting down between KIT and MAGDALENA*): Are you visiting here?

MAHLER: I'm staying with a friend.

FRANCINE: Oh? Where?

MAHLER: In the building with the new iron fence: the address I cannot recall.

KIT: That sounds like my apartment building.

MAHLER: Is it? It's no inconvenience, I trust.

KIT: Not at all. I'm just surprised, that's all. You're staying with the man on the third floor, I take it?

MAHLER (*cutting her off*): Yes. And, perhaps, now would be an appropriate time to introduce myself. My name is Mahler Peri.

MAGDALENA: Magdalena Lima.

KIT: Kit Mason, Mr. Peri.

FRANCINE: Will you be with us for long, Mr. Peri?

MAHLER: I'll be leaving in a few days.

FRANCINE: To return home?

MAHLER: I have no home.

FRANCINE: Oh?

MAHLER: I have been away for a very long time.

FRANCINE: To Europe? You seem very continental.

MAHLER: I lived in Germany for many years.

KIT (*glancing at her wristwatch*): Shouldn't we be going about now? I'm anxious to get started.

MAHLER: I hope I haven't detained you.

MAGDALENA: Not at all. We've just opened shop and are very excited.

MAHLER: May I ask the nature of your business?

MAGDALENA: We've recently purchased a book shop. We're expecting our first shipment of books today.

KIT: We really should be there when it arrives. Ready? (*The book shop had been purchased despite the missing partner. Had the murdered woman meant so little in the fabric of time? The answer seemed pathetically obvious.*)

MAHLER: The very best of luck to you both. Will you be open for business soon? I would like to be a customer.

MAGDALENA: We may open this afternoon.

KIT (*excitedly*): A test run. It's Friday and business usually is good on that day of the week. At least we hope it will be. I'm a little nervous, to be honest.

MAHLER: I love book shops and I always buy at least one volume. Is the Bard on your inventory?

MAGDALENA: Of course. A book shop wouldn't be complete without him.

MAHLER: I will purchase a copy of "Hamlet."

KIT (*flirting with MAHLER*): Why thank you, Mr. Peri. I feel much better talking to you. Really. (*MAGDALENA gets up to leave. FRANCINE begins clearing away the cups and saucers.*)

MAGDALENA: Kit, I've just realized that I've forgotten the ledger book. I left it on the kitchen table. Would you lend me your house keys? I won't be a minute.

KIT: I'll come with you.

MAGDALENA: That won't be necessary. I won't be long.

KIT: I could stand another cup of coffee. (*MAGDALENA exits stage left.*)

MAHLER: May I join you?

KIT: Please do.

MAHLER: (*sits down opposite KIT*) So, you ladies live in this area? Of course you do. You mentioned that, didn't you?

KIT: I own the building you're staying in. When my parents died, I was left some money. It was a complicated business. The estate had to be settled and the lawyers were at it for years.

MAHLER: Complicated? Yes. Matters of inheritance often are.

KIT (*looking inside her purse*): My sister disappeared shortly before they died: that didn't help matters.

MAHLER (*raising an eyebrow*): Disappeared?

KIT: Without a trace. It was odd. We'd been thinking of buying that particular building and she was on her way to it the night of her disappearance.

MAHLER: Was there any evidence of foul play? (*FRANCINE joins them.*)

KIT: There was no evidence of anything. I'll be blunt, Mr. Peri, my sister was strange and not a very nice person. She may have gone off without telling any of us; and, it would be just like her to do something vindictive like that. But, it's strange that no one's heard from her in all these years. She must be dead.

MAHLER (*changing the subject*): What other types of books will you be selling?

KIT: All sorts of a literary variety. We're going to try to appeal to the university students, that can be a very profitable market, I'm told.

MAHLER: I am a student of the occult. I am in search of some difficult to locate books and, perhaps, you could help me.

FRANCINE: Kit! Let's tell Mr. Peri about the séance last night.

MAHLER: You actually held a séance?

KIT: I don't-

MAHLER: Was it of a very personal nature?

KIT: Quite frankly, rather strange things have been happening in my apartment building lately, and I wanted an explanation. I was pretty desperate for one, in fact.

MAHLER: What strange things?

FRANCINE: Tell him, Kit. Maybe Mr. Peri can help us -- his being a student of the occult. I read the cards and the tea leaves. Tell him, Kit, or I will. It started before your sister disappeared. You weren't living here at the time, but I was. I've lived here all my life. Have you ever been in this neighborhood before?

MAHLER: No.

FRANCINE: Oh. Well, anyway, the house was always strange, you know. Always having mysterious visitors and tenants that no one ever saw before or ever saw again.

MAHLER: But, is that so unusual?

FRANCINE: To me it is. These people always keep to themselves and make themselves unapproachable. You look doubtful, Mr. Peri.

MAHLER: Many could be accused of that crime.

KIT: Francine exaggerates. There've only been a few such people, at least, since I've owned the building.

MAHLER: Go on, please. I'm sure your story doesn't end there.

FRANCINE: Well, a man had been seen coming out of the cellar that evening: a man who some say later returned.

MAHLER: It's all rather vague and circumstantial. And, it does lack a singular purpose.

FRANCINE: What was he doing down there in the cellar like that? And, he was familiar with the neighborhood. He was later seen talking to a woman…a woman nobody had ever seen before.

MAHLER: And, never seen again, I take it?

FRANCINE (*triumphantly*): Exactly! We speak the same language.

KIT: It's intriguing enough. I'll say that.

FRANCINE: And, Kit's sister disappearing like that. Some say they actually saw her enter the building, but never leave it!

MAHLER: Would they be likely to?

FRANCINE: No…but, no one ever saw her again. Period.

MAHLER: What other strange things have gone on inside that dwelling?

FRANCINE: Sounds coming from the cellar, movements of strange men in the night.

MAHLER: It doesn't really add up to very much. It may all be true, but it sounds explainable.

KIT: Maybe. But, I don't see the explanation.

MAHLER: I've not convinced you, then?

KIT: See how you feel about the place in a few days, Mr. Peri. I'd appreciate your observations. I'd like to get a man's point of view.

MAHLER: Fair enough. But, in the meantime, I will drop by your book shop.

KIT: Whatever happened to my sister defies logic. Perhaps it goes beyond the bounds of logic. I don't know. Francine? It's so cold in here! I'm freezing!

FRANCINE: I'll turn the heat up.

KIT: Thank you. My nerves are on edge as it is.

MAGDALENA (*entering from stage left*): Now, that didn't take too long, did it?

MAHLER: We missed your company. (*KIT gets up to leave.*)

MAGDALENA (*stopping at the door*): It's very strange, but no one is outside. The streets are completely deserted.

FRANCINE: That can't be. It's a work day and people should be about their business. What do you make of it, Mr. Peri?

MAHLER: I don't know, but one should not give way to fear.

KIT: Why do you say that?

MAGDALENA: I didn't mean to alarm anyone. I'm sure there's a logical explanation for it. Well, Mr. Peri, we'll see you later? Francine, we'll drop by later.

KIT: So long Francine. It was a pleasure meeting you, Mr. Peri. (*The two women exit stage left.*)

MAHLER: Do you mind if I smoke?

FRANCINE: Not at all.

MAHLER: Tell me...whatever became of the people that night? The people who allegedly saw Kit's sister and the mysterious man.

FRANCINE: I don't know. I was much younger then and involved with other things. I had my own set of friends. I wasn't the busybody that I am now. Why do you ask?

MAHLER: Are you suspicious of my questions?

FRANCINE: Frankly, yes. But, I'm suspicious of everyone.

MAHLER (*taking a long drag on his cigarette*): Indeed.

FRANCINE: Why do you ask? Did you know that man?

MAHLER: Yes. You're very perceptive for a Fool.

FRANCINE (*standings up*): Why-

MAHLER (*standing up*): Do I offend you? Allow me to apologize as one Fool to another. You see, I had in mind the symbolism of the Tarot. It is your card?

FRANCINE: Why, yes, it is, as a matter of fact.

MAHLER: My offense was meant as the highest of compliments for this is the Fool who is the very center of the universe. He is God.

FRANCINE (*sitting down*): You understand the cards, don't you?

MAHLER: I have a certain knowledge of the cards and their initiation rites.

FRANCINE: Who taught you them?

MAHLER: A beautiful woman by the name of Millette.

FRANCNE: A very beautiful name.

MAHLER: It suited her.

FRANCINE: Is she still with us in this world?

MAHLER: I believe so; but, I have lost contact with her.

FRANCINE: Was that from choice or circumstance?

MAHLER: Perhaps, from intent that was misguided. Strange that no other customers have entered your store. Is it some holiday that I am not aware of?

FRANCINE: Well, it is the day after Thanksgiving. But, I don't see-

MAHLER: I've taken up enough of your time. I trust that we'll see each other quite soon.

FRANCINE: Hopefully!

MAHLER (*a deadly silence hovers in the air*): Listen to me: something quite extraordinary is happening here and I've no explanation for it. It may very well be a matter of life or death.

FRANCINE: Mr. Peri, I'm frightened. Where is everybody?

MAHLER: You're not in any danger, at the moment.

FRANCINE: What does that mean? It means that we're in some sort of danger, doesn't it?

MAHLER: That was phrased awkwardly. Forgive me.

FRANCINE: Mr. Peri, look! The girls are back! Maybe, they can tell us something. (*KIT and MAGDALENA rush in out of breath.*)

MAHLER: Magdalena, what's happened?

MAGDALENA: I'm not sure. There was no traffic at all. The traffic lights were not working and the few people we did see were wandering about aimlessly.

KIT (*close to hysterics*): They were like zombies!

MAHLER: Did these "zombies" seem at all dangerous? Did they threaten you?

KIT (*leaning against a table*): Yes! Is this some terrible nightmare? What could have happened to cause all this?

MAHLER: You may not be too far from the truth.

KIT: Then, why can't we wake up from this horror?

MAHLER: Because we've entered another man's dream? Perhaps, we've bridged that chasm that separates the creation of another reality from our perceived reality?

KIT: Has another God taken over?

MAGDALENA: The universe that we knew was only a pure thought. Have we been taken into another's thought? That could mean that there's no escape for us.

FRANCINE: No! There must be an escape!

MAHLER: Magdalena, I must ask you a question and, then, we must go back to the apartment house.

MAGDALENA: What is it?

MAHLER: Last night, you held a séance. I know of it.

MAGDALENA: We tried to contact Kit's sister, Corinne.

MAHLER: Did you?

MAGDALENA: Yes.

MAHLER (*inhaling deeply*): My God! And?

MAGDALENA: She had been eliminated. I believe that was the word she used. She'd been "eliminated" from a plan.

MAHLER: What plan? Tell me!

MAGDALENA: We couldn't find that out. But, there was cruel laughter on her part.

MAHLER: Was anything else said; anything of import that could help us?

MAGDALENA: Beware of someone who is not what he appears to be: do you know what Corinne meant by that?

MAHLER: I'm that man. Perhaps, I've succeeded in destroying us all for the crime I've committed.

FRANCINE: What crime? Can you tell us?

KIT: Don't.

MAGDALENA: What was your crime?

MAHLER: An obscenity. Look. It's growing darker as we speak.

KIT: I can actually see the shadows lengthening.

MAGDALENA: Where are we? Is there no escape?

MAHLER: None that I'm aware of.

MAGDALENA: How does one escape from another's dream?

MAHLER: Through death, I imagine.

FRANCINE: No!

KIT: We can't be dead!

MAGDALENA: The séance…there was something odd about it. I didn't go home because of the late hour and as we left Francine's apartment, I had the strangest feeling of being isolated, cut off from the world, as if the three of us had vanished or the world about us had ceased to exist.

MAHLER: Perhaps, your séance propelled you to this desolation.

MAGDALENA: Are we dead? Or am I insane to even ask such a question?

MAHLER: Each of us still possesses a soul and a dead man would not have such a possession. Come. We mustn't stay here.

ACT THREE
Scene Two

The four people are just arriving in KIT'S apartment.

FRANCINE: It's freezing! It feels like the inside of a tomb. (*The three ladies sit down while MAHLER remains standing. They hear footsteps on the stairs and a banging on the door commences.*) Don't answer it!

MAGDALENA (*going over to the door*): Who is there? (*No answer.*) Please, answer me. Who is there?

ANNE: My name is Anne Terrell. Mr. Peri knows me. Is he in there? Please, let me in. We're all in terrible danger!

MAHLER: Let her in, Magdalena. She's either the friend we need or a trickster. (*MAGDALENA opens the door. ANNE is wrapped in a cloak with a hood draped about her head.*)

ANNE (*breathless*): Please, may I sit down?

MAHLER: Anne, you must tell us everything and quickly.

ANNE: I've been deceived. The invasion is finished. Your world is lost. It is now populated by the few remnants of my own people. I've been consigned to this hell. (*FRANCINE makes to interrupt her.*) Let me continue, please. The people of your world have either been slaughtered or absorbed or placed elsewhere.

MAHLER: Such as here?

ANNE: Yes. But, better off dead. At least the soul is released.

FRANCINE: What are you telling us? Are we all dead?

ANNE: No. We have been placed into another's dream. The god you once worshipped is no more. You must erect a monument to your new god.

FRANCINE: Are you insane? Do you expect us to believe any of this?

MAHLER: And, what god is this?

ANNE: We are part of a new thought.

MAHLER: What are the soulless people out there?

ANNE: The new creations.

MAHLER: But, they're imperfect. They're monsters. The dead that have been awakened?

ANNE: Yes. Monsters.

MAHLER: How were you deceived?

ANNE: I was tricked into coming through.

MAHLER: What will happen to us now?

ANNE: I was waiting…assuming that our new god would be walking amongst us. But, he's not appeared and the soulless ones are seeking us out.

MAGDALENA: To kill us? Why? What would that accomplish?

ANNE: Nothing. But, how do you reason with a mindless primitive?

FRANCINE (*screaming*): They'll kill us all!

KIT: How can we stop them?

ANNE: I don't know.

MAGDALENA: Mahler, we have no world to go back to? I don't believe this woman.

ANNE: I've told you no lies.

MAGDALENA: But, have you told us the entire truth? A half truth can be much more misleading than a lie. Why didn't your people invade this place?

ANNE: I don't know. But, your own world hasn't been destroyed. Life and its culture move forward and thrive.

MAHLER: So, just now you were lying? We can return to our world?

ANNE: Yes.

MAHLER: And, this place-

ANNE: Is an experiment. More may arrive through natural death or imposed sleep.

KIT: She's still lying. I don't believe a word of it.

ANNE: Whether or not I'm lying doesn't matter, but our survival does. (*The sound of loud scraping is heard.*)

KIT (*terrified*): What was that? It came from downstairs.

FRANCINE: I think someone's trying to get in.

KIT: It sounds like more than one person.

MAHLER: Is he still here? The man who brought me back?

ANNE: Go and see. But time is very much against us. Hurry!

MAHLER: Everyone stay here. (*He exits. The sound of pounding fists can be heard.*) You in there! Answer me! Answer me! Damn you! (*He kicks the door in and, then, his footsteps can be heard on the stairs.*) He's gone. The filthy bastard is gone!

KIT: Now, what do we do?

ANNE: Deceiver! I knew this would happen. We must make our way into the cellar before it's too late. (*More scraping sounds can be heard.*)

MAGDALENA: Mahler, look outside! It's nightfall. How can that be? (*The sound of shattering glass is heard.*)

ANNE: They've broken in! (*The lights go out.*)

MAHLER: We must head for the cellar before they cut us off. Quickly! (*Black out.*)

FRANCINE (*screaming with both hands clasped together*): We're doomed!

KIT: Francine, get a grip.

MAHLER (*switching on the light bulb*): If my theory is correct, we may be able to bridge the chasm back into our own world.

KIT (*putting her hand to her mouth to stifle a scream*): They're down here with us.

MAHLER: Kit, give me your hand. (*He places KIT'S hand on the light bulb and she vanishes.*)

FRANCINE: You did it! But, what if-

MAHLER: My dear, be the Fool no more. I'm sending you back. (*He places her hand on the light bulb and she, too, vanishes.*

He turns his attention to ANNE.) And, what of you? What am I to do with you?

ANNE: What are you saying? Keep away from me!

MAHLER: Magdalena, you must now trust this murderer.

MAGDALENA: Who are you?

MAHLER: I killed Kit's sister. (*ANNE reaches up and touches the light bulb. She vanishes.*) Good riddance to the bitch.

MAGDALENA: Have you destroyed them all?

MAHLER: I've saved them. We must hurry -- the monsters are closing in upon us. (*He touches the light bulb. Black out.*) We're back in our own world.

MAGDALENA: Who- what are you?

MAHLER: One of those who came to dwell amongst you. Corinne had stumbled on to certain facts and had to be killed.

MAGDALENA: She would have murdered you in time to come?

MAHLER: And, now young, Mahler Peri will never be born.

MAGDALENA: What of that other place we've just escaped?

MAHLER: An empty pocket of reality, perhaps, or a universe governed by some obscene god?

MAGDALENA: Is Corinne buried in this cellar?

MAHLER: Yes. (*Carefully, MAGDALENA makes her way out of the cellar as another figure approaches from upstage.*)

THE STRANGER: You've found your way back. And, what of Anne? Did you leave her to rot in that phantasmic world?

MAHLER: She escaped.

THE STRANGER: We must go into hiding and wait as immortals must. Do not attempt assimilation, again.

MAHLER: You mention the need to hide.

THE STRANGER: Not a need, but a device that will camouflage our intent.

MAHLER: What is that intent?

THE STRANGER: To conquer this race. And they will welcome us as only the handlers of appeasement are able to. It could be done tomorrow, but the hordes are not yet ready.

MAHLER: Is Anne to be contacted?

THE STRANGER: Despite her talents, she's troublesome.

ANNE (*entering from stage right*): I'm here. I've been here all the while.

THE STRANGER: Let us leave Mahler to ponder his purpose.

ANNE: Has he recovered his senses? He doesn't look well at all.

THE STRANGER: Being reborn is not a simple task.

ANNE: We'll have to watch him closely. He'll make the same mistake, again. I know it.

THE STRANGER: We could eliminate the woman, Magdalena.

ANNE: Would that solve anything? I'm not opposed to it; but, I don't think it's the solution.

THE STRANGER: The alternative?

ANNE: He could be isolated for a time.

THE STRANGER: Difficult.

ANNE: Shall we leave him to his thoughts?

THE STRANGER: Briefly. On his own, he may be dangerous.

ANNE: I thought you had discarded us. I knew what fear was. It was very disconcerting to feel that emotion. Was that your intention? (*Not waiting for an answer.*) Does he hear us?

THE STRANGER: I don't think so. Come, let us leave him for a few moments. (*He and ANNE exit the cellar.*)

MAHLER (*taking the knife from his jacket*): I am now the dominant imagery. Young Mahler is only a shadow thought in the dark chamber of my heart. My son was never born. Corinne was right to fear me. I am not human. I will murder, again. I will murder…anyone

End of play.

THE DYING GOD:

A Vampire's Tale

A Play in Three Acts

by

Gerard Denza

THE DYING GOD: A Vampire's Tale premiered at the
Common Basis Theatre in New York City on October 7, 2004
with the following cast:

DAMIEN	Brian Townes
ANTONIA	Marie Lazzaro
	(followed by Sharla Meese.)
COLETTE	Catherine Crawford
BAYLA ORTIZ	Jamie Oberlee
SAMUEL	Michael Vitiello
CORNFIELD	Phil Strumolo
DEANNA*	Meredith Napolitano

*A character that has since been eliminated from the revised version.

Set by Phil Strumolo.
Directed by Gerard Denza.

PLACE
The action begins in Damien's apartment in New York City,
an almost bare room where he has practiced the black art of
dreaming.

TIME
The recent past brought forward to the recent future.

SCENES

Act One
Scene One: Damien's apartment in New York City.
Scene Two: Colette's apartment in the same
building. It is the following evening.
Scene Three: Samuel's apartment that same evening.
Scene Four: Damien's apartment on the following morning.
Scene Five: Colette's apartment, later on the same day.

Act Two
Scene One: A rented flat in one of London's run
down districts. Three months have passed.
Scene Two: A flat in one of London's more
affluent districts. It is the following evening.

Act Three
Scene One: Bayla's apartment and
several months have passed.
Scene Two: Bayla's apartment one month later.

Epilogue
The following morning in Bayla's apartment.

CHARACTERS

DAMIEN, a cynical vampire.
ANTONIA, Damien's girlfriend.
COLETTE, a Frenchwoman and Damien's enemy.

BAYLA ORTIZ, a Magus of the highest degree.
SAMUEL, a young man who befriends Damien.
SAMUEL'S FATHER, a learned and unusual man.
CORNFIELD, a Magus of the highest degree.

ACT ONE
Scene One

DAMIEN is sitting on the floor with his right leg bent close to his chest. He is naked. A red spotlight is on this figure of a man and the rest of the stage is veiled in darkness. One can see and even sense the power within the strong, lean frame of the man.

DAMIEN: I am alone. There is no God in this place. Have I found my spirit? Does even that remnant of myself still exist? I fear not. I have been dreaming for a long time, but I have now awakened from my dream. A dream has a memory of its own and this memory is independent of the dreamer for it has a life and a place and a framework in the scheme of one's life. It is a fragile reminder of the impermanence of creation. A dream is created and destroyed for it must be destroyed if one is to awaken. It has power and death. Death. A word that I have come to embrace and to feel sublimely comfortable with and to long for. (*He hugs his arms about his torso as if he feels a coldness.*) It's still dark outside, but there is light in the room. I lift my arm to place my hand in front of my eyes and the light vanishes completely and the room becomes a pitch-black void of nonexistence. The terror that I feel takes a grip on my body, and every muscle shudders as a cold spasm sweeps through me. I try to cry out. Did I moan in agony or in ecstasy? Or was it just my imagination? (*He gets up and pulls his pants on. He places his hand to his mouth while suppressing the urge to laugh hysterically.*) I've bitten myself, again. (*He turns about and circles the stage in the opposite direction, occasionally glancing at the audience.*) When I was a small boy, I would receive communion. The little, blessed wafer: the body and the blood of the Christ: a holy ritual of magic is what it was and remains. It was my favorite part of the Mass, kneeling before the priest and feeling the cold marble beneath my knees. Everyone would be looking at you. You were holy and they were not. (*Staring incredulously at the audience.*) Was that when my life began to be cursed? a jealous onlooker? a darkness that had entered the receptacle of the church...a darkness that had been allowed inside? Yes. The blasphemers within would permit such a thing. A darkness that would crawl along the tiled floor and wind its way down the central aisle...only the central aisle...neither to the right nor to the left. Coiling its way and alerting any sensitive person to its presence. It coiled its way down looking for me. It saw me and struck at me when I was kneeling. The wafer fell to the ground and the snake lodged itself in my throat. The priest looked at me with contempt and moved on to the next little boy. Didn't he see what had just happened? Was he not a magician? A sage? A sinner? He would admit to nothing. The fool. Fool! (silence) Antonia is due to arrive soon. I hope she remembers to bring some food with her. Was that the door I just heard? Antonia? (*ANTONIA enters from stage right. She is young and attractive and has a touch of arrogance to her. She is carrying a brown, paper bag.*)

ANTONIA: Who else would it be? And, you left the door unlocked.

DAMIEN: Have you brought any food for a starving man?

ANTONIA: Yes.

DAMIEN: Good. Do you hate me?

ANTONIA: Yes. And, I resent you.

DAMIEN: Does it border on hate?

ANTONIA: And, respect. I respect your perverted talents.

DAMIEN: Get me my cigarettes, will you?

ANTONIA: No. I have to get the food ready.

DAMIEN: Then, get the food ready. I'm starving. (*ANTONIA exits.*) Soon, the full moon will be rising and we'll be able to see it from the parlour window. The summer solstice is only three days away. What irony!

ANTONIA (*enters*): I'm expected to wait on you? Yes?

DAMIEN: You don't have to. You don't even have to be here.

ANTONIA: Take a joke. It's almost done. How do you want your vegetables, a little burnt?

DAMIEN: Yes, please.

ANTONIA: I'll be right back. (*Exits.*)

DAMIEN: Antonia and I are like a flame when we have sex. The fire shoots into the sky burning away the air in its path. But, then, it would fall by degrees back down and the air would cool once again. Ah! She brings the food. (*ANTONIA enters with a tray of food.*) Nice job. You know how to be good to a man.

ANTONIA (*sitting down next to DAMIEN*): I know how to be very bad, also. But, you like that, too.

DAMIEN: I do. That's one reason why we put up with each other.

ANTONIA: I can think of many more. But, Damien, I want to talk about something else.

DAMIEN: I don't like discussions, so get to the point.

ANTONIA: You're in a mood, tonight.

DAMIEN: The point?

ANTONIA: The ritual. I've invited Colette. You mind?

DAMIEN: Not at all. I don't find that French whore too offensive.

ANTONIA: Is that what you think she is: a whore?

DAMIEN: A French whore; yes. But, what of it?

ANTONIA (*glancing out the window*): Eat your food. There'll be a full moon, tonight. It'll be glorious!

DAMIEN: Um…hmm.

ANTONIA: Um…hmm. You making fun of me?

DAMIEN: Can't take a joke?

ANTONIA: Touché.

DAMIEN: Eat your food.

ANTONIA: I'm going to look at the moon. Come?

DAMIEN: Not yet. I'm still a bit hungry. I'll eat your portion.

ANTONIA: What are you thinking of?

DAMIEN: I'm eating.

ANTONIA: Tell me what you're thinking of?

DAMIEN: You and myself.

ANTONIA: Not just me? That's all right; I'll settle.

DAMIEN: Keep me company while I eat. I'm enjoying your company tonight, rather.

ANTONIA: I want you to meet some people.

DAMIEN (*continuing to eat*): Interesting people?

ANTONIA: I only know interesting people.

DAMIEN: You know me.

ANTONIA: You most of all, my love. Still doing your rituals?

DAMIEN: Best not spoken of. I stopped. Never again.

ANTONIA: Damien! Couldn't have surprised me more. Won't tell me why, either? Huh? But, I also don't believe you. But, one last one, tonight? Okay?

DAMIEN: Maybe. Now, we must go to dear Colette's.

ANTONIA: No.

DAMIEN: No? But, I thought the gathering was at her place? Was I mistaken or misled?

ANTONIA (*sitting down beside him*): Both. Colette will be coming here. Do you mind, terribly?

DAMIEN: I should kill you for this.

ANTONIA: Later.

DAMIEN (*walking to the edge of the stage and addressing the audience*): I don't trust Colette. It's as if she had been standing just behind the door lying in wait. She flings it open for it's not good enough to just open it. She insists that we meet two very dear friends of hers; one of whom she's just met herself. His name is Samuel; but, I'll call him the Jew boy. The woman who brought him is Bayla Ortiz. Bayla is so completely a woman. She has an exotic, yet a somewhat European look to her. I cannot do her proper justice. Her scent is magnificent. I cannot place it. It was not meant to be placed. When she moved, she left behind a scented cloud of spice. Ravishing. How did she and Samuel meet? Their paths should never have crossed. (*The guests are now seated. COLETTE is a native French woman who dresses very chic despite the limits of her budget. SAMUEL is wearing black slacks and a white shirt. BAYLA is dressed in the "little, black dress."*)

BAYLA: I enjoy the company of interesting people. Colette has assured me that I am in such company. Am I?

COLETTE: My dear…

DAMIEN (*addressing SAMUEL*): My name is Damien. You know that already, but I think it sounds better coming from me. Tell me your name.

SAMUEL (*in almost a whisper*): My name is Samuel.

DAMIEN: Samuel?

SAMUEL: Yes. Samuel. I am named after my great-grandfather.

DAMIEN: How did you come to be here, tonight? Mind my asking?

SAMUEL: Miss Ortiz brought me. It was at her suggestion that I came.

DAMIEN: How did you come to meet Miss Ortiz? Where did you meet? When did you meet -- the circumstances, please?

SAMUEL: She came to visit the synagogue. We spoke at some length about Judaism and the Qaballah. I am a student of the

Qaballah and religion; it is a deep interest of mine that almost borders on a passion. Miss Ortiz was kind enough to invite me to your place. Do you mind my being here?

DAMIEN (*in an incredulous tone of voice*): And, you came?

SAMUEL: I am here, no?

DAMIEN: Why?

SAMUEL: I am not sure of the reason. I gave into impulse which I very seldom do. Perhaps, it is out of a sense of curiosity. I really don't know why.

BAYLA (*interrupting the conversation*): I wanted Samuel to meet you, Damien. Colette has told me so very much about you. Your pastimes…

DAMIEN (*responding too quickly*): I've retired from my pastimes.

BAYLA: That is unfortunate. You may want to resume the practice. Have you decided upon a new pastime? A progression from the old one?

DAMIEN: Yes. It may even kill me.

COLETTE (*very sweetly*): Or even worse.

BAYLA: If he's worthy of it.

DAMIEN: Samuel?

SAMUEL: Yes?

DAMIEN: Damien.

SAMUEL: Damien.

DAMIEN: What has Bayla told you about me? I don't know anything about you. That's not entirely true. I know you're Jewish. I was once mistaken for being a Jew. It rankled me quite a bit.

SAMUEL: Why should it "rankle" you? I do not understand that statement. Perhaps, you feel that people liken you to a caricature. You find that insulting.

DAMIEN: Not insulting. I wouldn't go to that length.

SAMUEL: To what other length would you take it, Damien? I am not judging your reaction because it is probably one that is based solely on emotion. You would do well to ask yourself the question: what is it that I feel and why?

DAMIEN: Interesting your saying that. I do play at being the intellectual; but, perhaps, my perspective is not as clear as I would have it be.

SAMUEL: As regards?

DAMIEN: My nature. My wants. My needs of spirituality and perversion.

SAMUEL: Perversion? That is not possible with spirituality; the two are opposites.

DAMIEN: That do meet at the crossroads of decision.

SAMUEL: Whose decision would that be and pertaining to whom or what?

DAMIEN: To me. I like you.

COLETTE (*casting ANTONIA a sidelong glance*): Damien? Tell Colette if we have interrupted a little tete-a-tete just now with you and Antonia.

DAMIEN: None of your damned business. Samuel? I thought Orthodox Jews grew full beards. Was I misled to believe that?

ANTONIA: I prefer clean shaven men, myself.

SAMUEL: There are points of energy contained within the beard. But, I am not Orthodox. What gave you that impression? My father is Orthodox; and, I am sure that he could provide you with an answer or at least with his own definition.

COLETTE: What points of energy? Tell me. I must know.

SAMUEL: I can't find the words. Energy for the light. My father could explain it better. I do not fully understand it, myself. It has to do with the godhead of Kether atop the glyph of life and death.

COLETTE: I understand!

DAMIEN: Who gives a crap?

BAYLA: Damien?

DAMIEN (*moving toward her for a cigarette*): May I have a drag on your cigarette? I gave them up, but I still smoke.

BAYLA: Good. No reason to give them up. Not really. I find them very satisfying. (*She holds out the black cigarette case.*) Yes. Black. My favorite color. (*She is staring at SAMUEL'S shirt.*) Is white yours?

DAMIEN: As a matter of fact, it is. But, black comes a very close second.

BAYLA: Red comes a very close second for me. Red. Red of the deepest and most beautiful fire. Red. When blood spills into daylight it is truly magnificent! No?

DAMIEN: I-

BAYLA: No?

DAMIEN: I'll take your word for it. Where do you come from, Bayla?

BAYLA: My current home is in London. A recent trip brought me to Israel. From there, I came to visit Colette. We met in Paris quite a long time ago.

COLETTE: Not that long ago.

BAYLA: A few years ago, perhaps. Does it matter?

COLETTE: Yes.

DAMIEN: How did you come to meet Samuel? Why did you bring him here?

BAYLA: I've answered these questions.

DAMIEN: Not satisfactorily.

BAYLA: I know. I am aware of that. Research and study, shall we say? Research into Judaism.

DAMIEN: Have you always had an interest?

BAYLA: No. I have always had a revulsion.

DAMIEN: And, now?

BAYLA: I find Samuel attractive.

COLETTE: Oh?

BAYLA: He is promised to another. A young woman. She wears the skirt.

ANTONIA: Do you mean to say that he's engaged to a woman?

DAMIEN: Samuel?

SAMUEL (*blushing*): We do not call it that. It's not an engagement, but a commitment between two people. I am explaining it badly. It differs from the Christian marriage because it is based on much history and the roles are clearly defined for both the man and the woman.

COLETTE: Is she pretty?

ANTONIA (*laughing*): You would ask him that.

COLETTE: But what is wrong with that? A perfectly natural question, no?

BAYLA: They'll be married soon.

DAMIEN (*to the audience*): Why is she completely ignoring the Jew boy. It's deliberate on her part. She's shedding him. She wants nothing more to do with him. Her task is complete and I'm positive that she'll leave without him. Nice of her. Why? A present for me? The Jew boy is for me.

BAYLA (*reaching for her bag*): May I?

COLETTE: Of course. The powder room is right over there, I believe. Please. (*BAYLA exits upstage.*)

DAMIEN (*taking a deep drag on his cigarette*): I think Bayla intends to leave us soon.

ANTONIA (*with a malicious smile directed at SAMUEL*): Yes. Will you be leaving with her?

SAMUEL: I assume so or I would not have come. It was not stated openly, but it was assumed, at least by me. Why do you ask that question?

COLETTE (*indignantly*): Of course he will. She brought him here; did she not? To abandon him? No!

ANTONIA: He could spend the night with you, Damien.

COLETTE (*in a state of almost complete distraction*): But, why? He comes with her. He goes with her. There! Simple! It is settled. No more talk.

ANTONIA: Samuel? Would you like to spend the night with Damien...

DAMIEN: Shut up -- the two of you. Let's wait for Bayla.

BAYLA (*a pronounced silence greets her*): Has there been an argument? Yes?

DAMIEN: That depends on you. Leaving?

BAYLA:. Yes. I've finished here.

DAMIEN: Finished with us?

BAYLA: Not with all of you.

COLETTE (*addressing SAMUEL*): My dear, you should get ready, then.

BAYLA: Samuel is not coming with me.

ANTONIA: Thought so.

BAYLA: I must go, how shall I put it, another way?

COLETTE: But, my dear, I do not have a car and it is very late. It would be unsafe for him to travel by public transport.

ANTONIA (*trying not to laugh*): Colette does have a point.

BAYLA (*looking directly at DAMIEN*): No. He shouldn't.

COLETTE: But, he cannot stay with Damien and, most certainly, not at my place. It is impossible!

DAMIEN: Scandal, Colette?

COLETTE: Son of a bitch! Go to hell!

DAMIEN: I will. But, I'll send you there just before me. You'll be my first, you French cunt.

COLETTE: Mon Dieu! I cannot bear anymore!

ANTONIA: Colette, lower your goddamned voice! Samuel? We can leave together.

COLETTE (*panic stricken*): No! You must stay.

BAYLA (*picking up her purse*): Good night, everyone. Samuel? Damien? I give you my love. (*She exits and a deafening silence follows.*)

COLETTE (*standing up*): I cannot believe she did this! I cannot believe it! Bitch!

ANTONIA: You're going to have a lodger tonight, Damien.

DAMIEN: Samuel? If you like, I'll take you home.

SAMUEL: I am afraid to travel at night. I would put you out, but I cannot think of an alternative. Miss Ortiz has disappointed me. What she did just now was very rude.

DAMIEN: No. You wouldn't be putting me out.

SAMUEL: The situation is awkward. It was made so by Miss Ortiz.

DAMIEN: Dear God! I could kill that woman who just left.

COLETTE (*standing too close to DAMIEN*): It is getting late. Antonia and I must leave.

DAMIEN (*nearly knocks COLETTE over*): You could have solved this. Enjoy your one night of pleasure. Now get out! (*COLETTE'S face is bloated with horror as she screams. He pushes her and ANTONIA through the door.*) Now, you're with me, Jew boy.

SAMUEL (*getting to his feet*): That is not my name. My name is Samuel. Are you anti-Semitic, Damien? Or do you just joke with me? But, the joke is at my expense.

DAMIEN: Relax. (*He beckons SAMUEL to sit back down.*) I think Colette's still screaming. (*He jumps over the couch and sits down next to SAMUEL.*) You're tired. It must be past your bedtime. Are you hungry?

SAMUEL: I've not eaten for quite some time. The thought of food is quite appealing.

DAMIEN: I've no food in the house. Get comfortable. I'll make up your bed. I'll sleep out here. It really is more convenient that way. No argument. If you like, you can use the bathroom. (*Exit SAMUEL.*) I feel myself weakening: a sign that I am beginning to lose control. I am becoming a vampire, but not in the conventional sense of that term. I have transformed myself into a predatory thing, but it is not complete. It needs the consecration of murder. For most of my life, I have been involved with the occult arts and with its dangers and promises and many misleading paths. If I could love a thing, it is this thing that would claim a love. It was during one, dark occult ceremony that I made my usual prayer, request if you would, of immortality. Not so much of eternal youth, but to see the world die about me and for myself to remain unchanged. It was a long ceremony with Colette and Antonia present to give it its needed momentum and female sustenance. We erected an unholy cross of supplication...yes... supplication to the gods of darkness who granted favors but not forgiveness...never forgiveness...never that. I placed myself upon this cross and prayed to be given immortality at any cost. An unholy messenger answered my plea. When the ceremony had ended, I arose naked from the cross. Colette and Antonia were exhilarated. And I? I felt nothing but coldness and, yet, my body was bathed in sweat...that had the odor of death about it. I touched my chest with my fingertips. Hard. Too hard. Something in me had changed. I knew that my prayers had been answered. A vampire who may dwell in the shadow of daylight and prey upon the living in the sanctuary of the night. (*A momentary silence.*) Perhaps, I will take Samuel with me tomorrow night to visit dear Colette. I like that idea, rather. I'll have an unpleasant surprise for her and Antonia.

ACT ONE
Scene Two

It is the following evening at COLETTE'S place. DAMIEN and SAMUEL are seated next to each other. ANTONIA is also there. COLETTE has not quite recovered from her encounter with DAMIEN the previous night.

DAMIEN: Colette?

COLETTE (*almost dropping her cake*): Yes?

DAMIEN: May I have another slice of cake? It's quite delicious and sweet. Do you think I'll sicken myself with another piece?

COLETTE: No! You may have even more than that!

DAMIEN: Such a gracious hostess.

ANTONIA (*picking at her cake*): How was your night?

DAMIEN: I love him.

ANTONIA (*seething with anger*): It must have been quite an evening. Really. I'm surprised he's still alive. I'm surprised you're still human. Are you? I think you are. You look warm blooded enough.

DAMIEN: Ask the Jew boy.

ANTONIA: I thought he was getting married to the girl with the skirt. Still is, I bet.

DAMIEN: Still is. I don't bet. You shouldn't either. You're lousy at it.

ANTONIA: Don't know that.

DAMIEN: I do. I know everything about you, my dear Antonia.

ANTONIA: Another lie. Liar!

DAMIEN: I didn't mean you to get angry.

ANTONIA: When did you ever love anyone? When? Tell me! Now! Tell me! You-love-someone? Monster!

DAMIEN (*staring at ANTONIA and addressing COLETTE*): Colette? Give Antonia some cake, please: a black and white slice. Shut her up. Shut this slut up!

COLETTE: Please! No quarreling. Why are you so angry, Antonia? Don't let him do this to you.

ANTONIA: I'm jealous. There. All of you surprised? Good. But, not in that way. I don't want you to love him- him. That Jew! That disgusting Jew!

COLETTE: Antonia, stop! At once!

DAMIEN (*getting to his feet*): Say it when Samuel leaves. Say it behind his back. Behind the veil. Let us not rent the veil, not again! (*ANTONIA gets up and he pushes her back down into her chair.*) I should kill you now. Rip your head off. (*He makes to leave and smacks ANTONIA hard behind the head. COLETTE burst into tears.*) Let's leave them to each other. (*Blackout.*) I fled into the courtyard. There was a fountain there that used to have running water but it had long since dried up. I leaned on it. My hands pressed against the warm stone, but I wasn't aware of the touch. The stone was smooth as my fingers gripped it. I was actually making indentations in the stone. I removed one hand from the fountain to place it against my mouth. It was beginning. Was it too late for the Jew boy? He followed me into my apartment...the courtyard...an illusion. My insanity is manifesting. Keep away!

SAMUEL: I cannot keep away. You need me.

DAMIEN: I don't need you. Now, get away.

SAMUEL: I do not turn my back on someone. You are suffering.

DAMIEN: I am...and I'm enjoying it. I take pleasure from it.

SAMUEL: Then, why do you warn me away?

DAMIEN: Because, I hate you. But, don't take it personally. I'm at odds with humanity, because I hate it. You're included in that, Jew boy. Hear what I'm telling you? Hear me?

SAMUEL: I am standing right behind you. Why don't you look at me? Look into my soul.

DAMIEN: Why should I look at you?

SAMUEL: Perhaps, Bayla brought us together because we need each other.

DAMIEN: Interesting. You've found your philosopher's tongue. But, which philosopher would that be? Aristotle? No. You make no sense. Good ole' Soren K.? You are religious; but, I think not. Ah! Thomas Mann. Yes! You would worship in the gondola of that lonely sage. Did I hit it right, philosopher?

SAMUEL: I wait. When something must be said, then I talk, and not to impress.

DAMIEN: That's what they all say. Leave me.

SAMUEL: I should be home. The Shabbat meal is very important. Come home with me, Damien. My father will welcome you. And, tomorrow we go to temple together.

DAMIEN: You must be mad.

SAMUEL: If it is madness that spurs one to be a human being, then, perhaps it has a nobility of its own.

DAMIEN: Why am I even discussing this insanity. I should end this filthy life. Go to your family, Samuel. They're your life.

SAMUEL: You've entered my life. I know of you now and that cannot be changed. Come, let us go home.

DAMIEN: All right. Lead the way...this night may still hold some promise.

ACT ONE
Scene Three

One hour later. DAMIEN and SAMUEL are in the latter's home. SAMUEL and his FATHER are on opposite ends of the dining room table with DAMIEN sitting on the father's right hand side.

DAMIEN (*addressing the audience*): Has it come to this? Is this what Bayla had in mind: the solace of religion and family?

FATHER: Young man, please speak to me.

DAMIEN: Could I have several desserts?

FATHER: You must have food first. You barely ate anything. Was it at least good?

DAMIEN: Delicious, in fact. You are an excellent cook. My compliments.

SAMUEL: My father's specialty is the haute cuisine. It was once his profession.

FATHER: Would you like something to drink?

DAMIEN: Thank you. No.

FATHER: Some wine?

DAMIEN: You're both being very kind.

SAMUEL: It is more than kindness. It is treating a human being as a human being.

FATHER: Samuel, what do we discuss, tonight? Perhaps, something that would interest your new friend?

SAMUEL: He has much on his mind; and, I'm sure that he would be the best judge as to what interests him.

DAMIEN: Is there a passage in the Bible that mentions the Valley of Shadows? I don't know what part it is: the Old Testament or the New Testament. But, you don't have a New Testament, do you? Sorry. I really don't know what I'm talking about. I'm quite ignorant of- well, let's just say that I'm quite ignorant.

FATHER: You are an intelligent man. Don't say such things about yourself.

SAMUEL: He is very intellectual; but, he lacks compassion for himself.

DAMIEN: The Fall. May we discuss that? Adam and the Fall. And, the Tree of Life. Tell me all that you know, please. The Tree of Life and the Tree of Knowledge.

FATHER: The saddest point in human existence.

DAMIEN: Where is the Tree of Life? Does it even exist? Can it be found?

SAMUEL: It can be found in the cave with Adam. I believe this.

DAMIEN: If we were to eat from its fruit would one be saved? I'm a sick man. If I ate from the Tree and if my intent were to save my life, would I be saved?

SAMUEL: Yes. You would be saved because you wanted to be saved. You would be your own savior; it could be no other way.

DAMIEN: I would be saving other people's lives, as well. Would that not be an act of giving?

FATHER: Do you really want to save lives? To save your life is an act of giving.

DAMIEN: Others would disagree.

SAMUEL: It would make me happy; but, that is of little import. It must make you happy.

FATHER: You know that Adam was a giant. Not even his skin was like ours.

DAMIEN: Tell me about him, please.

SAMUEL: He will. My father is a scholar in his own right and has even lectured on many topics.

FATHER: He glowed. His skin was like that of this candle.

DAMIEN: Where is he now?

FATHER: I like your questions. You are a very perceptive young man.

DAMIEN: What of the Tree?

FATHER: The fruit would be huge. You couldn't even hold it.

DAMIEN: Then, if I took only a portion…the very smallest of portions.

FATHER: It would be missed. I can tell you that it would be missed.

DAMIEN: But, I need it desperately. The Tree…where is it?

FATHER: With Adam in the cave.

DAMIEN: Bayla would know where it is.

FATHER (*in a sharp voice*): What did you just say?

SAMUEL: You don't need the Tree to cure you. Simply turn your back on the evil. Evil is impotent: you don't need it. It needs you.

DAMIEN (*turning to the FATHER*): You seem so peaceful. That's wonderful.

FATHER: Peaceful? But, there's always a tiny fire lit from within.

SAMUEL: I did not know this. You seem different tonight; is something wrong?

FATHER (*angrily*): There is nothing wrong with me.

DAMIEN: I was once told that there was nothing within me but fire. A woman told me that.

FATHER: A girlfriend?

DAMIEN: From that moment on, she wanted nothing more to do with me.

FATHER: What nonsense! And, how did she know this?

DAMIEN: The Tarot cards. She read my fortune...my destiny? My fate? But, it was my soul that she saw and it frightened her.

FATHER: Evil. They are evil and should not be used.

SAMUEL: You are familiar with them, father? I didn't know this. You've never mentioned this to me. Have you actually used them in divination? This, I cannot believe.

FATHER: Believe what you will, but the truth is never unbelievable. Now, tell me, what is your affliction?

DAMIEN: A fear of God. And, lest I forget, a hatred, also.

FATHER: Never have I heard such an answer. I like your honesty. We will discuss this more. But, first, tell me how you came to meet my son? He tells me nothing.

SAMUEL: That is not true. Why do you say that? I tell you everything. What secrets do I keep from you?

FATHER: I assume many, young man; but, they are not secrets. Perhaps, you think me ignorant of your desires?

SAMUEL: I do not know what you are saying to me.

FATHER: But, I do. And, don't look so uneasy.

DAMIEN: A woman introduced us: a woman who until that moment, I had not met. She and Samuel supposedly met at a synogugue. It wasn't your usual chance meeting.

FATHER: My son with a girl? How did this come to pass?

DAMIEN: I've no idea, really. From what I gathered, she was in town, briefly. She left. And, that's a pity because I still have questions for her.

FATHER: She sounds very mysterious. Was she pretty?

DAMIEN: Extraordinarily so. One really can't do her justice. I shan't try.

FATHER: Please try.

DAMIEN: Perhaps, one could liken her to the Biblical Lilith or, perhaps, Salome would be more apropos.

FATHER: Indeed. Did my son like her?

DAMIEN: I will not presume to answer for him.

FATHER: Well, Samuel?

SAMUEL: She was not to my liking. She veiled her motives with cleverness and spoke in well phrased riddles. She concealed much of herself.

DAMIEN: I really should go.

FATHER: You will stay the night. I'll get everything ready. It is no trouble your staying the one night. (*Exits.*)

SAMUEL: Excuse me, please. I must speak to my father. (*Exits.*)

DAMIEN (*addressing the audience*): I saw my bare feet as they gently touched a ground covered with leaves of red and gold. As I walked, my gaze fixed upon the opening at the end of a path. The Tree of Life was there. Would I be allowed to touch it? And, if so, would I be punished? (*Black out.*)

SAMUEL: You were sleeping. What did you dream about?

DAMIEN: The Tree of Life.

SAMUEL: You willed yourself to dream of it. That means that you are in control of your deepest thoughts. You have a powerful mind.

DAMIEN: It put things in perspective. I can think more clearly, now.

SAMUEL: Did you eat of the fruit? But, I can see that you didn't. A second chance, perhaps?

DAMIEN: Yes. I think it was a second chance. I do believe that it was.

SAMUEL: Please, continue.

DAMIEN: I was almost saved, but the dream was disturbing. There was a presence in it that I couldn't quite make out... but, I have my suspicions. I could have been saved. But, to have been saved would be to give up much. (*Walking behind the sofa.*)

SAMUEL: Give up the demon, you mean. That would be ridding yourself of evil intent.

DAMIEN (*clenching his fist, he grabs SAMUEL*): It's too late, brother. Control is what I would have to give up. Are you capable of understanding that? (*Black out, as SAMUEL is murdered.*)

ACT ONE
Scene Four

Early morning of the following day in DAMIEN"S apartment.

DAMIEN (*addressing the audience*): It felt heavy on my shoulder. Was it the weight of the body or was the sin pressing itself upon me? The sun had not yet risen, but I could see as if it were merely dusk. I could see all those uneventful things that no ordinary person could. I did not feel privileged or even exhilarated. I was strong and immortal, but the vitality of life had gone from me. (*Looking toward stage right.*)

COLETTE: Why doesn't the damned key work? It mustn't be the correct one. Try another. Quickly!

ANTONIA: Would you please get a grip. Do you want to wake up the whole building?

COLETTE: Do I care about others? Let them all hear! They will not understand.

ANTONIA (*still struggling with the lock*): You don't know that. Come-on! There!

COLETTE: Mon Dieu! Such a musty smell. Come, let us go in before anyone comes into the hallway.

ANTONIA: I thought you didn't care?

COLETTE: Close the door. There is much that I want to see.

ANTONIA: Say it.

COLETTE: What are you talking about?

ANTONIA: Say it!

COLETTE: I say what needs to be said. You should learn that and practice it. (*A strange sound can be heard in the room.*) Hear what I tell you. What must be said- what was that?

ANTONIA (*all her limbs ache with a fever*): Probably nothing.

COLETTE: What is wrong with you? I hope for your sake that you are not ill for that is the very last thing we need. We have a ritual to perform tonight.

ANTONIA: Oh, God! Don't remind me.

COLETTE: You need reminding. Where did he practice his magic? Did he keep a journal? If he did, I must have it.

ANTONIA: I don't think he kept one.

COLETTE: What about notes on his rituals? They could be of great import if what I suspect is true.

ANTONIA: And just what is that?

COLETTE: Haven't you noticed the change in him as of late? I think Damien may have within his grasp the very key to immortality. Mark what I am telling you.

ANTONIA: He can have it.

COLETTE: And, I intend to have it, as well. Come. Now, where did he practice his rituals?

ANTONIA: In his bedroom.

COLETTE: A strange place for it..and, yet, it could be most effective, but very dangerous. It could invade one's dreams.

ANTONIA: I'm sure that's what my ex-boyfriend had in mind.

COLETTE: But, did he succeed? We must find out for certain.

ANTONIA: I don't want to know. I really don't want to know.

COLETTE: That noise! It never stops.

ANTONIA: It sounds like dripping water.

COLETTE: Impossible. It's too loud. It frightens me.

ANTONIA: I think we should leave.

COLETTE: But, why? He is with his new friend, no?

ANTONIA: This place feels like it's been empty for years. And, did you have to mention Samuel? Let's just get this over with.

COLETTE: That noise…it is in this very room.

ANTONIA: You just guessed that?

COLETTE: The light switch? Where is it?

ANTONIA (*moving toward the edge of the sofa*): Just reach up and switch it on.

COLETTE: Have it! (*The light doesn't come on.*) Damn it! Something is on the floor. What is it?

ANTONIA (*looking over the sofa*): Oh, God! Oh, God! (*She runs off stage.*)

COLETTE: Antonia, what is it? I still cannot see. No! The boy! It is Samuel! All of us are doomed. Mother of God protect your daughter, I beg of you. Damien is here! (*She screams and flees the apartment.*)

ACT ONE
Scene Five

COLETTE locks the door to her apartment and stands motionless. It's as if she were afraid to move.

COLETTE: Decisions must be made. There is much that I must do and there is very much that I must not do. Yes. So important as to what one should not do- (a loud knock on the door) Who is there?

ANTONIA: Me, you idiot! Let me in!

COLETTE: She calls me the idiot. (*She opens the door.*) Where have you been?

ANTONIA: Waiting for you. I didn't just want to stand in the middle of the hallway. Someone might see me.

COLETTE: Yes. It is that time when people are getting up. (*Carefully, she closes and locks the door.*) Sit down. There is much for us to do and to discuss. I will make us some coffee.

ANTONIA: And, food -- I'm starving.

COLETTE (*offstage*): A good French breakfast. It will take only a few moments. Speak to me.

ANTONIA: What do you want to talk about?

COLETTE: You are joking with me, of course? What are we to do? And, you know what I am referring to.

ANTONIA: Nothing.

COLETTE: Nothing? Foolish girl. Don't be flippant with me and do not waste my time.

ANTONIA: I mean it. We shouldn't do anything. We don't know anything, not really.

COLETTE (*bringing in two cups of coffee*): Now, let us talk. We must both leave this place. I will go back to Europe. Yes. But, for now, we must decide what to do about the boy.

ANTONIA: Don't say his name. Don't say it.

COLETTE: As you wish. But, we know nothing at all. What happened or how it happened would be conjecture and no one would understand.

ANTONIA: So, we don't call the police?

COLETTE: Are you insane? We would be drawn into the web. No! We say nothing. What would we say? Tell me, please.

ANTONIA: Put the lights on. It's too dark in here.

COLETTE: Very well. (*Switching on a lamp.*) Better? Now, drink your coffee. It will give you strength. Damien could be anywhere. Yes. He could be anywhere.

ANTONIA: I wonder about that.

COLETTE: He got what he wanted. Now, let him torment himself with it! He got his wish!

ANTONIA: Colette, the police might come soon and there'll be trouble and probably for us.

COLETTE: But, we are innocent! We've done nothing. They will know who it was, surely.

ANTONIA: Maybe an anonymous call-

COLETTE: Forget it! Not on this phone. I should involve myself in some stranger's death? Yes. A stranger. You make me laugh.

ANTONIA: I guess- but, he was a human being.

COLETTE: Indeed.

ANTONIA: That's how Damien felt. I know he did.

COLETTE: You still love the bastard. He didn't love that boy. He said that to torment you.

ANTONIA: I'm not so sure about that.

COLETTE: It's understandable your still loving him. But, would you betray Damien by calling the police?

ANTONIA: Is this how it ends?

COLETTE: Hardly the end.

ANTONIA: I think we should call the police- no, listen. I'll do it. I want to get this done with.

COLETTE: No! They will suspect us!

ANTONIA: But, we probably left a hundred clues behind upstairs. Footprints, fingerprints, landmarks. The police can detect anything.

COLETTE (*calming down*): You may be right. Perhaps... Do it now, and let's be done with it. Hurry, before I change my mind. (*Black out.*) I thought they would never leave! I do not enjoy being questioned like a common criminal. I find it very insulting. You are to blame for this.

ANTONIA: Oh, come off it. At least we can breathe easy, sort of. I can, anyway.

COLETTE: How very lovely for you. But, perhaps, you are right. Yes. You may be right.

ANTONIA: Colette?

COLETTE: Yes?

ANTONIA: Why did you say what you did to the police?

COLETTE: What is it that I have said? Tell me.

ANTONIA: Why did you do it?

COLETTE: Do what? What are you talking about?

ANTONIA: You know what I'm talking about.

COLETTE: Say it, damn it!

ANTONIA: You implicated Damien. He'll know. He'll find out and kill us both.

COLETTE (*attempting to exude a confidence she does not feel*): How will he find out? Listen to yourself. How was it to be avoided? The body is found in his apartment. What are the police to think? I merely mentioned the possible motive.

ANTONIA: Oh, is that all? I'm sure Damien will forgive you for it. I forget how close you two were. Oh, God! I'm terrified! What exactly has he turned into?

COLETTE: Try not to think about it. The police already had their suspicions.

ANTONIA: Did they? How?

COLETTE: Do not dwell on this, Antonia. It can do no good.

ANTONIA: All right. Then, there's just one thing left.

COLETTE: What is that?

ANTONIA: Why little Samuel's relatives. What about his girlfriend?

COLETTE: We have nothing to do with that. The police will handle that.

ANTONIA: They may drop by...

COLETTE: And, I will not let them in! They will not set foot in this apartment! No!

ANTONIA: Oh, get a grip. I'll talk to them.

COLETTE: And, what will you say? Tell Colette.

ANTONIA: That their dear and precious son was my former boyfriend's lover. Oh, God! I can't wait!

COLETTE (*approvingly*): Yes. Revenge can be so sweet, no? Interesting that the police did not mention the parents. Had they even alluded to another murder? Had Damien killed the parents, as well? I wouldn't put it past the bastard.

ANTONIA: That was odd, wasn't it? I think they mentioned his dad. Do you remember what they said? I was too nervous to really listen.

COLETTE: He was mentioned, but I also forget the context. It doesn't matter. And, now that damned blackness outside. It is total blackness out there, but no rain. Anyway, tomorrow I must prepare to leave this country.

ANTONIA: Why are you in such a hurry?

COLETTE: You would do well to come with me. But, with or without you, I will soon leave this wretched country.

ANTONIA: For where? Surprise me.

COLETTE: I go to London.

ANTONIA: Why? Because Bayla is there?

COLETTE: How very little you know me. No. I go to one who makes even Bayla tremble. I go to my Master: Cornfield! (*Black out.*)

DAMIEN (*standing at center stage*): Light a match and see the fire burn white and orange and blue all suspended on a little stick of paper whose life is being burned away. But, the stick of paper doesn't mind, because for a moment, it is a glorious and wonderful glaring point of light and heat. It is transformed from compressed paper and just a bit of sulfur into a fabulous living and dying creature and, then, into a charcoal blackness like a dead star of the sky. Before that final moment, I place the burning star next to the end of the cigarette and puff. With the tips of my fingers, I extinguish the match and crush it into the street pavement. It's good to be smoking, again. I've always enjoyed the taste of tobacco and there's no longer any reason to give them up. Do I offend anyone? Too bad.

ACT TWO
Scene One

Three months later in a rented flat in London.

COLETTE: His image still haunts you.

ANTONIA: Every night, I dream of him and he's killing me and enjoying it.

COLETTE: Such a fantasy world you live in.

ANTONIA: It was a mistake coming to London. I don't need this.

COLETTE: Oh? And, what is it that you need? Tell Colette.

ANTONIA: A man. You know: a real honest-to-goodness man who'll at least make a pretense of protecting me. I'd act my part and he'd act his. Fair stuff, huh?

COLETTE: It is Damien whom you long for. This is Colette you are talking to, my dear.

ANTONIA: Let's go out to eat. I hate eating in this filthy place. I hate it!

COLETTE: Again? No. It is much too expensive and this English food is terrible. They know nothing of the haute cuisine! They lack culture as all barbarians do.

ANTONIA: Well, what are we going to do for supper?

COLETTE: I am going out. There is an errand that must be attended to.

ANTONIA: Have fun. And, if you happen to run into dear Bayla, give her my deepest shit and tell her that I won't be hanging out here much longer. Did you get all that?

COLETTE: You are impossible. And, I am not your messenger, so tell her yourself.

ANTONIA: How? I never see the bitch.

COLETTE: How you exaggerate. You have seen her several times. Yes…she is not so easy to know or to contact. Believe me, for years I have known her and, yet, I do not know her at all. That is how she chooses to be.

ANTONIA: And, I choose to leave this damned place.

COLETTE: I would be careful about that. You had better watch what you say and to whom you say it.

ANTONIA: Is that a threat?

COLETTE: I do not make threats. However, there are those who would be upset at your departure -- your very sudden and unexplained departure.

ANTONIA: Who? Bayla? Don't make me laugh.

COLETTE: Ha! She could care less about you or anyone else. No. Others.

ANTONIA: Like who?

COLETTE: You know of him. Cornfield.

ANTONIA: I- I don't know him. I've never even seen him. How could I? Have you?

COLETTE (*answering too quickly*): I've no need to.

ANTONIA: He's your master, isn't he? You told me that once.

COLETTE: He is part of the Order that we are privileged to be members of.

ANTONIA: Oh, get off it!

COLETTE: Why do you tremble so? You are afraid. You are very smart to be afraid for it keeps things in their proper perspective, as the English would say. And, now, my sweet, listen to your friend Colette. It would be very unwise for you to leave right now for things are yet expected of you. Learn from them, Antonia, learn all that is necessary and rise up in the ranks. And, then, one may leave on one's own terms; that is what Bayla did and I am now doing the same.

ANTONIA: So, why can't I leave?

COLETTE: I have just told you why! Tell me that you will stay. You must!

ANTONIA: I'm leaving.

COLETTE: There is some coffee, shall I heat it up for you?

ANTONIA: No. I'll do it.

COLETTE: I must leave.

ANTONIA: Just where are you going?

COLETTE: Out.

ANTONIA: All night?

COLETTE: Not all night; but, I may not return until quite early in the morning.

ANTONIA: When?

COLETTE: I do not report to you, my dear. I'm ready to leave. And, Antonia, re-think your position. Goodnight. (*Exits.*)

ANTONIA (*a loud knock on the door*): Who's that?

DAMIEN: Be a good girl and let me in.

ANTONIA: Damien. (*She goes to the door and lets him in.*) Did you run into Colette on your way up? You must have passed each other on the staircase.

DAMIEN: No. I didn't see her. I didn't intend for her to see me. Offer me some hospitality.

ANTONIA: You must have seen each other.

DAMIEN: Ask me another question. Do you mind if I take my jacket off? It's pretty hot in here. May I smoke?

ANTONIA: Go ahead. Damien-

DAMIEN (*taking off his jacket and sitting down*): Yes, Antonia? You weren't expecting my visit. Why should you? We didn't part under the best of circumstances -- circumstances that I brought about. Are you holding a grudge? I would.

ANTONIA: Yes.

DAMIEN: Good. We always did share that kind of anger...an anger that is deliberately self fed and sustained.

ANTONIA: I've thought about you.

DAMIEN: I know. Has dear Colette thought about me?

ANTONIA: No. Why are you here?

DAMIEN (*unbuttoning his shirt, but not taking it off*): To fulfill your desire.

ANTONIA (*sitting down next to DAMIEN*): Like Samuel?

DAMIEN: No. He was the sacrificial virgin. You will be merely another victim. Delightful, but merely a victim, nonetheless.

ANTONIA: I'm no one's victim. I hate your stinking guts!

DAMIEN (*laughing*): Good. And, that is because you "get" the joke. I hate you, but you are delicious to hate. It nourishes me. That's why killing you will be so satisfying.

ANTONIA: Go to hell, you freak! You're a monster! A condemned man!

DAMIEN: A monster that you still desire. And, you are condemned, as well.

ANTONIA: You wish!

DAMIEN: Don't end your last moments in lies. You're still in love with me.

ANTONIA: And, I hate you for that. Yes! You rotten bastard!

DAMIEN (*grabbing her by the nape of the neck*): You always liked to feel pain. Here! Taste my tongue on your neck. I'll take a bite out of it soon. Very painful!

ANTONIA (*trying to pull away*): Oh, God!

DAMIEN: Even vampires get hard.

ANTONIA (*gets up but DAMIEN pushes her back down.*): Just get the hell out of here!

DAMIEN: Sit back down. It still may not be too late for you.

ANTONIA: Just keep out of my life, damn you!

DAMIEN: Foolish, foolish girl. You've just signed your own death warrant. You are a fool. But, anyone who wants to die is a bit of a fool. I should know.

ANTONIA: You don't know anything. Colette is right to despise you. (*She makes her way toward the door, but DAMIEN grabs her by the arm.*)

DAMIEN: Look at me. I'm hard for you. But, I've got to kill you…bitch. Stay still…stay still. (*ANTONIA'S death cry can be heard. Black out.*)

COLETTE: Antonia? Antonia? Are you here? Colette is back and all is forgiven. I forgive you, do you hear me? I have brought some sweets for you to enjoy. (*Looking about the empty room.*) She must have decided to go out. It is for the best. She has not been very good company these past few days. The dear girl is terribly unhappy. How she longs for Damien- (*There is movement on the fire escape.*) Who is there? Antonia, is that you? Answer me at once. Who is that? (*The window opens and the sound of laughter can be heard.*) Mon dieu!

DAMIEN (*climbing into the apartment*): Good evening, dearest Colette. Do not scream. It will do you no good. Were you calling to me just now?

COLETTE (*staggering back*): You have come back from hell! But, why?

DAMIEN: My mortality has been wrenched from my soul.

COLETTE: You are the one who has given up your mortality. I've done nothing to you. Nothing. Always you have hated me.

DAMIEN: You really don't know anything, do you? It was not my choice to come here this evening. Had it been left to me, I would have tormented you for the rest of your pathetic life: a slow torture is what I would have preferred. I would have reduced you to a dribbling idiot. But, I will make the most of this night of killing.

COLETTE: Antonia? Where is she? No! You've killed her! Monster!

DAMIEN: No. Vampire.

COLETTE: Vampire! Of course! Mon Dieu!

DAMIEN: The taste was quite delicious. She told me that I would enjoy myself.

COLETTE: Antonia? No! Whom do you mean? Tell me! I don't understand. (*She moves toward the sofa where she has placed her bag. DAMIEN follows her. Carefully, she reaches for the bag and extracts a crucifix.*)

DAMIEN: Do not shout at me, Madame. Your friend sent me.

COLETTE: I don't believe it. You're lying to torment me. Bayla would not do this. And, you don't dare kill me -- not a member of Cornfield's Order. If anyone can stop you, he can and will! (*She thrusts the crucifix close to his face and he recoils in horror.*) And, now, it is Colette who has the upper hand. Yes. You think me unprepared, eh? No! Colette has been well trained by her Master. It is he whom you must answer to now. You thought to murder Colette like some animal? Forget it! Cornfield will see you burn in hell first if he is merciful. And, now, cherie, I will phone him and he will know what to do with you. Vampire! (*She glances away from DAMIEN to reach for the phone. With one quick gesture, he strikes the crucifix from her hand.)* No!

DAMIEN: Nice try. Maybe in the next lifetime, you'll have another go at me. What say? (*Taking his belt off, he wraps it around his hands.*)

COLETTE: No! He will come after you. No! Keep away! I will place my dying curse on you!

DAMIEN: I'm listening. (*COLETTE makes for the door, but he grabs her and wraps his belt about her neck. COLETTE collapses to the floor. He turns from her and sees the box of chocolates on the coffee table, opens it, and pops one in his mouth.*)

ACT TWO
Scene Two

It is the following morning in BAYLA'S apartment. A well dressed man is standing beside her and a very pointed conversation is about to begin.

CORNFIELD: Bayla, I was afraid that you might not have me. It pleases me to see you, again.

BAYLA: Refuse you entrance? The thought would never occur to me. You do yourself a disservice, Cornfield.

CORNFIELD: No, my dear. Never that. You look lovely. Tell me: how have you been?

BAYLA: I have been, shall we say, learning?

CORNFIELD: Of course. And, what degree of initiation are you now?

BAYLA: At this point, degrees have no value to me. I am a Magus, but you must be aware of this, surely.

CORNFIELD: I am. I am also aware that you wouldn't tell me anything that you weren't certain I already had knowledge of. I have thought about you of late; does that interest you at all?

BAYLA (*gesturing for him to be seated*): It does.

CORNFIELD: Why?

BAYLA: Our paths need no longer cross, therefore, what is it that you want? I've no patience for this.

CORNFIELD: Good. It is the response that I would have expected from you. I am expecting a visitor shortly. She will be arriving before the Autumnal Equinox. I want you to take her into your care. It was not an easy matter in extricating her from her present life. There were a great many difficulties; difficulties that may cause a great deal of unrest within her former sphere of existence. Are you following the thread of what I'm saying to you?

BAYLA: You look tired. Is the strength that is needed for life leaving you?

CORNFIELD (*ignoring her query*): She is not to be a part of my Order. She is to remain outside of it like yourself. But, unlike yourself, she will be kept close to activities that concern me. Are you able to have her?

BAYLA: Perhaps. But, I need to know more. I am still very much a student myself, and I may not achieve everything in this lifetime.

CORNFIELD: You will not: not as things stand with you now. You will make the fatal mistake.

BAYLA: And, what "fatal mistake" is that? Do tell me.

CORNFIELD (*lighting a cigarette*): A successor must be left in your stead and, like all of us, you will fail to train a proper one who is worthy of you. The window will be closed to you. Cigarette?

BAYLA (*withdraws a cigarette from her own case*): What is her name? And, how do you come to know her?

CORNFIELD: Questions already? Am I to bore you with so many details?

BAYLA: There are many more. What is her name?

CORNFIELD: I'm glad you didn't wear your usual veil. I might have thought you were trying to conceal your soul from me. Her name is Deanna.

BAYLA: A very lovely name. Is she attractive? But, she must be, mustn't she?

CORNFIELD: She is beautiful; but the beauty has not quite fully surfaced. I have waited years for the moment that is about to come and nothing must prevent it. I have had her watched since birth. It was not easy to find a loyal servant to attend to this, but it was done and the task is almost complete.

BAYLA: I detest riddles. Come to the point and explain all of this.

CORNFIELD: I am placing her under your tutelage; is that not enough for now?

BAYLA: But, why not yours so that she may learn at the feet of the Master-

CORNFIELD: Not until she is ready. You will see to that.

BAYLA: Do not interrupt me, again, Cornfield. I will not tolerate that.

CORNFIELD: Careful.

BAYLA: What of my own work?

CORNFIELD: It will not be impaired. If anything, it will be enhanced. I trust that I am making myself quite clear.

BAYLA: I want no attachments to your Order. I want to make that quite clear.

CORNFIELD: You have many times. And, I have not forgiven you for that trespass. Mark those words well.

BAYLA: I have chosen a guardian.

CORNFIELD: He is worthy of you.

BAYLA: Yes. A girl…perhaps. I must meet her and judge her.

CORNFIELD: She may judge you.

BAYLA: She may, if she's interesting. You are rather keen on her, aren't you?

CORNFIELD: Begin your preparations now for you haven't much time.

BAYLA: They've already begun.

CORNFIELD: Excellent.

BAYLA (*smiling charmingly at him*): There was a murder last night and a rather brutal one at that. You are aware of it, I assume?

CORNFIELD: There was a murder last night and a rather strange one: scratch marks on the dead woman's body. You are aware of it, I assume. Answer me.

BAYLA (*stops smiling*): How long, Cornfield?

CORNFIELD: You will tell me. I trust to your expertise.

BAYLA: I am not amused.

CORNFIELD: You aren't expected to be amused. No. You shouldn't be amused.

BAYLA: Will she be coming into the country very soon or is this also a carefully guarded secret?

CORNFIELD: I never told you she was out of the country.

BAYLA: I am telling you.

CORNFIELD: I will take my leave of you. And, by the way; where is your guardian? Are you concealing him from your old friend? Do we have secrets from each other? I don't like secrets...don't deceive me.

BAYLA: You presume far too much! You drive me to anger. Leave. You're beginning to bore me quite a bit.

CORNFIELD: Last night I lost a valued member of my lodge. What do you know of that? Was it your doing? That is a rhetorical question, my dear, for I do not expect an answer from you. However, I will have my vengeance upon Antonia's murderer.

BAYLA: Is this an interrogation? Get out of my house. Now!

CORNFIELD: If I bore you, have your guardian remove me. But be careful. I am not so vulnerable a picking as was Antonia. If you were behind that slaughter, you will pay for it dearly.

BAYLA: I'm not impressed with so hollow a threat.

CORNFIELD: It is not a hollow threat. I carry out my word to the specified letter. And, now, where is he?

BAYLA: "He?"

CORNFIELD: Your guardian.

BAYLA: He does not keep specific hours. I call him when he is needed. He is certainly not needed now.

CORNFIELD: You are correct. He is not needed…now. But, keep him close to you, Bayla.

BAYLA: I believe you were on your way out? I don't want to detain you. I'm sure you've appointments to keep.

CORNFIELD: Colette had conveyed some rather interesting information to me. She fled to London in fear of her life with the young girl, Antonia. From whom was she fleeing and why?

BAYLA (*genuinely surprised*): Didn't she tell you?

CORNFIELD: She told me what he was, but did not reveal his actual motive. Do you know of the motive? Why would he want to kill her?

BAYLA: The loyal Colette was hiding something from her Master? Why? Perhaps, you were unsatisfactory to her that night?

CORNFIELD: It won't be difficult to trace him. She provided the clues, but feared to tell me more. I'm not certain why. I think it may have been out of a misplaced loyalty to you.

BAYLA (*putting out her cigarette*): She was never loyal to me. She was a user. I tolerated her.

CORNFIELD: You tolerate someone only for a specific reason. What was that reason?

BAYLA: I'm sure I don't remember. Does it matter? She's dead.

CORNFIELD: But, she is not dead.

BAYLA (*taken aback*): What are you saying?

CORNFIELD: She hovers near death; but, I believe she will recover…and soon.

BAYLA (*recovering her composure*): I'll send her flowers.

CORNFIELD: Who attempted to kill her?

BAYLA: I've no idea.

CORNFIELD: Was it your guardian, Bayla?

BAYLA: Am I on trial, Cornfield?

CORNFIELD: Yes. You are. I'll be sending Deanna to you shortly.

BAYLA: Aren't you afraid that I might turn the girl against you? I could, you know. Easily.

CORNFIELD: To what end? And, besides, you are assuming that I would underestimate an enemy. I hope that Deanna doesn't pick up too many bad habits during her stay.

BAYLA: Good day.

CORNFIELD: You are still of use to me, for even when you serve your own needs, you satisfy mine. The day will soon come when I will no longer have any need of you. I shall enjoy that day, Bayla. (*Exits.*)

ACT THREE
Scene One

Eighteen months have passed. It is early morning and DAMIEN is standing down stage with an unlit cigarette in his right hand and a tiny globe of the world in his left. BAYLA, CORNFIELD, and COLETTE are drinking together at stage right.

DAMIEN: An Earth shift. The planet is going to roll over on its damned axis. (*Looking heavenward.*) On that day, it was as if the sun had never set. The air was stagnant. There were no waves upon the shore. The Earth had stopped moving or so it seemed. For a moment, there was that blind panic that feeds itself to the primitive emotions of terror. Anything that had been in motion now seemed to quiver and want to topple over. The axis began to shift. The planet was balancing itself to a new position in its never ceasing orbit. The oceans began to render their destruction: first along the sea coasts and, then, stretching into the interior of the continents. Landslides, volcanic eruptions, and earthquakes rocked the globe as continental plates shifted and pressed against each other pushing to make room for their own land mass. (*He drops the globe to the floor.*) The Earth was cleansing itself.

BAYLA: Pick that up, please? (*DAMIEN pointedly ignores her.*)

CORNFIELD: Well, together once again. How are you all coping with the global disaster?

DAMIEN: We're alive and drinking.

CORNFIELD: That is a state of circumstances, young man. You could easily end your life. The question is: how are you getting on?

BAYLA: Such a simple question, Cornfield. Are the answers to be as simple? If they are, perhaps, I should leave.

COLETTE: I feel as if our work is progressing. At first, I was disoriented and it was difficult to adjust.

CORNFIELD: Listen to her, Bayla, and you may still learn something from my student.

BAYLA: Nothing has changed for me. The shifting, if you would, was neither abhorrent nor exhilarating. It was an event and no more. Does that answer your question?

CORNFIELD: How convincingly you lie, my dear. And, why is it so convincing? Because, I'm not quite certain that you are lying.

BAYLA: Could we stop this little game, please?

CORNFIELD: Not enjoying yourself? I thought you'd become used to me by now.

COLETTE: Shouldn't we be discussing things that really matter? The change has affected me. I'm not quite certain just how; but, something is very different in my reactions and moods. And, must this murderer be present? I hate him!

CORNFIELD: Ignore him, my dear. What is it that's troubling you.?

COLETTE: The directions have shifted and the focal points are no longer where they were. How confusing it is!

CORNFIELD: The old landmarks, are no longer at the same focal points in relation to the stars. A whole new cosmology may have to be erected to replace the old one: new charts of the heavens to coordinate with the gods' new domains. It will take generations to set in place; and, yet, the challenge of such an undertaking is nothing less than epic in nature. It is the celebration of both a death and a creation. What will emerge from the new heavens? It staggers the imagination.

DAMIEN (*lighting a cigarette*): I've had enough of this. I think I'll go for a stroll: a long one. And, don't tell me when I'm needed. I'll let you know. (*Exits.*)

COLETTE: Good riddance!

BAYLA: Such a strange man. Where does he truly fit in?

CORNFIELD: Tell me about the current events of your life.

COLETTE: I keep written records of everything that I do.

CORNFIELD: To what end?

COLETTE: Someday, someone will read them and know of Colette. I am preparing myself for death.

CORNFIELD: Is that your ultimate goal?

COLETTE: I don't want to incarnate, again. I am quite sick of this existence.

CORNFIELD: Your hope is that of any enlightened barbarian; for that is what we all are: cretins upon this planet. Our very presence here is a testament to our barbarism. Physical life is a test and a mockery. How I loathe it! We are, all of us, groveling idiots upon a piece of stone that floats upon a vacuum of space. How very pathetic it all is. (*He spits on the floor.*) And, don't bore me with your objections.

BAYLA: Was I about to object?

CORNFIELD (*ignoring the question*): It is because of you, Bayla, that I almost wish I were staying.

BAYLA: Oh? Going somewhere, Cornfield?

CORNFIELD: And, very soon.

BAYLA: Do write.

CORNFIELD: Ah! Dear Bayla…one day, very soon, you must allow me to embrace you so that I may crush the very life from you.

BAYLA (*sipping her absinthe*): You don't bore me, Cornfield. You amuse me.

CORNFIELD: And what of your male slave? Does he amuse you, as well?

BAYLA: You are jealous of him. How easy it is to see now. You envy his youth.

CORNFIELD: His youth? A rather strange word to use on him.

BAYLA: Why have you asked us here?

CORNFIELD: Don't you know? Or is it that you don't dare to even hope for it? Stuck for words, my dear? I never thought I'd live to see the day: the great Bayla Ortiz, an Adept of the highest grade, no less. Have I underestimated your hatred of me? I surely cannot believe it.

BAYLA (*putting down her glass and speaking almost to herself*): You are going to die. You want us to help you cross over in order to give your consciousness strength in the astral plane; the strength that it needs to avoid its own self-imposed hell.

You want to incarnate, again, but with full consciousness. (*Turning to face him.*) I think I despise you!

CORNFIELD: Plotting against me, Bayla? You've been plotting against me for years and to no avail. I will take my leave of you now. The ceremony is to take place at your apartment on the night of the full moon. I'll be in contact. (*He and COLETTE exit.*)

BAYLA: He is going to die, but it will be no ordinary death. Before his last breath, he will leave his body and with the aid of the magic triangle he shall be brought to the astral plane with consciousness and identity. He will re-enter the physical plane in like manner. I must stop him. It has come down to this. He wants me to attempt to thwart his final plan. It would be a glorious moment for him, truly: to defeat me and to cross over with my aid. He would have it no other way. The thorn in his side would be finally removed and he will come back to settle scores with me. I accept the challenge. It could mean my own death, but what of it? (*She drains the last of her absinthe.*)

ACT THREE
Scene Two

BAYLA: Awake? What a pleasant surprise.

CORNFIELD: How very sweet of you. I wanted to save you the burden of hauling me bodily into the temple.

BAYLA: I understand. I've not yet cleansed and sealed it.

CORNFIELD: It's early, yet, and that can be done later.

BAYLA: I'd prefer to do it now.

CORNFIELD: Are you here to kill me?

BAYLA: You make my motives seem so devious. I'm quite certain that you don't want to offend.

CORNFIELD: Offending someone is a rather primitive weapon.

BAYLA: I agree.

CORNFIELD: Do you need a weapon, Bayla? If you do, take your choice and I will supply you with one. Name it if you would: a spear, a dagger or poison, perhaps?

BAYLA: My weapon? My weapon is yours, for I am as clever as you.

CORNFIELD: Do you think you will succeed tonight? You won't.

BAYLA: In stopping you?

CORNFIELD: No. In preventing me giving up the ghost; in willing my own death.

BAYLA: Yes. I will.

CORNFIELD: You are not as well informed as you may imagine. You believe yourself to be the initiator of certain past events. In that, you are correct; but, you've not gone unobserved. I know of your trip abroad and your visits to various synagogues. What strength that must have taken! How did you ever manage it? (*Not waiting for a response.*) I know of your brief liaison with Samuel and how you placed his life in danger without so much as a blink of the eye. Murderer. We always did have that in common. Your plans were carefully laid. You had heard that a human being was transforming himself into a blood thirsty vampire and you seized the opportunity. I congratulate you. Do you like the robe?

BAYLA: It's stunning.

CORNFIELD: It was woven for me by a woman many years ago. She had been a mystic and an Adept in her own right who had foretold of my death.

BAYLA: Why do you tell me this?

CORNFIELD: I will soon die. Is that not reason enough? I find the prospect exhilarating. I will conquer my passing and come back fully cognizant of myself. Full power in the guise of a child who is hidden from his friends and hidden from his many enemies.

BAYLA: Hidden from me, Cornfield?

CONRFIELD: Hidden from you most especially. (*Black out.*)
(*When the lights come up, he is seated on a throne of sorts with BAYLA and COLETTE on either side of him.*)

BAYLA: I, High Priestess, daughter of night, send my prayer to that which cannot be conceived of upon this plane. Hear the plea of your daughter. May my words reverberate upon the sphere called Earth. Hear me, father of the heavens. Protect me. Protect my disciples within these sealed walls as I invoke the four corners of the created universe.

CORNFIELD (*to COLETTE*): Wait for me.

BAYLA: Colette, he has murdered your father.

COLETTE: And, you had Antonia murdered.

BAYLA (*taken by surprise*): Do you hear me? He murdered your father -- violating him. The man whom he had you abandon: butchered. He did it. And, you did nothing except to sleep with him.

COLETTE: I'd almost-

BAYLA: Forgotten? How very convenient for you. How very dreadful for your father. It was a very slow murder, my dear. Decapitation is not quick. It is a horrendous deed. The victim is conscious of everything...your father was aware. The henchmen enjoyed the task. The cretins found his body entertaining...the rhythm of the torso during the separation. His daughter bought for so many pieces of silver.

COLETTE: What are you accusing me of?

BAYLA: Why do I tell you all this? To avenge his death! To kill the swine who is before you now. To dispense justice. Can you even ask that question?

CORNFIELD: Colette, do not listen to this woman. She will poison your mind against me. Beware of her treachery. It had to be.

BAYLA: Committed?

CORNFIELD (*raising his arm*): Filthy bitch!

BAYLA: Take this dagger. Kill this man. Take it! Colette? Now! It must be now. Why do you hesitate? Were we not friends once?

COLETTE: You take me for a fool.

BAYLA: Indeed. I will guide your hand. (*Now, she is too close to CORNFIELD. He grabs her by the wrist.*) No!

CORNFIELD: We shall leave together. Traitorous bitch! And, to think that it was I who taught you the sacred arts of darkness. Where's your henchman?

BAYLA: Damien! Damien! Leave your hiding place- answer my prayer- to the one who gave you immortality.

CORNFIELD: You are the fool! Your vampire boyfriend is nowhere to be found. Did you not think that I knew of his consecration? The consecration that consisted in ripping Samuel's throat. I helped pave the way for it. I was in the next room listening, waiting for Damien to strike the mortal blow. I even had dinner with the two young men. Surprised? "My son with a girl? How did this come to pass?"

BAYLA: You! It was you who killed Samuel's father.

CORNFIELD: The deception was quite easy. Even young Samuel never guessed, not completely. He was far too involved with Damien. I knew all along about your plans.

BAYLA: Damien! The dagger, Colette. Strike!

CORNFIELD: She will not.

COLETTE (*obediently*): I will not.

BAYLA: Damien!

CORNFIELD: Call to him, but his kind do not remain slaves for very long.

BAYLA: No! It cannot end like this.

CORNFIELD: A pity. You came so close.

DAMIEN (*appearing from behind a pillar*): As one murderer to another. (*He takes the dagger from COLETTE, who tries to stop him, and plunges it into CORNFIELD.*) Bayla, your wrist.

BAYLA: I shall recover. Do not look about. His presence is still in this room. We have been successful.

DAMIEN: But-

BAYLA: He was powerful...too powerful. Even in the face of victory, one must be careful of him. And, by the way, you took your time getting here.

DAMIEN: I hadn't quite decided whose side I should take.

BAYLA (*massaging her wrist*): I shall remember that.

DAMIEN: Fair enough. Bayla- look! (*CORNFIELD is rising from the floor. COLETTE goes to him.*)

CORNFIELD: Thank you. I did warn you that I would not be so vulnerable as you may have thought. And, now, I will take Colette and leave you with your henchman. I'm sure you've much to say to each other, but the tone of that conversation may not be entirely to your liking. How quickly you've forgotten your lessons: never underestimate an enemy. Did you think that I did not linger at the door to listen to your pompous speech of betrayal? I told you once that you were flawed, but your vanity wouldn't hear of such a thing.

BAYLA: Colette, we are now enemies.

COLETTE: We have always been enemies. You sent this monster to kill me and Antonia. And, for that, I shall always hate you, Bayla. You say that we are enemies? So be it!

CORNFIELD: Good day, Bayla. And, just one more thing. Never allow an enemy to enter your home. "Deanna" never existed. (*He glances over at DAMIEN.*) Damien? (*He and COLETTE exit.*)

EPILOGUE

It is the following evening and DAMIEN is standing just behind the sofa with BAYLA seated to his left.

BAYLA: Your company stimulates me, Damien. Are you happy that you've stayed with me?

DAMIEN: Happy? A rather unusual word applied to the likes of me. I am not discontent. I am glad, rather, that I made the journey here to the continent those seemingly long months ago. Or is it years or days?

BAYLA: But, did you stay to remain content? Or are you happy that you've stayed with me?

DAMIEN: I thought you wanted me to stay.

BAYLA: But, that is not the reason that you did. Is it out of gratitude?

DAMIEN: I am not grateful.

BAYLA: No? I have given you immortality. It was I who placed Samuel before you. It was you who made the choice.

DAMIEN: The choice? A choice that one is driven to? The choice of an addict who needs his fix?

BAYLA: Yes. And, the little tricks that I've taught you. Priceless.

DAMIEN: A gifted student does not leave a gifted teacher.

BAYLA: A wise man, like yourself, should not.

DAMIEN: You see? I'm still here. (*BAYLA sips her absinthe.*) How's your supply holding up?

BAYLA: Quite well, actually. One must be-

DAMIEN: Please. That's the first thing you taught me. What's the key to it? Self discipline. Christ! You're never wrong, are you? Or are you? (*He starts to make a slow circuit about the room.*)

BAYLA: Damien?

DAMIEN: Umm?

BAYLA: Are you happy to be alone with me?

DAMIEN: That word, again. You keep using it and it's simply not your style.

BAYLA: Please answer the question.

DAMIEN: A Mass only needs a priest and priestess.

BAYLA: True. So true.

DAMIEN (*stopping his movement, abruptly*): What are you up to? Come on, out with it.

BAYLA: Damien, never completely trust me.

DAMIEN: I never have. What about Cornfield?

BAYLA: I beg your pardon? His whereabouts are unknown to me, for the present time. Don't speak to me of him. Now, Damien, do get ready. I want to finish the Mass a bit earlier this evening. Then, the night will be ours completely.

DAMIEN: Fair enough…for now. (*Turning to face the audience.*) And, what of me? My claws and my cunning have been sharpened by experience and the necessity of the kill. I enjoy myself, but not wholeheartedly for there is a futility to it all. One cannot gloat over a corpse. It is a pleasure that is denied to the killer who possesses an intellect. I am immortal, but I can choose to die. When will that day be? I don't know. And there-in lies the filthy rub. One gets used to the physical life and one gets attached to it. Dangerous! The desire to rip the soul from the body diminishes and one loses the thought of even attempting it. (*Turning his attention to BAYLA.*) And, Bayla, what of her? Who is this woman who seeks to hold me? Hold me? No. That will not do. That will not do at all. (*Slowly, he moves toward BAYLA, dropping the cigarette butt on to the floor. He is now facing upstage and blocking BAYLA from the audience's view. His hands are reaching for her throat.*)

End of play.

SHADOWS BEHIND THE FOOTLIGHTS

A Play in Three Acts

by

Gerard Denza

SHADOWS BEHIND THE FOOTLIGHTS premiered at the ATA Theatre in New York City on November 1, 2006 with the following cast:

NICHOLAS GASPARI	Phil Strumolo
THOMAS MALKIN	R. Ross Pivec
RAMONA CHEN	Megina Tsai
MANUEL ROMA	Brandon DeSpain
REGINA ROMA	Lisa Peart
CLAIRE SANTONI	Diane Ordelheide
JOE	Malcolm Ehrlich
FRANK HOLDEN	J. C. Whittaker
JUSTIN KANE	Jeff Topf

Set by Phil Strumolo.
Directed by Gerard Denza.

PLACE
The action begins in Martin's Bar in Manhattan.

TIME
The play begins in the year 1949.

SCENES

Act One
Scene One: Early evening at Martin's Bar in June of 1949.
Scene Two: One week later in the Roma apartment.
Scene Three: Martin's Bar that same day.

Act Two
Scene One: 1953 at Martin's Bar.
Scene Two: Late night in Claire's apartment.
Scene Three: The following day at the Roma apartment.

Act Three
Late afternoon at Martin's Bar in 1955.

THE SUSPECTS

NICHOLAS GASPARI, a dedicated opera singer.
THOMAS MALKIN, ruthless agent.
RAMONA CHEN, artist and blackmailer.
MANUEL ROMA, frustrated matinee idol
REGINA ROMA, former Paris model.
CLAIRE SANTONI, destitute novelist.
FRANK HOLDEN, mysterious drifter.
JOE, nosey bartender.
JUSTIN KANE, ambitious actor.

ACT ONE
Scene One

The bar is on stage left and it is well stocked. Three tables are set downstage at stage left, center stage, and stage right. There is a door leading to the back room that is just behind the bar. Three stools are set up at the bar and some colored lights are on the counter. NICHOLAS has just finished singing.

MALKIN (*leaning on the bar*): Not bad, Gaspari. "Tell Me That You Love Me Tonight," isn't it?

NICHOLAS: I beg your pardon?

MALKIN: I said, "not bad." Not suprerlative, but usable enough on the stage.

NICHOLAS: Do I know you?

MALKIN: Thomas Malkin before you. We've not met formally, but my reputation usually preceeds me.

NICHOLAS: You're Manuel's agent. He's mentioned your name a few times.

MALKIN: I am Regina's agent, as well; although, she needs my services less than her husband.

NICHOLAS: I don't understand that statement.

MALKIN: I don't intend you to. Although Manuel is the less demanding of the two, it is Regina's ambition that I prefer.

But, that's not the reason I've been listening to you sing in this rather quaint bar.

NICHOLAS: What is the interest?

MALKIN (*begins to circle around NICHOLAS*): Don't be so damned defensive. You don't even know my motives; not yet, anyway. You're a new hand at this game, Gaspari, and you'd better learn some of the game's tactics. You need help...my help...savvy? I don't hear you.

NICHOLAS: Please continue.

MALKIN: You've had some success. Let's see...I want to recite my facts on a precise note: you've sung under Serafin in Europe. Good start, that. Then, it was on to the weekly broadcast at CBS, hack work, that.

NICHOLAS: Not when it's done properly and respectfully.

MALKIN: I will continue: more work at CBS with something called "Musical Tidbits" and, then, it was on to the Milwaukee Opera. You, then, did your military service until your discharge last year: a respectable, but hardly outstanding career. Let me put the question to you: are you a singer or an artist?

NICHOLAS: An artist.

MALKIN: I liked your Erik in The Dutchman. It has distinction, character, and the full bodied expression of a performance. My client, Gaspari, is concerned about you.

NICHOLAS: That is his problem.

MALKIN: You've just made the mistake of your career.

NICHOLAS: My career. You do your job as an agent and I'll do mine as a singer.

MALKIN: I am now your enemy. Talent is only one requirement. How many people end up as panhandlers or decaying corpses that are never fished out of the river?

NICHOLAS: Are you threatening me?

MALKIN: You apologize?

NICHOLAS: What do you want, Malkin?

MALKIN: Nothing.

NICHOLAS: Then, why are you here listening to me in Martin's Bar?

MALKIN: Are you being flippant with me, Gaspari? I want you to do nothing. You are to allow my client to eclipse you.

NICHOLAS: No.

MALKIN: Don't be too hasty. We can work out some advantageous details for you.

NICHOLAS: If your client has a better voice than mine, then so be it. It's up to the audience and, perhaps, the critics to decide that. I don't know the mechanics of it. I don't think I like you, Malkin.

MALKIN: You shouldn't have stated that so bluntly. Are you getting ready to leave?

NICHOLAS: Yes.

MALKIN: Anything the matter?

NICHOLAS: I thought I heard a movement in the back room. Anyway, would you like to share a cab? No hard feelings.

MALKIN: No. Thank you. I've my own car.

NICHOLAS: Goodnight, Malkin.

MALKIN: So long, Gaspari. (*NICHOLAS exits.*) All right. Who is here with me? (*A very beautiful Asian woman emerges from the bar's back room.*)

RAMONA: I overheard your conversation with Mr. Gaspari. So? What have you got on him?

MALKIN: Good evening, Miss Chen. Was it necessary to hide out like that? Spying on your old friend and savior? That's not very sporting.

RAMONA: I didn't want either one of you to see me.

MALKIN: Why are you here? Tell me.

RAMONA (*putting her purse down on to the bar*): The door was open, but the bar was closed. I didn't want to just help myself to a drink. And, then, I heard voices and hid in the back room.

MALKIN: You weave a plausible tale. You're a good liar, but let's try that, again, shall we?

RAMONA: Maybe, it's none of your business why I'm here. Always asking questions like a magistrate. I think I hate you a little bit.

MALKIN: You're English is improving. Careful.

RAMONA: Of you? Don't make me laugh.

MALKIN: What are you doing here? Don't let me have to ask it a third time.

RAMONA If you must know, I came here to meet someone and, then, I decided to spy on the very interesting Nicholas.

MALKIN: On a first name basis already?

RAMONA: He's good and you know it. I like him.

MALKIN: I'm actually glad to hear that. He's good, all right.

RAMONA: Not too good, I hope. That might panic some of your sniveling clients.

MALKIN: You're in a combative mood, tonight. And, don't take that tone of voice with me.

RAMONA: What tone of voice?

MALKIN: Go home. You have your commission. Surely, your work is not completed. I won't have you rushing it.

RAMONA: I'm no hack. And, besides, the night is still young.

MALKIN: I forget about your nocturnal hours. Going straight home?

RAMONA: Where are you going?

MALKIN: Possibly home. See? How simple it is to answer a direct question with a direct answer. Now, answer mine, please.

RAMONA: I- I need a drink. I'll wait for the bar to open.

MALKIN: Yes?

RAMONA: I've answered your question.

MALKIN: Make it one stiff drink and, then, head straight home.

RAMONA: Go to hell!

MALKIN: Careful, Miss Chen, the debt has yet to be repaid. We'll need to talk at length about that someday, but not here.

RAMONA: Oh? Too open for you? Afraid someone might hear us? Poor Malkin. So many people hate you; you know that, don't you?

MALKIN: Goodnight, Miss Chen. And, remember: I want it done properly as a commissioned work ought to be done. I need that portrait to be your finest work of art.

RAMONA: You don't scare me. Maybe, I know a few things about you that might not look so good in print.

MALKIN: Don't be a bore, Miss Chen.

RAMONA: I need more money. (*MALKIN grabs her roughly by the left arm.*) You might have to wait a long time- oh! You're hurting me!

MALKIN: Cheap, little blackmailer! Ingrate! You forget who took you off the street and bought your "contract." You'll do as you're told!

RAMONA: Let me go!

MALKIN (*releasing her*): There. And, now, my dear, I bid you goodnight. And, remember: one drink.

ACT ONE
Scene Two

A week later in the ROMA apartment. It is late afternoon. The apartment is stylized and the furnishings are spare, but speak of impeccable taste. MANUEL is sitting on a chair at center stage and staring at the audience. REGINA is sitting behind him and watching her husband intently while pretending to read a magazine.

REGINA (*looking up from her magazine*): Manuel, are you giving up on that already?

MANUEL: Already? I've been at it for the better part of the afternoon. I can't stand listening to myself, anymore. What's that magazine you've been looking at: the latest Paris fashions?

REGINA: As a matter of fact, it is. Some of the new models are making their Paris debut. They're quite nice.

MANUEL: You still miss it, don't you?

REGINA: I do. One never completely gets used to the idea of having to give it up. But, if one uses her brains, she develops other interests.

MANUEL: Like me?

REGINA: Of course, darling. You were an interest to be cultivated. You've a great deal of potential to you. So, why do you make things so difficult? You have a fine voice and a rather magnificent figure. Malkin and I have your best interests at heart. Everyone will gain from your success: you most of all.

MANUEL: What about my rival: Mr. Nicholas Gaspari?

REGINA: He doesn't matter. You will be the next matinee idol. You will be remembered -- not him.

MANUEL: Do you know what Gaspari is doing about now?

REGINA: I don't care.

MANUEL: Polishing an already perfect aria, probably Erik from The Dutchman.

REGINA (*flinging down her magazine and getting up*): No! That is one of your arias! Take a look at yourself in the mirror. You are Erik. Don't worry about the details, just concern yourself with charming the audience. An aria doesn't have to be sung perfectly because most of the audience won't even know the difference. Save that for the recording studio. You're afraid; aren't you? Don't deny it, Manuel. You can tell me everything. It's only when you don't confide in me that I am unable to help you.

MANUEL: We must be honest with each other, is that it, Regina?

REGINA: You doubt me? I can see it in your eyes.

MANUEL: You don't see a thing in my eyes. I-

REGINA: Say it.

MANUEL: It's our damned agent.

REGINA: Malkin? What about him? You don't like him, but he's the best there is. We're lucky to have him.

MANUEL: He's a cold blooded bastard.

REGINA: He's an agent, so put your dislike of him aside. You don't have to like him.

MANUEL: I don't trust him. There's something wrong about him.

REGINA: What?

MANUEL: I don't know.

REGINA: That's what I thought. You're inventing things in your mind to dislike him.

MANUEL: That's not true. I spoke to Claire-

REGINA (*sitting down, again and picking up her magazine*): Oh? When was this?

MANUEL: It was some time this afternoon -- maybe around one o'clock. I was waiting for you, as a matter of fact.

REGINA: The time doesn't matter. You've been seeing that writer? If anyone is strange, it's she. What did she say to you?

MANUEL: We spoke of Malkin.

REGINA: She doesn't like him because he doesn't like her work and has put that in print. Don't trust her.

MANUEL: She's an intellect, that's for sure.

REGINA: And, she knows it and flaunts it. She thinks the rest of us are quite stupid and that's very, very funny. She's always broke; destitute, in fact, and no one buys her books.

MANUEL: I always feel uncomfortable around Malkin and so does Claire.

REGINA: He's interesting and arrogant. Now, tell me about your luncheon date with dear Claire. (*The cast gathers in the bar as the lights dim in the ROMA apartment.*)

MANUEL: We were having a drink at Martin's when I spotted Malkin at the bar.

REGINA (*handing him a drink*): Here. Take this. You look as if you need it. How fascinating that Malkin's activities were observed. He knows so much about everyone else. (*At this point, MANUEL steps toward center stage to join CLAIRE.*)

JOE: Let me know if you folks need anything else. Miss Santoni, when's the new book coming out? I can't make heads or tails of them myself, but my daughter is a big fan of yours. She's an intellectual, like yourself.

CLAIRE (*lighting a cigarette*): Good for her. Is she in college, Joe?

JOE: Going to Barnard. She wants to major in philosophy and teach it. Is that practical, though? Teachers don't get paid very much, do they?

CLAIRE: If it's what she wants, it's practical. Bring the book here sometime and I'll autograph it for her.

JOE: I'll be sure to bring it with me, Miss Santoni.

CLAIRE: And, you encourage her with her goals.

JOE (*heading back to the bar*): Promise. She's a good girl. I'm very proud of her.

MANUEL: Well, weren't you chummy with Joe just now. I thought you didn't like him?

CLAIRE: I don't have anything against him, really. He's a gossip, but I guess that goes with the trade.

MANUEL (*distractedly*): Claire?

CLAIRE: Manuel, are you all right? You've just turned chalk white.

MANUEL: Over there, by the bar. Isn't that Malkin talking with someone?

CLAIRE: So it is. I wonder if it's one of his many friends whom no one ever sees? Don't stare so much, Manuel. He'll take notice.

MANUEL: I'm sure he's noticed us already.

CLAIRE: He's too engrossed in his conversation. Who is that with him? He gives me the creeps.

MANUEL: Pardon me for a second, I need a refill.

CLAIRE: Manuel-

MANUEL: I'll be right back. I don't want Malkin to get the idea that his client is trying to avoid him. Wait here. (*He crosses to the bar and orders a drink.*)

JOE: Mr. Roma, can I hit you, again?

MANUEL: Please. Malkin. I didn't expect to see you here at this time of day.

MALKIN: I see you're with our novelist friend. How is the dear girl these days? Still pounding out potboilers on her typewriter?

MANUEL: She wouldn't call them that.

JOE: Here you go, Mr. Roma. Mr. Malkin, here's your drink: just enough Scotch to cover the ice. I remembered from the last time.

MALKIN (*coldly*): Thank you.

MANUEL: Thanks, Joe.

JOE: I was just telling Mr. Roma that my daughter likes Miss Santoni's books. She's up all night with them; studying them.

MALKIN: Indeed.

JOE: Don't you like them, Mr. Malkin? I've heard Miss Santoni say that it takes her years to write just one and even then she's never satisfied with it.

MALKIN: Fascinating. Well, I won't keep you, Roma. Regards to Regina.

JOE: Will I be collecting your records soon, Mr. Roma? I've heard rumors, you know.

MANUEL: I hope so, Joe. Thanks for asking.

JOE (*turning to MALKIN'S companion*): Can I get you another drink, Mister- (*MANUEL returns to the table.*)

CLAIRE: Well, that was fast. How many words did you exchange with your agent?

MANUEL: Not too many. He was too engrossed in his conversation to be charming.

CLAIRE: Look. He's coming this way -- that friend of his.

FRANK: Good afternoon.

CLAIRE: Good afternoon. (*FRANK exits.*) What was that about?

MANUEL: I don't know. I don't care, actually.

CLAIRE: Oh, Manuel, where's your sense of curiosity? Look! Malkin is coming over now. Brace yourself.

MALKIN: (*standing over them*): Claire? Manuel? You two out for a bite to eat?

CLAIRE: I'm thirsty. Who was that friend of yours? I've never met any of your friends, Malkin. Didn't know you had any.

MALKIN: You mean that I've never invited you to one of my parties? Pity.

CLAIRE: Don't be condescending. Who is he?

MALKIN: Manuel? Do you share Claire's curiosity?

CLAIRE: Quit stalling, Malkin. Always the enigmatic one. You really can be a bore, you know.

MALKIN: You should know. And, try minding your business in future.

CLAIRE: How've you been, Malkin?

MALKIN: Quite well, actually...and busy. Very busy.

CLAIRE: That's the spirit.

MANUEL: He's kept me busy. Thank God.

MALKIN: Thank me. Not Him.

MANUEL: He's coming back.

MALKIN (*looking over his shoulder*): Whom do you mean?

MANUEL: Your friend. He's coming back to the table.

CLAIRE: Quiet, the two of you!

FRANK (*speaking to MALKIN*): I beg your pardon, but you have my cigarette case. Please?

MALKIN (*fumbling in his jacket pocket*): You left it at the bar, I think. I didn't want to just leave it there. It looks expensive, rather.

FRANK: Thank you. May I join your party for a moment?

CLAIRE: Please. Claire Santoni.

FRANK: I already know your name.

CLAIRE: Then, you're one up on me. What's yours?

FRANK: Holden. Frank Holden. I am an acquaintance of Mr. Malkin here.

JOE (*walking over*): Pardon me, folks, but can I get anyone another drink?

MANUEL: I don't think so, Joe. I don't want to get too tight.

JOE: And, you, Mr. Malkin-

MALKIN: No. Thank you. Isn't it time you were on your way, Holden?

FRANK: Yes. I've no appointment to keep; but I should go. We will meet, as they say, in Hell. (*Exits.*)

CLAIRE: What did he mean by that?

MALKIN: I must be going, as well. Good day. (*Exits.*)

JOE (*squinting his eyes, as though in pain*): Well, if nobody wants anything else-

MANUEL: Are you all right, Joe? You're not in any pain, are you?

JOE (*sweating*): Oh, no. No. I just felt a bit queer for a second, but it seems to be easing now. Boy! It took me by surprise there. I think I'll get myself a glass of water. Excuse me, folks. Sorry about that.

MANUEL: Take it easy, Joe. Is your shift almost done?

JOE: Not yet, Mr.Roma. Martin should be here in a couple of hours. He still likes tending bar.

CLAIRE: You don't look so hot, honey. Maybe, you should see a doctor?

JOE: Not a chance. I'll be okay without some witch doctor prescribing pills for me. And, besides, I've never left before my shift is done. Excuse me.

CLAIRE: What do you make of that?

MANUEL: Nothing, really. Joe will be okay. And, anyway, I better be off. I don't think Regina's coming.

CLAIRE: Wait. We've got to talk.

MANUEL: About what? About Malkin's crackpot friend? I've better things to do and so have you. Come on.

CLAIRE: If I'm not mistaken, the great agent was chasing after him.

MANUEL: I've no comment to make about a man I've only just met.

CLAIRE: Is everything all right with you, Manuel? Wife not giving you any problems, is she?

MANUEL: Let's go, shall we?

CLAIRE (*getting ready to leave*): Well, I've no one waiting for me at home.

MANUEL: Your work is waiting for you.

CLAIRE: Thanks. I'm ready- well, it looks like I'll be going home alone. Your wife just arrived. She's over there by the door. Snob. (*She picks up the cigarette case and drops it in her pocketbook.*) She's going over to the bar pretending that she doesn't see us. She'll probably chat it up with Joe. I think I'll just slip out the back way. (*MANUEL moves back to stage left as CLAIRE exits stage right.*)

REGINA: Interesting. I wasn't pretending not to see her. I actually didn't notice her. And, you didn't mention that she'd been there with you. Interesting. Not her, but that man: the mysterious man at the bar. When you first mentioned him, it sent a chill up my spine for some reason.

MANUEL: I know what you mean. Well, what are we doing for dinner, tonight.

REGINA: Let's go out, shall we? I need a breath of fresh air.

MANUEL: As you like. We can take in that new play at the Music Box and, then, go to dinner from there. And, afterward, we can stop off for a nightcap at Martin's.

REGINA: And, maybe run into Malkin and his mysterious friend? My husband does have a sense of curiosity.

ACT ONE
Scene Three

Later that evening at Martin's Bar.

CLAIRE: Like melting ice going down: ice with a kick, that is. I respect you, Gaspari. I respect your fine talent as an artist.

NICHOLAS: Thank you.

CLAIRE: I ran into Malkin this afternoon and he had that self satisfied grin on his face. I despise that man.

NICHOLAS: He'd like to have me as a client, but I turned him down.

CLAIRE: Mistake.

NICHOLAS: I'm not worried.

CLAIRE: He's dangerous.

NICHOLAS: I'm sure that's the impression he wants to give people.

CLAIRE: Don't take Malkin too lightly. He's vindictive.

NICHOLAS: He can't hurt you. He can't hurt anyone.

CLAIRE: Order me another drink, will you? He knows things. He collects dossiers on people. I'm sure of it!

NICHOLAS: Bartender? Another scotch, please?

CLAIRE: Thanks. Sorry about the little outburst. Oh, that's good. I spend a great deal of time by myself. I do a great deal of research. My plots are very detailed and accurate, painstakingly so.

NICHOLAS: Claire?

CLAIRE: In my own way, I'm sensitive to things and it tends to make me appear a trifle unstable.

NICHOLAS: Are you a prophetess?

CLAIRE: Don't be impudent, young man. No! I am not a prophetess! But, I surmise trends in the interplay of people. I see the distinct possibilities of what could happen.

NICHOLAS: And what exactly could happen?

CLAIRE: I can tell you this much: the minute you turned down Malkin's proposal was the moment he started plotting against you.

NICHOLAS: Claire, do you actually believe that?

CLAIRE: He's already slandered me in print.

NICHOLAS: Libeled you in print.

CLAIRE: He hates my books. He hates my mind because he doesn't have one of his own.

NICHOLAS: You may be right about that. He does seem to collect people; but, the people he collects are weak -- weak like he is. You may be giving him more credit than he deserves. (*Taking note of the new bartender.*) What's become of Joe?

FRANK: I don't know. I got the call from Martin and showed up an hour ago for work.

NICHOLAS: Do you know Martin?

FRANK: Yes.

NICHOLAS: Have you tended bar here before? I hope you don't mind my asking.

FRANK: Not here. But, I've poured shots in my life.

NICHOLAS: I beg your pardon. Nicholas Gaspari.

FRANK: Frank Holden.

NICHOLAS: This is Claire Santoni, the writer.

FRANK: We've met.

CLAIRE: You're Malkin's friend. How about pouring me another drink?

FRANK: Scotch, I think.

NICHOLAS: A ginger-ale for me.

CLAIRE: Coward. So, Holden, how do you come to know the owner of this establishment?

FRANK: Here's your drink, Mr. Gaspari.

NICHOLAS: Thank you.

CLAIRE (*gulping down her drink*): Nice! Now, answer my question, bartender.

FRANK: Holden's the name. And, I don't snap to command.

CLAIRE: I don't care for your tone of voice, bartender.

FRANK: Try it on this side of the bar, lady.

CLAIRE: Touché. Well?

FRANK: What?

CLAIRE: You're an obstinate little fellow. How do you come to know Martin: owner of said bar?

FRANK: None of your damned business. Satisfied?

CLAIRE: Just watch it, brother. I've stepped on better things than you.

FRANK: I doubt it.

NICHOLAS (*running interference*): Who is that rather attractive woman who just came in?

CLAIRE (*still glaring at FRANK*): Where?

NICHOLAS (*nodding toward RAMONA*): Right over there.

CLAIRE: Do your stuff, bartender. The lady obviously needs a drink.

RAMONA: Good evening.

NICHOLAS: Good evening.

CLAIRE: Claire Santoni. My friend, Nicholas Gaspari.

RAMONA: I know Mr. Gaspari. I heard you sing the other night.

NICHOLAS: When was this?

RAMONA (*evading the question*): You were in fine voice. I admire fine things.

NICHOLAS: Thank you.

RAMONA: You've told me your name; but, I haven't told you mine. Ramona Chen. I am a friend of Malkin's.

CLAIRE: Isn't he just dripping with friends, lately.

RAMONA: Yes. If you'll excuse me, I'll take my drink to my table. A pleasure meeting you, Mr. Gaspari.

CLAIRE: Get a load of her. Bitch! And, stop laughing, Gaspari.

NICHOLAS: I'm not laughing.

FRANK: Another double?

CLAIRE: Single. Thanks.

FRANK: A double, I think. You can hold your liquor.

CLAIRE: Just watch that rotten attitude.

FRANK: No. Then, I needn't be civil to you; but, I will be. You know, the sympathetic bartender who consoles the lush posing as an intellectual. An author of books that no one understands or gives a crap about. To your health, Miss Santoni.

CLAIRE: Fuck you!

FRANK: A rather guttural retort. Almost unworthy of you. No intellectual arguments to spit out? Shall I fetch you some paper and this way, perhaps, you can write them out in your usual mumbo-jumbo?

NICHOLAS: That's enough, Holden.

CLAIRE: Cretin! Philistine! I'll have your goddamned job!

NICHOLAS: Easy, Claire. I'll speak to Martin. This is inexcusable behavior, Holden. You owe Miss Santoni an apology.

FRANK: I'm not sorry.

CLAIRE: You will be, brother!

FRANK: I will be, but not in the way that you think. Do you think? (*Before CLAIRE can respond, NICHOLAS pulls her away and sits her down at a table on stage left. REGINA and MANUEL enter stage right.*)

REGINA: Look. There's Gaspari and that's dear Claire with him. An improbable couple.

MANUEL: Lower your voice, they might hear you.

REGINA: You worry too much. Who's the new bartender?

MANUEL: My God! That's Malkin's friend -- the one I told you about. What the hell is he doing behind the bar?

REGINA: Ask him. And, while you're at it, get me a drink. The usual.

MANUEL: I'll be right back. (*Crossing over to the bar and speaks to FRANK.*) Good evening. Holden, isn't it? We met today. Manuel Roma.

FRANK: What can I get for you?

MANUEL: Two bourbons, please.

FRANK: I'll bring them to your table. Is that Mrs. Roma with you?

MANUEL: My wife...yes.

FRANK: She's quite striking. She does you justice.

MANUEL: We met in Paris. She did quite a bit of modeling there. She's given it up, though.

FRANK: She has you to look after, now.

MANUEL: Yes. Of course. Bring the drinks over, will you, Holden? (*Joining REGINA at center stage.*)

REGINA: Well, who is he?

MANUEL: I don't know.

REGINA: Did you ask him what he's doing here?

MANUEL: No. I thought it might be rude.

REGINA: My husband's sense of propriety is astounding. Here he comes. (*FRANK places the drinks on the table.*) Thank you, Mr. Holden. You're a friend of Malkin's?

FRANK: Yes.

REGINA: Do you usually tend bar for a living? You don't seem the type.

FRANK: Not usually.

REGINA: A sideline, then?

FRANK: Yes. You'll excuse me, please?

REGINA: Of course. What is your usual occupation, Mr. Holden?

FRANK: It would mean nothing to you.

REGINA: Try me.

FRANK: I am an epistemologist.

REGINA: How very fascinating. A branch of philosophy, isn't it? A very complex branch of philosophy.

FRANK (*impressed*): Extremely. I've underestimated your wife, Roma. Please accept my apologies. And, now, if you will excuse me? (*He goes back to the bar.*)

REGINA: Do you see how easy it is? He felt himself superior to me. And, now look at him slither back to his bar. He's repulsive.

MANUEL: What makes you say that?

REGINA: Because he's obviously up to something.

MANUEL: I think I might agree with you on that.

REGINA: And, now that I have my drink safely in hand, why don't you go over there and invite Gaspari and dear Claire to join us. We'll make a party out of this.

MANUEL: If you insist.

REGINA: I suggest it. And, I have my reasons.

MANUEL (*notices RAMONA sitting in the corner quietly drinking*): Gaspari? Claire? Come on over to our table. Let's make a night of this.

NICHOLAS: Claire, are you game?

CLAIRE: Well, I never could resist a party atmosphere. And, Regina is looking so lovely, tonight.

MALKIN (*entering stage left, he stops short at seeing RAMONA*): What the hell are you doing here?

RAMONA: I'm tired of working. I needed to get out and have some fun. And, I'm not your slave.

MALKIN: Why this particular bar, Miss Chen?

RAMONA: I like the customers who come here.

MALKIN: I am now going to ask you to leave of your own volition.

RAMONA: I'll leave when I'm good and ready to leave.

MALKIN: How many drinks will that take?

RAMONA: I'm a pretty slow drinker. I might be here all night.

MALKIN: Leave.

RAMONA: No.

MALKIN: Miss Chen, you are truly beginning to annoy me. Now, get up and leave as quietly as I'm sure you came.

RAMONA: Get me another drink, please.

MALKIN: Don't you dare signal to him- That was a mistake.

RAMONA: What's the matter? Ashamed to be seen with Ramona? (*FRANK walks over.*)

MALKIN: I'll do the ordering. Two scotches, please.

RAMONA: I love to see you so uncomfortable. The great Malkin: agent of the world. Maybe you're afraid of me? Maybe, I know about you and your boy-

MALKIN: Shut up! (*Spotlight is now on center stage.*)

CLAIRE: What's the Asian beauty to Malkin?

REGINA: A "friend?"

CLAIRE: She seems to be holding her own with him.

REGINA (*approvingly*): She is. But, for how long, I wonder?

CLAIRE: I think he's trying to get rid of her.

MANUEL: That would be a shame.

REGINA: Do you find her attractive?

NICHOLAS: It's amazing bumping into two friends of Malkin's in the space of one evening.

CLAIRE: They don't look so friendly to me.

REGINA (*jealousy creeping into her voice*): When he's through with her, he'll come over here to join us. I've always found his company stimulating.

CLAIRE: I haven't.

REGINA: Why is that, Claire?

CLAIRE: Because he's a rotten, egotistical bastard.

MANUEL: Gaspari, I heard you in The Dutchman the other week over the radio. Nice job of it, man.

REGINA: We both heard your performance. Your German's getting better, much better, in fact. You're studying quite hard, I take it. Putting in the long hours. You look a little tired.

NICHOLAS: I am tired; but, I'm satisfied with my progress.

REGINA: Good. You're dedicated. Manuel will be ready to sing Don Jose next season. He's very modest about it, but he fits the role to perfection; don't you think?

NICHOLAS: Does Manuel think so?

REGINA: Do you?

NICHOLAS: Well, Regina, you put me on the spot. It's a plum role that any tenor would want to sing. Manuel, do you think you're up to it?

MANUEL: I'm still doing some minor repairs on the part. Regina shouldn't have brought it up.

REGINA: My husband talks nonsense. Someone had to replace McEwen and they chose you.

MANUEL: It's not in the Fall schedule, yet.

REGINA: It will be. (*Spotlight on stage right.*)

RAMONA: Why don't you introduce me to your friends? They've been watching us, you know.

MALKIN: You're joking, surely.

RAMONA: Maybe, I'll go over there and introduce myself.

MALKIN: What would you say to them?

RAMONA: Just small talk, for now.

MALKIN: You don't know any small talk.

RAMONA: I'll talk about you, maybe.

MALKIN: Why don't I take you home? Where are you living these days?

RAMONA: Brooklyn.

MALKIN: Christ!

RAMONA: I know. It's all Ramona can afford. Times have been very hard for me.

MALKIN: You've just received a sizable commission.

RAMONA: Half a commission. I want the rest of it.

MALKIN: Finish the damn job.

RAMONA: It's taking longer than I thought.

MALKIN: How much longer?

RAMONA: Oh…a few years, maybe.

MALKIN: What was that? Are you trying to swindle me?

RAMONA: I think the bartender is trying to get your attention. Why don't you go over there and see what he wants. Might be important.

MALKIN (*getting up*): I'll be right back. (*Spotlight on center stage.*)

REGINA: Tell me, Gaspari, are you excited about next season?

NICHOLAS: Every season is exciting.

MANUEL: I wish I could be more excited and less nervous about openings.

REGINA: It's good to be excited. Keeps you alert to the audience.

CLAIRE: Well, I'll have to be content with hearing these boys on the radio.

REGINA: Books not selling?

CLAIRE: My books aren't meant for the general public.

REGINA: Is there another kind of public I don't know about?

CLAIRE: As a matter of fact, there is.

REGINA: Let us know when you find them. Perhaps, we'll see you at the box office?

CLAIRE: Don't bet on it.

REGINA: Don't be cross, Claire, it's very unbecoming.

CLAIRE: Well, pardon me!

NICHOLAS: Here comes your agent, Manuel.

MALKIN: May I join this party standing up?

REGINA: Of course. But, why don't you get a chair and really join in the fun?

MALKIN: Fun? I do not believe in "fun." No. There is no "fun" at a party that I herald. Here! This drink is not to herald "fun.." (*Taking his glass and raising it to eye level.*) Interesting substance, eh? A beautiful liquid that redefines one's sense of proportion and sobriety. It penetrates the air that hovers just above its tiny ripples of intoxication. One cherishes its impact upon the senses even before the first swallow. It touches one's lips like a stinging and breathless kiss of abandon. It hurts the mouth. It should hurt for it is penetrating. And in its penetration, it enfolds the body and mind and heart and…the emotions. That beautiful liquid with a kick that can stain one's virtue or liberate it. Cheers!

CLAIRE (*applauding*): Good speech. Impromptu, too. I can tell. May I quote you in my next book?

MALKIN: I don't give a damn. You see, a man who is on his way to being drunk does not care of such trifles. Oh, not that your books are trifles -- pretentious rot, yes, but not trifles. No. I read all your glorious works. I must do another column on them soon. I've neglected you for too long. When's the next magnum opus coming out? Pub. date all set? Presses rolling?

CLAIRE: Not yet, but soon. A plot is just taking hold in my head.

MALKIN: Excellent!

CLAIRE: Isn't your friend lonely sitting all by herself? (*Beckons RAMONA to join them.*)

REGINA: Manuel, get the lady a chair, please? (*She makes all the introductions.*) I've not seen you at Martin's before.

RAMONA: I rarely come. I live- far away, and my work keeps me very busy.

MALKIN (*standing almost directly behind RAMONA*): Miss Chen is an artist in the Vermeer style.

REGINA: Have I seen any of your work?

RAMONA: No. I've not been exhibited.

NICHOLAS: Are you working on anything now, Miss Chen?

RAMONA: Yes. A commissioned work.

REGINA: Commissioned by whom, may I ask?

RAMONA: His name would mean nothing to you. I should go. I've much work to do.

REGINA: So soon? But, you've only just arrived.

RAMONA: Yes. I know. But, I must go.

REGINA: Malkin, stop her.

MALKIN: I?

CLAIRE: Who else? She is your "friend."

NICHOLAS: Perhaps, Miss Chen, feels a bit uncomfortable among so many strangers. I know I would.

REGINA: Stay, Miss Chen, please. I am enjoying your company. We so rarely get a chance to meet any of Malkin's "friends."

MALKIN: We are not "friends." And, you may take the quotations off that word. (*During this scene, FRANK leaves the bar and slips out unnoticed.*)

NICHOLAS: Well, it's past my bed time. If Miss Chen is leaving, perhaps, we can share a cab for a part of the way?

REGINA: The party seems to be breaking up. Perhaps, we should all call it a night? Manuel?

MANUEL: I could use another drink, actually. (*He turns toward the bar.*) Hello? No bartender. (*Everyone at the table turns to look.*)

CLAIRE: What do you make of that, Gaspari?

NICHOLAS: Very, very odd. But, so much of tonight-

RAMONA (*looking at MALKIN*): I must go. Goodnight. (*The phone behind the bar starts to ring.*)

CLAIRE: Someone should get that. Gaspari, go and see who's calling.

NICHOLAS (*crossing over to the bar and ducking behind it*): Hello? Martin's Bar. No. The bartender just left. Martin? It's Nicholas Gaspari. I'm standing behind the bar. Why? Because your bartender just took a Steve Brody. Your bartender: Frank Holden. (*Placing his hand over the receiver.*) It's Martin calling. Yes. Some of the gang's with me. What's happened? Are you joking with me? You can't be serious. But, why? The police were called in? What in God's name for? It looked suspicious, you say. Go on. Yes. We're all leaving now. I really don't know what to tell you. We'll turn the lights out and lock up. Of course, but- You're sure this is no joke? Sorry. All right. Goodbye.

CLAIRE: What is it?

NICHOLAS: It's the bartender, Joe. He's been murdered.

REGINA (*standing up*): Murdered?

CLAIRE: Who in hell would do such a thing?

NICHOLAS: The police said that Joe had been poisoned.

CLAIRE: Poisoned? Here? When?

NICHOLAS: Today. And, apparently only a few hours ago. It seems that we missed all the excitement by minutes. As a matter of fact-

CLAIRE: Go on, man!

NICHOLAS: Martin was surprised at my picking up the phone just now. He rang because he thought the police might have sent someone around by this time.

REGINA: That's quite understandable under the circumstances.

RAMONA: That's not what Mr. Gaspari means, is it?

NICHOLAS: That's not what I mean, Miss Chen.

MANUEL: Then, what do you mean, damn it? Don't keep us in suspense.

RAMONA: It's frightening!

NICHOLAS: When they took Joe off to the hospital, the bar had been closed.

REGINA: What are you telling us? What are you talking about? Tell me.

MALKIN: Yes. Tell me.

NICHOLAS: There should have been no bartender because none had been called for. That man -- your friend, Malkin -- was an impostor.

REGINA: This makes no sense at all. You mean to say-

NICHOLAS: I mean to say this: Frank Holden, who's just been serving us drinks, may be a cold-blooded murderer.

ACT TWO
Scene One

The year is 1953 at Martin's Bar.

JUSTIN: That was a very nice song.

NICHOLAS: An aria from the opera "Fedora." And, thank you. What's your name, young man.

JUSTIN: Justin Kane. And, you're Nicholas Gaspari. I've heard of you. I'm not so keen on opera, but I know your name and your agent.

NICHOLAS: I don't have an agent. Whatever gave you that idea?

JUSTIN: Isn't Malkin your agent?

NICHOLAS: No. Surely Malkin didn't state that he was my agent.

JUSTIN: Not really. No offense, Mr. Gaspari.

NICHOLAS: I didn't take any. Not much of a crowd here tonight.

JUSTIN: It's early.

NICHOLAS: Yes? You wanted to ask me something, Justin?

JUSTIN: My predecessor, Joe, he was killed here wasn't he? Never caught the murderer.

NICHOLAS: A little before your time.

JUSTIN: A few years, I guess. It was pretty exciting. I read the newspaper clippings.

NICHOLAS: The whole affair was disturbing. None of it made any sense. Excuse me, would you? (*REGINA and MANUEL enter.*) Good evening.

MANUEL: Good evening, Gaspari.

REGINA: Hello, Gaspari.

NICHOLAS: How about joining me, Regina? Manuel? I'm all by myself.

REGINA (*putting her bag on the table*): Of course. Manuel can order the drinks. We're expecting Malkin to join us soon; but, he may be a little late. How have you been.

NICHOLAS: Thankfully, busy.

REGINA: Good for you. Who's the new bartender?

NICHOLAS: A young man by the name of Justin Kane.

REGINA: Rather friendly, isn't he?

MANUEL: He's young and wants to make a good impression.

REGINA: Yes. Young and ambitious, I'm sure. He's quick with the drinks.

JUSTIN: Here you go. Let me know if you need anything else.

MANUEL: We will, Justin.

REGINA: The place hasn't changed very much.

MANUEL (*trying not to look at JUSTIN*): New bartender.

REGINA: Yes. The new bartender. Have I seen him before? Not here, surely.

MANUEL: How could you, Regina? You haven't been near the place for years. He's a kid; leave him alone.

REGINA: I don't care for your tone of voice.

NICHOLAS: You said you were expecting Malkin, Regina?

REGINA: He ought to have been here by this time. Always late. Always keeping you waiting. Oh, by the way, Gaspari, we're having a party at our place this Friday. You're invited.

MANUEL: And, don't say that you can't make it. I know your schedule better than mine.

NICHOLAS: I'll be glad to come. What time?

REGINA: Cocktails at seven. Dinner at eight. We'll have to find someone to tend bar.

MANUEL: What about young Justin over there? I'm sure he could use the extra money.

REGINA: You like him, don't you?

MANUEL: What of it?

REGINA: Why are you being so defensive? And, again, that tone of voice.

MANUEL: What do you have against that young man?

REGINA: You mean that handsome, young man? Nothing, of course. I barely know him.

MANUEL: And, don't take that tone of voice with me. Save it for Malkin -- not me! Do you hear?

REGINA: The whole damned bar hears you. Finish your drink. You're making a spectacle of yourself.

MANUEL: In front of whom? There's no one else in this dump, but us.

REGINA: And, Gaspari? Is he of no account?

NICHOLAS: I'm not insulted. And, Justin hasn't missed a word of this conversation. I'll order another round of drinks.

REGINA: Please. My husband could use another one.

NICHOLAS: And, you can tell me more about this party of yours. What's the occasion?

REGINA: A simple affair, really: a friendly gathering of colleagues.

MANUEL: Well...a gathering. I don't know how friendly it will be. And, believe it or not, there is a point to it.

REGINA: How cynical you are, tonight. What's gotten into you?

MANUEL: The point will be an unveiling of a masterpiece of sorts.

NICHOLAS: A portrait of Manuel?

MANUEL: We really don't know; do we, Regina?

REGINA: My husband is being unnecessarily mysterious. It's a work that's been commissioned by Malkin, in a sense.

NICHOLAS: You've piqued my curiosity. It's exciting.

MANUEL: Yes. Exciting.

REGINA (*spotting MALKIN framed in the doorway*): Malkin's arrived. (*They all turn in MALKIN'S direction.*)

MALKIN: Good evening. Gaspari? You're looking well.

REGINA: We've been waiting for you. Perhaps-

MALKIN: Gaspari, would you mind terribly if I spoke with Regina and Manuel in private? I don't have very much time and it is urgent, rather.

NICHOLAS: I'll just take my drink over to the bar.

MALKIN: I do apologize, but I am in a bit of a dilemma.

NICHOLAS: You, Malkin? I'd have never thought it. I'll try not to eavesdrop.

MALKIN: I heard your Don Jose the other evening. Quite good. But, I sense a futility to your efforts.

NICHOLAS: What efforts, Malkin?

MALKIN: Why your efforts toward immortality. You won't make it, Gaspari...not without my help. You play it role by role, performance by performance, season by season; but, your name, Gaspari...your name has not been emblazoned on the wall of Olympus. It is a mere scratch mark; mind you, a very nice and respectable one that abounds in the precise details of craftsmanship; but, it will fade. I tell you that it will fade...

NICHOLAS: Good evening, Malkin. And, by the way, have you ever heard from your friend: Frank Holden? I've got a few questions for him still.

MALKIN: Go to hell.

NICHOLAS: And, not Olympus?

MALKIN: Only the gods may enter.

NICHOLAS: Are you a god, Malkin?

MALKIN: Why don't you socialize at the bar? (*NICHOLAS walks over to the bar.*)

MALKIN: Now, we can talk.

REGINA: Was that necessary?

MALKIN (*ignoring her question*): The recording contract with RCA is a good one. Come to my office tomorrow morning and sign it.

REGINA: I'll be there, as well.

MALKIN: Ah! The devoted wife, or is it that you simply don't trust me?

REGINA: I trust you implicitly; but, I'd like to be there for the coronation.

MALKIN: Not quite.

REGINA: I disagree. The race is over and Manuel has won. His recordings will be a testament to my- to his talents.

MALKIN: Caught yourself, Regina?

MANUEL: I'm glad of this recording opportunity. It's like being-

REGINA: Immortalized, darling. Quite magnificent, really.

MALKIN: Another god being created. We seem to be stuffed with gods in this quaint, little bar, tonight.

REGINA: Manuel, I'm thirsty. Get me another drink, will you?

MANUEL: The same?

REGINA: The same, please. (*MANUEL joins NICHOLAS at the bar.*)

MALKIN: Why did you get rid of him?

REGINA: Don't mock me like that in public. I don' like it.

MALKIN: I was being facetious.

REGINA: Then, don't be facetious with me, again. You can be very annoying.

MALKIN: Part of my charm.

REGINA: Why did you insist that we meet you here, tonight? I would think that this is the last place in the world you'd want to visit.

MALKIN: Do you mean that unfortunate business some years ago? Ancient history, that. Forgotten.

REGINA: Not to the police.

MALKIN: Do you know many cops, Regina?

REGINA: I'm quite fond of detective novels.

MALKIN: Christie? Kendall? Sayers? Conan Doyle?

REGINA: I love Sherlock Holmes. And, don't mock me.

MALKIN: We are the sensitive one, tonight. When have you started to develop this thin skin?

REGINA: I may know more about your mysterious friend, Frank Holden, than you think. Don't underestimate me, Malkin. That, I would find insulting; and, you don't want to insult me, do you?

MALKIN: What do you know?

REGINA: A few details that I assume you've shared with the police.

MALKIN: You're being evasive.

REGINA: To be one up on you, Malkin. Gaspari would appreciate this.

MALKIN: I think…yes. I know the event you're talking about.

REGINA: Who is Frank Holden? The police gave you a hard time about him, didn't they?

MALKIN: I'll repeat myself: ancient history.

REGINA: Who was he? Did he actually kill the bartender?

MALKIN: You're turning into a first rate bore, Regina. Give my farewells to Manuel.

REGINA: Don't go. How was it done? You can tell me. Why was it done?

MALKIN (*getting ready to leave*): Goodnight, Regina. I'll see you at my office tomorrow. Party still on for Friday?

REGINA: Of course.

ACT TWO
Scene Two

CLAIRE'S apartment. At stage right there's an end table with an old Remington typewriter. The love seat is stained with liquor.

CLAIRE: Where in hell is Ramona? It's almost midnight. I think I need a drink. (*She moves toward the drinks table, but reaches for a pack of cigarettes and lights one.*) What luck! Bumping into Malkin and bumming a whole pack of cigarettes off him. (*She takes a deep drag on the cigarette.*) Better. It's so lonely here. I used to actually like that. It was like being in my own private office in a skyscraper. (*There's a sharp knock on the door.*)

RAMONA: It's Ramona.

CLAIRE (*opening the door*): You're late; but, at least, you're here and I'm still sober.

RAMONA: You keep house like me: sloppy. I like your place.

CLAIRE: Drink?

RAMONA: Whatever you're having.

CLAIRE: Cheap whiskey.

RAMONA: So, Claire, what is on your mind. Tell Ramona.

CLAIRE: Here's your drink.

RAMONA: Cheers!

CLAIRE: I'll get straight to the point: Malkin.

RAMONA: How boring. Everyone is so obsessed with him. Maybe your interest in him gives him so much power.

CLAIRE: I'll rephrase my statement: Frank Holden.

RAMONA: He's much more interesting. Do you know him?

CLAIRE: Do you?

RAMONA: Why should I know him?

CLAIRE: I met him. Manuel and I. We were having drinks at Martin's and he actually comes over to the table and introduces himself.

RAMONA: You're joking! I don't believe it.

CLAIRE: Thanks for calling me a liar.

RAMONA: What did he say to you? I must know.

CLAIRE: That's just it. I can't remember.

RAMONA: You're supposed to be a writer. You must remember.

CLAIRE: Why does it mean so much to you?

RAMONA: If he murdered that bartender-

CLAIRE: I know. Why all the pretense? Why stick around?

RAMONA: Good questions. So? Do you have the answers?

CLAIRE: It's almost like he was...

RAMONA: Waiting for someone. Yes. I had the same feeling. And, you want to know something even more frightening? I know he's been watching me.

CLAIRE: Christ! Don't say that.

RAMONA: Why not? It's true. You're trembling. Fix yourself another drink.

CLAIRE: Thanks. I think I will. Want another?

RAMONA: No. One of us should stay sober.

CLAIRE: When did you meet Malkin? You don't seem his type.

RAMONA: No woman is.

CLAIRE: I see.

RAMONA: He commissioned me to do a portrait of Manuel Roma.

CLAIRE: Does Manuel know about it?

RAMONA: He knows nothing. I did the portrait from press photos.

CLAIRE: Are they lovers?

RAMONA: I guess. Do you like Manuel? He's very handsome, but Nicholas is a much better singer.

CLAIRE: And, dear Malkin knows it.

RAMONA: So does Manuel.

CLAIRE: And, his wife.

RAMONA: You don't like her, do you?

CLAIRE: I despise her.

RAMONA: I think she has to put up with a lot.

CLAIRE: Opportunists usually do. She's so damned shallow.

RAMONA: Who isn't? So, who is Frank Holden? You know something, don't you? What do you have there?

CLAIRE (*fumbling in her overstuffed pocketbook*): A souvenir.

RAMONA: Let's have a look. Very nice. Solid gold. Yours?

CLAIRE: Frank Holden's, I think.

RAMONA: Where did you get it? He gave it to you?

CLAIRE: I stole it.

RAMONA: When? Tell me.

CLAIRE: After Holden left the bar, Malkin comes over to our table and makes up some small talk and, then, Holden comes back- that's it! Holden came back in the bar and starts chatting us up. Malkin tosses the cigarette case on to the table and said something like he thought it looked valuable and didn't want to just leave it at the bar.

RAMONA: What happened next?

CLAIRE: Holden leaves and Malkin chases after him. And, that's when I pocketed the case. I waited for Manuel to turn his back; lucky for me that Regina decided to make an appearance just about then.

RAMONA: Holden left without his cigarette case? Why?

CLAIRE: That was the odd part…doesn't make sense.

RAMONA: Maybe he just forgot to take it with him. You said he was in a hurry. Have you pawned it?

CLAIRE: Once or twice.

RAMONA: It's not Malkin's. I've seen his cigarette case: it's silver and gold. You thought it was Malkin's, didn't you?

CLAIRE: Guilty of a false assumption. It just doesn't add up.

RAMONA (opening it up): Empty.

CLAIRE: Yeah. Well, I won't keep you.

RAMONA: Throwing me out?

CLAIRE: I think I'll try and do some writing.

RAMONA: Next time, I'll invite you over to my place and, then, I can throw you out. I think you wasted my time. Here's your cigarette case. (*She exits, flinging the cigarette case at CLAIRE who picks it up and places it on the drinks table. The door opens.*)

FRANK: You shouldn't leave your door open like that.

CLAIRE (*spilling her drink*): Christ!

FRANK: You're spilling good liquor on to your tacky, worn out carpet. Careful.

CLAIRE: What-

FRANK: What am I doing here in this hovel? I've come for that cigarette case. The one you stole.

CLAIRE: It's not yours.

FRANK: It's not yours. I'll be stealing from a thief? A thief stealing from a thief? Not quite. I'll be fetching for someone.

CLAIRE: How sweet! A dog playing fetch for his beloved master.

FRANK (*moving toward the drinks table*): I'd be very careful if I were you, Miss Santoni. As a writer, you stink. As a woman, you're pathetic. And, as a strategist, you're an idiot.

CLAIRE: Get out!

FRANK: No. I've a few things to say to you. Get away from that door. Don't try to open it. You won't.

CLAIRE: Say what you have to say and get the hell out!

FRANK (*looking about the room*): This place is a pig's sty.

CLAIRE: I'm a bohemian. We do things differently.

FRANK: How many books have you sold lately? Three?

CLAIRE: You like insulting people. You're not looking so great either. Yes. I'm a writer and a damned good one!

FRANK: And an alcoholic. Let's not leave that out of the equation. Yes. A writer who is making a feeble attempt at playing detective. You know exactly nothing, Miss Santoni. But, here, I'll freshen your drink for you. Here. I'll start to pour. But, when should I stop? Huh? I could pour the whole bottle down your throat and it wouldn't be enough. Look, Miss Santoni, liquor! Come on! It's good stuff! Down the hatch! I insist. You stole that cigarette case. You invited Miss Chen here, tonight, to quiz her on...me! You ask too many questions for your own damned good and find out nothing. Always alert. Always posturing. Too bad it doesn't translate into anything useful. When I came here, tonight, I was undecided: terrify her, threaten her, steal back what she stole, or kill her? Drink up, Miss Santoni, it'll help deaden the nerve.

You see, I'm not unlike yourself. Our futures are decided. The fateful third sister is about to cut the dreaded thread on both of us. You suffer. I suffer. I walk the streets at night: a long and lonely dreadful affair. It is preferable to your flop house or train station or a park bench. Address: unknown but malleable. Identity: uncertain. Past: nonexistent. Present: classified. Future: cement slab in the city morgue. I want company on that slab, Miss Santoni. Claire! (*He smashes the bottle and holds the jagged edge toward her.*) Keep me company? (*CLAIRE screams. Black out.*)

ACT TWO
Scene Three

The ROMA apartment on the next day.

REGINA: Well, that should just about do it. The guests will start arriving soon.

MANUEL: Don't ask me to sing, tonight.

REGINA: I won't. I think it's rather distasteful for a host to sing at his own gathering. Shall I ask Gaspari to sing? He wouldn't, you know.

MANUEL: He doesn't sing on command. He's too much of a professional for that.

REGINA: Correct. And, take a page out of his book. (*She changes the subject.*) Is your writer friend coming this evening? I do hope she dresses properly. I don't want to feel embarrassed for her.

MANUEL: I don't think so.

REGINA: You don't sound very sure of it.

MANUEL: I've tried calling and she hasn't answered the phone.

REGINA: She could have been out.

MANUEL: She doesn't go out much. I think she's pretty destitute, actually.

REGINA: Have you dropped by her flat?

MANUEL: Yes. I dropped by this afternoon, but there was no answer.

REGINA: Did you knock loud enough? Perhaps, dear Claire was nursing a hangover.

MANUEL: Don't be cruel.

REGINA: It's not very becoming, is it? You could have asked the landlady to let you in.

MANUEL: I was going to, but thought better of it. If Claire were indisposed, she wouldn't appreciate unannounced visitors.

REGINA: I certainly couldn't blame her for that.

MANUEL: I did slip a note under her door.

REGINA: You were determined, weren't you?

MANUEL: I was concerned.

REGINA: Well, enough of her. (*The doorbell rings.*) I'll get it. Good evening. You're right on time. (*The guests arrive: NICHOLAS, MALKIN, and RAMONA.*)

RAMONA: I love your place, Regina. It's so modern and chic and cold. Did you decorate it yourself?

REGINA Thank you. I must admit that I borrowed from the Paris magazines quite a bit.

RAMONA: I love it. So, why are we here this evening?

REGINA: You ask very direct questions.

RAMONA: Is it for the unveiling? How very flattering.

REGINA: Not quite. But, the announcement may come as a shock to some.

RAMONA (*caught off guard*): What announcement?

REGINA: You'll have to be patient and wait.

RAMONA: Not too long, I hope.

MALKIN (*sauntering over from stage left*): Not too long for what?

REGINA: Our announcement.

RAMONA: "Our" announcement?

MALKIN: Yes. And, by the way, Miss Chen, who invited you?

REGINA: Ramona is here as my guest.

MALKIN: Would you excuse us, please?

RAMONA: Of course. (*Moving to stage left.*)

MALKIN: What are you trying to pull off here?

REGINA: Lower your voice!

MALKIN: Answer my question, please.

REGINA: The portrait, of course. What else?

MALKIN: You mean to say that our resident artist has actually completed it? When was this miracle performed? I may actually start believing in God.

REGINA: That's not what I'm talking about.

MALKIN: Then, what?

REGINA: Don't take that tone of voice with me.

MALKIN (*grabbing her by the elbow*): Do you think that you've removed yourself from my influence? You're mistaken. As your husband's agent, I control him and you! I can push him forward or destroy the both of you: humiliate the two of you! It would give me profound joy to do either one. You'd better decide which, Regina.

REGINA: You can't touch us now.

MALKIN (*releasing her arm*): I see. Your husband, Manuel Roma, matinee idol, will be remembered as nothing more than a "flash in the pan." You are a fool, Regina. I gave you credit for more intelligence.

REGINA: If that's a challenge, I accept it.

MALKIN: Not a challenge: a pre-ordained fact!

NICHOLAS (*walking over*): You two seem to be in deep and intense conversation.

MALKIN: Gaspari, your debut at the Met is this fall. Outstanding.

NICHOLAS: Thank you.

MALKIN: I've heard you sing Don Jose. It's your role.

REGINA: Others have sung it, as well.

MALKIN: Not like Gaspari, here. Again: outstanding.

REGINA: Excuse me, please. I think our bartender is being neglected.

NICHOLAS: Regina's upset.

MALKIN: With good cause.

NICHOLAS: I don't see Claire about. I've wanted to ask, but-

MALKIN: She was actually invited?

MANUEL (*joining the group*): I invited her.

MALKIN: Translated as: Regina did not.

MANUEL: Have you heard from her at all, Gaspari?

NICHOLAS: Claire's done this sort of thing before: dropping out of sight. I think it gives her a vicarious thrill to be the center of attention and, then, feign indifference when she decides to make a triumphant reappearance. You're worried about her, aren't you?

MANUEL: Concerned.

MALKIN: Worried. Claire has always been in love with Roma here.

MANUEL: Shut up, Malkin.

MALKIN: It's an open secret -- even Regina knows it. As a matinee idol, you should be used to that sort of thing.

MANUEL: Go to bloody hell.

NICHOLAS: Gentlemen! Let's maintain the civilities, please. This is supposed to be a party. (*Looking over at the make-shift bar.*) Justin seems to be having a good time. I think he's excited just being here.

MALKIN: Well, I need a drink. Roma? Keep me company, will you? Your "duty" as a host. (*The two of them walk over to the bar.*)

REGINA: Everyone? Please? Thank you for coming to our little party, tonight. As you know, I've planned an unveiling, but that must wait.

RAMONA: I thought-

REGINA: Please, dear. As I was saying, I've an announcemnt to make. This Fall season, Manuel will begin his recording career with RCA records. The long term contract has been signed and his first recording will begin next month! (*A respectful applause followed by the obligatory congratulations.*) It's exciting, no? A performance is so very nice, but soon lost and forgotten. But, a recording is a piece of immortality: history, in fact. So very sweet. Manuel, say a few words to our guests. (*The door is flung open and CLAIRE stumbles in. MANUEL rushes over and helps her to a chair.*)

CLAIRE: Am I late?

MANUEL: What's happened to you?

REGINA (*coming over with a drink*): Here. Give her this.

MANUEL: Should I get a doctor for you?

CLAIRE: A doctor? No...no doctor.

REGINA: Manuel, call one. Or get her out of here. Do something!

JUSTIN: I think she's in shock.

CLAIRE: Shock? No. I'm- I've been poisoned.

NICHOLAS: Somebody phone for an ambulance.

JUSTIN: Where's the phone?

NICHOLAS: Over there. Hurry, Justin.

RAMONA (*moving closer to CLAIRE*): I think it's too late. Look at her complexion: it's like a death mask.

CLAIRE: Die? Yes- but-

NICHOLAS: What is it, Claire? Tell us.

REGINA: Manuel, why are you just standing there?

NICHOLAS: Claire, would you like to lie down?

CLAIRE: No. I'll never get up, again.

JUSTIN (*rushing back in from stage right*): They're on their way. She looks like she's had it.

MANUEL: Shut up.

NICHOLAS: Claire, who did this to you?

REGINA: Or did she do it to herself? I smell liquor on her breath.

CLAIRE: He did it.

NICHOLAS: Whom do you mean?

CLAIRE: He's insane.

REGINA: She's talking gibberish. Always dramatizing.

CLAIRE: He thought I knew something. I didn't…not then.

NICHOLAS: And, now? What do you know, now? Tell us.

CLAIRE: He's not alone.

MALKIN (*holding on to his drink with his arm fully extended*): Who is not alone?

REGINA: What nonsense! I won't listen to any more of it.

MALKIN: Whom did he kill?

RAMONA: Why is she looking at me that way?

JUSTIN: Does she know what she's saying? She looks pretty delirious to me.

CLAIRE: It wasn't just Holden.

MALKIN: Holden? Where is he? Tell me! (*CLAIRE slumps heavily into the chair as she tries to point to the guilty party.*)

NICHOLAS: She's dead.

JUSTIN: It was that murderer's accomplice she was trying to point to, wasn't it? Which means-

NICHOLAS: Someone in this room has been an accomplice to murder-

MALKIN: Or?

NICHOLAS: -or has actually murdered Claire. (*MALKIN smashes his glass with his hand. Black out.*)

ACT THREE

Martin's Bar in late September of 1955.

NICHOLAS: I think it's time for another murder.

JUSTIN: Are you serious, Mr. Gaspari? What makes you say that?

NICHOLAS: I've been trying to weave a pattern to past events and, I think another murder is going to take place.

JUSTIN: But, why?

NICHOLAS: The first murder occurred when I was about to resume my career. The second murder occurred just before my debut at the Met. And, now, I'm about to sign up with London Records. I think I may have been the intended victim.

JUSTIN: Kind of makes sense. But, if you put it like that, the same thing could be said of Mr. Roma. He was just starting out when that bartender was killed, wasn't he? And, he'd just signed a contract with RCA Records when Miss Santoni was killed.

NICHOLAS: Perhaps, we were both the intended victims.

JUSTIN: What made you think about all this, Mr. Gaspari?

NICHOLAS: Miss Santoni came to mind the other day.

JUSTIN: Wasn't she kind of down on her luck?

NICHOLAS: She was suffering. For much of her life, she was suffering. She was a lonely and vulnerable woman despite the bravura.

JUSTIN: So, Mr. Gaspari, what's your theory about Miss Santoni's murder?

NICHOLAS: Claire knew too much.

JUSTIN: Knew what?

NICHOLAS: That, I don't know, Justin. But, her murder and Joe's are clearly connected.

JUSITN: But, don't forget that Joe was killed in '49 and Miss Santoni's death came four years later. Our killer must be a very patient man.

NICHOLAS: Or extremely cunning and insane.

JUSTIN: Insane…never thought of that. But, even the insane have their motives, don't they? Why the bartender and Miss Santoni? What's the connection?

NICHOLAS: Perhaps, our killer is a very clumsy man?

JUSTIN: Clumsy or cunning?

NICHOLAS: Both Claire and Joe were killed by a slow acting poison or so the police said. I wonder whom they suspected?

JUSTIN: Well, I wasn't around for Joe's murder; so, that let's me out, doesn't it?

NICHOLAS: Does it? They suspected Malkin and myself. And, Manuel.

JUSTIN: Any female suspects?

NICHOLAS: Miss Ramona Chen.

JUSTIN: The enigmatic artist. My money's on her.

NICHOLAS: And, Regina.

JUSTIN: Another good suspect.

NICHOLAS: And, talk about enigmas, what about Mr. Frank Holden?

JUSTIN: From what I hear, he is the obvious one. But, what about his accomplice?

NICHOLAS: Holden is the accomplice, the fall guy, if you would. But, the cold blooded murderer; he's the one walking amongst us: quite dangerous and quite insane.

JUSTIN (*laughing nervously*): Well…nice talking to you, Mr. Gaspari. (*MANUEL and REGINA enter stage right.*)

NICHOLAS: Here's Manuel and Regina. Regina, come to the table with me. Manuel can order the drinks.

MANUEL: And, good afternoon to you, Gaspari. Kane? Two whiskeys and sodas, please.

JUSTIN: Sure thing, Mr. Roma.

MANUEL: Well, Kane, any luck with the acting?

JUSTIN: None so far.

MANUEL: What are you aiming for?

JUSTIN: Television and the movies. It's pretty wide open.

MANUEL: You might have better luck with the theatre; that should be your foundation.

JUSTIN: Doesn't interest me. Theatre just leaves me cold. Sorry.

MANUEL: Don't be. It was only a suggestion.

JUSTIN: Isn't opera a form of theatre? That's what they tell me.

MANUEL: In a sense, yes; but, if it's not your preference, then you're quite right not to pursue it. Have you found yourself an agent, at least?

JUSTIN: Sort of.

MANUEL: What does that mean?

JUSTIN: It means that it's kind of unofficial.

MANUEL (*raising an eyebrow*): Unofficial?

JUSTIN: Here are your drinks, Mr. Roma.

MANUEL: Polite way of telling me to mind my own business? But, really, it's not very polite, young man. Remember your place!

JUSTIN: I didn't mean any offense, Mr. Roma. I just-

MANUEL: You were being evasive. I was taking a genuine interest in you. And, for the record, your "unofficial" agent is Malkin, bartender. (*He joins NICHOLAS and REGINA.*)

REGINA: Are you all right? Did you just have words with young Justin?

MANUEL: I slapped him hard across the wrists, if that's what you mean.

REGINA: Dare I ask why?

MANUEL: I don't like impertinent young men.

REGINA: What did he say to you?

MANUEL: It's what he didn't say. Here's your drink. (*MALKIN and RAMONA enter stage right.*)

NICHOLAS: Look who just walked in.

MANUEL: Malkin openly admitting to a friendship -- and with a woman.

REGINA: Don't be catty, Manuel.

NICHOLAS: He happens to be right.

REGINA: I must admit you've said what's been on my mind for quite some time.

MANUEL: And, you would know, Regina. Tell us; when did your feminine charms fail you with Malkin?

REGINA (*slapping MANUEL hard across the face*): How dare you?

NICHOLAS: Manuel, is anything wrong?

MANUEL: Not a damned thing. Not a goddamned thing.

RAMONA: Your friends are staring at us.

MALKIN: Are they?

RAMONA: I hear that Nicholas is signing with London Records. You never did get him to be your client, did you?

MALKIN: No.

RAMONA: How long has Manuel been your client?

MALKIN: Years. I've lost count.

RAMONA: You make a lot of money off him?

MALKIN: Money? Plenty.

RAMONA: Not enough for you, though? Not enough fame, maybe?

MALKIN: He's a flash in the pan, if it must be said. The matinee idol of today: period.

RAMONA: Does he know that?

MALKIN: He knows it.

RAMONA (*indicating REGINA*): Does she know that?

MALKIN: She's ambitious.

RAMONA: Does her husband appreciate that? Some men wouldn't, you know.

MALKIN: He probably hates her for it.

RAMONA: Why would he hate her?

MALKIN: No man wants his deficiencies brought home to him. Manuel is flawed.

RAMONA: What do you mean?

MALKIN: He's spoiled. On stage, he's got his good looks and charisma. You can't see those on a recording disc, unfortunately.

RAMONA: But, the critics seem to like his records. I've read some of the reviews. They're pretty good.

MALKIN: It's called praising mediocrity. Get used to it.

RAMONA: So why is mediocrity praised?

MALKIN: You're lucky I'm in a talkative mood. Because, Miss Chen, greatness is so damned rare. And, if people actually learned to tell the difference, your theatre halls would be empty. Manuel packs them in. When he retires, he'll be forgotten, and he knows it.

RAMONA: Does he care?

MALKIN: He cares. He's a vain bastard. You want another drink?

RAMONA: A sherry, please. (*MALKIN walks over to the bar.*)

JUSTIN: Hi, Mr. Malkin.

MALKIN: One sherry. One scotch and soda.

JUSTIN: How's Ramona? I haven't seen her since that night at the Roma's-

MALKIN: She's fine.

JUSTIN: Any news for me?

MALKIN: No.

JUSTIN: Just, "no?"

MALKIN: Yes.

JUSTIN: Thanks for nothing, man. I really appreciate it.

MALKIN: Have you been sending your head shot out like I've told you to?

JUSTIN: I-

MALKIN: You haven't. Don't even try to lie to me. You have to push yourself, Kane.

JUSTIN: Aren't you supposed to be doing that? Aren't you my agent?

MALKIN: Where are the drinks that I've ordered?

JUSTIN (*in a petulant manner*): I'm out of ice. I'll have to go back to get some. Sorry.

MANUEL: Malkin.

MALKIN: Manuel. How are you?

MANUEL: Same.

MALKIN: Something wrong?

MANUEL: Nothing. I'm the same. Stagnant. Frustrated out of my damned mind, thanks to you.

NICHOLAS: Easy, Manuel.

MALKIN: What's his problem?

NICHOLAS: A bad day, that's all.

MANUEL: A stinking career, that's all. A contrived and hollow career.

MALKIN: You're an ingrate, Roma. You've done better than most.

MANUEL: Thanks to you?

MALKIN: Thanks to me.

MANUEL: You're nothing but a rotten egotist.

NICHOLAS (*interrupting*): Where's Justin? He didn't go off duty, did he? Here he is. Justin, we all need refills at my table. (*JUSTIN prepares the drinks and MANUEL almost knocks MALKIN'S over.*)

MANUEL: Sorry, Malkin. I didn't spill any of it.

MALKIN: Forget it. I'll go back to my table now. Excuse me.

MANUEL: Good riddance.

NICHOLAS: Manuel, he hasn't done too shabbily by you. I may not like his tactics, but he gets things done.

MANUEL: I'm- I'm not myself tonight. I need this drink. (*Downing it in one gulp.*) Hit me, again, will you, Kane?

NICHOLAS: Try to nurse the next one.

MANUEL: I'm making a pretty spectacle of myself, aren't I? Don't even bother to answer that question.

NICHOLAS: Manuel, what is it? It seems that ever since you signed that recording contract with RCA Records, you haven't been yourself.

MANUEL: You.

NICHOLAS: I beg your pardon?

MANUEL: You. Your genius. Your dedication and hard work. You've never been afraid of the hard work. I have. I wanted the fame and the recognition and, of course, the adulation. Oh, how I wanted that!

NICHOLAS: And, you've achieved that.

MANUEL: He's achieved it! And, Regina.

NICHOLAS: You're excluding yourself, Manuel. You may be better than you think.

MANUEL: It's too late, Gaspari. I've been thinking too much, lately; and, that's a bad thing for a man with very little intellect. But, you have mastered your technique. You make it seem so effortless that the audience takes it for granted you'll hit every note. With me, they sit on the edge of their seats waiting for my voice to crack or a missed note or the elimination of a difficult piece of music.

NICHOLAS: There are many men who envy you.

MANUEL: I've thought a good deal about my career and about Claire.

NICHOLAS: Her death hit you pretty hard, didn't it?

MANUEL: Some things you never recover from.

NICHOLAS: I don't understand.

MANUEL: You do not understand.

RAMONA: Are you all right? You don't look so great.

MALKIN: I feel nauseous. I feel god awful, as a matter of fact.

RAMONA: What are you saying?

MALKIN (*staring at the glass that's still in his hand*): Ramona- I- the drink…

RAMONA: What is it? What's the matter with you?

MALKIN (*dropping the glass*): My shoulder…

RAMONA: Malkin, what is it? Are you ill?

MALKIN (*falling face down on to the floor*): I can't-

RAMONA (*screaming*): Help me, please. (*Everyone rushes over at once.*)

NICHOLAS: Give him some room to breathe.

REGINA: What happened?

RAMONA: I don't know. Suddenly, he started to feel ill and just fell over on to the floor. (*NICHOLAS and JUSTIN are leaning over MALKIN'S inert body. MANUEL is standing at a slight distance from the group.)*

REGINA: Is he going to be all right? (*FRANK emerges from upstage center unobserved.)*

NICHOLAS: He's dead.

JUSTIN: Dead? He can't be dead.

RAMONA (*pointing at JUSTIN*): You! He was trying to tell me something about his drink. It must have been poisoned. You did it. Murderer!

JUSTIN: Go to hell, lady! You're not pinning this on me. Who's to say you didn't slip a "mickey" into his drink. The man was my agent, why would I murder him?

NICHOLAS: Take it easy. No one is accusing-

JUSTIN: This bitch is! And, for that matter, you were at the bar when I served those drinks.

NICHOLAS: Take it easy, Justin. We'll have to notify the police and, then, we'd better try and keep our wits about us- (*Noticing FRANK.*) When did you get here?

FRANK: Good evening.

REGINA: You! Have you done this? Have you killed this man?

FRANK: I've killed no one.

MANUEL: Liar.

RAMONA: It must have been him; but, I don't see how.

MANUEL (*pointing an accusing finger at RAMONA*): Maybe, it's not Holden. Maybe, it's you!

RAMONA: What are you saying? Why would I kill him?

MANUEL: I've no idea. But, I think it's curious how you always show up for these morbid festivities, Miss Chen.

NICHOLAS: She's not the only one who can be accused of that. When it comes to being at the wrong place and time, aren't we all guilty?

MANUEL: I'd be damned careful of that if I were you, Gaspari. You and Malkin weren't exactly friends, as I recall. As a matter of fact, enemies would come closer to the mark.

REGINA: What are you saying, Manuel?

MANUEL: That we're all suspect. I exclude no one.

REGINA: You're accusing me? Your own wife?

MANUEL: You've got the temperament for it.

NICHOLAS: Justin, call the police, will you? We need them here.

JUSTIN (rushing over to the bar's phone): Sure thing.

RAMONA: I'm leaving. No one can keep me here.

REGINA: And just where do you think you're off to? You'll stay here like the rest of us.

RAMONA: I want to leave.

MANUEL: Thinking of taking a powder, Miss Chen? Forget it!

NICHOLAS: We'll all wait until the police arrive and that includes you, Mr. Holden.

FRANK: I've no intention of leaving, Mr. Gaspari. Bartender? May I have a brandy, please? (*Black out. Lights come up to find NICHOLAS, JUSTIN, and RAMONA at the bar.*)

RAMONA: We can go now? The police said that it looked like a heart attack.

NICHOLAS: And, I suppose there's no connection between Malkin's and Claire's death?

RAMONA: I don't know.

JUSTIN: I think Mr. Holden's getting quietly drunk. I thought for sure the police would hold him for questioning. They're still outside, you know.

RAMONA: They are? Can we leave?

NICHOLAS: I don't think so. And, I wouldn't appear too anxious to.

RAMONA: So, Justin, was Malkin your agent?

JUSTIN: Yes.

RAMONA: Did he do you any good?

JUSTIN: No.

RAMONA: Did you sleep with him?

JUSTIN: No!

RAMONA: Too bad. He might have done you some good, then. He was like that, you know: cruel to those who really needed him most and indulging dilettantes like Manuel Roma.

JUSTIN: You've a low opinion of Mr. Matinee Idol, don't you?

RAMONA: Don't you? You should. Malkin raised him up to what he wasn't and could never be on his own.

JUSTIN: And, what's that?

RAMONA: An artist like Nicholas, here. (changing the subject) I don't like sitting around like this.

NICHOLAS: Let's ask the police if we can leave. Come on. (He, JUSTIN, and RAMONA exit.)

MANUEL (staring into the audience): Did someone just leave?

REGINA: Justin and Ramona-

MANUEL: And, Nicholas?

REGINA: They've gone outside. Perhaps, they're talking to the police.

MANUEL: Perhaps.

REGINA: Manuel, are you all right?

MANUEL: I'm fine.

REGINA: No. You're not fine. How could you be with all this horror? After Malkin's funeral, we'll go to Majorca for a few weeks. A holiday. Yes. That's what we need: a holiday.

MANUEL: Have you convinced yourself of that?

REGINA: It's what's needed. Why?

MANUEL: I'm glad Malkin's dead.

REGINA: Manuel, have you taken leave of your senses? The police could overhear you and become suspicious.

MANUEL: Would that really matter?

REGINA: Of course. You've your reputation to think about.

MANUEL: I hated Malkin. I hated his charm and his depravity: in short, my dear, I'm relieved that I'm rid of him.

REGINA: I'll get you a drink.

MANUEL: No. Stay where you are. I've something to tell you. (*He extracts the gold cigarette case from inside his jacket.*) Cigarette?

REGINA: That cigarette case…it belongs to Holden, doesn't it? (*She glances over at FRANK who, like MANUEL, is staring out into the audience.*)

MANUEL (*slamming his fist on to the table*): No! It-belongs-to-Manuel-Roma! Your husband -- your puppet -- has a confession to make to his devoted wife. It was I who murdered Joe. It was I who murdered Claire. And, it was I who murdered Malkin. How utterly delicious the complete satisfaction that I feel at this moment. I-love-killing! It's a really very clever and dangerous game.

REGINA: My God…what am I married to?

MANUEL: Joe's murder was an accident. On that day, I intended to kill Malkin, but Holden fucked it! Frank didn't know that Joe kept a glass of booze for himself. I put the poison in, but the glasses got switched. Joe thought it was his and I had to let him drink it. Holden went to frighten Claire that night in order to get back the cigarette case. Poor bitch was desperate for money and kept pawning it. Finally, I had a chance to get it back. Holden took it that night, but I couldn't take a chance on what Claire had surmised. I calmed her down and made love to her and, then, poisoned her. Didn't put enough in…too bad. And, that brings us to this evening. To see that dickless bastard writhing on the floor in agony; I could barely keep a straight face. Dead. Dead like I am. Dead like Gaspari will be. His career is complete while my pathetic career is a damned shambles. Read the backs of those record labels, Regina. The reviews filled with apologies for the tenor's voice, but superlatives for his diction and passion. The mediocrity held up in front of gauze to conceal the imperfections. It's all on record and immortalized! That was Malkin's doing and yours! (*FRANK gets up and exits.*) He's leaving you with me. Regina. Stay put. Let him go.

REGINA: Who is he?

MANUEL: My accomplice. I picked him off the gutter: dressed him, paid him, serviced him, and supported him all these years. I let Malkin think he had influence over him. He didn't. (*Standing, he picks up the cigarette case.*) Here. This little mechanism opens it. The poison is in here. (*He puts some in her drink.*) Now, drink it. Drink it!

REGINA (*getting up*): Manuel, we must go to the police.

MANUEL: Drink it, Regina.

NICHOLAS (*rushing in with RAMONA, JUSTIN, and FRANK*): Manuel!

REGINA (*running over to them*): Thank God! He killed Malkin and was going to kill me!

NICHOLAS: Manuel, there'll be no more killings. We'll get you help.

MANUEL (*holding on to the glass*): I'm holding that in my hand now, Gaspari. You see, I've never had the luxury of fooling myself. I've stared into the mirror too many times.

NICHOLAS: Put the glass down, Manuel.

MANUEL: Of course. (*He gulps down its contents.*) There was enough poison in that little drink to kill five men. It's burning me alive! What have I done? Please-! (*He collapses to the floor.*)

FRANK: I waited too long. That day when Joe took the poison by mistake, I knew it had all gone horribly wrong. I came back that night to face Manuel with what we'd done; but, I couldn't get him alone, and he wasn't about to acknowledge me in public.

RAMONA: And, what about Claire? Did you kill her, too?

FRANK: I didn't kill anyone.

NICHOLAS: Don't be so easy on yourself, Mr. Holden.

FRANK: I'm not excusing myself, if that's what you mean. I went in to get the cigarette case from Claire that night. I waited until Miss Chen left and, then, when I'd gone, Roma went in. I should have stopped him.

NICHOLAS: Why didn't you? You knew the man was unbalanced.

REGINA: Please...I can't take any more of this.

RAMONA: He was nothing but a murderer. I liked Claire and he killed her. I don't feel sorry for him.

JUSTIN: He got off pretty easy, if you ask me. He killed my agent. Bastard!

NICHOLAS: That's enough of that, Justin. There's an officer outside, would you mind getting him? (*Black out. Some time later at the bar.*)

RAMONA: Do you think Manuel would have gone on killing?

NICHOLAS: There was no other way out for him.

JUSTIN: But, how did it all begin?

NICHOLAS: He resented the manipulations of Malkin.

JUSTIN: So, he kills the guy?

NICHOLAS: A man who can't stand on his own is a pretty vulnerable target.

RAMONA: He was a very vain man. I never liked him.

NICHOLAS: Malkin spoke of immortality that day and Manuel took him seriously. Malkin should have reminded Manuel that the gods of Olympus were flawed.

RAMONA: What about Regina? I feel a little sorry for her.

NICHOLAS: At least you know where you stand with Regina. She's ambitious and for any other man she would have made a good wife.

JUSTIN: So what happens now?

NICHOLAS: You move forward and never look back on the memory.

RAMONA: That's not so easy.

JUSTIN: It all seems so unreal.

NICHOLAS: The truth is real, Justin. It's that truth that killed Manuel. In a sense, it also set his demon free.

End of play.

THE HOUSEDRESS

A Play in Three Acts

by

Gerard Denza

Copyright 2007

THE HOUSEDRESS premiered at the Producer's Club on November 1, 2007 with the following cast:

SYBIL SCHMIDLAP-SCHWAB	Rachel Green
SAMANTHA SCHWAB	Melissa Mercedes
SAM SCHWAB	Phil Strumolo
GRANDPA SCHWAB	Malcolm Ehrlich
SOLOMON SCHWAB	Jeff Topf
CARL CONTINENT	R. Ross Pivec
GRANDMA SCHWAB	Jeanne Pearson
OLIVE K. SCHNEER	Josie Rose-Forde

Set by Phil Strumolo.
Directed by Gerard Denza.

PLACE
The action takes place in the Schwab's living room.

TIME
On a late Wednesday afternoon before Thanksgiving.

SCENES

Act One
Late afternoon in the Schwab's house.

Act Two
The following day in the Schwab's house.

Act Three
The evening of the same day.

CHARACTERS

SYBIL SCHMIDLAP-SCHWAB, housewife and novelist.
SAMANTHA SCHWAB, daughter and semi-recluse.
SAM SCHWAB, husband and trouble maker.
GRANDPA SCHWAB, freeloader and blackmailer.
SOLOMON SCHWAB, mother's boy.
CARL CONTINENT, con artist.
GRANDMA SCHWAB, hateful mother-in-law.
OLIVE K. SCHNEER, back stabbing friend.

ACT ONE

The day before Thanksgiving in the SCHWAB'S living room. The room is in complete darkness as a flashlight's beam makes its way across the floor and traces a path to SYBIL'S tonic water. A gloved hand drops two pellets into the glass. The flashlight's beam makes its way off stage. The lights go up and SYBIL is seen at her writing desk speaking on the telephone.

SYBIL: Oh, Olive! How are you, dear? I really haven't the time to chat. Tomorrow is our Thanksgiving meal and I must give last minute instructions to my rather helpless family. And, one must begin dressing for tonight's Ball. Weren't you invited, dear? Oh? What a pity. You'll be missed. Is my husband, Sam, coming with me? You're joking, surely? I think it rather chic and daring to go by one's self. Samantha? My daughter? You must be mad. My timid, plain daughter would come apart at any formal gathering. Now, Olive, I really must- Oh, yes! I've just sent the manuscript off to my editor. And, I simply adore the title: Toxic Cherry. Isn't it divine? And, everyone laughed at my first novel: Glazed Doughnut. Why the public simply went wild for it. Mind you, some thought it was a cookbook; but, of course, it wasn't. It was quite political in its own way. And, now, Olive- what? The reason for your call? You think that someone is out to kill me? Are you joking? Why, you must be- well, if you must come over, it's perfectly fine. Mind you, I'll be rushed. What do you mean that I'd better not go out until you get here? Very well, I'll wait, dear. Now, I've a million things to do. Goodbye. (*Slowly, she hangs up the receiver.*)

SAMANTHA (*entering from stage left*): Mother?

SYBIL (*standing up*): Oh! I didn't hear you come in. You startled mother.

SAMANTHA: Forgive me, but I wanted to speak to you about a very grave matter.

SYBIL: Dear Samantha, how you do dramatize.

SAMANTHA: Yes. It is dramatic, mother, and I need your full attention.

SYBIL: And, so you shall have it. But, there is an errand that I need you to run for me.

SAMANTHA: I don't dare leave the house. It's too frightening.

SYBIL: Now, dear, we've been through this before. There is no danger from any falling meteorites or stray comets.

SAMANTHA: I'm frightened for us all.

SYBIL: Listen carefully to mother: I need you to go to the corner bakery and fetch a dozen orange, cream pastries for tomorrow's dessert. Do you think you can do that?

SAMANTHA: It's such a very long way to the bakery.

SYBIL: It's right on the corner.

SAMANTHA: And, that horrible Herr Kraut. He frightens me.

SYBIL: Herr Kraut is perfectly harmless if somewhat of an imbecile. He'll give you no trouble because mother happens to know that the dear man is in hospital having a kidney stone removed.

SAMANTHA: But, Frau Kraut doesn't speak English.

SYBIL: You simply point to what you want -- point -- like that. Frau Kraut is harmless for a moron. The fact that she's an American citizen is rather unusual, given that she can't speak or understand a word of English, but such are the oddities of life. Now, Samantha, get mother's purse and, then, off you go. And, not another word of protest. I mean it. You must conquer your fear of walking short distances. There's a technical term for this type of phobia; but, I can't quite call it to mind.

SAMANTHA: But, mother-

SYBIL: Get out! (*SAMANTHA exits stage right. SAM, SOLOMON, and GRANDPA enter from stage left.*)

SAM: What is all this shouting about?

SYBIL: What?

SAM: Where has Samantha gone off to?

SYBIL: Where you were supposed to go and didn't: to the bakery.

SAM: She's in the house too much. The fresh air will do her a world of good.

SYBIL: Why don't you join her at the bakery? Get some of that fresh air.

SAM: Shouldn't you be in the kitchen scrubbing a pot?

SOLOMON: Mother, may we see your gown for tonight's Ball? I'll be taking up fashion design at the Institute next Fall and I'm simply dying to see your new frock.

SYBIL: Come and sit next to mother, dear. Sam, get up.

SOLOMON: Not until you show us your new frock.

SYBIL: But, Solomon, I want you to get the full effect when mother makes her entrance later.

GRANDPA: Hey, Syb, how about lending your favorite father-in-law a couple of bucks. And, how about a sip of your tonic water?

SYBIL: You may not take a sip of my tonic water. And, here's your money. Take it!

GRANDPA: Thanks, Syb.

SAM: My throat feels parched, rather. Perhaps, just a drop of your rose tonic water for medicinal purposes?

SYBIL: No!

SAM: Well!

GRANDPA: Hey, Syb, maybe a few more bucks for the road?

SYBIL: Bloodsucker.

GRANDPA: Just hand it over, Syb, like a good girl. I think I'll go for a stroll to Herr Kraut's for some of those rum balls.

SYBIL (*under her breath*): Choke on them! (*Aloud.*) You may run into your granddaughter.

GRANDPA: I'll send her straight home where she belongs.

SYBIL: Perhaps, an afternoon outing with her grandfather wouldn't be amiss?

GRANDPA: Her place is at home. It's dangerous for a girl like that to be wandering the streets all by herself. What the hell is wrong with you, Syb? Give me another buck, will you?

SYBIL: Drop dead.

GRANDPA: I might have to bribe her to come back.

SYBIL: I doubt it.

GRANDPA: The money, Syb?

SYBIL: No.

GRANDPA: Syb? Don't let me ask, again.

SYBIL: Get out!

GRANDPA: We'll talk later. And, have that money-

SYBIL: Get out! (*GRANDPA exits stage right.*)

SOLOMON: Mother, shouldn't you be getting ready for tonight?

SYBIL: Dear boy, so considerate. But, I must attend to things in the kitchen, first.

SOLOMON: Samantha and I can do all that for you. I want my mother to be the belle of the Ball, tonight. No one must eclipse you; even though your family won't be there to bask in mother's glory.

SAM: Yes. We weren't invited.

SYBIL: Too bad.

SAM: How do you rate an invitation; if you don't mind my asking?

SYBIL: Well, one doesn't like to brag, but I am a world famous author. Does that answer your rather naive question?

SAM: A world famous author with no escort? It's scandalous. I'm coming.

SYBIL: You are not coming.

SOLOMON: Mother? You seem a bit on edge this afternoon. Is there anything troubling you?

SYBIL (*answering too quickly*): No, of course not.

SOLOMON: What is it, mother? Tell Solly.

SYBIL: Well, dear, there have been those anonymous phone calls, lately. And, I feel that mother is being watched; spied upon!

SOLOMON: But, by whom, mother?

SYBIL: I've no idea. But, it's most disconcerting.

SOLOMON: Poor mother.

SAM (*Ignoring the above conversation.*): Should I wear a black tie?

SYBIL: You are not coming!

SOLOMON: Was that Miss Schneer on the phone before?

SYBIL: Yes. Yes. It was. How did you know? She's coming over to discuss something with mother. She insisted.

SOLOMON: Is it serious?

SYBIL: Nothing for you to worry your head over.

SOLOMON: I think I'll go to my room and have a lie down. Let me know when my missing sister returns.

SYBIL: Mother will awaken you before she leaves. Now, run along and give mother a great, big kiss. (*SOLOMON exits stage left.*)

SAM: What did Olive want?

SYBIL: I didn't want to say anything in front of Solomon and especially not in front of your rotten father, but Olive thinks that my life may be in danger.

SAM: In danger from whom?

SYBIL: I don't know. (*Suspiciously.*) Do you have any idea who it might be?

SAM: None.

SYBIL: Indeed…

SAM: You haven't libeled anyone in your latest novel, have you?

SYBIL (*guiltily*): Of course not. Why do you ask? Whom would I libel?

SAM: Well, aside from your immediate family, no one in particular.

SYBIL: Just what are you hinting at?

SAM: Well, Sybil, some of your characters do resemble certain people.

SYBIL: Whom?

SAM: Oh…Samantha, Grandpa, Olive, Solomon-

SYBIL: Enough! That's a lie!

SAM: Is it?

SYBIL: A dastardly distortion.

SAM: Down, girl.

SYBIL: All my characters are fictional: all of them. I can't help it if my imagination runs rampant. Who am I to suppress my artistic talents?

SAM: It's only a theory.

SYBIL: No. I won't give into denial because there is nothing to deny.

SAM: Of course.

SYBIL: And base my immortal characters on my useless family?

SAM: You're digging yourself into a crater.

SYBIL: You made me say that!

SAM: I?

SYBIL (*getting to her feet*): You ingrate! How I support you and everyone! A virtual slave! A drudge!

SAM: A "drudge," dear?

SYBIL: A drudge no more! I am Sybil Schmidlap-Schwab: authoress extraordinaire. My works will live when the rest of us are dust!

SAM: Perhaps, if you tried on your Ball frock, you'd feel a trifle better?

SYBIL (*sits back down*): Shut up! I'll get ready when I damned see fit. And, don't think that I haven't noticed you turning Samantha against me. Don't deny it. I don't care. Solomon will always favor his mother. We're bonded.

SAM: That's what Olive- oops!

SYBIL: What was that?

SAM: Nothing, dear, nothing.

SYBIL: What did that little tramp say?

SAM (*leaning forward*): Well, she said that your relationship with your son was...now, how shall I phrase this?

SYBIL: Spit it out!

SAM: Unnatural.

SYBIL (*taken aback*): Did she? I'll ask her myself about this-this outrage! And, you'd better not be lying to me.

SAM: Perish the thought. Now, I do believe I hear Samantha returning from Herr Kraut's.

SAMANTHA (*entering from stage right*): Mother? Mother!

SYBIL: Mother is right here. Now, I must get ready for tonight. Perhaps, a small sip of my rose tonic water? I've so much to do.

SAMANTHA: Mother, I must tell you of my adventure.

SYBIL: An adventure, dear? Did you manage to pick up mother's orange creams like mother asked you to?

SAMANTHA: My adventure goes beyond orange creams. Oh, father, I'm so glad you're here to witness this.

SAM: Don't tell me that Frau Kraut can actually speak English?

SAMANTHA: Oh, not a word. I started pointing to items like mother instructed me to and she got very cross.

SAM (*laughing*): Why? Can't she understand that?

SAMANTHA: I don't believe she can. I do believe the poor woman is very simple-minded.

SAM: I think "imbecile" is the word your looking for.

SYBIL: Don't be cruel to the poor idiot.

SAMANTHA: Mother? Father? I must tell you at once. I cannot delay any longer.

SYBIL: Please.

SAM: Take your time. I'm enjoying this.

SAMANTHA: Oh, father, do try to be serious.

SAM: Did you run into Grandpa?

SAMANTHA: I saw him, but I did not actually run into him.

SYBIL: Where did you see him?

SAMANTHA: With his bookmaker.

SYBIL: I knew it! He'll come home broke, again, and put the bite on me for more money.

SAM: Why do you give it to him? I've always suspected-

SYBIL: What?

SAM: Oh…blackmail? What has he got on you?

SYBIL (*deliberately changes the subject*): Samantha, dear, tell us all about your little adventure. Don't keep us dangling so; that's very naughty of you.

SAMANTHA: I met a man.

SYBIL (*incredulously*): You met a man?

SAM (*incredulously*): You met a man?

SAMANTHA: Yes! My Prince Charming!

SAM: Tell us about Prince Charming.

SYBIL: Yes. Please. I've more time than I thought.

SAMANTHA: He's tall, blonde, and handsome and his name is Mr. Carl Continent. He's very European. And, mother, he's a big fan of yours.

SYBIL: Indeed.

SAMANTHA: Yes. And, he's waiting outside. May I bring him in?

SYBIL: Of course. (*SAMANTHA exits stage right.*)

SAM: This I've got to see.

SYBIL: Can you believe it? Our daughter finding a man?

SAM: No!

CARL: Mrs. Schwab! Mr. Schwab! Allow me to introduce myself: Mr. Carl Continent.

SYBIL: Good afternoon, Mr. Continent.

SAM: Hello.

CARL: Such an honor, Mrs. Schwab. I've read your book, Glazed Doughnut: a masterpiece! It glowed with literary enterprise. You're magnificent. Allow me to humble myself before you. (*He gets down on bended knee before SYBIL.*)

SYBIL (*pretending to be flustered*): Really, Mr. Continent, that's quite unnecessary.

SAM: Yes. It is.

CARL: I disagree. It is necessary.

SYBIL: Well, if you insist.

CARL: I do.

SYBIL: Are you from Europe, Mr. Continent?

CARL: Carl, please.

SYBIL: Carl.

CARL (*standing up between SYBIL and SAM*): I am a world traveler.

SAM: Where have you been, lately?

CARL: It all seems of no consequence, for this moment is the crowning glory of my life. Again, I bow to you, Sybil. Forgive the familiarity.

SAMANTHA: Mother, isn't he just too wonderful?

SYBIL (*getting up*): Oh, dear, look at the time. It's nearly six o'clock. I must get ready for tonight's Ball. Would you please excuse me, Mr. Continent? Samantha, be a lamb and help mother get ready?

SAM: I'll look after our guest.

SYBIL: Do. (*She and SAMANTHA exit stage left.*)

SAM: Well, Mr. Continent, have a seat. Would you like a drink?

CARL (sitting down at the writing table): No. Thank you.

SAM: Mr. Continent?

CARL: Yes, Mr. Schwab?

SAM: What's your game?

CARL: My "game?"

SAM: Your angle?

CARL: My "angle?"

SAM: You met my daughter at Herr Kraut's Bakery and just out of the blue, you start chatting her up?

CARL: She was enchanting!

SAM: Try, again. My daughter's a bit of a frump.

CARL: Mr. Schwab, I don't share your harsh opinion about Samantha. She has deep potential.

SAM: You'd need a Geiger counter to find it. Now, what exactly are you up to?

CARL: I am "up to" nothing, as you so quaintly put it.

SAM: And, you've read darling Sybil's first novel?

CARL: "Glazed Doughnut." It was fascinating!

SAM: It stunk. A great many people were rather annoyed with her for writing it. Her so-called characters were pretty thinly veiled portraits of family and enemies.

CARL: I would have been honored!

SAM: Hmm...

CARL: Mr. Schwab, just exactly what are you driving at?

SAM: The point to your being here. How shall I phrase it? It doesn't add up.

CARL (*opens the bottle of tonic water and sniffs it*): Perhaps, you're a poor mathematician?

SAM: The equation is a bit lopsided, and that could mean an explosion. Now, if you'll excuse me, I think I'll hunt down Grandfather Schwab and, perhaps, stop at Herr Kraut's for a pastry or two? Pardon me?

CARL: Of course. (*SAM exits from stage right as CARL breathes a sigh of relief.*)

SOLOMON (*enters from stage left*): Did father just leave?

CARL (*startled.*): Yes.

SOLOMON: You must be Mr. Continent. I'm Solomon Schwab. (*Very gingerly, he sits down in the center of the love seat.*)

CARL: Pleased to meet you, young man. You're very fortunate in having a mother like Sybil.

SOLOMON: Yes. What's your line of work, Mr. Continent?

CARL: I've private means.

SOLOMON: I see.

CARL: You don't; but, then, it's none of your business.

SOLOMON: I see.

CARL: You don't.

SOLOMON: What don't I see?

CARL: Into my affairs, young man. Now, don't be impertinent.

SOLOMON: I didn't mean to be, really. I was just curious, that's all.

CARL: I took no offense. Now, be a good boy and go fetch your mother. I must be leaving soon and I'd like to arrange a luncheon date for tomorrow. (*SOLOMON remains seated and staring at him.*) Well? What are you waiting for? And, stop staring at me like that.

SOLOMON: Mother is a married woman.

CARL: Don't be a bore.

SOLOMON: May I come to luncheon, as well?

CARL: Are you mad? Absolutely not.

SOLOMON: Why not?

CARL: Would you please get your mother?

SOLOMON: She may be in a state of undress.

CARL: Knock on the damned door, first! Now, be off.

SOLOMON: Mother and I do everything together.

CARL (*nodding*): I'm sure.

SOLOMON: We're inseparable.

CARL (*loosing his accent*): Hey, bud, cut the umbilical cord and get Sybil down here, okay?

SOLOMON: I don't like you.

CARL: Good. Now, beat it!

SOLOMON: I love my mother more than life.

CARL: You've gotta' be kidding me.

SOLOMON: I never joke. I take life very seriously.

CARL (*getting back his accent*): So do I. Now, seriously, get your mother, little boy.

SOLOMON: I'll be right back. Excuse me, please? (*He exits stage left. The doorbell rings and SYBIL shouts from off stage.*)

SYBIL: Oh, Mr. Continent, would you please get that?

SAMANTHA (*running in*): Forgive mother's familiarity, Mr. Continent. She's very Bohemian.

CARL: Of course.

SAMANTHA: Grandfather Schwab! Why on earth did you ring the doorbell?

GRANDPA (*enters from stage right and goes over to the armchair, but does not sit down*): Forgot my keys. I met your father at the bakery. He was pointing at Frau Kraut and laughing. He'll be here in a minute. Where's Syb?

SAMANTHA: Mother is dressing.

GRANDPA: Who the hell are you?

CARL: Continent. Carl Continent.

GRANDPA: What the hell are you doing here?

SAMANTHA (*sitting down on the love seat*): Grandfather Schwab, really! I invited Mr. Continent here.

GRANDPA: You've gotta' be kidding me.

SAMANTHA: We met at Herr Kraut's Bakery. And, I'm not sure that I care for the tone of your voice.

GRANDPA: Sounds more like Syb every day. And, speaking of whom, I've got some news for her, and she won't like it.

SYBIL (*enters from stage left and stands close to SAMANTHA*): What won't I like?

GRANDPA: Someone's out to kill you. The whole neighborhood's talking about it.

SAMANTHA: Mother, can this be true?

CARL: I shall protect you, Sybil.

SYBIL: This is very upsetting. My girlfriend, Olive, mentioned as much to me over the phone only today. But, who? And, why?

GRANDPA: The "who" is anyone's guess. The "why"…well, Syb, you've got enemies.

SOLOMON (*enters from stage left and goes to stand upstage between the desk and loveseat*): Don't listen to him, mother. You are the most beloved person I know of.

SYBIL: Envy. It must be envy. The burden of fame.

GRANDPA: The only burden is in your midsection, lady.

SYBIL: Just watch that mouth

SAM (*enters from stage right and sits down on the love seat*): Sybil, you'd better forget about that Ball, tonight. I've just heard that you're a dead woman. It's all over the neighborhood.

SYBIL: So, that's it! This is all a plot to keep me home. Well, it won't work. I will be the belle of the Ball. I will triumph!

CARL: You're perfection! And, I must be going. Tomorrow? Luncheon? Noon? The Tip Top Club?

SAMANTHA: But, mother, tomorrow is Thanksgiving-

SYBIL: Yes! The Tip Top Club! Until tomorrow, Carl.

CARL: Until tomorrow, mon petit! (*Exits stage right.*)

GRANDPA: I think I'll go to my room.

SYBIL: Please. (*GRANDPA exits stage left.*)

SOLOMON: I've homework to do. Excuse me, mother?

SYBIL: Of course, dear. (*SOLOMON exits stage left.*)

SAMANTHA (*standing*): Why not put those ice cucumbers on your eyes, mother: a little perk up before you leave?

SYBIL: But, dear, there's simply no time.

SAMANTHA: Oh, I think we can manage. You put the eye packs on and father and I will have your dress ready for you when you come out.

SYBIL: Well, if you think there's enough time.

SAMANTHA: Of course there's enough time; isn't there, father?

SAM: Of course.

SYBIL: I won't be a moment. (*She exits stage left.*)

SAM: She fell for it.

SAMANTHA (*sitting down next to SAM*): How completely delicious! To put one over on dear, clever mother. Really! Going off to a Ball and leaving us behind. That will never do.

SAM (*reaching down under the loveseat*): Here's the housedress. It weighs about the same as her tacky gown.

SAMANTHA: This will work?

SAM: It's too late for cold feet. You just slip the housedress on her and make sure she keeps those cucumbers over her eyes and, then, help her into her cape. Cape!

SAMANTHA: Will it completely conceal the housedress?

SAM: It's full length. The only problem might be Solomon.

SAMANTHA: He's studying. Won't be out of his room for hours.

SAM: Perfect. Little bookworm

SYBIL (*shouting from off stage*): Samantha, dear, mother needs your help.

SAMANTHA: I'm coming, mother.

SAM: Here, take it. No- wait! She's coming down. (*SYBIL gropes her way into the room from stage left.*)

SAMANTHA: Mother, be careful! You'll trip and fall. (*She takes the housedress from SAM.*) Let's get you ready. Come along.

SYBIL: Such a dear, thoughtful girl.

SAM: Isn't she, just? And, be sure to put mother's cape on. We don't want any dust particles marring her gown. Now, go! Be off! (*SYBIL and SAMANTHA exit stage left.*) It's almost too easy. How will my pompous ass of a wife react when she unveils herself? She'll try to bluff her way out. She'll swear that's she's an eccentric: a trailblazer of the avante garde. The question is: will she stick it out for the entire evening? The cow will have to. (*He bursts out laughing. SYBIL enters wearing her cape. SAMANTHA is looking visibly nervous and goes to stand near the armchair at stage right.*)

SYBIL: I am running late. Samantha, dear, call mother a cab.

SAM: I'll call. (*He rushes over to the phone on the writing desk.*) A cab, please, and make it snapy. They're on their way.

SYBIL (*suspiciously*): How thoughtful.

SAM: Thank you. (*A car's horn is heard.*)

SAMANTHA: Mother, that must be your cab. Hurry!

SYBIL: Perhaps, one final glance in the mirror?

SAM (*pushing her out the door*): No! I mean, you have no time. You might muss yourself. Now, quick! Quick!

SYBIL: Perhaps, you're right. Well, I'm off! (*She exits stage right.*)

SAMANTHA: Oh, father, have we done the right thing?

SAM (*sitting down on the love seat*): No!

SAMANTHA: Oh, how terribly wicked of us. Will there be photographers there?

SAM (*in a wistful tone of voice*): One can only hope.

SAMANTHA (*pacing back and forth*): But, she'll know that we did it.

SAM: Too bad. Publicly, she'll have to laugh along with us.

SAMANTHA: And, privately?

SAM: Well…we'll have to just brace ourselves for that one. But, your mother's a good sport. She'll get over it in time.

SAMANTHA: How much time?

SAM: Oh…ten or twenty years.

SAMANTHA: I've got a very bad feeling about all this.

SAM: Let's look on the bright side: maybe, she'll be hit on the head by one of your meteorites.

SAMANTHA: We don't dare go to bed; do we?

SAM: I wouldn't. Your mother's got her hammer in her pocketbook.

SAMANTHA: How perfectly bizarre.

SAM: I wonder if she'll stick it out for the entire evening? She's the unpredictable type. (*SAM and SAMANTHA sing and dance to "After the Ball."*)

SAMANTHA: Shall we play a game of cards, father? It will help pass the time.

SAM: You're on. (*Lights fade. The ticking of a clock is heard. Lights go up and they're still playing cards.*) If she's coming back, she should be here any minute.

SAMANTHA: I can't play anymore. (*She puts down her cards and SAM takes a peak at them.*) The time is moving so incredibly slow- what was that?

GRANDPA (*enters from stage left*): Only me. Waiting up for Syb?

SAM: You mean your meal ticket?

SAMANTHA: Really, Grandfather Schwab, you should be ashamed of yourself: blackmailing your own daughter-in-law.

SAM: What have you got on her?

GRANDPA: Oh, a little doctor's report that might prove mighty embarrassing to dear Syb.

SAM: Like what?

SAMANTHA: Yes. You must tell us.

GRANDPA: All in good time. Someone's at the door. Can't be Syb coming back; too soon for the belle of the Ball to return.

SAM: Well…

SAMANTHA: Oh, father!

SAM: Brace yourself...here we go.

SYBIL (*enters from stage right*): Good evening.

GRANDPA: Why good evening, daughter-in-law. What brings you home so soon? They run out of food?

SYBIL: Shut up.

SAM: Don't tell me somebody was wearing the same dress?

SYBIL: I'll get to you in a second.

GRANDPA: Syb, as long as I'm up and you're here, can you spare a couple of bucks?

SYBIL: Get upstairs before I kick you out into the street. Get out!

GRANDPA: Sour puss. (*He exits stage left and can be seen eavesdropping.*)

SAM: I can explain-

SAMANTHA: Oh, mother, it's just awful what we did.

SAM: She put me up to it.

SAMANTHA: Father! It was your idea. You're the one who picked out the housedress.

SYBIL: And, you slipped it on! You spineless, little wallflower!

SAMANTHA: Mother, how unkind! That's very hurtful.

SYBIL: Good! My own daughter jealous of her mother's beauty and status. From him, I would expect this; but, from you, Samantha...

SAM: Now, Sybil-

SYBIL (*taking her hammer from out of her pocketbook*): You rotten, little mouse. I'll have your head on a platter. Stand still like a man so I can flatten you!

SAM (*getting up as SYBIL starts chasing him about the room*): Now, let's not be rash!

SYBIL: I said stand still!

SAM: Sybil, dearest! Sybil! Oh!

SYBIL: Stop saying my name!

SAM: Sybil!

SYBIL: I said stop saying my name!

SAMANTHA: Oh, mother, do try to control yourself. Why at any moment, a meteorite may come crashing down-

SYBIL: I hope it hits and wipes out the damned planet! (*SOLOMON and GRANDPA enter from stage left, carefully avoiding the combatants.*)

SOLOMON: Mother, has father upset you, again? I've told you time and again to divorce him. He's no good for you.

SYBIL: That you can say, again!

GRANDPA: Syb. Syb. What's the matter? Why only a few hours ago, you thought you had the world at your feet.

SYBIL (*stops chasing SAM*): Yes. Yes, I did. No real harm has been done.

GRANDPA: Take off your cape, Syb, you're overheated.

SYBIL: Later.

GRANDPA: Now, Syb.

SYBIL: Later!

SAM: Oh, come on, take it off.

SYBIL: I want you out of this house!

SAMANTHA: Mother, it was only a practical joke: admittedly, in questionable taste. You really should take off your cape. It's quite hot in here.

SYBIL (*in a pompous tone of voice*): Very well.

GRANDPA: What the hell have you got on? It's one of your tacky housedresses.

SOLOMON: Mother, is that how you actually went to the Ball? How very eccentric of you.

SAM (*moving to stage left to be clear of SYBIL*): Oh, eccentric is the word.

SOLOMON: Father, this is your doing, isn't it? You were the mastermind behind this. What a horrid thing to do. And, Samantha, you are no better than he.

SAMANTHA: Oh, dry up.

GRANDPA: Hey, Syb, how about a couple of bucks?

SYBIL: That does it! (*She lunges for GRANDPA who sidesteps her. Instead, she pushes SAM down the flight of stairs on stage left.*)

SAMANTHA: Mother! I'll see if father is hurt. (*She screams from off stage.*) He's dead!

GRANDPA: Syb... (*Black out.*)

ACT TWO

Thursday afternoon in the SCHWAB'S living room. The room is pitch black as a flashlight's beam makes its way acroos the stage. A hand drops two pellets into SYBIL'S tonic water. The flashlight's beam exits stage right. Lights go up to reveal a makeshift funeral.

SYBIL: How dreadful that death should come to each mortal.

SAMANTHA: Mother, how insincere!

SYBIL: Was I being insincere? Pity. Look at him. Look at how peaceful he looks. He should have looked that peaceful when he was breathing. Too bad.

SAMANTHA: Mother, really.

SYBIL: Yes, dear?

SAMANTHA: Nothing.

SYBIL: Yes. He's dead and I'm alive. I could drop dead right now, but I saw him go first.

SAMANTHA: Behave yourself, mother. People may start arriving soon.

SYBIL: What of it?

SAMANTHA: You are being impossible.

SYBIL: No. You're wrong. I'm being very practical. (*GRANDPA enters from stage left, unobserved, and goes to stand behind*

SYBIL and SAMANTHA.) In fact, I'm celebrating. Yes. It's a celebration of life: my life. I'm still young and immensely talented and…yes!…beautiful! I can conquer the world. I, Sybil Schmidlap-Schwab, will conquer the world!

GRANDPA: Hey, Syb, can you spare a couple of bucks? (*The mood is broken and SYBIL bursts into tears.*) Come on, Syb, you're loaded.

SYBIL (*fumbling through her pocketbook*): Here! I should pound you on the head with my hammer; but, I seem to have misplaced it.

GRANDPA (*goes over to the writing desk to count his money*): I'll just have a seat over here in case you should need me.

SYBIL: I should live so long.

SAMANTHA: Mother, someone is coming. Sit down and behave yourself. I mean it.

SYBIL (*sitting down on the love seat*): Kill joy. (*GRANDMA and SOLOMON enter from stage right.*)

GRANDMA: My son! My dead son! It can't be! It just can't be! How is it possible? Why you? Why not her? Murderess!

SOLOMON: Grandmother Schwab, please, control yourself. Sit down over here.

GRANDMA: When I broke my ankle, he ran to me! He ran to me when I broke my ankle!

SYBIL: Too bad it wasn't her neck.

GRANDMA: His eyes! They flickered! Have I been granted a miracle?

SYBIL: Hardly.

SOLOMON (*trying to catch his breath*): I don't think so, Grandmother Schwab.

GRANDMA: My hopes dashed to pieces. Oh, I knew it. I knew something like this would happen. I had visions, I tell you. I'm a religious woman: devout and pious...so very, very pious; not like some heathens I could mention. Fiend! Murderess! Yes. I'll say it, again. Oh, how it bears repeating.

SYBIL: Got any proof?

GRANDMA: The facts speak for themselves. You shoved him down the stairs.

SYBIL: An accident. The circumstances were quite extenuating.

GRANDMA: I'll see you hang!

SYBIL: Will you?

GRANDMA: Righteousness is on my side. And, God is on my side.

SYBIL: Pray tell?

GRANDMA (*sitting down defiantly next to SYBIL*): Did you love my son?

SYBIL: I hated your son.

GRANDMA: How dare you!

SYBIL: Come, again?

SAMANTHA: Stop this, at once! The two of you are behaving like children.

GRANDMA: Shut up.

OLIVE (*enters from stage right*): Sybil, darling, you look simply dreadful. I couldn't make it last night because something quite interesting came up, very interesting, in fact. I'd like to tell you all about it. May we speak in private, dear?

SYBIL: I'm afraid not, Olive. I do have certain obligations.

OLIVE: Oh? I did mention that someone is out to kill you? You haven't forgotten, have you?

SYBIL: Hardly.

OLIVE: Good. But, dear, I really must speak to you in private. I couldn't possibly say what I have to say out in the open. It would be awkward.

SYBIL: Stick around, Olive. We'll talk later.

OLIVE: But, the matter is so dreadfully pressing. I must speak of it now or I will burst. Sybil, do offer me a drink. (*Looking about the room.*) My God! But all your guests seem so stern.

GRANDMA: My son is dead.

OLIVE: How depressing for you.

GRANDMA (*turning to SOLOMON*): Who is she? What is she doing here?

SOLOMON: She's a friend of mother's.

GRANDMA: I hate her. She's a slut. (*OLIVE and SYBIL move upstage and begin a very earnest conversation. SYBIL starts dipping into her pocketbook and extracts a wad of money, handing it over to OLIVE.*)

SYBIL: Olive, do make yourself comfortable. We're having champagne in a little while; a domestic brand, but it will do.

OLIVE: How very decadent! I approve. One should celebrate.

SYBIL: Sit next to me, Olive. You can perch yourself on the arm like an alley cat.

OLIVE: Briefly, of course. I only dropped by to remind you that your life may come to a rather abrupt end. I don't mean to alarm you, but my sources are very reliable. The entire neighborhood knows about it. And, of course, there was a matter of the other business.

GRANDMA: Who's out to kill the bitch?

OLIVE: I'm afraid that Sybil has libeled someone.

SYBIL: I've libeled no one!

GRANDMA: She's libeled everyone. How else do you think she writes that trash?

OLIVE: You must be Grandmother Schwab.

SYBIL: Enough of this chit-chat. I've an announcement to make.

OLIVE: Sybil, you may not have much time.

SYBIL: Oh, you're so very wrong. I feel immortal: invincible, in fact. I believe that I'm actually made of titanium.

GRANDPA: You mean helium, don't you?

OLIVE: You do have a flair for the exaggeration.

SYBIL (*getting up to view the corpse*): No. It's a fact. And, now, I must have one final view of him. Pardon me. I intend to have my husband cremated, tonight!

GRANDPA: Cremated?

GRANDMA: Cremated!

SOLOMON: Cremated.

SAMANTHA: Cremated!

SAM (*sitting up*): Cremated! But, you can't. I'm still alive. (*There are various cries of astonishment, disbelief, and snickering.*)

GRANDMA: I knew it! God has granted me a miracle!

SYBIL: What is the meaning of this outrage?

SAM (*flinging a lily at her*): You tried to kill me so I had to get even with you -- so there!

GRANDMA: Come to mother! Get away from that cow.

SYBIL: He'd better get away from me -- pronto! (*SAM sits down next to his mother.*)

OLIVE: Sam, this is going too far. You should be ashamed of yourself. You should be. What a dreadful fright I just suffered!

SAM: I am ashamed.

SYBIL (*moving toward SAMANTHA*): Were you in on this, lady? I thought you were taking it rather well, a little too well. I hope you and your father will be very happy together because you're both getting tossed into the street! Get out! It's all too much. My rose tonic water; I simply must have a sip. Solomon, help mother!

SOLOMON: Solly is here for you, mother.

SYBIL: Dear boy.

CARL (*enters from stage right*): Sybil!

SYBIL: Oh, Mr. Continent, how good of you to come. I am in dire need of a man's assistance.

SOLOMON: But, mother, Solly is here.

SYBIL: You're only a boy, dear. You're mother's little man.

CARL: Don't drink that tonic water. I've reason to believe it's been poisoned.

SYBIL: Poisoned?

GRANDMA: Don't believe him; drink it.

SAM: Oh, go ahead and take a sip.

CARL: Sybil, darling, your husband's childish joke is unimportant. It's your life that we must protect at all costs. You're very precious.

GRANDPA: I'll say. Hey, Syb, can you spare another couple of bucks.

SYBIL: Carl, please, stop that man. He's crucifying me.

CARL: Ignore him, dear Sybil. If he's been blackmailing you-

SYBIL: He has!

CARL: -well, that's a matter best handled by the police. We'll attend to him later.

SYBIL: Yes…later.

GRANDPA: You'll attend to me, now. Cough up that money, Syb.

SYBIL: Not one more frigging dime!

GRANDPA: Suit yourself. Here's a medical document that I just happen to have on me.

SYBIL: Carl, grab it! (*CARL rushes across the room, but SAM is too quick for him.*)

SAM: I've got it!

SYBIL: Carl, break his neck!

SAM (*blocking CARL'S way*): No!

GRANDMA: Good boy. Now, let's have a look.

SYBIL: I don't care.

GRANDPA: She will.

GRANDMA: Hmm…suffering from adiposity? Good heavens, Sybil, what on earth is that; some kind of social disease?

OLIVE: Sybil, would you like a breath of fresh air?

SYBIL: No. But, I do want certain people dead.

GRANDMA: Samantha, get grandmother a dictionary like a good girl.

SAMANTHA: Of course.

SYBIL: Don't you dare!

SAMANTHA: Mother, please.

GRANDMA: Touchy little thing, isn't she?

OLIVE: Must you embarrass this woman? I see the dictionary. It's over there, Samantha.

SYBIL: Why thank you, Olive

SAMANTHA: Here you are Grandmother Schwab.

GRANDMA: Excellent. Now…adiposity…yes. Oh, this is too rich. Really, Sybil, we are vain. And to allow oneself to be blackmailed? How much did you get from the bitch?

GRANDPA: Plenty.

GRANDMA: Serves her right.

SAMANTHA: Grandmother Schwab, don't keep us in suspense.

GRANDMA: I won't; that would be very mean of me if I did. It means that she's fat! She's suffering from fatness! Cramming food down her throat.

CARL: An obvious misdiagnosis.

GRANDPA: He's after your money. He'll say anything.

SAMANTHA: Isn't that the pot calling the kettle black? It does put an end to your blackmailing days, Grandfather Schwab.

SAM: Enough with the fat talk. What's all this about someone wanting to put the kibosh on Sybil? I won't hear of it.

SOLOMON: I hate to admit it, but for a change, father is right. Shouldn't that be our priority right now; now that Grandfather Schwab's blackmailing scheme has been exposed? How disgusting.

GRANDPA: Show some respect, whippersnapper.

SYBIL: I am not fat! I intend to sue that doctor for malpractice.

SAMANTHA (*incredulous*): Someone has in all probability attempted to poison my mother and all she can think of is some inane diagnosis by a quack doctor. You can't be serious?

SYBIL: But, it implies that mother is fat: such a vulgar word. You know that mother is not fat. Samantha? Solomon?

SOLOMON (*evading the question*): Mother, calm yourself down.

SAMANTHA (*evading the question*): It's your life, mother, that you should be concerned about.

GRANDPA: The kids are right, Syb. We want you alive and fat. I'm sure I speak for us all.

SYBIL: I truly loathe you.

OLIVE: Enough of this nonsense. You are not fat, Sybil. A trifle overweight, yes, that is quite undeniable; but, you have yet to reach the gargantuan stage. Don't bother to thank me.

SYBIL (*plopping down in the arm chair*): Would someone please hand me my rose tonic water: the one that's been poisoned?

CARL: Sybil, I notified the police before I came. They're outside now and no one may enter or leave the premises.

SAM: Trapped like rats!

SYBIL: You would say that. But, what good will that do? It may not be anyone in this room.

OLIVE: It is certainly not I. As your best friend, I am above suspicion.

CARL (*moving to where OLIVE is perched*): No one is above suspicion. I'm sorry; but, we haven't been properly introduced. Carl Continent before you.

OLIVE: Schneer, Olive K. So very enchanted to meet you, Mr. Continent, at such close proximity. You know, I am simply dying for a piece of chocolate! And, would you believe that at one time I loathed the very sight of chocolate? Yes. It is true. But, dearest Sybil informed me of the many sexual benefits that it bestows on a woman and, so, now, I eat chocolate.

CARL: Yes. Of course. How very fascinating. As I was saying, no one is above suspicion.

SAM: Does that mean you, too, Mr. Continent?

CARL: Mr. Schwab-

SAM: Call me Sam.

CARL: Sam. Let's try to get organized, shall we?

SAM (*standing to attention*): Your wish is my command, mon Capitan!

CARL: Will everyone, please, take a seat?

GRANDMA: I don't think I like this foreigner. Who the hell is he, anyway?

SOLOMON: A friend of mother's…a rather recent friend.

SAMANTHA: He's my friend. I found him.

CARL: The assassin-

GRANDPA: Assassin?

GRANDMA (*flirting with CARL*): Aren't we being just a tad melodramatic, Mr. Continent? Carl?

CARL: Not at all. If what I believe to be true is correct then only someone who is well acquainted with Sybil's daily habits could be the assassin.

GRANDMA: That leaves me out. I hate the bitch.

CARL: Precisely. Sybil, do you have enemies in this room?

SAM: You might say the room is filled to overflow with them.

CARL: Very well. We have Samantha, Solomon, Grandfather Schwab, Grandmother Schwab, Sam, and Miss Schneer.

OLIVE: But, Mr. Continent, you exclude yourself. How very convenient for you.

CARL: It's simply a fact, Miss Schneer. Now, I propose a test of wits. We'll set up two tables and we will each take our allotted places. A glass of rose tonic water will be placed on each table. Yes, Sam?

SAM: One of which is poisoned?

CARL: Good man! But, no one will know which is which.

GRANDMA: Sounds stupid to me.

SAMANTHA: Grandmother Schwab, we should listen to what Mr. Continent has to say. Perhaps, he's falling in love with mother.

SAM: He can have her.

GRANDMA: Now, you're talking sense. You can come home to mother. I'll make you one of those nice chicken pot pies that you love so much.

CARL (*standing at center stage*): Of course. Now, everyone, set up two tables. Myself, dear Sybil, Olive, and Samantha on one table. Sam, Grandfather Schwab, Grandmother Schwab, and Solomon on the other. A bottle of rose tonic water will be placed on one table and this poisoned bottle on the other table.

GRANDMA: The one that you think is poisoned.

CARL: Of course.

SAM: And, then?

CARL: Each one will taste from the bottle on his or her table.

SAM: And, then?

CARL: The one who hesitates is our assassin.

SAM: I'm missing something here. No one in his right mind will drink out of this glass: it might be poisoned!

CARL: I'm going to switch bottles and, then, they'll be switched, again, until no one knows which is which.

OLIVE: And, you expect us to taste from a bottle that may be poisoned? You're insane!

GRANDPA: You can say that, again, Olive. I think your plan stinks, Mr. Continent. No offense.

CARL: Do you have a better suggestion?

GRANDPA: Let Syb over here fend for herself.

SAM: Or…let's see who has the best motive for wanting her dead.

GRANDPA: I wanted her alive for blackmailing purposes.

SAM: She's cut me out of her will. I bribed her attorney to find that one out. Her darling son is her sole beneficiary. I want her alive for sponging purposes.

SAMANTHA: I'm in the same boat as father. We're both left penniless. My rotten brother gets everything. He must be your assassin, Mr. Continent.

SOLOMON: Mother, is it true that I get everything?

SYBIL: You know you're the apple of mother's eye.

GRANDPA: Sickening, isn't it?

GRANDMA: A mother should love her son above all else. I know I do.

GRANDPA: As I was saying…

SAM: But, wills can be changed, eh, Mr. Continent?

CARL: Miss Schneer?

OLIVE: I will bask in Sybil's glory.

GRANDPA: Like a leech to a blood vessel.

OLIVE: Son of a bitch! Blackmailer!

GRANDMA: That leaves you, Mr. Continent.

CARL: I? I want my darling to live!

SAM: Well, for at least a few more days.

CARL: We must get organized! I know my little scheme will work. (No one moves.)

SAMANTHA: I don't think I like you anymore, Mr. Continent.

GRANDPA: Who the hell would be crazy enough to take a chance on sipping a bottle full of poison? Solomon, take a sip for Grandpa.

SOLOMON: You are totally without scruples, Grandfather Schwab. (*He sniffs the bottle.*) Harmless.

CARL: Aha! Murderer! It was you, boy!

SYBIL: Solomon? Enough! I'm going to call the police.

OLIVE: But, Sybil, they are outside. If you like, I will bring them in.

CARL: I shouldn't bother about that, Miss Schneer.

OLIVE: And, why not Mr. Continent? Have you something to hide?

CARL: There's no one out there. I lied.

OLIVE: You are a very convincing liar.

CARL: I did it for Sybil's sake.

OLIVE: Only a complete idiot would believe that.

SYBIL: I believe it- never mind. I'm calling the police. (*She rushes over to the phone.*) Hello? Operator? Get me the police. Now, we'll get to the bottom of this. Hello? Police? This is Sybil Schmidlap-Schwab: authoress extraordinaire. I've reason to believe that an attempt has been made on my life. I'm quite desperate. What? What did you just say? How dare you! What do you mean I sound like I'm fat? Drop dead! (*She slams down the receiver.*) Carl, take me away from all this.

CARL: That's what Carl is here for.

GRANDMA: I knew it! Harlot! And, she's fat, too.

SAMANTHA: This is getting us nowhere.

SAM: Oh, I think it's getting us somewhere. Listen up: I know who the murderer is.

SAMANTHA: Tell us father. Show them all how very clever you are. And, won't mother be very grateful.

SAM: But, will she be generous?

SAMANTHA: Good point.

SOLOMON: What are you two going on about? You're always leaving me out. Well, I don't care.

SAM: Hmm...

SAMANTHA: Father, be careful. I think I'm beginning to get your drift.

SOLOMON: Careful of what? Say it! Go on, say it!

SYBIL: Solomon, what's wrong, dear?

SOLOMON (*turning on his mother*): I'll tell you what's wrong. I'll tell you all what's wrong! My mother is wrong! Her career-

SAM: Such as it is.

SOLOMON: -her morals are obscene! She is a heathen who has revealed herself at Satan's altar!

GRANDMA: A heathen...heathen!

SOLOMON: "Toxic Cherry" a vile title brimming with sexual innuendo. It's evil! I had to stop it. I had to stop her!

GRANDPA: Hey, kid, you're blowin' your inheritance.

SOLOMON: It is tainted money fit only for a Sodomite. It was I who poisoned your precious tonic water. I was wrong to do it. I should have insisted you enter a convent.

SYBIL: He is insane.

SAMANTHA: A convent? Sister Sybil? My brother really has flipped. And, you are admitting you're guilty of attempted murder?

SYBIL: We'll get you help, dear. I'll just make one little phone call to the Mad House and the men in the white jackets will come and fetch you. (*Aside to CARL.*) Watch him. He's out of his mind!

GRANDMA: Grandmother Schwab will visit you. It's all this creature's fault. So young…so demented.

OLIVE (*getting off the couch*): I assume that one is free to leave, now?

CARL: Of course, Miss Schneer.

OLIVE: Good riddance. And, by the way, Sybil?

SYBIL: What is it, Olive? I'm rather busy.

OLIVE: Don't trust this man. There is something very unscrupulous about him. I leave you. I must purchase some chocolates before going home. And, Sybil, I will be in touch about the next payment.

SYBIL: And, you're calling Carl unscrupulous? Bitch!

SAM: You wouldn't be taking up where Grandfather Schwab left off, would you?

OLIVE: I can say no more. Goodbye. (*She exits stage right.*)

GRANDPA: So long, Olive!

SAM: Maybe, we can put Solomon in the attic?

SOLOMON: No! Not that! Give me a few hours head start. I promise never to come back.

SYBIL: But, dear, I couldn't possibly allow that. No. I insist on having you committed.

SOLOMON: You'll have to catch me, first! (*He pushes past CARL and exits stage right.*)

CARL: I'll call the police.

SYBIL: And, I'll call the papers: this is priceless publicity!

ACT THREE

Later that evening.

SYBIL: Dearest Carl! Come in.

CARL: Is everyone asleep?

SYBIL: Yes. Or pretending to be. It doesn't matter.

CARL: We must be careful. The slightest mistake could be costly.

SYBIL: I don't make mistakes.

CARL: Are you packed?

SYBIL: Of course. And, how easy it all was -- except for that dreadful prank of my husband's.

CARL: Your soon to be ex-husband.

SYBIL: A divorce, at last!

CARL: As a matter of fact, that prank of his and Samantha's bolsters your mental cruelty case against him.

SYBIL: It does; doesn't it? And, then, my glory as a writer will be unquestioned. I'll take back my maiden name. Yes. Sybil Schmidlap: so much more melodious to the ear, don't you think?

CARL: Sybil Continent would sound better.

SYBIL: Would it? Perhaps. We'll see. And, now, we must be on our way.

CARL: A toast with the so-called poisoned tonic water.

SYBIL: That was rather clever of you.

CARL: To us!

SYBIL: To my future- our future. (*SAM and SAMANTHA are seen listening behind the couch.*)

CARL: Poor Solomon. He actually convinced himself that he was the guilty party. Stupid bastard!

SYBIL: Now, Carl, don't be unkind.

CARL: But, he is rather odd.

SYBIL: He is my son. Shall we drop this topic, please?

CARL: He's on the loose. He could be dangerous.

SYBIL: Nonsense. He's harmless and really a dear boy. Now, shut up about him, Carl. I mean it.

CARL: And, as for your daughter-

SYBIL (*trying not to laugh*): Well, dear Samantha is very...shall we say, easily manipulated? She really thinks that she met you at Herr Kraut's Bakery by accident. How amusing!

CARL: Little realizing that her mother had arranged it all... and her mother's lover.

SYBIL: We had to get you into this house by some means. And, dear Samantha proved so effective. It was almost too easy.

CARL: A simple plan for the simple minded.

SYBIL: Frankly, yes! Oh, I'm being cruel!

CARL: It becomes you, dear. (*He drinks the tonic water and promptly collapses to the floor.*)

SYBIL: Carl? Carl, darling? You're not-

SAM: Well, not yet. Your lover has several more seconds to live.

SYBIL: Where's my hammer?

SAM: I took the liberty of removing it from your pocketbook. Now, you may leave-

SYBIL: I may leave? I may leave? Who in hell are you?

SAM: Your loving husband.

SYBIL: Not for much longer.

SAMANTHA: Really, mother, how pedestrian all this is.

SAM: Let's have a family chat, shall we? Mr. Continent does not, well, did not, love you. Tut-tut ! Let me finish. He was after your money.

SYBIL: That's a lie.

SAM: It's the truth, dear.

SYBIL: What of it?

SAM: Aha! You admit it.

SYBIL: So you poisoned my Carl- Oh!

SOLOMON (*enters from stage left*): I did that, mother. As usual, father is lying to you. I've been hiding in the basement. I knew it wasn't I who had done anything wrong...until now. You were both supposed to drink the poison and, then, I would inherit.

SYBIL: I'm surrounded by fiends!

SAM (*leading SOLOMON to the basement door*): Why don't you lie down on the couch in the basement like a good boy? That's it. (*He slams the door shut.*) Samantha, call the cops. Quick! (*He and SYBIL continue their conversation completely ignoring the corpse on the floor.*)

SYBIL: The drama is over. I must unpack.

SAM: I've already done that for you. I did leave one housedress in your overnight bag, just in case you did fly the coop.

SYBIL: Perhaps, a late night repast? A snack might cheer me up.

SAM: I think I'm coming down with a cold. Samantha, get daddy some aspirin, please? (*SAMANTHA hangs up the phone and looks in the table's drawer for some aspirin.*)

GRANDPA: What's going on down there? What's Syb up to now?

SAM: We're once again a happy family.

GRANDPA: Goodnight!

SAMANTHA: Here are your aspirin, father.

SAM: Thank you.

SYBIL: Samantha, dear, why not fix us all a midnight snack? I have some anchovies and petit-fours in the refrigerator. Hurry! Mother is feeling quite ravenous. (*SAMANTHA exits stage left.*) Well, how do you feel?

SAM: Mmm.

SYBIL: I said: how do you feel?

SAM: Mmm.

SYBIL: Are you trying to be funny? How do you feel, damn it!

SAM: Mmm.

SYBIL: What the hell are you saying?

SAM: You're not supposed to talk when you take aspirin.

SYBIL: Good God! Where is Samantha with the food? Well, can you talk now?

SAM: If you insist.

SYBIL: How long did you know about Carl?

SAM: I had my spies out.

SYBIL: Olive?

SAM: Perhaps.

SYBIL: The bitch is trying to blackmail me.

SAM: She is your best friend.

SYBIL: I knew Carl was a cad and a bounder. But, it was such fun!

SAM: It was fun. And, now you have your career, such as it is, and I have your money. Tut-tut! No arguments.

SYBIL: Well...all's well that ends well! (*Turning to the audience.*) Until tomorrow!

End of play.

EDMUND:

The Likely

A Play in Three Acts

by

Gerard Denza

Copyright 2009

EDMUND: The Likely had a script reading at the Producer's Club on June 20, 2009 with the following cast:

MARLENA LAKE	Susan Gazzolo
MITCHELL SOAMES	Brandon DeSpain
EDMUND HOLDERMAN	Nick Arens
DICK MILLOT	Brett Jaspers
RODDY CERVANTES	R. Ross Pivec
COACH MASCAGNI	Malcolm Ehrlich
JEANNE MANTEE	Natasha Gilgen
LINDA MASCAGNI	Khris Foster
MICHAEL MILLOT	Ron Schnitt
RITA MILLOT	Linda Rosen
DET. THOMAS	Phil Strumolo
AGENT VOGEL	Diane Ordelheide

EDMUND: The Likely was recorded for radio in September 20013 with the following cast:

MARLENA LAKE	Pooya Mohseni
MITCHELL SOAMES	Brandon DeSpain
EDMUND HOLDERMAN	Ed Newman
DICK MILLOT	Daniel Dambroff
RODDY CERVANTES	Johnny Castillo
COACH MASCAGNI	Alfred Rosenblatt
JEANNE MANTEE	Katie Fanning
LINDA MASCAGNI	Eileen Maher
MICHAEL MILLOT	David Shakopi
RITA MILLOT	Gulshan Mia
DET. THOMAS	Phil Strumolo
AGENT VOGEL	Susan O'Doherty

PLACE
Downtown Manhattan in a run down gymnasium.

TIME
Early winter of 1947.

SCENES

CHARACTERS

MARLENA LAKE, a fascist.
MITCHELL SOAMES, Marlena's partner in crime.
EDMUND HOLDERMAN, a young bodybuilder.
DICK MILLOT, Edmund's gym buddy.
RODDY CERVANTES, Edmund's gym buddy.
COACH MASCAGNI, Edmund's coach.
JEANNE, Roddy's girlfriend.

LINDA MASCAGNI, Coach's daughter.
MICHAEL MILLOT, Dick's father.
RITA MILLOT, Dick's mother.
DET. THOMAS, Edmund's interrogator.
AGENT VOGEL, Immigrations Officer.

PROLOGUE

MARLENA LAKE'S apartment on the upper east side of Manhattan.

VOICE: Are you prepared to die?

MARLENA: No.

VOICE: You disappoint me. It is your duty to die, unquestioningly.

MARLENA: The work is not yet completed.

MITCHELL: Will there be no negotiations?

VOICE: None.

MITCHELL: I understand.

VOICE: Annihilation and, then, our terms will be met.

MITCHELL: Or?

VOICE: Or the carnage will continue until every major city in America is destroyed.

MARLENA: But, that is self-defeating and a waste of resources.

VOICE: You question the syndicate's methods, Miss Lake?

MARLENA (*frightened*): No.

VOICE: You and Mr. Soames are expendable.

MARLENA: We have the plan for the advanced atomic detonator. It will leave the country soon.

VOICE: It will make the blast that will soon destroy New York City look like a mere pin prick. The city will be leveled as an example of what any act of defiance will cost them.

MARLENA: Our agents are in place and have their orders.

VOICE: Has a courier been chosen?

MARLENA: He has.

VOICE: There is very little time. These plans must leave the country and soon.

MARLENA: They will.

VOICE: They must!

MARLENA: Mr. Soames and I will not fail you.

VOICE: You will not fail us!

ACT ONE
Scene One

December 26, 1947

EDMUND, RODDY, and DICK are working out. EDMUND is posing and scrupulously examining himself in the mirrors. He is not vain, but all too critical of his progress as a competitive bodybuilder. DICK, his workout buddy, is watching his friend. RODDY, another bodybuilder, is lifting weights in another part of the gym.

EDMUND: Okay. You've been watching long enough. So, what do you think?

DICK: You're maintaining yourself, Edmund. You're toned and defined and ready to compete. Do you really need me to tell you that?

EDMUND: As a matter of fact, Dick, I do. You've got a critical mind and your mouth matches it: that's a compliment, by the way. I think I may be walking on a plateau.

DICK: No. You haven't hit a plateau, man. You've peaked. There's a big difference.

EDMUND: Is there?

DICK: I don't have to explain it to you, Edmund. You'll win a few more competitions and, then, you either call it quits or go to the senior level if your prospects hold out.

EDMUND: My prospects?

DICK: Your overhead, man. Your maintenance. The cost of living.

EDMUND: You mean like getting a decent job?

DICK: No. That's not what I meant I meant living well and not worrying where your next buck is coming from.

EDMUND: I always worry.

DICK: I used to know what that was; worrying, I mean.

EDMUND: Oh? Are you suddenly flushed with money, Dick? How so?

DICK: Would you mind so much if I didn't go into it? It's really none of your business, anyhow.

EDMUND: You brought it up. Frankly, I don't give a crap about your personal life.

DICK: Thanks.

EDMUND: I don't like being baited.

DICK: I didn't-

EDMUND: You did.

DICK: Take it easy, man. Here. Put your sweatshirt on. You're gonna' catch a chill.

EDMUND: Thanks. And, I've actually got a modeling job for tomorrow: a full layout plus a shot at the cover.

DICK: Good for you, man!

RODDY: (*putting down the barbell*): Did I just hear right, Ed? What's the magazine? Have I heard of it?

EDMUND: You've heard of it: Man of Tomorrow.

RODDY (*impressed*): That's top of the line. You've made it, Ed. I'm proud to know you. Wait'll I tell Jeanne. She'll probably buy a dozen copies and have you autograph each one.

DICK: Hey, Edmund, you don't tell this to your best friend? You've been holding out on me.

EDMUND: Not really. I would have told you tomorrow. You two guys are the first I've told.

RODDY (*extending his hand*): Congratulations. I am so impressed and, a little jealous, you prime piece of beef.

DICK: Hey, here comes Coach Mascagni. I think we better hop back to the weights. What's he bringing in?

COACH: It's called a projector. Edmund? Help me set up this contraption, will you? I want to show you characters some old time bodybuilders and how the sport's changed over the years. (*To DICK, whom he doesn't like.*) Think you can take it?

DICK: Try me, Mr. Mascagni.

COACH: He's respectful, today. Good.

RODDY: I'm not sure I can stay. My girlfriend's probably outside waiting for me.

COACH: I invited her in. Edmund? I invited Linda in, too.

EDMUND: Why tell me?

COACH: I won't answer that question.

DICK: I will.

COACH: Shut up. (*Enter JEANNE, LINDA and MICHAEL MILLOT.*)

JEANNE: So, this is the fabled gymnasium. It's quite masculine!

LINDA: It's pretty Spartan. It suits you to the "T," Edmund.

EDMUND: Thank you.

LINDA: So, how's my dad's protégé? You look healthy and fit.

EDMUND: Again, thank you.

LINDA: My compliments make you uneasy? They just happen to be on the level, you know.

EDMUND: I didn't mind.

MICHAEL: Dick, I hope you don't mind your dad showing up? I ran into Eduardo and he invited me along.

DICK: You're always welcome, Dad. Mom's not with you? Is she?

MICHAEL: Absolutely not. She's home and up to her ears in paperwork: business, she tells me.

DICK: I'll bet! Monkey business, you mean.

JEANNE: Dick, your mom sounds interesting. Is she educated?

DICK: She's a character is more like it.

JEANNE: Don't you like her?

DICK: No. And, please shut up about her.

JEANNE: What's eating at him?

RODDY: Skip it. Sore topic, that's all.

COACH: Okay. We're ready. Somebody get the lights.

JEANNE: I will. (*The room is plunged into darkness and the projector starts up.*)

EDMUND: When does the film start?

LINDA: Dad? This is nothing but blank film. I don't get it.

DICK: Here's something coming on the screen. What the- What is this? Is this some kind of a joke or something?

EDMUND: Hey, Coach? I think somebody's having one on you. It looks like a cheap gangster movie but-

DICK: -but real.

LINDA: But, it can't be real. That would mean-

JEANNE: -that we're witnessing an actual murder! I don't want to see anymore! Stop it!

COACH: The damned mechanism is jammed.

MICHAEL: Let me try. If this is actual footage, we've got to notify the police. Here…this switch. (*The projector shuts down and they are now in total darkness. A shot rings out.*)

EDMUND: Somebody switch on the lights. We're being shot at!

LINDA: Everyone be careful. (*Another shot rings out.*)

JEANNE (*screaming*): There's blood on me!

EDMUND (*stumbles toward the light switch as another shot rings out, just missing him*): Is everybody okay? Has anyone been hurt?

LINDA: Dick! Your dad's been shot! Someone help me.

DICK: Somebody get to a phone and call an ambulance.

JEANNE: Call the police! There's a killer on the loose! Hurry up! Roddy, you go: there's a pay phone right by the staircase. I saw it on my way in.

RODDY: Stay here. (*Exits.*)

COACH: Give him room to breathe. He took that shot in the back. I don't like the look of it.

LINDA: But, he's alive?

DICK: Who'd want to do this? My dad's the nicest guy in the world.

EDMUND: He's gonna' be all right.

LINDA: Of course, he'll be all right. Help will get here soon. We just have to keep our heads.

JEANNE: Oh, Roddy, hurry up! What's taking him so long?

LINDA: He just left. Give him a chance.

JEANNE: What's to prevent that trigger happy bandit from coming back?

EDMUND: I doubt if he's still in the building. But, you're right, we can't afford to take any chances. There's always the risk-

LINDA: Don't say it, Edmund.

RODDY (*running back in*): They're on their way. How is he? He's not-

JEANNE: Roddy, let's go outside and wait for them. Come on! I don't want to stay here. (*She and RODDY exit.*)

EDMUND: He's coming around. Mr. Millot, try not to move.

MICHAEL: I think I've just been grazed. I must have passed out.

LINDA: Don't get up, Mr. Millot. Lie still.

MICHAEL: Who did this to me?

EDMUND: We don't know. Try to relax. You're gonna' be okay. (*Black out. When the lights come up only EDMUND and LINDA are in the gymnasium. MITCHELL SOAMES can be seen hiding in the shadows.*)

LINDA: Edmund?

EDMUND: Yes?

LINDA: Would you mind if I kept you company for awhile?

EDMUND: No.

LINDA: You sure?

EDMUND: I'm pretty upset right now.

LINDA: I know. Dick's dad wasn't hurt too bad.

EDMUND: I don't understand any of it.

LINDA: Edmund, are you angry with me?

EDMUND: No.

LINDA: Are you angry about anything I've done? Will you be up front with me?

EDMUND: You haven't done anything.

LINDA: Maybe, that's the problem. Take me to a nightclub, Edmund. I've never been to one.

EDMUND: I wish I could, Linda. I can't afford it.

LINDA: Then, take me to a movie.

EDMUND: Why do you waste your time on me?

LINDA: Is that what I'm doing? I kind of enjoy your company.

EDMUND: That's very nice of you; but, I don't believe you, Linda. I'm a very boring bodybuilder who doesn't know how to do anything else. My father was a laborer and didn't leave his son very much.

LINDA: Oh, baby, you're so wrong. He left a pretty wonderful son to carry on his name. He'd be so proud of you.

EDMUND: I have no background-

LINDA: You're your own man. You don't need to stand on the shoulders of some dead ancestors. You're your heritage. And, for that, I love you -- you idiot!.

EDMUND: I don't know what to say.

LINDA: Just look at me, Edmund. Just look at me and I'll see the answer in your eyes.

EDMUND: My bodybuilding career isn't going much further than it already has.

LINDA: Is that what's bothering you?

EDMUND: Yes!

LINDA: Is that so terrible?

EDMUND: Yes! Damn it! It is!

LINDA: Who's to tell you that it can't go any further? I'm sure my dad doesn't agree with you. I know I sure don't.

EDMUND: Thank you. Truly.

LINDA: We've had a pretty bad shock with the shooting and the questions by the police. They want us to make sense out of something that doesn't make any sense to anybody.

EDMUND: The police took the film and, maybe, they can learn something from it.

LINDA: Did you notice the man in the film: the murderer? He was wearing a pretty clever mask. It looked like- he looked like-

EDMUND: Like who?

LINDA: Like you, Edmund. That man, or whoever it was, looked like you. (*MITCHELL slips out unseen.*)

ACT ONE
Scene Two

December 26, 1947

RITA and DICK are having a heated discussion in Jimmy's Bar. EDMUND and MITCHELL walk in and sit down. MARLENA is sitting by the bar watching all that is going on. DETECTIVE THOMAS and AGENT VOGEL are also there.

RITA: Well? Answer me. Where did that passbook come from? Who sent it to you and why? How was it earned?

DICK: None of your dmaned business, lady. Just lay off my back.

RITA: I'm waiting for an answer. Bartender? Another scotch, please? Well?

DICK: How did you find out about it?

RITA: That little tramp came by and dropped it off.

DICK: Who? Jeanne?

RITA: That's her name.

DICK (*incredulous*): And, she gave the passbook to you? I can't believe it.

RITA: No. She gave it to your father who thought I was asleep.

DICK: Up to your old tricks, huh? You're disgusting, ya' know?

RITA: What did my son do to earn twenty grand? Hmm...?

DICK: It's for services rendered and- and it's a part of a membership fee.

RITA: Oh, really? It's a member who usually pays a fee to join an organization. What makes you so special?

DICK: Like I said, it's for services rendered. And, you can wipe that smile off your face. No. I don't go in that direction.

RITA: You don't have to "go" in that direction to benefit from it. You're a smart boy and handsome. And, I think for once in your life, you're starting to use your brains instead of your biceps. Good! Now, tell me: where did that money come from?

DICK: No.

RITA: I can help-

DICK: To do what? Spend it?

RITA: Invest it. Bankroll it. Parley it into something even bigger. Let me have some.

DICK: Forget it.

RITA: Does Edmund belong to this club of yours?

DICK: No.

RITA: Good. Who is that man sitting with him: a client?

DICK: You've got a filthy mind.

RITA: Your friend, Edmund, is a loose cannon -- keep your eye on him and I'll keep my eye on you!

MITCHELL: To your health, Mr. Holderman.

EDMUND: Thanks.

MITCHELL: Thank you for joining me for this drink. I needed it.

EDMUND: Don't mention it.

MITCHELL: I have seen you workout in your gymnasium. You are a very focused athlete. I admire that. I have also been informed that you have won several titles as a bodybuilder contender. Outstanding!

EDMUND: You seem to know a lot about me, Mr. Soames.

MITCHELL: It is more or less public information. Do you mind my frankness?

EDMUND: I don't think I do. Not yet.

MITCHELL: As a bodybuilder, your future must somewhat be assured, is it?

EDMUND: No. Not really. I'm twenty-seven.

MITCHELL: Not old, certainly, but no longer in the full bloom of youth. Are you well off, Mr. Holderman?

EDMUND: No. I live by my body and beauty.

MITCHELL: Do they fetch very much for you?

EDMUND: You've got a lot of pretty faces out there.

MITCHELL: The competition must by quite intense. Have you thought about another kind of support: a livelihood, if you would?

EDMUND: I don't follow you.

MITCHELL: And, that is precisely what I and my employer want to do for you, Mr. Holderman: follow us toward a destiny worth gambling on. The stakes are quite high and the road ahead is treacherous. You interested? Say, yes.

EDMUND: Maybe.

MITCHELL: Not good enough, Mr. Holderman. It is a yes or no proposition. Say no, and I will pay for our drinks and leave. Say yes, and I will take you to my employer who is a very interesting person. Well? I need your answer.

EDMUND: Yes.

MITCHELL: That didn't sound too convincing. Say it, again, please.

EDMUND: Yes.

MITCHELL: A little better, that. Now, you need to change your circumstances. And, how does one go about doing that? I'll tell you. Look at my hands: are they empty or holding hundred dollar bills in them? Here. Look closely. I'm counting out thousands of dollars, aren't I?

EDMUND: No.

MITCHELL: But, I am, Mr. Holderman. Look. If I say it is thus, don't I make it a reality? You must learn to manipulate your reality and the perceptions of others. Do you understand? In time, you will. (*RODDY and JEANNE enter.*)

EDMUND: What good will it do: to fool people? I mean, that is what you're talking about, isn't it?

MITCHELL: It goes much deeper than that. The ramifications are intense and significant. And, to alter your environment is to take command of it; but, that is only one thing you will learn, Mr. Holderman.

EDMUND (*eyeing him suspiciously*): There was a shooting at the gym this afternoon. You wouldn't know anything about that, would you?

MITCHELL: It doesn't concern me. I was aware of an occurrence, that is all.

EDMUND: Is that all?

MITCHELL: Listen to me, Mr. Holderman: the day after tomorrow at my employer's apartment: be there promptly at 9 PM. Impress her with your punctuality, intelligence, and-

EDMUND: Desperation?

MITCHELL: If you like. It's not the word I would have chosen. Determination is a far better choice of words. Determination and even ruthlessness. And, now I must take my leave. Good evening. (*He exits and is followed by AGENT VOGEL. JEANNE and RODDY, who have joined RITA and DICK, gesture EDMUND over to their table.*)

EDMUND: Dick, how's your dad?

RITA: He'll live.

DICK: It was just a flesh wound..

RITA: How are things with you, Edmund?

EDMUND: About the same, I guess.

RITA: Who were you with just now?

DICK: Edmund, just ignore my mother.

JEANNE: I hear you have a job lined up for tomorrow, Edmund. Muscle magazine?

EDMUND: That's all I do.

RODDY: Ed's the best. He's a perfectionist.

RITA: My son, Dick, doesn't share your dedication to fitness. He seems to be occupied in other areas.

DICK: Shut your mouth.

RITA: Temper. Yes. He's investing himself in other areas. Do you share his varied interests, Edmund?

EDMUND: I don't know what you're talking about, Mrs. Millot. Dick and I are gym buddies and that's it.

RITA: But, you are "buddies." Interesting.

DICK: You can only guess at what my dear mother is hinting at. Stop it. Stop it, now!

JEANNE: I can guess what she's hinting at. And, for the record, I don't believe it.

RITA: You have doubts, dear?

JEANNE: Don't you?

RITA: None.

EDMUND (*getting up*): Mrs. Millot, I don't like you. Some people stink from the outside and some stink from the inside. You get my drift?

DICK: My mother's impervious to insults, Edmund, even when it's the truth.

EDMUND: So long. And, your son's business, Mrs. Millot, is his own and not mine.

RITA: His business is my business. And, I'll thank you to keep out of my affairs.

EDMUND: Or what?

RITA: Or else! Keep out of my way!

EDMUND: With the utmost pleasure. (*Exits.*)

DICK: Was that necessary?

RITA: Yes. It was.

JEANNE: Why? For pity's sake!

RITA: I think Edmund's just shown his hand-

DICK: Shown what?

RITA: I'm interested in him, now. I wasn't before; but, now I am.

JEANNE: Dare I ask why?

RODDY: Are you trying to be mysterious or something, Mrs. Millot?

RITA: Cautious. By the way, does anyone know who shot my husband?

JEANNE: Does your husband have any idea?

RITA: None. And, he wasn't lying. I would know if he were lying.

RODDY: You're pretty sure of yourself, huh?

RITA: I'm never wrong.

RODDY: Get a load of her!

DICK: Cool it, Roddy.

RODDY: What am I doing?

DICK: You're laughing at my mother.

RODDY: There's a lot to laugh at. I noticed you didn't seem to mind it when Ed was sparring with her.

DICK: I said shut up!

RODDY: Make me. I hadn't figured you for a momma's boy. And, just watch your friggin' mouth. Savvy?

DICK: I dig. Now, shut up.

RODDY: Make me, baby. (*DICK jumps up to confront RODDY.*)

JEANNE: Oh, God, stop it! Roddy, let's go. This is so unnecessary.

RITA: To a man, it isn't.

JEANNE: Mrs. Millot, don't encourage them. You don't understand-

RITA (*catching her up*): What is it that I don't understand? (*RODDY jumps up and throws a right hook at DICK'S chin. DICK staggers back and, then, rushes RODDY. The two of them fall to the floor and tumble over each other. DICK pins RODDY down and starts choking him.*)

JEANNE: Stop it! You're choking him! Let him go! (*She rushes over to the bar and grabs a bottle and smashes it over DICK'S head. He lets go of RODDY, turns on his side and starts nursing the back of his head.*) Roddy, are you all right?

RODDY: Fucking maniac! This is not finished. You hear me?

JEANNE: Get up! We're getting out of here. Come on. Come on!

RODDY: Okay. Man! He was gonna' kill me!

JEANNE: I know.

RODDY: Am I bruised?

JEANNE: Mrs. Millot, you could have helped, you know.

RITA: I don't understand.

JEANNE: It shouldn't have gone as far as it did.

RITA: No one was hurt.

JEANNE: Dick? Dick?

DICK: What?

JEANNE: Are you cooled off now? Are you okay?

DICK: I'll live.

JEANNE: Are you bleeding? I'm sorry I had to do that.

DICK: Don't worry about me.

JEANNE: Think about things and try not to be so hot-headed. (*She and RODDY exit.*)

DICK (*getting to his feet*): You're a troublemaker.

RITA: If I am, I had help.

DICK: Meaning?

RITA: You know what I mean.

DICK: I don't know anything about you, mother.

RITA: But, I know a great deal about you. Who is that woman by the bar?

DICK: Who? Never seen her before.

RITA: She's leaving. And, this is the second time tonight that you've lied to me. (*MARLENA exits and is followed by DETECTIVE THOMAS.*)

ACT ONE
Scene Three

December 27, 1947

EDMUND and LINDA are sitting on one of the work-out benches in the gym.

EDMUND: It's supposed to snow, tonight.

LINDA: I don't like snow.

EDMUND: Funny. I didn't think there was anything you didn't like.

LINDA: Only things, not people. Not usually.

EDMUND: Why don't you like snow?

LINDA: It belongs in the country where it can melt gracefully. In the city, it's beautiful for about one second.

EDMUND: Savor the second, then.

LINDA: Oh? How about going up on the roof with me and watch it come down? I'll race you up the stairs.

EDMUND: Maybe a little later. I don't think it's started yet.

LINDA: It sure has. It was coming down like fine, white powder. And, for some reason-

EDMUND: Yes?

LINDA: Don't laugh; but, it kind of gave me the willies. I don't know why.

EDMUND: You're being silly. Is your dad coming to pick you up?

LINDA: He worries about my walking home alone.

EDMUND: Did the police keep him for very long?

LINDA: They had an awful lot of questions for him.

EDMUND: I'll bet they did. Is he okay? Were his answers acceptable?

LINDA: He wasn't arrested, if that's what you mean. So. I guess they must have been acceptable. Edmund? What's that thing over there?

EDMUND: What thing?

LINDA: Over there by the wall. It's propped up against that barbell.

EDMUND: It's a spear. What is it doing here. Man! This thing feels like it's charged with electricity.

MARLENA (*walking into the gym*): It is a spear, young man. And, it happens to belong to me.

EDMUND: I beg your pardon, but this is a private gym. What are you doing here?

MARLENA: Don't be impertinent, Mr. Holderman.

EDMUND: How do you know my name?

MARLENA: By your photograph on the wall by the stairwell. You're an accomplished bodybuilder. I congratulate you. I am Marlena Lake. You met my employee, Mitchell Soames, yesterday evening. We have an appointment for tomorrow night. Now, would you please hand me the sacred object, Mr. Holderman?

EDMUND: Here. It feels almost weightless.

LINDA: A "sacred" object?

MARLENA:: Yes. Now, good evening. And, about tomorrow, be prompt. (*Exits.*)

LINDA: Who in the world was she, Edmund?

EDMUND: Honestly, I know nothing about her.

LINDA: But, she knows you. Who's Mitchell Soames?

EDMUND: No one in particular.

LINDA: I can take the hint. I won't press you; but, I don't trust that woman.

EDMUND: When I know more, I'll give you more details.

LINDA: You haven't given me any details, but that's okay. I believe you when you say you're in the dark.

EDMUND: Has anyone ever told you that you're an extremely perceptive young woman?

LINDA: My teacher once told me that I'm a master of deductive reasoning.

COACH (*enters*): Hello, Edmund. Linda, would you mind if I spoke with Edmund here for a couple of minutes?

LINDA: Yes, but that's okay. I'll go up to the roof and watch the snow come down.

COACH: Be careful and stay near the door. It's coming down harder now.

LINDA: Call me when you're ready to go. (*Exits.*)

EDMUND: What's on your mind, Coach?

COACH: You.

EDMUND: Glad to hear it; even though I'm twenty-seven and with one leg over the hill.

COACH: Whining is not your style, Edmund. Stop it or get yourself a new coach.

EDMUND: It's officially stopped.

COACH: That's better.

EDMUND: What's on your mind?

COACH: I'll get straight to the point. You're at the top of your form. Keep in shape and you'll have another five, six years on top. You've got muscle and you're sculpted. In short, you're a god-damned Adonis. You're a beauty. And, when you're on top of the heap, you're fair game for the spoilers. Keep yourself clean and don't trust your best friend.

EDMUND: I think I know what you mean.

COACH: Do you, Edmund? I wonder. At your age, no one could tell me anything I didn't want to hear. But, I want you to listen; to really listen. Trust no one.

EDMUND: Not even Linda?

COACH: It's easier to trust no one than to try to be selective about it. It's hard to read character, almost impossible, so don't waste your time. And, people can turn on you; jealously will always do that -- always. (*The lights go off and, then, back on.*) Hey! What gives here?

RODDY (*walking in with DICK*): Mr. Mascagni? What's wrong?

COACH: Who's fooling with the lights?

DICK: Not I. Could be the snowstorm outside.

COACH: It's a snowstorm, now?

DICK: Looks that way. Kickin' up something fierce. Hey, Edmund, how about coming with us for a drink before heading home?

COACH: He's in training: not so much as a beer.

DICK: You can "nurse" a ginger-ale. We'll settle for your company, man. What say?

EDMUND: Not tonight, guys. I think I'll walk Coach and Linda home.

DICK: Suit yourself; but, all I'm having is a ginger-ale, too, man. You won't be lonely.

RODDY: The boy said "no." Let's beat it to the bar. I hope that friggin' snow lets up.

DICK: Goodnight, Edmund. Mr. Mascagni. (*He and RODDY exit.*)

COACH: Good riddance. I just came from that bar. Dick's mother is over there getting herself plastered.

EDMUND: Close call! You might have mentioned that.

COACH: I ducked out before she could corner me. I thought she was coming after me.

EDMUND: She probably was. Poor Dick!

COACH: Don't feel too sorry for the bastard.

EDMUND: You don't like him, do you?

COACH: No. Now, let's you and me beat it. (*As he and EDMUND about to leave, the lights flicker and go out.*)

EDMUND (*meeting up with DICK and RODDY outside*): I thought you boys left already.

RODDY: Are you kidding? Look at that blizzard out there.

DICK: Come on. Let's make a dash for the bar; it's just across the street.

RODDY: In a minute. Did you just hear something? It came from upstairs. Let's have a look around.

DICK: In the dark?

RODDY: Scared?

DICK: Go to hell.

RODDY: Hey, buddy, we're supposed to be friends, again; right?

EDMUND: Where's Coach and- Linda! I forgot all about her. She must be still on the roof. (*He makes a mad dash up the stairwell.*)

DICK: Let's follow him.

RODDY: You follow him. I 'm going across the street for a drink. Here comes your mom. So long, pal. (*Exits.*)

DICK: What are you doing here?

RITA: I saw you and your buddy from across the street. I was in the bar having a nightcap.

DICK: In the middle of a blizzard?

RITA: Why not? (*A scream is heard.*) Sounds like somebody getting killed.

DICK: Where did it come from? I couldn't tell.

RITA: The roof. (*A loud thump is heard nearby.*)

DICK: What was that?

RITA: It sounded like something hitting the pavement.

DICK: I didn't see anything.

RITA: How could you in all this damned snow? (*COACH rushes past them and offstage.*)

DICK: What is it? What's going on?

COACH: It's my daughter, Linda. She's been killed!

ACT TWO
Scene One

December 28, 1947

At the gym, a small table and three chairs are set up with an overhead light focused on EDMUND.

DET. THOMAS: Edmund Holderman: that is your name?

EDMUND: Yes.

DET. THOMAS: What's your occupation, Edmund?

EDMUND: Bodybuilder and physique model.

DET. THOMAS: Is that steady employment?

EDMUND: No.

DET. THOMAS: Do you have other means of support?

EDMUND: Personal trainer.

DET. THOMAS: Have you won many awards.

EDMUND: Mr. New York, twice. I placed second in Mr. Muscle Beach. What does this have to do with anything?

AGENT VOGEL: Edmund? My name is Tracy Vogel. We're trying to get to know you; try to be patient with us.

DET. THOMAS: What is your work-out schedule like?

EDMUND: I work out two hours a day, six days a week.

DET. THOMAS: You're in the gym most of the time, then?

EDMUND: It's my life. I'm rarely not here.

AGENT VOGEL: That's very admirable.

DET. THOMAS: Even past regular hours; you would still be in the gym?

EDMUND: I have my own key.

DET. THOMAS: How long have you had your own key?

EDMUND: Since I started winning titles. You might say that my reputation lends a little status to the gym. I earned that key: it wasn't just given to me.

DET. THOMAS: Who else has a key?

EDMUND: The owner, Coach Mascagni, and the janitor.

DET. THOMAS: Shouldn't the gynasium have been closed last night due to the blizzard?

EDMUND: I don't think anyone saw that blizzard coming. The weather report said a chance of snow flurries.

DET. THOMAS: And, you were here, working out?

EDMUND: I was still here, but not working out.

AGENT VOGEL: You were about to say something else, Edmund.

EDMUND: I met Linda at the gym. She was waiting for her dad to show up.

DET. THOMAS: Did he show up?

EDMUND: Yes. He wanted to talk to me alone. That's when Linda went up on the roof.

DET. THOMAS: In the middle of a blizzard?

EDMUND: We didn't know how bad it had been snowing. Her dad, Coach Mascagni, warned her to be careful.

DET. THOMAS: What did you and Coach Mascagni talk about?

EDMUND: Tips on competing and working out: things like that. You wouldn't understand.

AGENT VOGEL: Edmund, make us understand.

EDMUND: It's a hard life. Every dime I make from modeling and coaching goes back into body building: gym membership, good food, and all the work-out gear: the gym gear, the posing trunks, body lotion, travel expenses, decent clothes. I have one suit, one pair of sneakers, and a pair of wing-tips that I picked up at a thrift shop. I've got one white shirt to go with the suit and a borrowed tie from my uncle: his only tie. Any book that I happen to read comes from the Public Library. The muscle magazines, I buy. They're like reference books for me: textbooks. I live in my uncle's spare bedroom in a working class neighborhood in Brooklyn; but, it's clean and it's right across the Williamsburg Bridge. Travel time is short and the subway fare is cheap. I happen to think it's worth it.

DET. THOMAS: And, you've got the trophies to prove it. Let's pick up the thread, shall we?

EDMUND: Okay.

DET. THOMAS: And, then, your two buddies come in?

EDMUND: Dick and Roddy.

DET. THOMAS: Mr. Dick Millot and Mr. Roderigo "Roddy" Cervantes. Anyone else around last night?

EDMUND: No. I don't think so- wait a minute. Dick's mom was outside. I ran past her.

DET. THOMAS: When was this?

EDMUND: When I- when I was following Coach- I ran into Dick and his mom.

DET. THOMAS: Were you and Linda fond of each other?

EDMUND: Yes.

DET. THOMAS: She admired you?

EDMUND: Yes. Her father's my coach.

AGENT VOGEL: Was she in love with you?

EDMUND: Yes. I think she was.

DET. THOMAS: Who would want to harm her?

EDMUND: I don't know.

DET. THOMAS: Tell me exactly what happened after you left your two not-so-good friends to go looking for Miss Mascagni.

EDMUND: I ran up the two flights of stairs.

DET. THOMAS: In the dark?

EDMUND: I know that place like the back of my hand.

DET. THOMAS: Go on.

EDMUND: I ran up to the roof's door and when I got there, I flung it open. She'd already gone over. Coach ran past me and pushed me out of the way.

DET. THOMAS: How do you know she'd gone over? How in the world could you know that?

EDMUND: I guess- Coach must have told me. It all happened so fast. My reactions seemed so damned slow.

DET. THOMAS: Did you go to the edge of the roof?

EDMUND: I nearly slipped over. I couldn't see anything in all that snow. I started to run back down.

DET. THOMAS: Where were your two friends: Roddy and Dick?

EDMUND: Dick was downstairs with his mom.

DET. THOMAS: And, Roddy?

EDMUND: I didn't see him.

DET. THOMAS: There was a blizzard last night, the worst to ever hit New York City, but, as far as we're able to ascertain only you and Miss Mascagni ever made it on to that roof. There was no trace of anyone else; except for her father.

EDMUND: But, the storm would have covered up anybody else's footprints.

DET. THOMAS: True. But, yours are the only footprints leading down from that top stairwell. Can you explain that?

EDMUND: Coach was there-

AGENT VOGEL: Edmund, are you acquainted with a Mr. Mitchell Soames?

EDMUND: He hangs out at the gym sometimes.

AGENT VOGEL: Mr. Soames is a very dangerous man. We know about your conversation at Jimmy's bar. Does Mr. Soames want you to meet with someone?

EDMUND: You tell me.

DET. THOMAS: No. You tell us.

AGENT VOGEL: Please, Edmund.

EDMUND: He wants me to meet his employer.

DET. THOMAS: Why?

EDMUND: I think he wants to teach me to manipulate the minds of other people. It was all pretty laughable.

DET. THOMAS: Mr. Soames is a manipulator.

EDMUND: He hinted at some kind of payoff. He was pretty vague.

DET. THOMAS: We'd like you to go to that meeting. It's tonight, isn't it?

EDMUND: Yes.

DET. THOMAS: Did Mr. Soames tell you his employer's name?

EDMUND: He didn't. But, I actually met her at the gym. Linda was there, too.

AGENT VOGEL: You saw her? She came to the gym?

EDMUND: She pushed her way in. I told her to get out.

AGENT VOGEL: Did she?

EDMUND: No. I was holding on to her property, I guess.

AGENT VOGEL: Her property? What in the world was that?

EDMUND: A spear.

AGENT VOGEL: My God!

DET. THOMAS: You gave her the spear?

EDMUND: Why not? I don't get it. That thing wasn't supposed to be in the gym in the first place.

AGENT VOGEL: You touched that spear? You held it?

EDMUND: Yes.

AGENT VOGEL: Did anything happen to you?

EDMUND: Nothing. It was an oversized javelin. She wanted it and I gave it to her. But-

AGENT VOGEL: But, what, Edmund?

EDMUND: It felt strange…like it was generating electricity. It was light as a feather.

DET. THOMAS: That was no ordinary spear, Edmund. It is, in fact, an allegedly very powerful weapon.

EDMUND: Looked more like a trophy to me.

AGENT VOGEL: You're not entirely wrong.

DET. THOMAS: Some people believe that that spear was used by Hitler to attain power.

EDMUND: What? I don't believe it.

DET. THOMAS: It was rumored that when he lost possession of it, his fall from sanity and power began. Many have tried locating that spear, but until now no one has succeeded. We suspected that Marlena had the spear, but we weren't certain.

AGENT VOGEL: That spear, Edmund, is supposed to be very ancient. It's said to date back to the time of Moses. It is said to have pierced the side of Christ.

EDMUND: I can't believe any of this. And, even if it were true, what does it really matter.

DET. THOMAS: It means that Marlena Lake may have been a traitor to her own Nazi party. She wants to recruit you to carry some crucial documents out of the country. These document contain the plans for an advanced atomic warhead and the triggering mechanism that Marlena and her cohorts plan to use against us and Great Britain. They've already assembled an atomic bomb and plan to drop it. We're pretty sure their target is Manhattan. We don't know when, but it's soon.

EDMUND: You want me to join her syndicate and get these documents for you?

AGENT VOGEL: We want you to find out more about Miss Lake and the spear and who else she's recruited: that is essential.

DET. THOMAS: And, the planned time for the attack on New York. If we know that much, we can at least put out the alarm.

EDMUND: This is obscene!

AGENT VOGEL: It's an obscenity that we've lived with for the past couple of years ever since the first failed attempt.

EDMUND: What attempt was that?

AGENT VOGEL: You must remember it, Edmund. It was in all the papers for weeks: a B-25 Army bomber crashed into the Empire State Building only weeks before the Japanese surrender: that was no accident.

DET. THOMAS: That plane rammed into the building because it was deliberately flying too low: it was on a direct trajectory over Fifth Avenue. A few documents were retrieved that hinted at an espionage network working here in Manhattan: a network that was to succeed Hitler if the Nazi movement failed in Europe.

AGENT VOGEL: Edmund, will you help us?

EDMUND: How? How can I?

AGENT VOGEL: Go to Marlena's, tonight. Ask questions about the spear: if you show an interest in Marlena's favorite subject, occultism, you'll win her over easily. If you can get into any other room of her apartment, have a good look around.

DET. THOMAS: And, don't be shy about helping yourself to any documents.

EDMUND: Would she be likely to keep them out in the open?

DET. THOMAS: She's a slob and she's arrogant. We hear she likes to hide things out in the open.

EDMUND: Like Sherlock Holmes would do.

AGENT VOGE: Exactly.

EDMUND: How much time do we have?

DET. THOMAS: Days…maybe.

EDMUND: Who was flying that B-25?

DET. THOMAS: The pilot was Lt. Col. William F. Smith; with him were two crew members; but we've reason to believe there was a fourth person on board that Billy Mitchell. Edmund, fourteen people were killed-

AGENT VOGEL *(interrupting)*: There was more to that incident than we can safely go into here.

EDMUND: Okay. I guess I break out my only suit for tonight's party.

DET. THOMAS: Good boy. I'll loan you one of my ties.

ACT TWO
Scene Two

December 28, 1947

MARLENA and MITCHELL are expecting guests to arrive at any moment.

MARLENA: It's nearly 9 o'clock. Do you think Edmund will show up? And, where is Roddy? He's late, as usual.

MITCHELL: I think Edmund is reliable. I'm certain that he'll be here.

MARLENA: Is he curious, as well?

MITCHELL: He tries to conceal it; but, I believe he's very curious and desperate.

MARLENA: Good. We need him and time is no longer on our side.

MITCHELL: I know. We must act quickly, but would failure be worse than not acting at all?

MARLENA: Let's not speak about failure. The time is set and the deadline must be met.

MITCHELL: You're starting to sound pretty desperate, yourself. I never thought I'd live to see the day. Your enemies would rejoice.

MARLENA: Indeed. I have many enemies, Mitchell.

MITCHELL: Marlena?

MARLENA: Yes?

MITCHELL: You have the documents: the design for the triggering mechanism.

MARLENA: Of course. You know this.

MITCHELL: It's just-

MARLENA: Frightening? Yes. It is frightening. That's a good word to use. I like it. Fear, Mitchell, is a most potent weapon. You want to ask another question?

MITCHELL: You knew Hitler, didn't you?

MARLENA: I was one of his advisors; although, my part was played out in the background.

MITCHELL: Lucky for you, that was.

MARLENA: At the time, I resented my unrecognized status; but, as you say, it was most fortunate.

MITCHELL: Was he obsessed with the occult? I've heard rumors about it.

MARLENA: Obsessed? Yes. I shared that obsession. I even reveled in it, at times.

MITCHELL: Were you very intimidated by him?

MARLENA: In his saner moments, I could influence him and even control him. But, those moments of sanity grew less and less. He became dangerous to us all. He became quite unstable and certain steps had to be taken.

MITCHELL: He was unstable? What steps-

MARLENA: I've said too much. Our guests will be arriving soon. Where is Roddy?

MITCHELL: But, Marlena, when will the plan be executed?

MARLENA: You are afraid, aren't you? Afraid that you will be left behind in this once impressive city.

MTICHELL: Frankly, yes. You're afraid, too. It is a terrifying prospect. Now, please, answer my question.

MARLENA: You're free to leave at any time.

MITCHELL: And suffer the consequences? Forget it. I'd sooner be left with the rest of them to be blown to kingdom come. When?

MARLENA: You're beginning to annoy me. Tomorrow. The plane will strike the skyscraper, the mechanism will be triggered and the city will be leveled. Nothing will remain standing. There will be few survivors.

MITCHELL: Tomorrow, you say? It can't be! The documents are still-

MARLENA: Here?

MITCHELL: Yes! (*The doorbell rings.*)

MARLENA: Get a grip. That was the doorbell. Answer it. We'll continue this discussion later. Now, get the door. Tell our guests that I'll be right out. Get the door! (*Exits.*)

MITCHELL: Of course. (*He brushes back his hair and takes a deep breath.*) Mr. Holderman, please come in. And, you've arrived promptly. You look very handsome in your suit. Nice tie. Marlena will join us presently. Make yourself comfortable. Please.

EDMUND: Thank you. I think there were a few more guests coming up the stairs.

MITCHELL: Excellent. May I get you a drink, Mr. Holderman?

EDMUND: Ginger-ale, please.

MITHCELL: Nothing in it?

EDMUND: I don't drink.

MITCHELL: The athlete in training, I dare say.

EDMUND: You could.

MITCHELL: Pardon me, please. Ah! The entire Millot family. Mr. Millot? Mrs. Millot? And, of course, your son, Dick. Dick, a friend of yours is here. Roddy? Come in, also. So many people at one time! You are late, Mr. Cervantes and Marlena is not pleased. Try to be more punctual. Jeanne, please come in. May I have a word with the two of you. Please, everyone, help yourselves at the drinks table. I must have a word with these two young people. (*Takes RODDY and JEANNE aside.*) Why weren't you here sooner? No excuses! I don't want to hear them! You don't have to listen to Marlena's rantings, but I do! Time is not to be taken for granted, not anymore. Apologize to her when she comes out and make it sincere.

JEANNE: Where is she? Don't tell me she wants to make an entrance?

RODDY: For whose friggin' benefit? And, why are all these people here? I thought this little get together was for Edmund? I don't like crowded rooms.

JEANNE: I love them: smoke-filled, crowded rooms are fun. And, everyone here looks intelligent enough, so the conversations should be pretty interesting.

MITCHELL: Smart girl. Come on, let's join the others.

MARLENA (*walking into the room*): Yes. Let's join them. And, Mr. Cervantes, I'll thank you not to question my guest list.

RODDY: Crowds make me a little uneasy.

MARLENA: Conquer that fear, Mr. Cervantes. My guest list is very selective. I do not gamble away my time. (*The guests drift into two groups: RITA, MICHAEL, DICK, RODDY, and MARLENA on stage left and EDMUND, JEANNE, MITCHELL on stage right but the conversations occasionally overlap.*)

MITCHELL: Mr. Holderman, are you looking for something?

EDMUND: No. Just admiring your apartment. Nice place you've got here, but a little cluttered.

MITCHELL: My room is over there. I keep it very neat. You would appreciate that.

EDMUND: Where are you from, Mr. Soames? I can't place your accent.

MITCHELL: I'm trying to get rid of my accent. I want to sound American.

EDMUND: Good for you.

JEANNE: I like accents. I find them very sexy and intriguing.

EDMUND: Even my Brooklyn accent?

JEANNE: Especially your Brooklyn accent. I like you, Edmund. You're an honest-to-goodness man and I appreciate that.

MITCHELL: You see, Mr. Holderman? You're building a fan club. I hope we're not embarrassing you.

EDMUND: Not at all. Jeanne? Are you from the Midwest?

JEANNE: Milwaukee. I grew up there, and worked my way to New York. It's sort of a dream come true for me. I love it here. And, I'll bet I've seen more sights than you have.

EDMUND: You probably have. Maybe, you'll take me to the top of the Empire State Building sometime. I hear the view is pretty spectacular.

JEANNE: Why there? You'll just run into a lot of tourists. I prefer the off beat spots. I'm very unconventional.

EDMUND: I'm not. I like the simple pleasures in life. I guess you'd find me pretty square and boring.

JEANNE: That I don't believe.

MITCHELL: Mr. Holderman is too busy to do any sightseeing. His bodybuilding is his life and must take up all of his time. I respect you very much for that. And, I don't know what you mean by "square." You're a very fascinating man. I like you.

JEANNE: So do I.

EDMUND: My work-outs are pretty time consuming. And, thank you for the compliment: the both of you.

MITCHELL: Don't mention it. (*The spotlight shifts to stage left.*)

RITA: My son tells me that you're a world traveller, Miss Lake. I'd imagine that your travels have been pretty limited lately with the war and all.

MARLENA: Not entirely. I was in Europe when the main conflict broke out.

RITA: What part of Europe?

MARLENA: Germany, Mrs. Millot.

RITA: That must have been interesting; was it?

MARLENA: Immensely. I never talk about it.

RITA: Why not?

MARLENA: Your questions are very direct. It's a pity that it's none of your business.

RITA: Something to hide?

MARLENA: Don't make the mistake of insulting me, Mrs. Millot.

RITA: Is that a threat?

MARLENA: A rather pointed warning.

MICHAEL: You must forgive my wife's curiosity; but, you are a rather interesting woman.

MARLENA: And, Mr. Millot, is your curiosity not also piqued?

MICHAEL: You put me in a difficult position, Miss Lake. When I am someone's guest, I keep the conversation to pleasantries. I go to parties for pleasure.

MARLENA: As do I. I attend and give parties for entertainment purposes only.

RITA: I don't believe that, Miss Lake. I think we're all here tonight for a purpose. I'd be disappointed if we weren't. (*Leaning forward in her chair.*) Are you a Nazi, Miss Lake?

MARLENA: I beg your pardon?

DICK: I'm actually glad my mother brought up the topic of Nazism: the Third Reich. I wouldn't be too quick to toss out some of their ideas. If that offends anyone, I'm not particularly sorry.

MICHAEL: What exactly is my son saying?

DICK: I'll tell you what I'm saying, Dad. The Third Reich had its points and we might do well to extract a few things from their philosophy.

MICHAEL: My God!

DICK: Don't be shocked. I'm not even asking you to be open-minded. Just look at their philosophy with a critical eye. (*The spotlight extends to stage right.*)

EDMUND: Some would say their philosophy was perverted.

DICK: But, its sources weren't.

MICHAEL: Ah! You mean Nietszche. Of course: the super man who is above good and evil: thus spoke their god of annihilation.

DICK: I'm impressed, Dad. Truly. Man is a self made god if he has the intellect to carry through with his moral convictions. And, don't confuse morality with good and evil.

EDMUND: You'll have to explain that one, Dick.

DICK: If a man is weak or if he refuses assimilation, he is dangerous: an outlaw. He has only one fate: elimination.

EDMUND: Meaning the Jews?

DICK: I won't deny it. But, not just the Jews. Let's be honest: races don't mix. They never were meant to. A purity of heritage should be a country's national anthem.

JEANNE: If there were another Reich, would it be called the Fourth Reich? I'm serious.

MICHAEL: So is my son, I'm afraid.

MARLENA: Don't judge him too harshly, Mr. Millot. His ideas may sound radical, but they are not without substance.

JEANNE: Would somebody please answer my question?

MARLENA: Yes, my dear, it would be the Fourth Reich. The Fourth Reich, that is, if we are successful.

EDMUND: "We?"

MITCHELL: Do not interrupt our hostess.

EDMUND: I'm asking a question, pal.

MITCHELL: I didn't mean to be so abrupt. You'll forgive me.

MARLENA: Success will procure for us what is rightfully ours to possess: power.

EDMUND: And, what exactly is power?

MARLENA: Order and discipline. A unity of mankind and not a so-called melting pot of civilization. There will be no god and no religion. A man's sole reliance will be on his comrades and the State. Worship will be replaced by duty.

MICHAEL: Miss Lake, you sound very much like a Nazi. I'm only a guest in your home; but, I reserve the right to absent myself from this company.

RODDY: Mr. Millot, I was in the Nazi Party right here in New York City. My Party card is still in my wallet.

MICHAEL: Roddy, I'd no idea. I don't mean to judge you, but-

RODDY: Mr. Millot, I'm still Dick's friend. And, would it help my reputation any if I told you that circumstance forced it on me? It did.

MICHAEL: And, now, Roddy? Does "circumstance" still force it on you?

RODDY: Yes. Yes, Mr. Millot, it does.

MICHAEL: I don't believe you.

RODDY: I'm sorry.

MICHAEL: So am I. I've lost all respect for you. Edmund, what about you?

EDMUND: I'm a little out of my depth here, Mr. Millot. And, this is news from left field.

DICK: Come on, Dad, Roddy's still my friend. His belief system is different from yours, that's all.

MICHAEL: No. His entire philosophy is obscene! Terrible. Terrible.

JEANNE: Mr. Millot, you're upset.

RITA: My husband takes his politics too seriously. I like you, Roddy.

MARLENA: To get back to the main topic: order and discipline in a chaotic world where the ruled seek to be the rulers and to dominate. This can never be permitted. If those who were once ruled were to be given any measure of power, they would exceed their former masters in cruelty and put forward a chord of distortion.

RITA: Miss Lake, are you trying to convert us?

RODDY: Does she need to?

MITCHELL: The concept of fascism has always fascinated me.

MARLENA: A person must willingly change.

MICHAEL: Your former Chancellor would have disagreed with you on that vital point. His methods were pretty dramatic!

MARLENA: I disagreed with my Chancellor methods; but, many of the Party's principles were sound enough.

MICHAEL: I think I've had enough of this.

RITA: The Fourth Reich…interesting.

MITCHELL: Perhaps, you would like to join?

RITA: I'd be open to it. I'm only half-joking.

MICHAEL: That's what upsets me. You don't know what you're saying. I fought against fascism in the war.

MARLENA: Mr. Millot, you look at me strangely. I have offended you. But, let me say this: I applaud your fight because the methods and the executions had to be stopped. It was madness.

EDMUND: What are your methods, Miss Lake?

MARLENA: My own methods would be termed cruel, but humane, in their own way.

MICHAEL: Do you actually believe that, Miss Lake?

EDMUND: Would purity of race be an ideal of yours?

MARLENA: I would not deny it.

DICK: People will always gravitate towards their own kind and that's just the way it is. Races don't share the same ideas. People like to share their ideas with like-minded people. It's called progress -- civilization. It's preserving a quality of life: a good quality of life.

EDMUND: Miss Lake, you came to the gym the other night to fetch a pretty curious object, something you referred to as a sacred object. Are you an occultist?

MARLENA (*smiling almost coquettishly*): I dabble.

EDMUND: That spear: was it the spear of Longinus? If it was, that's a pretty powerful occult symbol you've got. I'm told that it pierced the side of Christ.

MARLENA: You're well informed, Edmund. Its history goes even further back than that event. It is said that it was used by Moses to combat Pharaoh. It is said to possess powers that are undreamt of by man!

EDMUND: You're pretty cavalier about where you leave it.

MARLENA: It was there for a purpose, I can assure you.

EDMUND: Did Hitler have it during the war? I have heard rumors.

MARLENA: He did. And, I will anticipate your next question: it was taken from him.

EDMUND: His descent from power came pretty fast. And, the Nazis were defeated.

MARLENA: Were they, Mr. Holderman?

EDMUND: Weren't they, Miss Lake?

MARLENA: No. They were not. The work goes forward until the end of the world.

EDMUND: Until the end of the world? My dad once told me that evil never dies.

MARLENA: I like your statements and the fact that you do not ask the obvious questions.

EDMUND: I say what needs to be said. The meanings usually speak for themselves.

MARLENA: Well said, young man. Mitchell did well to invite you.

MICHAEL: Well, Miss Lake, I think I'll say my goodbyes.

MARLENA: But, Mr. Millot, it's still early. You mustn't leave.

MICHAEL: It's late. And, you may want to discuss your plans without a dissenter in the room

MARLENA: I understand. Your decision is made, then?

MICHAEL: Oh, yes, Miss Lake. My decision is made.

RITA: I'll be in touch. Goodnight, everybody. (*She and MICHAEL exit.*)

JEANNE: I like Mr. Millot. He's got guts. Well, now what?

MARLENA: I've no idea what you mean, my dear.

JEANNE: Oh, come off it, Marlena! I didn't come here tonight just to debate politics in this freezing apartment.

MARLENA: Shall I turn up the heat for you?

JEANNE: Go to hell!

RODDY: Easy, girl. I think Marlena might be even more upset than you. One bird just flew the nest.

JEANNE: I doubt it.

MARLENA: Jeanne, dear, you're cold and tired and ill tempered, why don't you and Mr. Cervantes go home?

JEANNE: What?

MARLENA: I'll send for you when I need you. And, of course, you will make yourselves available. (*JEANNE is about to answer, but RODDY cuts her off.*)

RODDY: We are kind of tired. And, Marlena, sorry I was late tonight.

MARLENA: I don't forgive bad manners. Goodnight. (*RODDY and JEANNE exit.*)

EDMUND: Would you like me to leave, Miss Lake?

MARLENA: No, Edmund. Can you spare us some time?

EDMUND: That's what I'm here for.

MARLENA: I do like your responses. A man of a few and carefully chosen words. Mitchell, fix Edmund a drink.

MITCHELL: Mr. Holderman doesn't drink. I've already offered him one.

EDMUND: He's right, Miss Lake, I don't drink.

DICK: Maybe, I should leave.

MARLENA: No. Stay. I want to talk to you. It's important. Edmund, I will be direct with my questions: will you join us?

EDMUND: I don't know who "us" is. But, you, Miss Lake, sound very interesting. I'd like to come back if I'm invited.

MARLENA: Excellent. You will be invited back, but unfortunately not to this flat. My address will soon change. My next question: would you be willing to relocate at a moment's notice?

EDMUND: I have very few ties here and every major city has a gym. Traveling wouldn't be too much of a hardship.

MARLENA: If I were to ask you to relocate within twenty-four hours, would that be a hardship?

EDMUND: Inconvenient, maybe, but why not?

MARLENA: I have only just met you, Edmund, and, therefore, I cannot be liberal with my trust; but tonight was a satisfactory beginning. Mitchell will be in touch with you first thing in the morning. Start packing, tonight. Can you be reached by phone?

EDMUND: My uncle has a phone. I live in his house. Here's his telephone number.

MARLENA: Good. Be at your uncle's house tomorrow morning. The phone call from Mr. Soames will come early. He will tell you where to go and by what means to get there.

EDMUND: This is embarrassing, Miss Lake, but-

MARLENA: Of course. (*She reaches into her oversized pocketbook.*) Here is some money for both traveling expenses and to help you find a suitable lodging until you are contacted.

EDMUND: One hundred dollars. I've never had so much money on me before.

MARLENA: Edmund, if you live up to my expectations, you will have so much more that you will wonder how you ever managed without it. Goodnight. Get home safely. I look forward to more discussions on the occult.

EDMUND: Goodnight. Dick? Mr. Soames? Goodnight.

MITCHELL: Oh, goodnight! (*EDMUND exits.*)

DICK: I'm glad he's gone. Now, what about the plans for the triggering device? Who's gonna' deliver them?

MARLENA: You don't waste any time.

DICK: I thought we didn't have any time to waste.

MARLENA: Mitchell will have to deliver them. We made contact with Edmund too late. He's yet to prove himself.

MITCHELL: That's too bad. But, I think your faith in him will be justified. The all-American boy: it's perfect.

MARLENA: If he proves trustworthy.

MITCHELL: I'm sure he will. A fine specimen.

MARLENA: You're quite taken with him.

MITCHELL: I don't know what you mean by that.

MARLENA: Never mind.

DICK: Where will the plans be delivered to? Not Germany. By the way, where did you get them? From here in America?

MARLENA: You ask too many questions.

MITCHELL: What Marlena is saying, Dick, is that tonight's events complicate matters. The garment has unraveled and the loose threads must be shorn off neatly.

MARLENA: Your father was very hostile. I don't like that. I don't like him.

DICK: He'll be okay. You'll see.

MARLENA: He's a principled man.

DICK: He's my dad.

MARLENA: And a potential danger to us.

DICK: I don't understand.

MARLENA: Don't you? When it comes time to make our "point?," shall we say, he could take it into his head to expose us.

DICK: He wouldn't do that.

MARLENA: He would. He is a weak, but honest man. I despise the type.

DICK: My dad isn't weak.

MARLENA: You admire him. Good. Then, when you've completed your task, you will be held in more esteem by us.

DICK: I'm tired. Can we talk about this another time?

MARLENA: No. Once the plans have been delivered the completion of more lethal devices will be relatively easy.

DICK: You don't mean to say-

MARLENA: New York City will be destroyed. Ours is no mere threat, you fool! The atomic device will be detonated. The plane will strike the Empire State building straight on.

DICK: When?

MARLENA: Tomorrow. But, before that day, you must kill your father and Edmund!

DICK: Edmund? But, just now-

MARLENA: I am no fool. I look into people's souls. I hear what they say, but their thoughts speak the truth. Edmund is as principled as your father, but unlike your father, he is no weakling. He spoke guardedly, tonight. Guardedly. He thought to deceive me? More fool him! And, for that I want him dead.

MITCHELL: But, Marlena, I think you're wrong about him.

MARLENA: You're infatuated with him. Find yourself another pretty face to fall in love with.

MITCHELL: I don't like when you speak to me that way.

DICK: I can't do it. Maybe Edmund- no not even him. He's my friend. I can't go through with this. It was kind of fun, but-

MARLENA: You must kill your father.

DICK: Okay…maybe…maybe, I can do it.

MARLENA: Are you certain?

DICK: I guess.

MARLENA: I don't believe you.

DICK: I better go.

MARLENA: Wait. Here's your weapon. Take it. Do you know how to use a handgun? Here. It's already loaded: just snap it in place like this.

DICK: (*moves toward the door, but MITCHELL shoves him forward*): No! Please! Daddy, help me! (*MARLENA shoots him in the chest. He staggers back and falls to the floor. Black out.*)

ACT THREE
Scene One

December 29, 1947

EDMUND is sitting at the bar.

JEANNE: Edmund? I didn't expect to find you here. Are you okay? You don't look so hot.

EDMUND: Oh? Jeanne. I didn't see you come in. I was on the phone just now with my uncle. The cops were over at his place looking for me.

JEANNE: Looking for you? Why? Was it about Linda's murder?

EDMUND: No. It was about Dick's murder.

JEANNE: What? Are you serious?

EDMUND: He'd been shot. The cops wouldn't say anymore. They wanted to know where I was and where I'd been last night.

JEANNE: I wouldn't worry about it. They're probably looking for all of Dick's friends. And, you were with me and Roddy last night.

EDMUND: You don't think Marlena is mixed up in this, do you?

JEANNE: Do you?

EDMUND: Yes.

JEANNE: Why, Edmund? Level with me. I mean it. If the cops are after you, I might be able to help.

EDMUND: How's that?

JEANNE: Talk.

EDMUND: Marlena gave me a lot of money last night before I left and told me to be ready to leave on a moment's notice. I packed a bag just for-

JEANNE: Go on.

EDMUMD: If you look at it one way, the way the cops are going to look at it, it's pretty incriminating: like I'm ready to skip town.

JEANNE: I wouldn't put it past her. She's a rotten double-crossing bitch, but she's smart. Look, here's Roddy. Roddy, over here.

RODDY: Hey, Ed, no work-out today? You're gonna' get soft, man.

JEANNE: That's enough of that.

RODDY: I just came from the gym. The cops are there looking through all the lockers. You got something to hide, Ed?

JEANNE: Just shut your mouth, Roddy. Dick was killed last night and they might try to pin it on Edmund. Marlena must have set him up. Just wait until I see that-

RODDY: Easy, girl.

JEANNE: We have to get Edmund out of town. We have to get ourselves out of town. Pronto!

RODDY: Cool it.

EDMUND: Jeanne, don't get involved in this. The police will probably be here soon enough and I've got enough on my mind as it is. I don't want to have to worry about you. Man, I feel like I'm on a one way elevator ride into Hell. First it was Linda and now Dick. Who's next?

JEANNE: Edmund, let me help. I have such respect for you, and that's something very new to me. I want to help. I like you an awful lot.

RODDY: That was pretty poetic.

EDMUND: Roddy, what did the cops say to you?

RODDY: Nothing. I ducked out. But, that detective what's-his-name was there and so was that agent dame.

EDMUMD: Let them come for me. I've nothing to hide.

JEANNE: It's not that simple, Edmund. If Marlena set you up, she probably did a thorough job of it. You can count on that. Roddy, don't your parents have a place out on Long Island?

RODDY: We could go there, but-

JEANNE: All we need is one day, just one day, and tomorrow everything will be different. No one will give a damn about Dick Millot.

RODDY: We'll be in it up to our necks.

JEANNE: We're in it up to our necks now. We've got to see it through.

EDMUND: You two are losing me on this.

JEANNE: Do you have any money on you?

EDMUND: Marlena's money.

JEANNE: Good. We'll use it to get out of town. She's gone too far this time. I won't have it!

EDMUND: Jeanne, I can't let you and Roddy do this. I'm heading back to the gym. I'm not running away. I appreciate all that you're trying to do. Really. You're okay, Jeanne.

JEANNE: No! Let me help you, Edmund. I want to.

RODDY: Maybe, I'm not needed here?

JEANNE: Don't be an ass. Stay. (*Turning back to EDMUND.*) Edmund, trust me. If Marlena is behind this, I'll set it right.

EDMUND: I think that only I can do that. I've got to stand my ground and face this. I think Detective Thomas and Miss Vogel are pretty decent people.

JEANNE: They stink! They're cops, aren't they? I hate all cops.

RODDY: Uh-oh. Here come two of them, now. Maybe, we should let Edmund do a solo on this?

JEANNE: Coward. Slip out the back if you want to. I'm staying.

RODDY: Don't call me a coward. I mean it! Take it back!

JEANNE: Make me. (*DET. THOMAS and AGENT VOGEL walk in.*)

EDMUND: Yes. My name is Edmund Holderman. And, I did not kill Dick Millot. My uncle gave me a heads up.

DET. THOMAS: You'll have to come with us for questioning, Edmund. I'm sorry.

JEANNE: Are you arresting him?

DET. THOMAS: Miss Mantee?

JEANNE: He doesn't have to say anything.

DET. THOMAS: I'd advise you, Miss Mantee, not to say anything.

JEANNE: I hate all you dirty cops.

AGENT VOGEL: You're not helping your friend any.

JEANNE: And, you are? Edmund didn't kill anyone. You know that as well as I do.

AGENT VOGEL: Maybe, we do. But, we have to do our job. Dick Millot was brutally murdered last night and we have to find his killer. We've already found the murder weapon.

JEANNE: It wasn't Edmund.

DET. THOMAS: Then, who was it, Jeanne?

JEANNE: I don't know.

DET. THOMAS: Roddy?

RODDY: Don't look at me, man. I'm innocent.

DET. THOMAS: Edmund? Come along, will you?

EDMUND: I'd like to call my uncle. He'll be worried.

DET. THOMAS: You can do that at the station house.

JEANNE (*in a panic stricken voice*): Then, you are arresting him. He was with me last night.

DET. THOMAS: Are you ready to sign a statement to that effect?

JEANNE: Yes.

EDMUND: Jeanne, stay out of this. Okay, detective, do your stuff.

JEANNE: No! Roddy, do something.

RODDY: Who? Me?

JEANNE: No. The man in the moon, you idiot!

RODDY: Watch your mouth. Hey, here comes Coach. He looks friggin' mad.

COACH (*storming in with clenched fists*): Just what the hell is going on here? You're not arresting Edmund, are you? You're an idiot, Detective and, you, too, lady.

AGENT VOGEL: Take it easy, Mr. Mascagni. You can come with us, if you like.

COACH: You're not going to push my boy around. Forget it!

EDMUND: Detective Thomas? Agent Vogel? I honestly don't know anything about Dick's death. Until last night, I thought he was a pretty decent kid. I didn't know about his politics. His dad was more upset about that than I was. He was young and hot headed, but he was my friend. He was Roddy's friend, too.

RODDY: Oh, yeah, I liked Dick.

DET. THOMAS: Edmund? Let's go.

ACT THREE
Scene Two

December 29, 1947

MARLENA is on the phone.

MARLENA: What are you saying? You can't be serious.

VOICE: You are to be left behind.

MARLENA: I'm to be left behind? No. You can't. You need me.

VOICE: Your part has been played out.

MARLENA: What do you mean my part is played out? I'll tell! I'm begging- how do you know about that? Yes. Yes. I understand. My duty, of course. Very well. I- I won't attempt to flee. Yes. Of course. I can take precautions. I'll hide in the cellar. No. No! I'm not afraid anymore. I've conquered my fear! Hello? (*Frantically, she starts throwing things haphazardly into a suitcase.*)

MITCHELL (*enters*): Marlena, what is it? You look pale.

MARLENA: It's nothing.

MITCHELL: That was him on the phone just now, wasn't it?

MARLENA: I must sit down. I have to think while there's still time.

MITCHELL: You're upset. Can I get you a drink?

MARLENA: A double. Thank you. (*She gulps down her drink.*) Better. I must make my own plans, then. They can't push me around like this.

MITCHELL: Careful what you say.

MARLENA: You're right. First things first: I must get you off. Take the bus to the airport. If it were prudent, I'd have that briefcase handcuffed to your wrist.

MITCHELL: Don't worry, it will never leave my side.

MARLENA: Do you have everything you'll need? Passport? Visa papers? Forged I.D.?

MITCHELL: Of course. And, don't worry; it's not your style.

MARLENA: Time has almost run out. It was sheer good fortune that we intercepted that busload of German scientists who were being transported to God only knows where behind the Russian lines.

MITCHELL: And how grateful they were!

MARLENA (*laughing*): They were for a few minutes! These papers will confirm the plans for more powerful weapons and a triggering mechanism that is simplicity itself.

MTICHELL: It takes your breath away, rather.

MARLENA: Doesn't it, just? And with suspicion diverted from us, we will be free to move about in this country.

MITCHELL: Are you ready to leave, Marlena? There's only a few hours left and you must be safely away.

MARLENA: I've some business to attend to here. Our so-called "cohorts" will be informed that the schedule has been "delayed?"

MITCHELL: I see...

MARLENA: They're too young and unstable. One of those loose threads that needs to be cut. You see, Mitchell, I'm quoting you. Well, you better be off. Good luck- (*A knock at the door.*)

MITCHELL: Who can that be? Not the police, surely?

MARLENA: You better go into the bedroom. Quick! I don't want you seen with that briefcase. Here! Take my gun.

MITCHELL: Get rid of them.

MARLENA (*opens the door to RITA*): Mrs. Millot, I'm afraid that I can't spare you very much time.

RITA: I won't take up much of your time, Miss Lake. What do you know of my son's murder?

MARLENA: Nothing, Mrs. Millot.

RITA: I don't believe you.

MARLENA: That surprises me. Truly. I would have expected your husband to be here. His accusastions would have been veiled with courtesy, at least.

RITA: He was my son.

MARLENA: Your tone has traces of guilt. You never cared a damn for your son.

RITA: He was in your employ and involved with you and your covert organization. Don't deny it. I know I ask too many question and- and I eavesdrop. How very uncivilized of me.

MARLENA: Would you care to join my little group?

RITA: I thought-

MARLENA: Yes, Mrs. Millot?

RITA: I was so sure last night…

MARLENA: What's altered your decision? Grief?

RITA: Maybe.

MARLENA: Or fear? You should fear me, you know. If I have my way, very little will remain in this city.

RITA: What are you saying?

MARLENA: I've said too much. It's time for you to leave.

RITA: I need time to think.

MARLENA: You disappoint me.

RITA: To commit a crime is one thing…even to betray a trust, but-

MARLENA: Murder is an expedient: a rather brutal one, but an expedient none-the-less. I do not justify my methods. I exploit them. I believe you were on your way out?

RITA: You murdered my son.

MARLENA: You're beginning to bore me, Mrs. Millot.

RITA: You murdered Dick.

MARLENA: How very tiresome. Please, leave.

RITA: When- when will it happen?

MARLENA: I beg your pardon?

RITA: The end?

MARLENA: Perhaps, what happened to your son was a mercy?

RITA: What's to stop me from going to the police?

MARLENA: That would be a very grave mistake, my dear. Listen to me: keep silent and you may still save yourself. You can prove nothing because all you've been privy to is talk that is vague at best. You have no real knowledge or proof. But, if you were to voice your suspicions, we would know it, Mrs. Millot. Do you understand what it is I am telling you? Answer me.

RITA: Yes. Perfectly.

MARLENA: You're an intelligent woman, so don't act like the fool. You've overstayed your welcome.

RITA: Edmund's been arrested.

MARLENA: How dreadful for him.

RITA: I don't understand-

MARLENA: Enough! Must I be more insistent, Mrs. Millot?

RITA: I'm going.

MARLENA: And, I suggest you go straight home and start acting the part of the bereaved parent. (*Exit RITA. MITCHELL is about to come out, but there is another knock on the door. She signals MITCHELL back into the bedroom.*)

DET. THOMAS: Miss Marlena Lake?

MARLENA: Oh! You startled me. May I help you.

DET. THOMAS: Detective Christian Thomas. My partner, Tracy Vogel.

AGENT VOGEL: Miss Lake?

DET. THOMAS: Miss Lake, going somewhere?

MARLENA: Why no, Detective. Of course not. What makes you ask?

DET. THOMAS: A nylon is sticking out of your suitcase.

AGENT VOGEL: May I have a glass of water, Miss Lake?

MARLENA: Help yourself. The kitchen is right off the corridor.

AGENT VOGEL: Thank you.

MARLENA: No! Not that door, Miss Vogel. The one to your right.

AGENT VOGEL: Sorry. (*Exits.*)

DET. THOMAS: Miss Lake, that nylon is still sticking out of your suitcase.

MARLENA: How careless of me. I'm simply taking some clothes out to be cleaned.

DET. THOMAS: I need to have a few words with you. It won't take long.

MARLENA: I am somewhat pressed for time, Detective Thomas.

DET. THOMAS: You don't plan on leaving town, do you?

MARLENA: What's it to you?

DET. THOMAS: You won't get far.

MARLENA: What the hell does that mean? And, get out of my way.

DET. THOMAS: Sit down. Now.

MARLENA: Get on with it. I've got things to do.

DET. THOMAS: Where were you last night, Miss Lake-

MARLENA: Here. If it's any of your damned business.

DET. THOMAS: I'll finish the question. Between the hours of 9 P.M. and 1 A.M. Think carefully. Did you ever leave your apartment last night?

MARLENA: No, Detective. I didn't.

DET. THOMAS: Were you alone for those few hours?

MARLENA: I had guests and, of course, my boarder, Mr. Soames, was here.

DET. THOMAS: Who else?

MARLENA: Mr. and Mrs. Michael Millot. Young people: Jeanne Mantee, Roddy Cervantes, and Edmund Holderman.

DET. THOMAS: An interesting group of people.

MARLENA: It was an interesting party.

DET. THOMAS: Who left first and when?

MARLENA: I believe Mr. and Mrs. Millot left around ten-thirty: that's not a precise time.

DET. THOMAS: And, the others?

MARLENA: It's difficult to remember.

DET. THOMAS: Try.

MARLENA: Jeanne and Roddy left shortly afterward. Yes.

DET. THOMAS: Go on.

MARLENA: I believe that Mr. Holderman, Mr. Soames, young Millot, and myself had a bit of a tête-à-tête.

DET. THOMAS: And, the next guest to leave?

MARLENA: Mr. Holderman.

DET. THOMAS: Which leaves Dick Millot alone with you and Mr. Soames. By the way, where is Mr. Soames?

AGENT VOGEL (*entering the room*): He wouldn't be hiding in that room on the left; would he, Miss Lake?

MARLENA: Just who the hell are you, lady?

AGENT VOGEL: I'm with the Immigrations Dept. And, we've reason to believe that you've been harboring an illegal alien. Have you?

MARLENA: I don't know what you mean, Miss Vogel. An illegal alien, you say? I'm at a loss.

AGENT VOGEL: Is he here, Miss Lake?

MARLENA: No.

AGENT VOGEL: May I have a look around?

MARLENA: Got a search warrant?

AGENT VOGEL: Yes.

MARLENA: I see. Well, then, I can't stop you, can I?

AGENT VOGEL: It would look very bad for you if you tried.

DET. THOMAS (*signaling to hold off*): Did Dick Millot leave by himself?

MARLENA: Yes.

DET. THOMAS: Why was that, Miss Lake?

MARLENA: You'll have to ask young Millot.

DET. THOMAS: Impossible. We found his murdered body in an alleyway not far from your place.

MARLENA: He was assaulted?

DET. THOMAS: Murdered.

MARLENA: By whom?

DET. THOMAS: Don't you know?

MARLENA: I do not.

DET. THOMAS: What was the reason for this party of yours?

MARLENA: Need there be a reason? Entertainment.

DET. THOMAS: Entertainment?

MARLENA: Unfamiliar with the term, Detective?

DET. THOMAS: Young people and older people mixing? Unusual. That doesn't happen very often.

MARLENA: I have many young friends. I enjoy their company.

DET. THOMAS: Was it a party, Miss Lake, or a meeting?

AGENT VOGEL: Was it for reasons of recruitment?

MARLENA: I don't follow any of this.

DET. THOMAS: I want to know why Dick Millot stayed on after all your other guests had left. Why, Miss Lake?

MARLENA: He had his reasons. If you must know, Detective, young Millot was a bit tight. He stayed for another drink and, then, I sent him on his way.

AGENT VOGEL: Was that very wise?

MARLENA: I am not his keeper.

DET. THOMAS: And, that left you by yourself?

MARLENA: Mr. Soames was with me. We cleaned up and, then, retired for the evening.

DET. THOMAS: How did you sleep?

MARLENA: I am a very light sleeper.

AGENT VOGEL: What was discussed at your party? Was there a general theme?

MARLENA: General theme, Miss Vogel? Not that I recall. Party talk.

AGENT VOGEL: Party talk?

MARLENA: Yes.

DET. THOMAS: Nothing of a political nature?

MARLENA: What exactly are you driving at?

DET. THOMAS: Are you well versed in politics, Miss Lake?

AGENT VOGEL: And, the occult?

MARLENA: So…you've had me investigated.

DET. THOMAS: What was discussed last night?

MARLENA: This dreadful weather: the blizzard. Really, Detective, why not come to the point?

DET. THOMAS: What do you know of Dick Millot's murder?

MARLENA: Nothing.

DET. THOMAS: Did you order it?

AGENT VOGEL: And, why?

MARLENA: How dare you? That's slander.

DET. THOMAS: It's a question.

MARLENA: Get out!

AGENT VOGEL: In a minute, Miss Lake. We'd like a look around first. Do you mind?

MARLENA: Drop dead, lady.

DET. THOMAS: Tracy, check out that bedroom.

MARLENA: No.

DET. THOMAS: Miss Lake?

MARLENA: Mr. Soames, please come out. These people have some questions for you.

DET. THOMAS: Tracy, get to the door!

MARLENA: Soames, they're armed! (*MITCHELL bursts out of the room knocking AGENT VOGEL to the floor. She recovers and draws her gun. MITCHELL stops and looks to MARLENA.*

DET. THOMAS sees this and draws his gun as MARLENA grabs for the light switch and plunges them into darkness. A shot is fired and, then, another shot. MITCHELL runs back into the bedroom and down the fire escape with DET. THOMAS in pursuit. MARLENA runs out the door. AGENT VOGEL fires a shot into the hallway.)

ACT THREE
Scene Three

December 29, 1947

The lights are flicked on by DET. THOMAS in Jimmy's bar. EDMUND and AGENT VOGEL follow him in.

DET. THOMAS: Edmund, sit down. We don't have much time and I've got a couple of questions for you. Did you kill Dick Millot?

EDMUND: No.

DET. THOMAS: Did you attempt to shoot Michael Millot?

EDMUND: No.

DET. THOMAS: I believe you; but, that's not going to be good enough. The circumstantial evidence against you is pretty steep.

EDMUND: Soames planted that gun in my locker.

DET. THOMAS: I'm sure he did,

EDMUND: And, what about that film? I've been thinking a lot about that. Is Coach involved in all this?

DET. THOMAS: Yes, Edmund, he is.

EDMUND: What are you saying: that he's some kind of a traitor?

DET. THOMAS: I'm saying that your line of thinking is correct; but, I can't say more than that right now.

EDMUND: Coach warned me that night of the blizzard not to trust anyone. I didn't know what he meant at the time, but I guess he was talking about himself. Not to trust him.

DET. THOMAS: Good advice, that was.

AGENT VOGEL: Tell us what happened last night at Marlena's, Edmund.

EDMUND: They wanted to involve me. She gave me money and said I was to leave town at a moment's notice. I think she meant sometime today.

DET. THOMAS: Do you know why?

EDMUND: Something horrible is supposed to happen today.

DET. THOMAS: Yes. Horrible. Mass genocide. What else went on last night?

EDMUND: Roddy and Jeanne are mixed up in it and so was Dick.

DET. THOMAS: We know that. That's probably why young Millot was killed. So, Marlena told you to be ready to leave and, then, she proceeds to frame you.

AGENT VOGEL: We made the mistake of underestimating her.

DET. THOMAS: We picked up Miss Lake and her henchman, Mr. Soames.

AGENT VOGEL: Edmund, it was Marlena who killed Dick Millot. We're positive of that. Christian, we haven't much time.

DET. THOMAS: You'd better go and fetch our two playmates.

AGENT VOGEL: I'll bring them in. (*Exits.*)

EDMUND: Why are you so sure that I'm innocent?

DET. THOMAS: I study character and integrity. You have both, Edmund. But, I have to find out the reason for the attempted murder at the gymnasium, and Miss Mascagni's involvement, and young Millot's murder. Blinds, all of them. A cover-up for what's to happen tonight.

EDMUND: Why not ask Marlena? Or Soames? He'll talk.

DET. THOMAS: He talked all right. But both he and Marlena are pawns themselves. They're being controlled.

EDMUND: Maybe, it's all a cover up for the end of the world.

DET. THOMAS: What made you say that?

EDMUND: It was something Marlena said.

DET. THOMAS: That film we confiscated told us something: someone went to a lot of trouble making a mask that was meant to resemble you.

EDMUND: That's what Linda thought.

DET. THOMAS: But, who was the man behind the mask? Did Linda have any idea?

EDMUND: I don't think she did. She would have told me.

DET. THOMAS: In a about one minute, guests are coming and I've got a surprise for them and you. Let me tell you this much: tonight we intend to break up the most dangerous spy ring we've ever come up against. Pray for the nine million people in this city. (*He signals for AGENT VOGEL to bring the "guests" into the bar. Enter RODDY, JEANNE, MICHAEL, RITA and COACH. AGENT VOGEL waits by the door keeping an eye, and her gun, on MARLENA and MITCHELL.*) Would everyone have a seat? I won't take much of your time because there isn't much time left; isn't that right, Roddy? Jeanne?

RODDY: What's this all about? You had one of your men pick us up at the Long Island Railroad. We just missed our train.

DET. THOMAS: Catch a later one.

RODDY: My parents are expecting us. They'll worry.

DET. THOMAS: Catch the train after midnight.

RODDY: We-

DET. THOMAS: Yes?

RODDY: Never mind. (*Catches sight of EDMUND.*) Ed, they let you out, man.

EDMUND: You could say that. Let's listen to Detective Thomas.

DET. THOMAS: A young boy was killed last night: brutally murdered. He was shot at point blank range and, then, dumped like so much trash into the gutter. We know who committed this crime: Marlena Lake and her associate, Mr. Mitchell Soames. Tracy, would you bring in those two, please? (*Enter MARLENA and MITHCELL.*)

AGENT VOGEL: Have a seat, Miss Lake.

MARLENA: Thank you, no. I must leave. I've business to attend to in Hoboken: it's most urgent that I be there tonight.

DET. THOMAS: You sound a little frightened, Miss Lake.

MARLENA: Merely rushed for time, Detective. Oh, Mr. Holderman.

EDMUND: Miss Lake? A little surprised to see your patsy?

MARLENA: I-

EDMUND: Don't know what to say? Mr. Soames? How's the set up business, pal?

MITCHELL: I've done nothing. You can't keep me here.

AGENT VOGEL: Shooting at people is a crime, Mr. Soames. And, you are an illegal alien. I'm afraid you'll have to be deported.

MITCHELL: Then, deport me tonight. Please!

AGENT VOGEL: These things take time, Mr. Soames.

MITCHELL: Surely, you can make an exception. Please! I'll confess everything! I must get out of this city!

MARLENA: Shut your mouth, you idiot!

DET. THOMAS: We're all staying. And, you're right, Mr. Soames, none of us may have much time left.

MTICHELL: Then, it is madness to stay. We must all run for our lives!

JEANNE: You're disgusting.

DET. THOMAS: We have an attempted murder to solve. We believe the motive was to implicate Edmund as a cover up for the dispatch of certain documents relating to fusion research. These papers reached Miss Lake and were to be taken to a Nazi syndicate in South America.

EDMUND: How'd they get these papers?

DET. THOMAS: By a citizen willing to committ treason. Those documents were obtained from a government facility and relayed to Miss Lake. We know who that person is.

EDMUND: And, their objective? To blackmail the U. S. government?

DET. THOMAS: No. To destroy New York City: a demonstration of power.

MICHAEL: Who is that person, Detective: the one who got the documents.

AGENT VOGEL: We're not at liberty to reveal that scientist's name. He's being watched and will be apprehended. His name, you would recognize.

MICHAEL: Then, who was the go-between?

DET. THOMAS: Someone in Miss Lake's little terrorist group. Someone in this room attempted to kill Dick Millot at the gymnasium. Yes. We're pretty sure that it was young Millot who was the intended victim: a weak link in their spy network. That same person would have also killed Miss Mascagni-

JEANNE: "Would have?" I don't get you, Detective. You mean to say that-

DET. THOMAS: She's not dead.

JEANNE: I don't believe it.

RITA: Mr. Mascagni, is your daughter alive?

COACH: Yes.

JEANNE: What kind of game are you playing, Detective? Two people are dead-

DET. THOMAS: One person is dead: Dick Millot.

RITA: Where is Miss Mascagni?

DET. THOMAS: Right over there. (*LINDA enters from the back room.*)

MARLENA: Miss Mascagni, you're looking very healthy. My congratulations.

EDMUND: Am I dreaming this?

LINDA: Dad, I think you'd better level with them.

MARLENA (*making for the door*): Detective, I've had enough. You've nothing incriminating on me or any associate of mine. Now, get the hell out of my way! I must leave! Get out of my way!

DET. THOMAS: Those papers, Miss Lake, proved to be very interesting: the papers we got from Mr. Soames' attache case.

MARLENA: Must we go into this now?

DET. THOMAS: The papers were blank, Miss Lake. They were blanks.

MARLENA: What of it?

MTICHELL (*standing up and moving toward MARLENA*): Blank pages, you say? You gave me blank pages to deliver? What-does-this-mean?

MARLENA: It means you're a fool. Do you think I would actually trust you with such an assignment?

MITCHELL: But, the documents-

MARLENA (*momentarily forgetting herself*): Were delivered safely weeks ago. Weeks ago, you idiot! I- but they were merely import papers on merchandise: Columbian coffee and sugar. And, now, I must leave.

AGENT VOGEL: You'll stay, Miss Lake, or else this gun goes off. And, I don't think I'll miss at this range.

MARLENA: No! (*She bursts into tears.*)

MITCHELL: I'll kill you! Rotten, stinking bitch! You were setting me up!

MARLENA: I was getting you out of town or had you forgotten that?

MITCHELL: I'll confess everything. But, please, I beg you; we must all flee this place.

DET. THOMAS: When is it to happen?

MITCHELL: Tonight. At 11 P.M. The plane is set to crash into the Empire State Building and that will trigger off the atomic bomb.

AGENT VOGEL: Why not just detonate it in the atmosphere above the city?

MITCHELL: Because they're incompetents. The triggering device wasn't completed. The only sure way of making certain of the blast was a direct hit on a specified target.

DET. THOMAS: Tracy, get the Air force on the phone. They're on standby alert. That plane will have to be shot down. (*AGENT VOGEL rushes over to the phone by the bar and starts dialing frantically.*)

EDMUND: Is there enough time? It's almost 11 P.M. now.

DET. THOMAS: People can still be moved to shelters. It's too late to evacuate the city.

AGENT VOGEL: I'm dialing HQ. They'll sound off the general alarm and broadcast it over the airwaves.

RITA: For God's sake, hurry!

JEANNE: I need a drink. Roddy get everybody a drink.

DET. THOMAS: Mr. Mascagni, you have something to tell us.

COACH: They wanted me to kill my daughter. It broke me. I came back to my senses and the love of my country. I went up to the roof. Linda was still there and I told her to hide on the second floor until I came back for her. I tossed a sandbag over and, then, went down past Edmund. When he came down to the street I kept him away and everybody else until the police arrived. I told them everything and they put me in touch with Detective Thomas and Miss Vogel. (*The general alarm is sounded. MITCHELL gets down on his knees and prays.*)

EDMUND: You were involved, Coach? I can't believe it. For God's sake, why?

COACH: Don't look at me that way, Edmund. I didn't know they were Nazis. On my life, that's the truth.

DET. THOMAS: Who wanted you to kill your daughter?

COACH: A voice…a voice over the phone. It was always that same voice: threatening and, then, promising and knowing everything about me. It was so convincing! It was like I was being hypnotized.

EDMUND: Linda, I still can't believe it. You're alive.

LINDA: I'm sorry I had to put you through this, Edmund.

EDMUND: You're safe and that's all that matters.

LINDA: Safe? Nobody's safe. Hold me, please!

EDMUND: It can't end like this. It won't end like this! (*Everyone is silent as the alarm continues. The phone rings.*)

AGENT VOGEL (*picking up the receiver*): Yes? I'm listening. I'll tell him.

DET. THOMAS: Who was it?

AGENT VOGEL: It's H.Q. The air force sent a squadron of fighters from Floyd Bennett Airfield to intercept. They're keeping the general alarm in place. They'll keep us notified.

EDMUND: Then, we're not out of it, yet. That plane could still get through our defenses.

AGENT VOGEL: I'm afraid so.

DET. THOMAS: Edmund? Do you remember what you told us about that night when Coach was getting the film ready?

EDMUND: I told you a lot of things.

DET. THOMAS: Who turned off the lights?

EDMUND: I don't remember.

DET. THOMAS: You do. Think, Edmund. Who shut them off? Who knew exactly where to go?

EDMUND: It was- Jeanne! She knew just where the light switch was.

JEANNE: Does it matter?

DET. THOMAS: I think it matters a great deal, Jeanne.

JEANNE: Why?

DET. THOMAS: Because you tried to kill Dick Millot. Oh, it was you, Jeanne. You'd never been to the gym before, but you knew exactly where the light switch was.

JEANNE: Roddy told me-

RODDY: Roddy didn't tell you. Bitch! I knew something stunk that night.

JEANNE: Why would I want to kill Dick? I have no motive.

DET. THOMAS: You were trying to frame Edmund. Edmund was the fall guy for your plan, not Marlena's. The police would be busy with Edmund and Dick Millot's death. Two birds with one bullet: a nice cover up to divert attention from your real objective. You knew Dick was in it only for the thrills: a boy's game. He wasn't so keen on murder.

RITA: But, the documents were blank.

DET. THOMAS: Marlena wasn't taking any chances. She'd already sent off the real papers via Jeanne here. Isn't that right, Jeanne?

JEANNE: Prove it, Detective.

EDMUND: He doesn't have to. You did it, didn't you, Jeanne?

RODDY: I really don't know you at all. You're just someone who came up to me one day at school. You started chatting me up like we'd known each other for years. Nice job. And, then, you recruited me and Dick.

JEANNE (*starts wiping off her make-up and removes her wig*): And, it was so easy. You sniveling simpleton. Yes. It was I

who pulled that trigger, but my aim was off. I don't usually miss, but the room was blacked out and there was a lot of confusion. And, you, Detective Thomas, are less stupid than I thought. The documents have been delivered. As a woman, I went virtually unnoticed and my affiliation with the Party is now solidified. (*She takes out a gun.*)

COACH: What about that film?

JEANNE: It's called a red herring. It kept you occupied and guessing. It had the same effect on the police. You were in it over your head.

LINDA: And, your day of reckoning is here.

JEANNE: Your petty life will soon be ended, you little fool. Too bad your half-wit father failed to obey orders that night. Edmund would've been mine!

LINDA: You're the fool, lady. Every morning I wake up and look forward to seeing my dad and all those people I love. Yes. I look forward to buying some foolish little thing that'll give me pleasure; to love someone is life and to betray that is something less than human.

MARLENA: The alarm is still going. We must get out of the city!

JEANNE: Poor, Marlena. You're flawed. You're clever, but your methods are sloppy.

MARLENA: You are my superior? I would have never guessed. It's-

JEANNE: Shocking? You flatter me. As your last act of duty: pray that the plane makes it through.

MARLENA: You're insane! You must be.

JEANNE: You are a disappointment.

EDMUND: And, you're the bottom of the barrel, lady.

JEANNE: Were you addressing me? As long as I have your limited attention, I may as well clear up one little mystery for you. I was the one in that film wearing the mask. It is I who will lead the slaughter when the first atomic warhead is unleashed. It will level this entire city. Yes, Edmund, the plane will get through because it must! And, now I must leave. It could have been you and I, Edmund. Truly. Out of my way.

EDMUND: Rotten traitor!

JEANNE: You imbecile! You muscle bound imbecile. How I loathe you and everything you stand for. (*She lunges for EDMUND as RITA throws her drink in JEANNE'S face. EDMUND belts her one.*)

RODDY: Jeanne girl is out for the count.

DET. THOMAS: Tracy, we're gonna' need some back up here. Marlena? Mitchell? Over there, please. What the-

RITA: Oh, my God!

AGENT VOGEL: It went off! That was the flash point. Look out! (*A blackout occurs as a blinding white flash is seen outside. A moment later, a powerful shock wave hits: the windows shatter, bottles explode and pieces of the ceiling collapse. Everyone in the bar is either knocked to the ground or takes cover under the tables. After a long moment, very slowly, everyone starts getting up.*)

DET. THOMAS: We may be all right, if it was far out enough over the water-

MARLENA: There may be fall-out.

DET. THOMAS: Pray that the wind current carries the radiation out to sea.

LINDA: Edmund! Are we safe? Is it over? (*The phone rings.*)

AGENT VOGEL (*picks up the receive*r): Yes. Yes. Thank God! Thank you so much. Of course, I'll tell him. We'll be over at Police HQ in a few minutes. (*Hangs up the phone.*) The plane was shot down a few miles off the Bay. The entire squadron was lost. The navy thinks we're safe. The wind currents should carry any radiation out to the North Atlantic. It was close. (*DET. THOMAS puts the cuffs on MARLENA and MITCHELL, much to their protestations. AGENT VOGEL drags JEANNE to her feet and pushes her out the door.*)

MITCHELL: Edmund, I've always had a great admiration for you. You will help me, surely. Such a beautiful boy. (*Two Police Officers enter and seize both him and MARLENA.*) Stop! You're hurting me! I want to talk to my friend, Edmund.

DET. THOMAS: Roddy, you'll have to come with us, son.

RODDY: I guess it's up with me. Put the cuffs on me, man.

RITA: Michael, let's go with him. He'll need somebody.

MICHAEL: He'll need his friends. Good girl. (*He exits with RITA, AGENT VOGEL, RODDY, and DET. THOMAS.*)

COACH: They'll want me there, too. Are you two gonna' be all right?

LINDA: We'll be okay, dad. I'll wait up for you. (*Exit COACH.*)

EDMUND: It's over, Linda. It's over.

LINDA: Is it? Those documents were delivered to those rotten people.

EDMUMD: We know about them now. And, I think Mr. Soames can be persuaded to do a lot of talking. We won't be caught off guard, again. It'll be a long time before they can try something else.

LINDA: How long a time?

DET. THOMAS (*enters*): Forgot my hat. Long enough to put up a strong defense and to let them know that we're on to them.

LINDA: But, who are they, Detective?

DET. THOMAS: Destroyers. Haters of the civilized world and every decent thing in it. They'll lose every time because their insides are hollow.

EDMUND: Detective? When I was in Marlena's apartment, I was looking for that spear. I didn't see it there.

DET. THOMAS: Tracy and I searched for it, as well. It wasn't there, Edmund.

EDMUND: Marlena seemed on edge that night. Do you think it was because of the spear?

DET. THOMAS: I think it's a possibility. That's when her plans began to go haywire. Coincidence?

EDMUND: They say that when Hitler lost it his plans started to go haywire. Do you think there's anything to it?

LINDA: Do you mean the spear that was in the gym that night? Does it wield that much power?

EDMUND: I don't know. But, I think Marlena thought so.

LINDA: If it should fall into the wrong hands-

DET. THOMAS: I'm not a superstitious man, but, I'd sure like to know where that spear is now.

LINDA: But, where did it come from? Who could've made a weapon like that and why? Marlena said it was a sacred object. What did she mean by that?

EDMUND: I get the feeling that it was taken from Marlena. I also got the feeling that she couldn't do anything about it. Maybe Jeanne would know where it is now? Maybe, she had something to do with its disappearance?

DET. THOMAS: If she does, we'll get it out of her. Well, see you two later. And, relax! For the time being, we're safe.

EDMUND: Inspector? Thanks. Thanks for everything. And, thank Miss Vogel, too.

DET. THOMAS: Don't mention it, Edmund. Take care. (*Exits.*)

EDMUND: You want to know something, Linda? For the first time in a long time, I'm looking forward to tomorrow. It's going to be a beautiful day because we'll make it so. I was afraid, but I'm not afraid, anymore. I felt alone; but I know that I'm not alone. There are some pretty decent people in this world -- a world that I'm getting a whole new outlook on. And, I think it's time I entered another competition: a competition that I intend to win: to be the best. It's what I love to do, and I'm not giving it up. So, if you can stand having a bodybuilder for a boyfriend...well, I'm your man. (*He kisses LINDA.*)

LINDA: Now, that's the man I love talking.

EDMUND: Come on. I'll walk you home.

End of play.

MOON STRIKE

A play in Three Acts

by

Gerard Denza

Copyright 2011

THE GUEST LIST

JAMES McAVEY, an ex-priest and a multi-millionaire.
PILAR GOMEZ, a jewel thief.
JAKE CHAN, a young, Asian actor.
ALEXIS TANG, an actress, but not as ambitious as Jake.
VALERIE CHRISTIAN, a respected screenwriter.
TOMMY MARCONI, a gangster who likes Valerie.
RANDY SULLIVAN, a young director.
ADELE EMERSON, is a newspaper reporter.
MITCH, an ex-convict and blind man.
MARLENA LAKE, a fascist.

PLACE
The story takes place in Manhattan.

TIME
Unknown.

SCENES

PrologueRandy and Alexis are stranded
on board James' yacht.

Act One
Scene One: A party in James' apartment in Manhattan.
Scene Two: Some party-goers are exploring
the basement of James' skyscraper.

Act Two
Scene One: James and Adele are in the former's apartment.
Scene Two: Adele and Pilar in the
basement of James' skyscraper.
Scene Three: The party-goers are on the pier.

Act Three
Scene One: Adele is in the basement of James' skyscraper.
Scene Two: Randy, Alexis, and James on board James's yacht.
Scene Three: Tommy and Adele are searching for the spear.
Scene Four: On board James' yacht.
Scene Five: Mitch is hiding in the shadows of the pier.

EpilogueThe party-goers are back on board James' yacht.

PROLOGUE

RANDY: Hello? Is anyone out there? Please come in. We're adrift in the Bay aboard the Phoenix. This is Randy Sullivan calling. We have casualties. Repeat. We have casualties. There are people in need of medical attention. This is an emergency, please respond!

ALEXIS: Randy? Randy! Is anyone out there? Look at the city, it's so deserted. There are no lights anywhere.

RANDY: There must be a power outage.

ALEXIS: And, there's no moon to guide us back. Look. It's just setting below the horizon. It's an evil thing.

RANDY: Alexis, see to the others. Give them water-

ALEXIS: What can I give them-

RANDY: We'll get through to someone. The radio's working.

ALEXIS: Are we drifting out to sea?

RANDY: I don't think so.

ALEXIS: If we are, tell me. Don't lie to me, please. Don't insult me like that.

RANDY: I'm not lying to you, Alexis. Look! Are those headlights near the Battery?

ALEXIS: I think so, but what good does that do us?

RANDY: Look around for some flares; get Tommy or Jake to help you.

ALEXIS (*looking toward the moon*): I'll look. But Randy, are we safe from-

RANDY: Yes.

ALEXIS: I'm still shaken by it. Are we really safe? Will it come back?

RANDY: Don't worry, that mystery's been solved for now. I saw a couple of bottles down below. James was well stocked for that party of his- party!

ALEXIS: I'll bring up a bottle. (*She goes below deck.*)

RANDY: Hello? Is anyone out there? This is Randy Sullivan. We're aboard the Phoenix...

ACT ONE
Scene One

A party is in full swing with about twenty guests and more anticipated. Everyone is dressed in formal evening wear with few exceptions. The party is in JAMES' townhouse. It's early evening on a July night. There is a large window looking out on to the street.

JAMES: I need another martini; just one more will put me on the periphery of intoxication, not drunk, mind you. A martini is effective because of its purity...the olive is added for aesthetic reasons only. Would you get me another martini, Pilar? Chill the glass.

PILAR: Right now?

JAMES: No. Ten years from now. I don't know where I'll be later.

PILAR: You will be here with me.

JAMES: This party of mine is boring. You say that I'll be here with you?

PILAR: Unless you tire of my company; I may prove to be too pedestrian for you.

JAMES: And, you will remain with me?

PILAR: Of course.

JAMES: I believe you.

PILAR: Look at me. You're afraid.

JAMES: I am afraid to look out the window. Yes.

PILAR: It will come to nothing.

JAMES: Are you afraid, Pilar? You must be honest with a priest.

PILAR: I don't like lying; not when I don't have to, for there is no gain to be made. The weather outside is strange…a stillness is in the air…and, yet, they tell me that storms are raging near the coastlines.

JAMES: The moon is moving away from the Earth.

PILAR (*glancing out the window and on to the street below*): No one seems to be about. The streets are deserted and there is no traffic. Yes. The Earth will be defenseless.

JAMES: Explain that, please.

PILAR: The shield which guarded us will be no more.

JAMES: The Earth will be defenseless as well as this great nation of America.

PILAR: What do you mean to say; that another war is imminent?

JAMES: I think it may have to come to that.

PILAR: And, whose side will you be on, James?

JAMES: I would be flexible.

(*Spotlight moves to center stage.*)

JAKE: Why don't you call me by my name?

ALEXIS: Why should I?

JAKE: Jake's the name. Is it too Anglo for you?

ALEXIS: No.

JAKE: Liar. Jake Chan: a good, strong Hollywood name.

ALEXIS: You like it?

JAKE: I chose it.

ALEXIS: I thought the studio did those things.

JAKE: They usually do. Jake Chan: four letters in each name; clean and neat and easy to remember. How about a martini for you? Make it a Manhattan for me. You know how to make one, Alexis? I'll show you how. I've tended bar in lime houses. Surprised?

ALEXIS: I've been in lime houses. Wait here while I get the drinks. Stay here. I want to talk to you some more.

JAKE: Look at the moon. I can see it from here…just barely.

ALEXIS: It's moving away. I don't like to look at it anymore.

JAKE: Don't worry. It will no longer influence the tides, that's all. Who cares? The scientists don't seem to be too worried about it. Better that it moves away from us and not closer, then, it would be the end. I'm thirsty. Get me my drink.

ALEXIS: Don't shout like that.

JAKE: No one here is listening; and, they should listen. I'm an Asian actor who will soon take second billing to no one. I walked in and they should have taken notice. They did not. Soon, I'll be famous; if not here, then in Europe. Even now, they're pretending not to notice. Who are you Alexis? What are your goals?

ALEXIS: I'm an actress, Jake. You know this. I wish I had your drive. It's the one thing I lack.

JAKE: You speak in direct sentences, but I still don't know you. We should make movies together in Europe and, then, Asia where the market is opening.

ALEXIS: Maybe James can help us do that. We could speak to him about it later on; get him alone and convince him. He likes me, and I'm sure your powers of persuasion are good. Do you want to try?

JAKE: Before the party breaks up, we can try and broach the subject...tactfully. I'll raise my voice now; get me my drink, please.

(*Spotlight moves to stage left.*)

VALERIE (*wearing men's trousers and a jacket casually thrown about her shoulders*): Poor Alexis, if a man shouted at me like that-

TOMMY: You'd belt him one.

VALERIE: That's right.

TOMMY: Drink?

VALERIE: Never touch the stuff. Tastes like poison.

TOMMY: Funny thing for an Italian gangster, I don't drink, either. How about steppin' out with me for some coffee and fresh air?

VALERIE: It is getting stuffy in here even with the windows wide open.

TOMMY: So, let's go.

VALERIE: I hate just leaving and, besides, Randy just walked in. I like him. He's just getting started and I'd like to help him get launched. I've seen some documentaries that he's directed. He's good.

TOMMY: Let's go, already.

VALERIE: It's dark outside with virtually no moon. And, those murders...all those people killed so brutally the other night.

TOMMY: Not to mention that museum heist. That was a pretty slick job. I'd like to know who pulled it off.

VALERIE: Even I have to admit that, but-

TOMMY: But?

VALERIE: Are the two connected: those murders down near Wall St. and the robbery at the museum?

TOMMY: Why would they be? Lots of crimes happen in this city. Thinking of writing a screenplay about it? It might be good. I'd be willin' to bankroll it. Now, let's get out of here.

VALERIE: James is on the Board of Directors of that particular museum.

TOMMY: Is he a suspect?

VALERIE: Some people seem to think so.

TOMMY: Then, he must be guilty. Don't like him. He's a slimy bastard.

VALERIE: Tommy!

TOMMY: I'll get my uncle to back your screenplay.

VALERIE: I just might take you up on that; but, first let me do some digging around. I know some of the board members of that museum. James isn't well liked. He was kicked out of the priesthood, you know.

TOMMY: I didn't know.

VALERIE: I shouldn't have brought it up; not here, anyway.

TOMMY: Ya' can't stop now.

VALERIE: James funded the expedition to the Mid-east with the sole purpose of bringing back Sumerian artifacts.

TOMMY: What of it?

VALERIE: Not too much is known about Sumer. It predates even the Egyptians and no one knows where they originated from.

TOMMY: Does James?

VALERIE: I doubt it. But, the relics they dug up were smuggled out of the country and into the United States. The Iraqi government wants them back real bad.

TOMMY: So James goes and steals his own loot? Clever. How do you happen to know all this? I must read the wrong papers.

VALERIE: This wasn't in the papers.

TOMMY: Ya' gonna' keep me guessing?

VALERIE: I'm afraid so. But, my sources are reliable.

TOMMY: Have it your way, baby, but I've got dibs on that screenplay. And, if ya' need protection-

VALERIE: I won't.

TOMMY: You might regret sayin' that. Don't be so friggin' sure of yourself. Here comes your director friend.

RANDY (*wearing a navy blue suit with an open collar shirt*): Party's really underway. Valerie, how are you?

VALERIE: I'm good. I think you know Tommy.

TOMMY: We've seen each other around. You been assigned to any movies, yet, man? I hear you've just been promoted to director.

RANDY: A director with no film assignment.

TOMMY: Here's my card. Call me tomorrow. Valerie here has got a swell idea for a screenplay.

RANDY (*very much interested*): Like what, Valerie?

VALERIE: It's barely an idea; but, I think it might be interesting and marketable.

RANDY: Don't keep me in suspense.

VALERIE: Tommy and I were talking about those murders and the museum robbery. There might be a connection or, at least, I can invent one.

RANDY: I like it: a murder mystery. Write an outline for me, Val, and I'll start blocking it.

TOMMY: Valerie, give it a title.

VALERIE: Well…how about: Murder. Murder. Murder?

RANDY: Kind of gruesome, isn't it? And, pretty effective. It'll look great on a movie marquise.

TOMMY: It is great, man. This is how things get started in this business: the writer, the director, and the man with the deep pockets. I think I'm startin' to sweat.

VALERIE: Cool it, boy. Let's go for that walk. I've got a lot of research to do. Randy? See you later. (*ALEXIS walks over and touches RANDY lightly on the shoulder.*)

ALEXIS: Here. A Manhattan for you.

RANDY: Thanks, Alexis.

ALEXIS: You're welcome. I came with Jake, but he's busy feeling sorry for himself. I overheard Valerie mention a screenplay. Is there room for a heroine in it.

RANDY: The sex angle? I think we can find a suitable part for you.

ALEXIS: Do you think Valerie was really serious about it, though? Sure it wasn't just talk? There's a lot of that at parties.

RANDY: Absolutely. She's not the type to talk through her hat. I'd love to work with her. What a break that would be for me. Valerie's respected in this business.

ALEXIS: Those murders were near here, weren't they?

RANDY: In the basement of James' new skyscraper on Water St. Why?

ALEXIS: Morbid curiosity, I guess. Let's change the subject, shall we? Look who just walked in: the gum cracking Adele Emerson. She's fun.

RANDY: She's also an ace reporter on The Tribune. Maybe, she's following a lead. And, maybe, we can get you some publicity.

ALEXIS: Too bad Valerie left. She could have saved herself a trip to the library.

ADELE (*sporting her "day" dress from the office*): Hi, folks! What's up?

ALEXIS: We've just been talking about those murders, Adele.

RANDY: Have you been assigned that story?

ADELE: Not officially. But, my typewriter seems to have a mind of its own. It keeps clicking murder, murder, murder. A scoop just might be on my horizon.

ALEXIS: What a coincidence your saying that. Valerie wants to do a screenplay of the murders and the museum heist with just that title. And, Randy wants to star me in it, of course.

ADELE: A screenplay based on my copy? Love it.

ALEXIS: It's all that anyone talks about. Well, that and the moon disappearing.

ADELE: The moon's old news.

RANDY: Is it? It's drifting is still affecting the earth's weather.

ADELE: Not for much longer.

ALEXIS: What caused it to drift off like that?

ADELE (*turning to RANDY*): Mix me a drink, baby? Scotch and soda. Struck by an asteroid: a pretty big one, knocked it right off its orbital plane or something like that. No one even saw it coming. The science boys could tell you more about it. (*RANDY comes back with her drink.*) Thanks, baby!

JAMES: Adele! So glad you could make it. No photographer along? No mention about me in tomorrow's paper?

ADELE: I'm writing the bit as we talk. Keep talkin' to me.

JAMES: May I date you some time?

ADELE: No.

JAMES: Go to hell. But, write my party up in tomorrow's paper, first.

ADELE: Of course, James. James?

JAMES: Adele?

ADELE: I do have some respect for you.

JAMES: A left handed compliment. I'll accept it.

ADELE: I apologize. You're one of the best hold-outs we've got in Manhattan.

JAMES: How's that?

ADELE: The ultra chic have all migrated to the safer haven of Europe. Why do you stay, James? I'll print your answer in tomorrow's paper.

JAMES: I like the anonymity of Manhattan, the loneliness, the crowds of people. I even ride the subway just for the hell of it.

ADELE: How interesting. I like riding them, too.

ALEXIS: No one in his right mind rides the subway for pleasure.

JAMES: When you don't have to, you do. But, to get back to your question, Adele, I plan on moving this party of mine to my yacht. Will you come?

ADELE: Well-

ALEXIS: Randy and I will come, James. And, Adele, if you could drop my name in your column tomorrow...

ADELE: Done.

RANDY: Why the change in venue?

JAMES: No reason.

ADELE: Have you got a short-wave radio on board?

JAMES: Of course. Do you know how to operate one?

ADELE: A boyfriend taught me how. When do we leave?

JAMES: I'll make the arrangements. (*The stage is now completely lit.*) Everybody, please, may I have your attention? A dramatic pause, if you would? The party's moving to my yacht which is moored just off the Battery. Are you all game?

PILAR: But, James, is there enough room for everyone?

JAMES: No. But, I've a small pavilion on the pier and it's well stocked. Are you game, Pilar?

PILAR: Of course. But, where are Valerie and Tommy?

JAMES: Don't know. Oh, and did I mention that we'll only be a block away from the murder scene?

ALEXIS: I hadn't thought of that.

JAKE: That's unnerving, James.

JAMES: Where's your nerve, Jake?

PILAR: Jake is right. With the city is so empty and everyone's nerves so frayed, why not stay here?

JAMES: You'll be near water. If anyone sets you on fire, just go for a dip in the harbor.

PILAR: That's not funny. (*MITCH enters.*)

JAMES: Mitch! Welcome to our party -- my party.

MITCH: Don't I get a drink?

JAMES: A quick one. I want you to meet someone.

MITCH: Here?

JAMES: At the dock.

MITCH: What's the rush?

JAMES: You're late, Mitch. I don't like people being late to my parties.

MITCH: Tough.

JAMES: Do you have any manners?

MITCH: I'll list 'em for you one at a time: none. Interesting mix, here.

ADELE: Don't you approve, Mitch?

MITCH: I've got mixed feelings on mixed company.

ADELE: That smacks of-

MITCH: Of what, lady?

ADELE: Intolerance. Haven't you seen that epic film?

MITCH: What the hell does that mean?

ADELE: It means you don't like half the world.

RANDY: Mitch? Randy Sullivan.

MITCH: The director.

RANDY: Well, the soon-to-be director.

JAMES: Everyone, let's start on our little pilgrimage. Pilar, are the stars favorable?

PILAR: No. They are not. This night is unlike any other, James.

JAMES: Ready?

ADELE: Ready for what?

JAMES: To leave, darling, of course. I've already told you that you can phone in your story from the boat.

ADELE: I'll use a pay phone.

JAMES: My lines aren't tapped.

MITCH: Don't trust him, Adele. As an ex-priest, he's given up religion. No religion, no ethics, right, pal?

JAMES: The two don't necessarily go together.

MITCH: So, even as a priest, you had no ethics. Is that what you're telling us?

JAMES: I wouldn't tell you anything, ex-con.

MITCH: An ex-con and an ex-priest. Hey, Adele, take your pick: the hypocrite or the thug?

JAMES: Careful.

MITCH: I can't stomach religious people. You make me puke.

JAMES: Then, leave. Or wait until we get to the boat. You can throw up in the bay.

MITCH: I'll meet you down at the pier. Adele, you coming?

ADELE: James, we'll catch up with you. (*She turns angrily on MITCH.*) Try to behave yourself, for Christ's sake! (*ALEXIS and JAKE move back to stage left.*)

ALEXIS: Did you hear that?

JAKE: I sure did. It sounds like entertaining stuff.

ALEXIS: I don't like that Mitch. He gives me the willies. I wonder-

JAKE: Wonder what?

ALEXIS: I wonder if he didn't have something to do with that museum theft the other night?

JAKE: Ask him.

ALEXIS: Very funny. Do you want to go over to James' yacht? It might be a lot of fun. It would be insulting to James if we didn't; and, he's a very influential man. Randy will be there.

JAKE: You like him; don't deny it. Try to get me a part, as well. Yes. I heard the talk of a screenplay. Valerie should be more discreet; her voice carries.

PILAR: Mitch, might I have a few moments alone with Miss Emerson? I won't keep her long.

MITCH: Sure. I'll wait for you downstairs. (*Exits.*)

ADELE: Maybe, he'll run into Valerie and Tommy. I'd like to ask her a few questions about that screenplay of hers.

PILAR: I may be able to give you some answers, as well. Don't trust that unnatural woman.

ADELE: Unnatural? I won't pursue that.

PILAR: You surprise me, Miss Emerson. Isn't your job one of fact finding? The woman is a lesbian. I despise the type.

ADELE: Why, Miss Gomez?

PILAR: I have my reasons. Are you going down to the yacht with us?

ADELE: Yes.

PILAR: Good. What do you know of those murders the other night? Or would you be violating a trust in the telling?

ADELE: Lady, you're assuming an awful lot.

PILAR: I knew those people who were killed. They were part of a syndicate that murders for reasons of hatred, expediency, and…ideology.

ADELE: Have you gone to the police with this?

PILAR: No. I come to you with quite a story.

ADELE: Who exactly were those people?

PILAR (*avoiding the question*): One more thing, don't trust anyone in this room, especially our host. (*JAMES walks over and places his hand on PILAR'S shoulder.*)

JAMES: Was my name mentioned and not in my presence?

ADELE: It's your party and that's one of the occupational hazards of throwing one.

PILAR: We speak of you only in passing.

JAMES: Why do you lie, Pilar?

ADELE: Mitch is waiting for me. Excuse me? (*Exits.*)

PILAR: We should also be leaving.

JAMES: I have a gift for you. Here.

PILAR: It's beautiful: an emerald broach of such beauty. I can't accept it.

JAMES: Don't be a bore, darling. It's yours. And, in the future, speak kindly of me. And, by the way, has there been talk about the spear- the museum heist?

PILAR: Gossip and conjecture, no one knows anything.

JAMES: I'm expecting another guest: Marlena Lake. She's a fascist; although, she'd deny it vehemently. She knows things and dangerous people. I need her here, tonight, because the moon is now at its furthest from the Earth. Tonight, it will begin to swing back.

PILAR: And, Miss Lake will furnish you with information?

JAMES: Oh, yes.

PILAR: Her name...I've heard it before. Do you think you can control her?

JAMES: She'll be our ally.

PILAR: I don't like it. And, you mentioned the spear just now. I've seen this spear. It's been written about in obscure literature.

JAMES: Has it?

PILAR: You know it has. Don't be coy with me.

JAMES: Perhaps, some of my guests will stop off at the murder scene.

PILAR: How very morbid. And, you have changed the subject.

JAMES: Some would call your pastimes morbid, Pilar: séances and the use of tea leaves...

PILAR: Parlor games, I admit it. People find them amusing and so do I. Now, tell me more about Miss Lake.

JAMES: I've corresponded with her and even spoken to her a few times.

PILAR: Then, you've never actually met her?

JAMES: No. Have you?

ACT ONE
Scene Two

*JAKE, ADELE, and ALEXIS are in the basement of JAMES'
skyscraper. There are a great many crates about and a large, roll
top desk in the corner. The spiral staircase is toward stage right.*

JAKE: What are we doing in this hole?

ADELE: Exploring. You know, looking around.

JAKE: Why?

ADELE: You're obviously not a reporter.

JAKE: I'm an actor. Surprised?

ADELE: Don't take out your hostilities on me, save them for
your girlfriend. I'm here to cover a story, a pretty gruesome
one.

ALEXIS: We should all go to the yacht. The party is being held
there and James is expecting us.

ADELE: A boat at anchor is a bore. We'll be okay.

ALEXIS: But, there's nothing here to see.

JAKE: And, I need a drink.

ALEXIS: So do I, Adele. Let's go. James will be wondering
where we are. I don't like this place.

ADELE: Not yet. Three people were murdered here and some rare museum pieces were stolen and this reporter wants to know why. There has to be a connection.

JAKE: What connection?

ADELE: Do I know?

JAKE: Do you?

ADELE: No.

JAKE: Then, how are you going to prove that there is a connection?

ADELE: Aren't we the kibitzer! Don't worry, handsome, I'll prove it.

ALEXIS: What exactly was stolen from the museum? There was mention of an ancient spear.

ADELE: You two don't read my column, do you?

JAKE: Should we, Miss Emerson?

ADELE: How about a slap in the face?

ALEXIS: Listen! What was that? I hear someone coming.

MITCH (*enters from stage right*): A blind man.

ALEXIS: You were going to the boat. You said so. Why did you lie to me?

MITCH: Go fuck yourself. lady.

ADELE: Mitch! You move like a cat. Only Alexis, here, heard you coming.

MITCH: Like a cat burglar, huh?

ADELE: Are you? You can tell me.

MITCH: Used to be, before my accident; but, I've reformed. Feel sorry for me?

ADELE: You want pity? You don't seem the type.

MITCH: From a woman, yes.

ADELE: And, from a man?

MITCH: I'd break his balls.

JAKE: You're crude.

MITCH: Careful, son. I can see pretty good for a blind man. My punches land right on target.

JAKE: I know how to handle myself. My knife is always with me.

MITCH: You were saying?

JAKE: It's gone! What is this?

ALEXIS: He probably stole it. I wouldn't put it past him.

MITCH: Feeling a little defenseless now, son?

ADELE: Gentlemen, please.

ALEXIS: Let's get away from this place.

MITCH: I'll take myself to the yacht.

ADELE: Please.

MITCH: Come with me. I think this party's unhealthy for you.

ADELE: Unhealthy?

MITCH: I smell blood.

ALEXIS: You're just trying to scare us.

JAKE: Don't believe him.

ALEXIS: I smell it, too, now. It's coming from one of the crates.

JAKE: Try to scare someone else, Mr. Tough Guy.

MITCH: You asked for it, you slant eyed pig! (*He and JAKE fight, throwing punches and falling over each other. They stagger back and go crashing into a crate, breaking it open. VALERIE'S body falls out.*)

ADELE (*running over*): It's Valerie! Is she-

MITCH: She's dead, all right. And, I thought corpses didn't bleed.

ACT TWO
Scene One

JAMES and ADELE are arguing in his apartment.

JAMES: You had to phone in that story?

ADELE: It's my job, sweetie.

JAMES: A real scoop for you, huh, Adele?

ADELE: What of it?

JAMES: Bad publicity and more of it.

ADELE: More of it?

JAMES: You haven't been doing your homework. I happen to own that particular skyscraper: four murders in the space of one week. The police will be crawling all over me. You should have come to me first, Adele.

ADELE: What was that screenwriter to you, James?

JAMES: Exactly nothing. Let's go down to the yacht. I'm expecting another guest.

ADELE: Who's that?

JAMES: A woman.

ADELE: Do I know her?

JAMES: Marlena Lake.

ADELE: Do I know that name?

JAMES: You should. Aren't you up on your current affairs?

ADELE: I've seen that name in print, somewhere. Who is she, James?

JAMES: An enemy to you.

ADELE: Meaning?

JAMES: You'll find out.

ADELE: I'll make it my business to find out.

JAMES: I wouldn't tangle with her.

ADELE: What is she; some kind of a thug?

JAMES: And, not your two-bit variety type, either. Don't take this warning lightly, Adele.

ADELE: I'm heading back to the scene of the crime.

JAMES: Again?

ADELE: James?

JAMES: Yes?

ADELE: Loosen up. (*Exits.*)

JAMES (*starts pacing the floor as JAKE and ALEXIS enter*): Jake? Alexis? What are you two doing here?

ALEXIS: I left my purse here. I'm going home.

JAMES: No. Don't do that. I don't want you to do that. I need you.

JAKE: She's upset. You need a drink. You'll feel better after you've had a drink.

JAMES: Make it a fast one. I'm expecting someone shortly.

ALEXIS: Ashamed to be seen with actors?

JAMES: Not tonight.

JAKE: Here. Drink this.

ALEXIS: Not joining me?

JAKE: No. Down the hatch.

ALEXIS: Don't rush me. This is straight scotch, it's too strong.

JAKE: Drink it in one gulp. It'll burn like anything going down. Bottoms up.

ALEXIS: Terrible stuff! (*MARLENA enters, unannounced.*)

JAMES: Ah, Marlena!

MARLENA: James, you have guests.

JAMES: They'll meet us down by the yacht.

MARLENA: Get rid of them.

JAKE: We're leaving. I don't like ill-mannered people.

JAMES: Alexis, make sure you both arrive at my yacht. Alexis?

ALEXIS: You like giving orders?

JAKE: Behave yourself. Let's go. James is entertaining.

JAMES: Alexis? Remember what I've said. (*ALEXIS and JAKE exit.*) Now, we can talk.

MARLENA: I've come for the spear. Where is it?

JAMES: You don't waste any time.

MARLENA: It's not wasted on trifles. Where is the spear?

JAMES: At the murder scene. It's safe.

MARLENA: There's been a lot of attention drawn to that building, lately.

JAMES: Can you think of a better hiding place for it? It's being well guarded.

MARLENA: Can we get to it?

JAMES: I own that building, so no one will question my being there at any time.

MARLENA: And the other artifacts?

JAMES: Can be disposed of easily. Pilar can see to that.

MARLENA: See to it. Now, let's go.

JAMES: You and Pilar Gomez should meet. The two of you are obsessed with the occult.

MARLENA: I am obsessed with power, not with the means of attaining it.

JAMES: You know, Marlena, I detect an accent in your speech.

MARLENA: I don't attempt to disguise it or my origins. I was born in New York City and raised there by immigrant parents. We were quite poor, but my parents saw to my education and that of my sisters. They chose a mundane life. I did not. My passion for knowledge occupied my every waking moment. Religion became my obsession and I've dedicated my life to its study. Politics has also been of keen interest to me; it's usefulness can be quite effective.

JAMES: No social life?

MARLENA: I married a Rabbi who is not unknown in the more powerful circles of that religion. This surprises you, James? I am also the mother of two children.

JAMES: Marlena, you are a repository of surprises. A Rabbi, you say, for a husband? How does he figure into your future plans?

MARLENA: The marriage has ended.

JAMES: Changing the subject, somewhat, has a puppet "leader" been found?

MARLENA: Yes. His mind borders on insanity and he may prove to be dangerous but, for the time being, he can be manipulated.

JAMES: For how long; until the strings are cut and he's dead?

MARLENA: There will be another war, even more devastating than the last, which will sweep across Europe and penetrate into Asia. And, that will only be the beginning. One man alone can't hope to accomplish all this. It's we, the manipulators, who will exert the power over humanity.

JAMES: Exert power over devastation? Exert power over rubble?

MARLENA: We'll have power over resources, James, human resources.

JAMES: You mean slaves?

MARLENA: Conscription is a more accurate term. The survivors will be grateful.

JAMES: You hope. Don't count on it.

MARLENA: Are you worried, James? Worried about the coming disruption? You shouldn't be. You should be prepared for it.

JAMES: Marlena, why do you want the spear?

MARLENA: The spear of Longinus is older that recorded history. The being who Adam referred to as God was said to have left it in the fabled Garden. It was taken from that place by an unknown Pharaoh who battled Moses for it. He lost it to that magician. It's even said to have pierced the side of Christ.

JAMES: And, you believe all that?

MARLENA: And, you obviously doubt it. A man of your religious background, that surprises me.

JAMES: Religion and fable.

MARLENA: The spear is not a fable.

JAMES: Have it your way. I won't argue the point.

MARLENA: You've held it. You've touched it. Did you feel nothing?

JAMES: It felt peculiar…as if I was close to being electrocuted.

MARLENA: Precisely. Now, what of those killings…by radiation.

JAMES: I know nothing about them.

MARLENA: They occurred the same night as the robbery. Were you testing the spear whose power you don't believe in?

JAMES: It may be some kind of bizarre coincidence. Who knows? By the way, there was another murder there tonight.

MARLENA: And, tonight, a ritual will be held…a ritual will be the deciding factor. I must be sure of the spear's authenticity.

JAMES: I'll gather the others aboard my yacht.

MARLENA: No. The spear must be placed on solid ground.

JAMES: It will have to be on the pier, then.

MARLENA: Who killed those people?

JAMES: I told you. I don't know.

MARLENA: I don't believe you. Anyway, within the hour I want us packed aboard your yacht and ready to sail. It must be tonight. The moon is at its most distant and will be brought back to its proper orbit.

JAMES: What in God's name are you saying: that that antique of a spear will pull the moon back to Earth?

MARLENA: Terrifying, isn't it, that such a seemingly mundane object possesses such power? Come, we've wasted enough time.

ACT TWO
Scene Two

ADELE and PILAR are in the basement of JAMES' skyscraper.

PILAR: All this waiting and to what purpose?

ADELE: Read our tea leaves, honey.

PILAR: Yes. Make fun of what is serious. I don't laugh at death and neither should you.

ADELE: I was only joking. As a reporter, I value every angle of a story.

PILAR: Murder is terrible and, yet, why don't I feel any sorrow?

ADELE: Didn't like our screenwriter friend?

PILAR: I didn't trust her. She never spoke of herself.

ADELE: Go on.

PILAR: She was not as she seemed. I was aware of her unnatural practices and even that seemed- I shouldn't say.

ADELE: Say it.

PILAR: A lie...a lie that she invented, but why? It makes no sense to me.

ADELE: It might just be an effective cover to draw away attention from something else.

PILAR: What?

ADELE: Don't know.

PILAR: But, you have suspicions?

ADELE (evading the question): Where's Tommy, by the way?

PILAR: On board the yacht. He was the last one to see her alive.

ADELE: He sure was.

PILAR: You suspect him? Somehow, I don't see him as a murderer.

ADELE: Neither do I, but he's not Mr. Nice Guy, either. What is it that bothers me about Val's death? She was robbed and murdered. Robbed...but, she never carried a pocketbook around. Why would a robber single her out to take a chance on a woman who didn't have any "bait?"

PILAR: She could have been a victim of a psychopath.

ADELE: Then, why was her body hidden so carefully?

PILAR: Just like the other murder victims.

ADELE: Maybe, she was carrying papers with her, like her screenplay? But to kill her for that?

PILAR: We assume these papers were harmless, were part of a screenplay. But, perhaps, like herself, they were something else altogether. My intuition tells me that we are meant to discover something of import.

ADELE: Let's take a look in one of those crates.

PILAR: There are too many of them to go through, and what would be in them?

ADELE: If Valerie wanted to hide something...if she were being followed...she'd have to think fast...real fast. Was this basement supposed to be used for office space?

PILAR: Yes. James was going to use it for that purpose. The desk is by that wall.

ADELE: It's a mess, like mine.

PILAR: James wouldn't have it that way. Someone else has been using it.

ADELE (*leaning on the desk*): Would it be likely that Valerie would have her work on her?

PILAR: Why not? Writers often do.

ADELE: But, they'd carry their work in a briefcase.

PILAR: She carried nothing on her, that one.

ADELE: Okay, she leaves Tommy and heads toward James' building. Why?

PILAR: To meet someone?

ADELE: Exactly. So, she gets here and the place is empty. She hears footsteps and she's not taking any chances so she hides whatever it is she's got on her and, then, the murderer shows up.

PILAR: But, what does she conceal?

ADELE: Easy. Her notes.

PILAR: Then, where are they?

ADELE: They must be in this desk. (*Looks around, startled.*) What was that?

PILAR: Someone is coming. We must leave.

ADELE: Too late. Pilar, you meet whoever it is. I'll hide under the desk.

PILAR: Quickly!

JAMES (*coming down the spiral staircase*): What are you doing here?

MARLENA: I know Miss Gomez.

PILAR: I came on my own.

JAMES: Why? And, try telling the truth for a change.

PILAR: Does it matter? I will leave.

JAMES: Excuse us, Marlena?

MARLENA: I'll wait outside. And, don't forget what we came for. (*Exits.*)

PILAR: Why are you so angry?

JAMES: Now, you may tell me the truth.

PILAR: But, I have told you the truth.

JAMES: You've told me nothing.

PILAR: Keep away from me.

JAMES: Frightened?

PILAR: How do you know Miss Lake?

JAMES: The "how" is none of your business. (*He walks over to one of the crates and takes out the spear.*): Come with me. (*He and PILAR exit. ADELE comes out from under the desk and starts going through its drawers. The typewriter catches her attention. She's about to snatch a paper from its carriage when footsteps are heard. ADELE ducks under the desk as a figure emerges from the dark. This figure looks about, but does not move from the staircase. It is a very tall figure...its movements are strange. In a moment, it leaves. ADELE snatches the paper from the typewriter and makes her way out of the building.)*

ACT TWO
Scene Three

The party goers are on the pier.

JAMES: Is everyone here?

ADELE: You tell us.

PILAR: People are here, but I don't like this, James. To hold a ritual near water is dangerous. Why in this particular place?

JAMES: You'll find out.

PILAR: But, water is unstable and anything could happen.

ALEXIS: I don't like the idea of a ritual.

JAKE: Are you afraid of the boogeyman?

RANDY: The only bogeymen are the live ones, pal.

TOMMY: You can say that, again. Let's get this game over with.

MITCH: What's the friggin' point of this spook game, anyway?

MARLENA: The "point" of this ritual is a demonstration of power. Perhaps, the term "ritual" is inaccurate.

RANDY: What would you call it, Miss Lake?

MARLENA: A controlled experiment.

RANDY: You lost me.

MARLENA: Soon, you'll see and no explanation will be necessary. Try not to be frightened.

JAMES: Let's begin. Everyone form a circle. Marlena, will you start us off?

MARLENA: The spear is placed at our feet in the center of the circle. Don't move for any reason; if you do, all could be lost. Look at the moon: a satellite knocked from its orbit which must now be brought back…carefully. Focus. (*A low rumble begins as the waters of the bay start to tremble, splashing higher and higher against the pier. The night sky becomes bright with the lunar light.*)

ALEXIS (*looking up*): Randy! Jake! The moon is moving closer to the Earth!

MARLENA: Quiet, you fool!

JAKE: My God! Alexis is right. Look at it!

TOMMY: Hey, baby, what the hell's goin' on here?

MARLENA: The spear is forcing the moon back into orbit.

ADELE: It's getting awful close. I hope it knows when to stop. It's incredible!

PILAR: We should not be doing this unholy thing. We are tampering with God's laws.

MARLENA: There! It's back in its proper orbit. I knew it! I was right. (*A movement catches her attention.*) What- what are you doing? Stop! You'll kill us all! (*JAMES bends down and touches the spear. The moment he puts his hand on it, there's a burst of light and a crash. Black out.*)

ACT THREE
Scene One

ADELE finds herself back in the basement of JAMES' skyscraper.

ADELE: What in the world happened? How did I get back here? I must have blacked out or something. (*She walks over to the desk and takes the paper out of its carriage.*) Wait a minute! I did this already. (*She reads from the paper, aloud.*) "The spear of Longinus plummeted from the heavens. Its power is limitless. It is a temptation to fools. It is a gift from the gods of the wandering planet. The ocean is its enemy. The Earth is its haven. It was fashioned from the Tree by Lucifer, the most beautiful of the gods. To Adam, he gave the weapon and from thence man has held the demon in his midst." (*She puts the paper down.*) Valerie's name is on this, but it's so unlike her style. It reads more like a cryptic telegram…a warning.

TOMMY: Is it?

ADELE: What? Tommy!

TOMMY: Is it a warning?

ADELE: You scared the hell out of me. Did you bring me here? Did I pass out on the pier?

TOMMY: I guess we both must've passed out. I found myself leaning against the door outside.

ADELE: Where are the others?

TOMMY: Beats me.

ADELE: Well, baby, you're a sight for sore eyes.

TOMMY: You makin' a pass at me?

ADELE: You wish. And, don't get fresh.

TOMMY: What are ya' reading?

ADELE: That's a damned good question. It's a piece of a script, I think; but, it reads more like some ancient, forbidden verse.

TOMMY: Come, again?

ADELE: Was Valerie religious?

TOMMY: I didn't know her too good; but, I'd say no.

ADELE: So would I. Who's there?

JAKE (Descending the spiral staircase.): It's I.

ADELE: Jake?

TOMMY: Where did you come from, man?

JAKE: I've been listening to your conversation. I heard you read that piece of script. It's very interesting. So, what do you make of it?

ADELE: You tell me, handsome. You know what it means, don't you?

JAKE: I don't. I'm not a religious man. If Alexis were here, she might know.

ADELE: I'll bet. How come James touched the spear?

TOMMY: We oughta' try and find him.

JAKE: I think we've more important things to do, tonight.

TOMMY: Like what?

JAKE: Like saving our bloody lives. Have either of you bothered looking heavenward?

ADELE: Why? What's out there?

JAKE: Take a look for yourself, Adele.

TOMMY: Just tell us and kill the suspense bit.

JAKE: It's moving closer to the Earth…too close.

ADELE: What are you saying?

MARLENA (*coming down the spiral staircase*): He's saying, my dear, that the end of the world may be upon us.

ADELE: The end of the world? What the hell is going on here?

MARLENA: I admire you, Miss Emerson. You have balls.

ADELE: Thanks. It was James who touched the spear and that's what's causing all this?

MARLENA: You catch on quickly.

ADELE: Where is he? Do you know, Miss Lake?

MARLENA: Close by; I'm certain of it.

ADELE: Why did James touch the spear? Does he know what he's done?

MARLENA: He knew. We have to find him. Have you any idea where he might be?

ADELE: Not a clue.

JAKE: The paper which you just read, did Valerie actually write it?

MARLENA: Does it matter, Mr. Chan?

JAKE: Not really, I suppose.

MARLENA: Then, don't waste our time with trifles.

TOMMY: Where do we start looking?

MARLENA: Here in this building, young man. The spear has placed us in this particular location for a purpose.

TOMMY: What about those murdered people-

MARLENA: Distractions -- all of it.

JAKE: Where are the others? What's happened to them?

MARLENA: I would assume that they are either back on the pier or aboard the yacht.

JAKE: Why not here with us?

MARLENA: They may well be somewhere in the building.

JAKE: If they're on board James' yacht, maybe the spear's there.

ADELE: Jake could be right about that.

MARLENA: It's doubtful.

TOMMY: I hate to interrupt, but I think we'd better start hunting for this thing.

JAKE: We'll split up into two groups: Miss Lake and I and Miss Emerson and Tommy.

MITCH (*He and PILAR descend the spiral staircase.*): Don't leave us out. Even a blind man can see.

PILAR: The moon -- have you seen it in the sky?

ADELE: We know, Pilar.

TOMMY: We're going on a treasure hunt to find that little ole' spear.

MITCH: A treasure hunt, you say? Pilar, let's you and me go back to James' place and, maybe, we'll find some buried treasure there.

ADELE: Mitch, what are you up to?

MITCH: You're a newspaper woman, lady, so you figure it out. The murders, the museum heist, the moon, and the God damned spear: all parts of some God damned jigsaw puzzle. So, what do the pieces spell out, huh?

ADELE: I'll bite.

MITCH: One piece is in back of all this. I know because an ex-con oughta' know. You, too, Tommy boy; savvy?

TOMMY: You're one up on me, man.

MITCH: I know who's behind that piece of the puzzle, the manipulator pulling all the strings on us puppets.

ADELE: Who is it, Mitch?

MITCH: First, I get me some priceless artifacts. I'm gonna' need you, Pilar. The rest of you can save friggin' humanity; but, if you do save it, I intend to keep my profit. Come on, baby, you can point out the best take.

PILAR: Good luck. I feel the spear is close by, but I also feel that death is close, as well.

MITCH: We're wastin' time.

ACT THREE
Scene Two

RANDY and ALEXIS find themselves on board JAMES' yacht.

RANDY: Alexis? Are you okay?

ALEXIS: What happened to us, Randy?

RANDY: We've set sail. We're moving out into the harbor.

ALEXIS: Are we being shanghaied?

JAMES (*coming on deck*): We've been set adrift, my dear.

ALEXIS: Randy, look at the water!

RANDY: There must be a storm ready to hit.

JAMES: If it were only that simple, young man.

ALEXIS: But, it's so clear and bright out.

RANDY: My God, Alexis, look up at the sky!

ALEXIS: The moon…it looks so huge.

JAMES: It's moving closer to the earth.

RANDY: On a collision course?

JAMES: The two planets will not touch. The gravity of the earth will rip apart the moon. There will be few survivors, if any.

ALEXIS: Are you telling us the truth or are you just trying to frighten us.

RANDY: How did this happen, James? You know, don't you?

JAMES: You're an intelligent man, tell me.

RANDY: The spear…that ancient spear is the cause.

JAMES: Yes.

RANDY: Then, where is it? We've got to find it.

JAMES: Do you know?

RANDY: Don't get smart, pal. Where is it?

JAMES: I don't have it.

RANDY: Then, who's got it? You're the one who touched it. I saw you.

JAMES: Perhaps, Marlena has it.

RANDY: Is she involved in this?

ALEXIS: She's a fascist, isn't she?

JAMES: What makes you say that, Alexis?

ALEXIS: She is, isn't she? I can smell one a hundred miles off.

JAMES: Good girl.

RANDY: And, what does that make you, James; some kind of a sympathizer?

JAMES: No.

RANDY: A collaborator, take your pick.

JAMES: An associate.

RANDY: You're full of crap.

ALEXIS: You're being disrespectful-

RANDY: Too bad. It's because of you that we're all going to get blown to smithereens.

ALEXIS: James, how much time to we have?

RANDY: Can the moon be sent back into orbit?

JAMES: It can be done, but we have very little time, not much more than an hour from the look of it.

RANDY: What?

JAMES: Maybe less. It will gain momentum due to the increase of gravity.

RANDY: Level with us; do we have a chance?

JAMES: If we can find the spear, yes.

ALEXIS: Why did you touch it?

JAMES: Impulse? The spear could have betrayed me and gone back into hiding.

ALEXIS: You talk as if it were alive.

JAMES: It is energy that has been harnessed by the ancient ones. It is alive.

RANDY: Steer this ship back to port. I just hope we can dock this boat in one piece.

ALEXIS: We've got to. There's the pier, it's not so far off. You can't miss it in all this moonlight.

RANDY: We're starting to slow down.

ALEXIS: The boat will crash against the pier!

JAMES: We've got to try. Why don't you two go below and have a look around for our missing souvenir? It just occurred to me that the spear might be on board ship. It's a long shot-

RANDY: It's worth a look. Come on, Alexis.

ALEXIS: I'll stay here with James. Maybe, I can help. I know how to pilot a boat. You look below.

JAMES: By the time you're done, we should be ready to dock.

RANDY: Call me when you're ready. We could help position the ship with the poles.

JAMES: It might work. Now, hurry! (*RANDY goes below deck.*) Let me take over.

ALEXIS: But-

JAMES: Do you presume to disobey me?

ALEXIS: Never! It was your safety and that of the yacht's that I feared for. The wheel's very difficult to handle.

JAMES: You disobeyed me.

ALEXIS: I didn't!. How can you say that? You made me into a thief and I should hate you for that.

JAMES: You were my confidante and my instrument of thievery. Look at the moon.

ALEXIS: Judgment Day is upon us! We've practiced black magic and are being punished!

JAMES: A fitting grave for a mutineer, wouldn't you say?

ALEXIS: I'm loyal to you!

JAMES: You've killed for me, as well.

ALEXIS: No! I didn't commit those murders. I know nothing of that! Nothing! I played up to Randy like you asked me to.

JAMES: We're veering off course. Give me the wheel.

ALEXIS: Take it! No! What are you doing? (*JAMES karate chops her on the back of the head. She collapses to the deck.*)

ACT THREE
Scene Three

TOMMY and ADELE are searching in the basement of JAMES' skyscraper.

TOMMY: Some treasure hunt, lookin' for a lousy spear.

ADELE: I wish Valerie were here. She could really help us.

TOMMY: How so?

ADELE: She knew about it and maybe she knew how to use it.

TOMMY: She'd still have to find it, right.

ADELE: Yes.

TOMMY: What exactly did Valerie know? And, don't play footsy with me.

ADELE: All right, handsome, I was her source material. We were working on a story that would have blown the lid off of James' little escapades. We both suspected him of treason, for starters.

TOMMY: Now, it's startin' to make sense; that friggin' screenplay was nothing but a cover. Cool. James must have overheard me and Val talkin'.

ADELE: Val was telling you all this at the party?

TOMMY: She sure was.

ADELE: Little idiot! Why?

TOMMY: Maybe, she wanted me to know just in case.

ADELE: Just in case she was bumped off, so she tosses hints like confetti?

TOMMY: What's on your mind?

ADELE: Do you trust Miss Lake?

TOMMY: No. She's a crook, like me.

ADELE: And, a practitioner of the occult.

TOMMY: You mean that supernatural jazz? Maybe.

ADELE: You don't think so?

TOMMY: That spear sounds like some kind of a weapon to me and that's hard, concrete stuff, not magic. If you know how to use it, you're in control, and control is what that dame is after.

ADELE: Smart boy.

TOMMY: Not so stupid as you thought, huh?

ADELE: There's a ticking brain inside that gorgeous head. Do you think Miss Lake knows where the spear is?

TOMMY: Yeah. I do.

ADELE: Then, why all the risk? Makes no sense.

TOMMY: She's lookin' to make points with someone.

ADELE: James?

TOMMY: Maybe. Now, let's find Marlena and Jake. I'll bet my life that chick knows where the spear is.

ADELE: And, if she doesn't?

TOMMY: We're dead.

ADELE: Come on!

TOMMY: I hope she hasn't been bumped off.

ADELE: Don't say that! We need her and her black magic skills. If the spear is here in this building, Marlena will know what to do with it. We don't.

TOMMY: That's not good, baby. I don't trust her.

ADELE (*hearing a rumbling sound*): Tommy…is the ground starting to shake? It is! Oh, my God, this is it! It's the end! (*They hurry up the spiral staircase.*)

ACT THREE
Scene Four

On board JAMES' yacht.

RANDY: It's not on board. It's just not here. Where's Alexis? (*Spotting her on the deck floor, he helps her up.*) What the hell just happened, James? Did you do this?

JAMES: What of it?

RANDY: Filthy bastard! You're behind all of this, aren't you. You wouldn't mind seeing us all dead.

ALEXIS (*recovering*): Randy, he killed Valerie and those other people. He's a murderer and a thief.

JAMES (*putting the boat on automatic pilot*): I'll tell you a few things, Mr. Director. Alexis, here, stole the artifacts to help finance the coming movement in this country. She betrayed me to Pilar, to whom she gave several of the stolen artifacts. More fool her! Pilar told me of her betrayal. Our darling Alexis is no innocent. Her hands are as filthy as mine.

ALEXIS: No! Don't listen to him, Randy. I did steal the artifacts. I don't deny it. But, I had nothing to do with the murders. I swear it! And, I'm no traitor.

RANDY: You killed Valerie and those other people. You did that.

JAMES: Yes.

RANDY: In God's name, why?

JAMES: A murder takes priority over a mere theft. It kept the police occupied on less pressing matters. And, besides, I had to test the spear's power as a weapon.

ALEXIS: He's a monster!

JAMES: An accurate statement, so what's the point in denying it? (*He lashes out at RANDY with a metal hook.*)

ALEXIS: Stop it, James, please. Randy, he'll kill you.

RANDY: James, back off! The whole, damned world is going to end soon enough.

ALEXIS: He doesn't hear you.

JAMES: Oh, I hear him. I'll satisfy myself with the killing sport.

ALEXIS: You're insane. Look at the moon! It's so close!

RANDY: James, listen to me; the boat's heading straight for the pier. It's going to crack up. There's no way we can dock it.

JAMES: Let it crash. I'll kill the two of you, first. (*He swings at RANDY and grazes him on the forehead. RANDY tackles JAMES and wrestles him to the deck. ALEXIS tries to grab the steel hook from JAMES, but can't. JAMES pushes her away as the two men struggle to their feet. RANDY belts JAMES in the jaw as the boat crashes into the pier.*)

RANDY: Alexis, jump!

ACT THREE
Scene Five

MTCH is hiding in the shadows of the pier.

MTCH: A blind man is gonna' lead 'em. Rot…I'm blind, but I can see the details of the pressure which holds the glue of this rotten universe together. Words…vibrations that resonate through infinity, but no one friggin' hears 'em! No one, except me! The lines of infinity meet at the crossroads of infinity. Is all this destined to repeat itself? Trapped in a rotating, infinite circle? Christ! Where the hell is Pilar? (*He hears JAKE and MARLENA enter, who discover the spear…exactly where it had been during the ritual. He ducks behind a parked car.*)

JAKE: You knew where it was all along, didn't you?

MARLENA: Call it a surmise, Mr. Chan. Pick it up.

JAKE: You pick it up. I don't want it.

MARLENA: Are you afraid, Mr. Chan?

JAKE: Yes.

MITCH (*comes out of hiding*): Leave that spear where it is.

MARLENA: Are you insane? We must-

MITCH: Use it? Then, I'll do the using, lady. (*He picks up the spear.*)

MARLENA (*lunges at MITCH and takes out a hand pistol*): Give it to me!

MITCH: Fuck you, lady. (*As the yacht crashes into the pier, JAMES grabs the spear from him. MARLENA fires a shot at him, and he is wounded.*)

JAMES: Good shot, Marlena.

MARLENA: Throw the spear into the water! (*ADELE and TOMMY run on stage.*)

JAMES: No. I'll see the damned world come to an end first.

ADELE: James, you've lost.

TOMMY: There's no use talkin' to him.

ADELE: Tommy, take it from him! It's our only chance! (*TOMMY rushes JAMES as RANDY and ALEXIS recover. TOMMY knocks the spear from JAMES' hand and RANDY picks it up.*)

MARLENA: Toss it in the water! (*RANDY flings the spear into the water. There is an explosion underwater as the moon stops its collision course with the Earth. Slowly, it drifts back into its proper orbit.*)

EPILOGUE

RANDY: We're drifting closer to shore.

ALEXIS: We were shifted back into James' yacht. Adele is radioing in her story. Randy, will James make it?

RANDY: He's strong. I think he'll pull through.

ALEXIS: And, the moon is safely back in its orbit. Is the spear lost forever? I hope it is.

RANDY: I doubt it.

MITCH (*comes on deck*): It'll turn up in somebody's backyard, someday.

ALEXIS: That's a frightening thought. I just hope it's the right backyard.

MITCH: I'm betting it won't be the right backyard.

RANDY: Try not to think about it.

MITCH: Marlena's thinking about it. I bet she starts hunting for it. Let her have it. A weapon like that is just what that bitch deserves. She's rotten.

RANDY: It's been a night to remember.

MITCH: If anybody remembers it aside from us.

RANDY: What do you mean, Mitch?

MITCH: Look at the Battery? Cars moving along, people walking late at night. I don't see any panic, do you? I didn't see a living soul the whole damned night.

ALEXIS: Come to think of it, neither did I. I didn't pay any attention to it at the time. (*ADELE and PILAR come on deck.*)

ADELE: Funny that you two should say that, Alexis; when I was trying to phone in my story, I got nothing but static. I only told James that I'd phoned it in. The police never did show up, but Valerie's body was…gone when Pilar and I went back to the skyscraper.

PILAR: And, when Mitch and I went to James' apartment, we encountered no one on our way there. The city seemed completely deserted and, yet, I felt…

RANDY: What, Miss Gomez?

PILAR: As though I were being watched from a distance. I felt that if I were to turn around quickly enough that I would see whoever it was. I was afraid.

ADELE: Pilar, when you left the skyscraper with James, did he come back down the stairs?

PILAR: No. We left for the yacht with Miss Lake.

ADELE: Well, someone did. Someone very tall and-

PILAR: Yes?

ADELE: And, strange…his movements were odd. It's like he knew I was there. (*She laughs nervously.*) I just gave myself the willies!

PILAR: It's as if we have all been manipulated.

ALEXIS: I have this terrible feeling that the spear will turn up, again. Who could have made such a thing?

MARLENA (*comes on deck with JAKE and TOMMY*): They were a race of beings, my dear, who were the forerunners of the ancient Sumerians. It was fashioned from the very Tree of Life which was not corrupted by Adam's touch.

ADELE: How do you know this, Miss Lake?

MARLENA: You doubt me, Miss Emerson?

ADELE: That's just it, lady, I believe you. And, by the way, weren't there two trees in that Garden?

MARLENA: Yes. But, the Tree of Knowledge was defiled by Man.

ADELE: And?

MARLENA: The trees were planted by an ancient race of beings mentioned in the Bible as the Nefilim. They were a race of gods who procreated with mortals. Fear them, Miss Emerson. Fear their return.

ADELE: A race of beings that came from another planet; but, from where?

MARLENA (*pointing to the setting moon*): There!

End of play.

SKYBLAZERS:

Jack Parsons Ed Forman

A Play in Four Acts

by

Gerard Denza

CHARACTERS

JACK PARSONS, a young and naive scientist.
ED FORMAN, an engineer and a man of strong convictions.
PROFESSOR VONKARMAN, a teacher at Caltech.
FRANK MALINA, a student at Caltech and a mathematician.
APOLLO "AMO" SMITH, a student at Caltech.
TSIEN HSUE-SHEN, a student at Caltech, from China.
JANE WOLFE, former silent movie actress.
GRADY MCMURTRY, an occultist.
CANDY CAMERON-PARSONS, an avant-garde artist.
RALPH BENTON, former police Captain and murderer.

PLACE
The action takes place in Pasadena, a suburb of Los Angeles, CA.

TIME
The play begins in 1952.

SCENES

Prologue
The year is 1952 just outside the lab at Caltech.

Act One
Scene One: In the Arroyo Seco just outside
the suburb of Pasadena in 1936.
Scene Two: A few days later in a lab at Caltech.
Scene Three: Later that evening in the lab at Caltech.

Act Two
Scene One: In the Arroyo Seco test site in 1939.
Scene Two: Early evening at the
Caltech lab. The year is 1940.
Scene Three: Later that year at the county prison.

Act Three
Scene One: At the Arroyo test site. The year is 1941.
Scene Two: Late evening at Jane Wolfe's apartment in 1943.
Scene Three: Early morning at the Caltech lab in 1943.

Act Four
Scene One: Visitor's room at the state prison in 1951.
Scene Two: Midnight at Jane Wolfe's apartment in 1952.
Scene Three: Late afternoon at the Caltech lab in 1952.

Epilogue
It's 1952 at the Arroyo Seco test site.

PROLOGUE

An explosion rips across the stage knocking down CANDY
CAMERON-PARSONS and ED FORMAN as they're
hurrying toward the laboratory at Caltech. The year is June
17, 1952, and it's just past 5 P.M. A second explosion almost
immediately follows. Smoke hovers over the stage as bits of
debris fall on to CANDY and ED.

ACT ONE
Scene One

In the Arroyo Seco near the suburb of Pasadena. JACK and ED are sitting on a sand dune with what looks like a metal rocket. JACK has his usual vest on and ED is wearing his white, driver's cap. The year is 1936.

JACK (*pointing to the moon*): We'll aim it toward the moon.

ED (*brushing off his pants with his white cap*): We'll hit it, man. We'll hit it and go beyond it.

JACK: Where'd you have in mind, Ed?

ED: To the edge of the Milky Way galaxy. I know we can do it, Jack. You just tell me what you want built, and we'll take it there. The moon's just a stop-off point. Once the barrier's taken down, anything's possible.

JACK: But, we need money. We're broke. And, we can't do this part time. It has to consume our lives, Ed. It has to take up all of our time and energy and money, which we don't have. Everything else simply doesn't count -- not even our jobs in the powder factory.

ED: What exactly do we need?

JACK (*picking up a handful of sand and letting it slip through his clenched fist*): Respectability, Ed. Everyone laughs at rocketry and says it's impractical and a fool's game. Look at how they mocked Robert Goddard, and his book is the only real textbook on rocketry out there. The man turned himself into some kind of a semi-recluse. He gave up. We won't give up.

ED: Maybe we should correspond with him, again? I know he was pumping us for our ideas, but we could do the same. Maybe even take a trip out to Roswell. It might be worth it.

JACK: It's not a bad idea. But, I don't think Professor Goddard is the type to share any of his discoveries. He doesn't trust anyone and that's a damned shame.

ED: He can trust us.

JACK: He won't. But, maybe a trip out to New Mexico is a possibility once we're really underway here. I'd like to talk to him about his "experience" sitting on that tree and his "revelation." It sounds almost spiritual.

ED: Or an encounter of some kind.

JACK: What kind of an encounter did you have in mind? Not extraterrestrial?

ED: Is it so far fetched? We read about it all the time in the science fantasy magazines, don't we?

JACK: We do. But...

ED: It's crossed your mind, too, that maybe Goddard was taken up by some kind of space craft. Think about it, Jack, it's not as crazy as it sounds. He was taken airborne in something... some kind of vessel that had terrific speed.

JACK: Maybe. But, just maybe. I'll admit that I'm open to the possibility. I'd have to be.

ED (*playing with the "rocket"*): Now, where do we go and get "respectability?"

JACK: Academia has to supply that. We're pretty big on hands-on testing and hardware, but we need the high-tech math to go with it. We need calculations on lift-off and speed and trajectory. I'm not up to that kind of math.

ED: You telling me that we need to go to the universities?

JACK (*taking the "rocket" from ED*): Yes. Caltech is the best place. I've heard of a Professor vonKarman who teaches there. He's supposed to be quite a character. He might be open to our ideas.

ED: Well, if he recognizes genius, he's sure to spot you. You're the explosives and chemical King. You're "it" on a stick of dynamite.

JACK: And, where do I put that dynamite? In one of your man-made contraptions, engineer. (*Tapping ED on the shoulder with the "rocket."*) You'd better start blowing your own horn or I'll just have to do it for you, Ed. We're a team. Period. And, nothing separates us. If we blow ourselves up, we'll both be headed for kingdom come together. And, if we should happen to land on the moon, we both touch down. We're like Romulus and Remus, only we're not stopping off at any one place. It's the uncharted galaxy we're after.

ED: You can do it, man.

JACK: We can do it. We're going to do it! But, we need help and a proper laboratory and funding.

ED: Will they take us seriously?

JACK: No. But, what of it? There has to be at least one or two daredevils at Caltech. We'll find them, Ed. Man has always looked up at the moon, but we're going to blast off and actually land there. Let's bring this rocket with us. Your handiwork, engineer.

ED: And, your explosives -- on paper, that is.

JACK: We could always threaten to blow up the place.

ED: Like the time your were at that military academy your mom sent you to? You blew up half the toilets!

JACK: Nothing to it. And, I blew up all the toilets.

ED: I know. And, if we just happen to get lab space, we just might have a couple of explosions at Caltech! (*Both men jump up and let out a shout.*)

ACT ONE
Scene Two

Takes place in a well equipped lab at Caltech, a few days later. The lab is brightly lit by the many windows and it is impeccably clean and well ordered.

JACK: Professor vonKarman? Jack Parsons. My friend, Ed Forman.

VON KARMAN: A pleasure, young men. Are you students here at Caltech? I don't know everyone, you know.

JACK: Funny that you should ask that, Professor. We're not Caltech students, Ed and I.

VON KARMAN: Are you thinking of enrolling?

ED: No.

JACK: We need your help, Professor. You see, it's like this: we need a good mathematician who can help get us to the moon.

VON KARMAN: To the moon, you say? You get straight to the purpose. Rocketry, is that what you're talking about, Mr. Parsons?

JACK: Yes, Professor.

VON KARMAN: You'll need a good mathematician and one with a good imagination. I might be able to help you. How far along have you gotten with your rocketry? That's a fine mock up of a space craft. You built this?

JACK: Ed, here, did.

ED: Jack launched it with his explosives.

JACK: But, we need a good science man --- a theorist -- and we need to use Caltech's facilities. Can you help us, sir?

ED: Say yes.

VON KARMAN: I can't sanction your rocketry experiments. The technology-

JACK (*picking up a test tube and pointing it at VON KARMAN*): Will exist! We're creating it just like the Wright Brothers did forty years ago with aerodynamics. Rocketry will surpass that branch of science because it must. The imagination is already there.

VON KARMAN: But the concretization of it is not.

JACK: But Robert Goddard's textbook of rocketry-

VON KARMAN: Theory. Some of it quite sound but, as yet, unproven.

ED: We'll prove it. (*A moment's pause.*)

VON KARMAN: A man of a few words, but very strong ones. I like you both and I like your sincerity. You'll be ridiculed by most people. You know this.

ED: We know it, all right.

VON KARMAN: And, that doesn't bother you at all?

JACK: Should it, Professor?

VON KARMAN: It doesn't. I can see that or you wouldn't have come here today. You know, this terrible Depression has affected even this great institution. I can let you use our lab facilities after hours and I can even recommend a young man for you to meet.

ED: That's why we're here.

VON KARMAN: Wait here, please, I won't be a minute. (*Exits.*)

ED: What do you think?

JACK: We've got ourselves a lab.

ED: But, who's this guy the professor's bringing in to meet us?

JACK: Beats me.

ED: Not knowing, makes me nervous; that's why I never go on blind dates.

JACK: Here they come. Be nice.

VON KARMAN (*beaming like a proud father*): Jack? Ed? Meet Mr. Frank Malina: a very level-headed, young man. He's just written a paper on space flight and its benefits for humanity. Frank?

FRANK: Well, Professor, my paper was kindly received, I daresay.

JACK (*hoisting himself up on one of the lab tables*): So, you believe that space flight is possible?

FRANK: Yes. It's only a matter of time and proper theory and formula.

ED: And, testing.

FRANK: Theory and calculation come first, even Jules Verne conceded that much.

JACK: You've read Verne's "From the Earth to the Moon?"

ED: You're our kind of man.

FRANK: Yes. Several times. Theory, calculation, ground testing-

ED: What?

FRANK: Ground testing. It's sort of an upside down motor to test acceleration, fuel consumption -- like going in the opposite direction, but still arriving at your destination.

ED: I don't like traveling backwards. Going forward gets you there a lot faster

FRANK: If you arrive in one piece. Once we establish the proper ratio of fuel to escape velocity, then we push forward even faster. You take a step backward, build the proper motor and triggering mechanism and...wham...from the Earth to the moon is no longer fiction.

ED (*doubtful*): I guess.

VON KARMAN: Jack, what do you say to Frank's approach? It's a sound, scientific method.

JACK (*jumping down from the lab table*): It's kind of frustrating, Professor. Ed and I like hard-core hands-on testing. I guess you'd call it trial and error.

FRANK: Errors cost time and money. If you gentlemen want academic blessings and the science community's endorsement, there's a proper way of going about experimentation. We need to keep records of everything: before, during and after actual testing. We need to work on theory and, then, formulate the equations and solve them. It's not as bad as it sounds, honest!

JACK: I guess we'll have to take your word for it.

VON KARMAN: Good! You won't regret it. And, now, you're all invited back here, tonight, for an informal gathering. All three of you will come and we'll talk some more. Okay? I can see that you two gentlemen are not entirely convinced; but, young Frank, here, speaks like a true scientist. And, he's a damned good mathematician.

ACT ONE
Scene Three

An informal gathering at the Caltech laboratory later that evening. There's a bucket of champagne at center stage and a table with various party food at stage left.

JACK: This lab looks better at night. It's like a pocket of refracted light off a diamond.

ED (*laughing*): I haven't seen too many diamonds.

VON KARMAN (*entering from center stage*): Gentlemen, do you prefer the night hours? So do I. The planet is turned away from the sun and, yet, that doesn't explain the darkness that we experience. In my opinion, more light should be reaching us. It's a phenomenon I'd like to investigate one day.

JACK: Maybe once on the moon, we can investigate it and come up with an answer for your question, Professor.

VON KARMAN: You never stop thinking about that celestial object, do you?

ED: Not if we can get there. Personally, I can't wait to take a ride in one of my rockets.

VON KARMAN: Oh? Do you have the blueprint for your space vessel?

JACK: As a matter of fact, he does. Tell him about it, Ed. (*AMO walks in.*)

VON KARMAN: Ah, Mr. Apollo Smith, I'd like you to meet Jack Parsons and Ed Forman: chemist and engineer.

AMO: Nice meeting you boys. Everyone calls me "Amo." I ran into Frank on campus today and he invited me along. Hope you don't mind, Professor.

VON KARMAN: You know better than that. You're always welcome. But, now we must listen to Mr. Forman. He's about to tell us of his rocket ship design.

AMO: No kidding? You've got the floor, Forman.

ED: Ed. It'd be a four tiered ship, if you would. In the nose of the ship, would be the pilot and co-pilot and navigator: this would be the "eyes" of the ship. The second level would be your auxiliary crew and back-up. The third level would be crew's quarters and galley. The lower level would house the motor, the oxygen supply and a sort of tool surplus. It's pretty basic, but it's a start. And, the ship would be in constant rotation.

AMO: It's a good start, Ed. And a trip to the moon would only take a couple of days once we reach escape velocity. After a couple flights, we could turn it into a "milk run."

JACK: It's the first step in reaching the stars and the outer solar system. It can be done.

AMO: But?

JACK: There are no "buts." Want to join our team, Amo?

AMO: Yes! Is Frank on the team, too?

JACK: Just about.

AMO (*glancing over his shoulder*): Hey, don't look now, but the "son of Heaven" just walked in.

ED: Who's that?

AMO: Mr. Tsien Hsue-shen. I don't fancy him much, but he's as close to a genius as you're likely to come across.

FRANK: And, doesn't he know it? But, he's a decent guy: strictly no nonsense.

AMO: And no sense of humor.

JACK: Is he a team player?

ED: I've never met a person I can't get along with. Let's ask him over. And, if I can't get along with this "son of Heaven," I'll just belt him one.

JACK: Behave, engineer.

VON KARMAN: Tsien? Would you care to join us?

TSIEN: Of course, Professor vonKarman. I hope you don't mind my appearance here, tonight. But, there has been talk on campus of rocketry and the use of our laboratory. It will be a future branch of science, I'm certain.

ED (*shaking hands with TSIEN*): Pleased to meet you Tsien. I'm Ed Forman.

JACK: Mr. Engineer to us. I'm Jack Parsons.

TSIEN: A pleasure. Frank? Amo? What has been discussed?

JACK: A trip to the moon, Tsien, and not on gossamer wings, either. The Professor, here, says we can use the lab and we've got sort of an unofficial test-site up in the Arroyo. Want to join our team?

ED: Say "yes."

TSIEN: Fascinating. Yes. I would love to join and be a part of your team. There are many challenges to meet, but I strongly believe in your idea of space travel. In theory, at least, the problems are not insurmountable. I'm honored. When can we get started?

JACK: Tomorrow night and right where we're standing. Isn't that right, Professor?

VON KARMAN: I'll see to the arrangements. But, remember, theory and then experiment -- controlled experiment and the results will further your work.

ED: That's not gonna' be easy. (*The group breaks up and he notices two new arrivals.*)

VON KARMAN: Hello? May I help you? I'm Professor vonKarman.

GRADY: Grady McMurtry. This is a friend of mine, Jane Wolfe.

JANE (*dressed casually and a just a bit unorthodox*): A pleasure, Professor. We're not party crashing, are we? We heard there was a science fantasy party going on. Grady here is quite the aficionado of the genre.

GRADY: You don't mind our being here, do you? We'll leave if we're not wanted.

VON KARMAN: Stay, young man. We're not a bunch of snobs, quite the contrary. Are you a student?

GRADY: No. Not here. I've just finished my undergraduate work at USC. So what's tonight's theme?

VON KARMAN: A research team into rocketry is being born. It's quite impressive, actually. Chemists, engineers, and mathematicians: tonight may be a benchmark in the annals of science.

JANE: It sounds like a momentous occasion, Professor. But, perhaps, it's all been done before?

VON KARMAN: What do you mean by that? What you just said can't be true. It's not possible.

JANE: I'm not referring to hard science, Professor. I'm referring to another science.

VON KARMAN: Go on, please. (*CANDY walks in and all eyes turn to her.*)

AMO: Get a load of her. Brother!

ED: She's a beauty. Who is she?

TSIEN: A very striking appearance.

JACK: She's got beauty and intelligence.

FRANK: You know her, Jack?

JACK: Can't you see? And, not yet, in answer to your question. The Professor is doing his stuff.

AMO: Bring her over here!

ED: Down, boy! You're dripping saliva.

AMO: That's not all I'm dripping.

FRANK: That's disgusting.

AMO: Isn't it?

CANDY (*walking over to JANE*): Hello. My name's Marjorie Cameron, but call me Candy.

JANE (*shaking CANDY'S hand*): Wolfe. Jane Wolfe.

CANDY: Don't I know you, Miss Wolfe?

JANE: Over-the-hill actress, honey. I worked in silent movies. Yes. I'm that ancient. Worked with Mary Pickford in "Rebecca of Sunnybrook Farm," and I've got a few other museum pieces to my credit.

CANDY: I know the movie. How do you come to be here, Miss Wolfe?

JANE: Jane. I love parties, especially intellectual ones.

CANDY: Is that what this is?

JANE: A scientists' party is what I'm told -- the hard-core stuff -- completely out of my depth. Me and Grady here come to terms with life from a different perspective.

GRADY: Grady McMurtry. Nice meeting you, Candy. And, no, Jane's the occultist here, but we do share an interest in science fantasy.

CANDY: What are the boys over there talking about: science, the "hard-core" stuff?

JANE: No, honey, their main topic is you. They haven't taken their eyes off you. Do you dabble in the occult, Candy?

CANDY: No.

GRADY: Jane's group, the OTO, is looking for new blood, if you'll pardon the expression.

JANE (*staring hard at GRADY*): Yes…an unfortunate choice of words, Grady.

CANDY: The two of you are talking over my head.

VON KARMAN (*taking advantage of an opening in the conversation*): Good evening. I'm Professor vonKarman.

CANDY: Candy Cameron. Nice meeting you, Professor. Is this a party or an august meeting of scientists?

VON KARMAN: You're a very perceptive young woman. Yes. I couldn't have phrased it better.

CANDY: And, the outcome, Professor?

VON KARMAN: A trip to the heavens and beyond.

CANDY: Wow! I'm glad I came. And, how will we get there?

GRADY: "We?"

CANDY: I don't like being left out. How, Professor?

TSIEN (*walking over*): In a rocket ship: very practical and feasible. I am Tsien Hue Shen. Are you interested in science, Miss Cameron?

CANDY: Let's stick with this rocket ship. Has it been built?

TSIEN: The blueprints and theory need to be worked out: tiresome but challenging. It will not take long. Within our lifespan, our goal will be realized.

CANDY: You're pretty sure of yourself, aren't you?

TSIEN: As a scientist, I must be.

CANDY: That was a compliment. I like you, Tsien. What's your field?

TSIEN: Mathematics. Here is Frank Malina, another mathematician.

FRANK: Hello.

CANDY: Nice meeting you, Frank.

FRANK (*blushing*): Thank you.

CANDY: Where exactly will your rocket ship take you? To the moon?

FRANK: Yes.

CANDY (*tossing back her head and laughing good-naturedly*): I knew it. And, I love it. You know what I think? I think you boys are scientists and romantics -- my kind of men.

VON KARMAN: They are romantics and just a bit insane, as well.

CANDY (*looking approvingly at FRANK and TSIEN*): The price of being a genius. My kind of men.

JANE: Does one need a rocket ship to leave the earth?

TSIEN: What other method would there be, Miss Wolfe?

VON KARMAN (*offering her a glass of champagne*): Please, tell us, Miss Wolfe. You broached this subject before.

GRADY: You may be sorry you asked.

JANE: Shut up, Grady. What about man's mind? Is there anything more powerful?

FRANK: You're not talking about levitation, are you?

GRADY: No...that's not what she means.

JANE: Get yourself some liquor, Grady. And, get me a refill. (*Addressing VON KARMAN.*) It's what will one day be termed science.

FRANK: I understand. Occultism. Astral projection of the etheric body.

TSIEN: You mean giving up the ghost? But, that is death.

FRANK: No, Tsien. You place yourself in deep meditation and out springs your astral phantom, if you would.

JANE: Very good. A little vulgar in the terminology, but you're right.

FRANK: It's the bunk. I don't buy this mysticism rhetoric.

TSIEN: Miss Wolfe, you state that one day it will be within the realm of science. Yes. Perhaps. I don't judge your beliefs for at the present moment in history, our talk of space travel is derided as the imaginings of small children.

VON KARMAN (*sipping his champagne*): Good point, Tsien.

FRANK: I'm still not buying it.

JANE: Why not? Tell me.

FRANK: I will. (*Forgetting his shyness.*) In a word, prove it. If the astral body can travel anywhere -- and I assume that it has that potential -- where are the records of its travels: the diaries, the charts? Where can they be found if they actually exist.?

JANE: Thanks. (*Taking a glass of champagne from GRADY.*) Maybe, they have been found.

FRANK: Now, you're just being enigmatic, Miss Wolfe.

JANE: No. Not at all.

FRANK: Then, where?

JANE: In the ancient library of Alexandria.

FRANK: Well, that's pretty convenient. It was destroyed two thousand years ago by the Romans.

JANE: No, Frank, it wasn't. (*Downing the remainder of her drink.*) And, aren't you the cynic. Hit me, again

CANDY (*walking over to where JACK, AMO, and ED are standing*): Hello, boys. I'm Candy.

ED: Ed Forman. My two friends, Jack Parsons and Amo. Nice meeting you, Candy. Looks like you just left a heated discussion back there.

CANDY: Hard science versus mysticism.

ED: Whose side were you on?

CANDY: I like rocket ships. I want you boys to build us one.

AMO: "Us?"

CANDY: Do you mind, Amo?

AMO (smiling like a schoolboy): Not at all.

CANDY: Jack?

JACK: We'll name the first rocket ship "Candy." Do you mind?

CANDY: No, Jack. I'd be honored. But, why not call it "Skyblazer?" (*Shifting back to the other conversation.*)

FRANK: What do you mean by that, Miss Wolfe: that the ancients made copies?

JANE: They were no one's fools.

FRANK: Copying scrolls was an art form, granted.

VON KARMAN: A very exacting labor and quite honored in its day. I believe what you say, Miss Wolfe, that somewhere, hidden, is a duplicate of the ancients' Alexandrian library. Do you know of its location?

JANE: No, Professor, I don't.

VON KARMAN (*pointing his champagne glass at her*): I don't believe you, Miss Wolfe.

JANE: Thanks a lot.

TSIEN (*puzzled*): But, the science of metallurgy was limited to jewelry and military weapons.

GRADY (*laughing and not good-naturedly*): That does seem a valid point, Jane. Rocket ships made out of masonry wouldn't get too far off the ground, I think.

JANE (*getting just a little angry*): Who said anything about ancient rocket ships. Their minds propelled objects: any objects of any size. They journeyed through space by means of hidden "doorways." They knew how to reassemble themselves through the folds in time and space which surround us. Rocket ships weren't needed.

ED: What's this about rocket ships not being needed? Who says? (*Helps himself to some food from the table.*) You trying to put me out of a job?

AMO: We need 'em, that's for sure. And, me and Ed are gonna' help build 'em. Right, engineer?

ED: You bet.

JANE: I'm not arguing with modern science, boys. I like hardware, and I wish you all the luck in the heavens.

VON KARMAN: A wonderful word that is.

AMO: I kind of like it, too.

TSIEN: The Milky Way galaxy will one day be charted through exploration. It will take special men and women to board these space ships, but they are here, present, in this room.

ED (clapping TSIEN on the shoulder): Good for you, man.

GRADY: You boys will chart the stars one day. But, don't look now, someone else has stars in his eyes.

JANE (looking over toward to where JACK and CANDY are talking): Don't embarrass them.

JACK: Where are you from, Candy?

CANDY: The Midwest, Iowa. Very boring and best forgotten. I just got out of the Navy. Jack?

JACK: Yes?

CANDY: I want to join your team here, but I don't have any training in science.

JACK: What did you do in the Navy?

CANDY: Photographer. I was pretty good at it, too.

JACK: You'll be the team's historian. You'll take photos of everything -- even our failures.

CANDY (sensing JACK'S vulnerable nature): There won't be any failures. Anything that blows up has a kick to it and anything that backfires can be righted. We won't fail, Jack.

And, thanks for having me on board. Thank you. (*JACK kisses her.*)

JACK: Thank you. I hope I take a good picture.

CANDY: Leave that to me, handsome-

JACK (*taking CANDY'S hands*): Candy? What's wrong. Your hands just went ice cold.

CANDY: It's nothing. No. It is something, but I'm not so sure what. It's like someone just stepped on my grave and I saw-

JACK: What? Tell me, baby?

CANDY: It's just too stupid. Let's join the others. They're trying not to stare.

JACK: Tell me what's wrong.

CANDY: I saw you sitting in a court room.

JACK: On trial?

CANDY: No. It wasn't like that. Please. Come on, let's join the others. I do have a wild and vivid imagination, you know. I'm an artist, too.

JACK: Okay. Your hands are warming up.

VON KARMAN: Ah! Jack and Candy, please join us. We need to make a toast.

JACK: Go ahead, Professor.

VON KARMAN: No, Jack. You and Ed. You two young men had the courage to turn a dream into a reality: the hard reality of science.

AMO: Was that the toast, Professor?

VON KARMAN: Don't be flippant. Jack? Ed?

ED: I'm no speech maker. And, besides, Jack speaks for me. Always.

CANDY (*addressing the group*): Everybody? Take a glass of champagne. (*She takes the bottle from the bucket and fills everyone's glasses.*) Come on, handsome, the floor is yours.

JACK: To a night of dedication to space travel. Rocketry will one day be a recognized science. Truly, this is an epic moment when mankind will advance toward the heavens…toward our destiny. (*Everyone raises his and her glass to shout "Cheers!"*)

ACT TWO
Scene One

Out in the Arroyo Seco test site. The year is 1939. The charred remains of an explosion are littered about the site. JACK and ED are picking up some of the debris.

JACK (*picking up a piece of debris and tossing it aside*): Okay. At least, it exploded. It would have gotten itself off the ground.

ED: Too bad it's pointing in the wrong direction.

JACK: Part of Frank's theory.

ED: Yeah. Ass backwards.

JACK: You don't like Frank much, do you?

ED (*dodging the question*): Where is he?

JACK: He'll be here with vonKarman.

ED: He oughta' be here now. Here's Tsien.

TSIEN (*running up to them, a little out of breath*): Forgive my being late for the test. I heard the explosion. Had it been pointing skyward, would it have been airborne?

JACK: Maybe.

ED: Yes.

TSIEN: What is wrong here?

ED (*pointing to the horizon*): Where's Frank? Where's Amo?

TSIEN: Amo cannot come today. He-

ED: I don't want to hear his excuses.

TSIEN: He has other commitments or so he said.

ED: This here is supposed to be his commitment. Where is he?

JACK: Down, boy. Next time we'll point the damned rocket right-side up.

ED: That suits me just fine.

TSIEN: Calm yourself, Ed. We are making progress. Our theories are working out in practice. Within the year, we'll be ready for an actual launch. I know this.

ED: I wish I did, Tsien.

JACK: Here's Frank and vonKarman. Hey, Candy's with them. Hello, baby! (*He and CANDY embrace and kiss. She is carrying a picnic basket on one arm.*)

CANDY (*looking about the littered landscape*): Was it a successful test? Looks like it.

JACK: You trying to be funny or something?

CANDY: Yes. I brought some food for you boys.

JACK (*taking the picnic basket from her*): Thanks. Did you bring some nice, greenbacks with you, too? We need 'em.

CANDY: As a matter of fact, I did.

JACK: It's cash money or nothing, baby. We need the dough. We're broke.

CANDY: I want you all to hear this.

JACK: Gentlemen? My girlfriend, here, has some news to tell. Candy?

CANDY: I was at the lab waiting for Frank and the Professor to show up when a stranger comes in: a young man by the name of Weld Arnold. He said he was an assistant from the astro-physics lab...I think.

ED (*inspecting the inside of the picnic basket*): Never heard of him.

CANDY: He's heard of you and he wants to help and with no strings attached, either.

ED: So where's the money?

JACK: Hey, engineer, simmer down. She's coming to that part, right, baby?

CANDY (*handing the money to JACK*): Here. One thousand dollars in cash money, of course.

TSIEN: Generous. Is it a loan or a gift?

CANDY: A gift, Tsien.

ED (*putting the picnic basket down*): I'd like to thank him. Truly. Man, this is friggin' great! Three cheers for Weld Arnold.

CANDY: I couldn't convince him to come. But, he wishes us luck in blasting off.

FRANK: Very strange.

VON KARMAN: Indeed, yes.

ED: Nice people aren't strange, pal. This is our first endowment so let's all try and be grateful, shall we?

FRANK: I wasn't being critical, Ed. But, it is coming from left field.

ED: What of it? Calling someone strange sounds pretty critical to me.

FRANK: To you, maybe, but I was just-

ED: Just being what? I've got a short fuse today. Me and Jack, here, are doing all the heavy stuff and you come waltzing in at the tail end. Yeah. I'm in a rotten mood!

JACK: Easy, engineer. We've got money now and man do we know how to spend it. Thank you, Mr. Weld Arnold!

VON KARMAN: Gentlemen and lady, we might also look to the government for funding.

CANDY: Will they take us seriously, Professor?

VON KARMAN: If the approach is correct, yes, Candy, I believe that they will.

ED: Meaning?

VON KARMAN: Watch that tone of voice. The propeller plane has gone as far as it can which is approximately four hundred miles per hour. Now, what about a jet propelled airplane? Have any of you thought of that?

ED: And, what about our trip to the moon?

VON KARMAN: It's impractical without sufficient funding.

FRANK: One thousand dollars won't get us past the stratosphere. And, I'm still wondering about this money. Was it obtained honestly?

CANDY (*staring meaningfully at FRANK*): I'm sure it was, Frank. I'm a pretty good judge of character most of the time.

ED (*glancing at FRANK*): I knew it. I just knew we could depend on you, hot shot Caltech man!

TSIEN: I must agree with Ed. I understand what you are saying, Frank. But, let me propose this: a rocket -- a missile, if you would --that can traverse the upper atmosphere: a rocket which can span the continents. Would that not be worthwhile? Would the government not also favor that, as well?

FRANK: Professor, tell them.

ED: Tell us what?

JACK (*patting ED on the shoulder*): Hey, hothead, simmer down!

CANDY: Let's listen, Ed.

VON KARMAN: I'm sending Frank to speak with Air Force officials. They're looking to solve two problems: de-icing at high altitudes and take-off from a confined landing space with heavily loaded cargo planes. We can solve the second of these problems. Jet assisted take-offs: JATOs for short. What do you think of the idea?

JACK (*stroking his chin*): It sounds feasible enough.

ED: We can probably do it right now.

TSIEN: It's within our immediate reach. Absolutely.

CANDY: If that explosion I heard today is pointed skyward, the problem's no longer a problem for the Air Force.

TSIEN: We must control the take-off and the fuel consumption and we'll need to find a suitable plane and someone to pilot it.

VON KARMAN: The Air Force will supply us with a pilot and an airplane that meets our specifications.

JACK: We'll need a more reliable binder for the fuel. What we've got now forms cracks and takes forever to pour into the rocket units.

FRANK: We also need a correct fuel formula.

JACK: That, I'm not so worried about. It's the fuse -- the binder that triggers it off. Like I just said, what we've got now is unstable.

CANDY: You'll find the solution, Jack. The answer is there.

JACK: Where, baby?

CANDY (*pointing to his temple*): There!

ED (*laughing*): Just don't blow it off.

ACT TWO
Scene Two

It's early evening at the Caltech lab. The year is 1940. CANDY is pacing the floor and smoking a cigarette..

CANDY: Jack, I'm worried.

JACK: Don't be, baby.

CANDY: Your testimony at the Ralph Benton trial got too much publicity. It was in all the papers.

JACK: Wasn't it great? I took a very nice photograph.

CANDY: I'm not joking with you. Ralph Benton is a dangerous man. He has a lot of friends in the L.A. Police Force. They're corrupt and ruthless and loyal.

JACK: Not all of them. I sure hope not.

CANDY: Enough of them. Some of the cops wouldn't even testify against Benton out of fear. Jack, he planted that car bomb and those two officers were killed. It's a miracle no one else was killed!

JACK: With any luck, Captain Benton is headed for prison.

CANDY (*pointing her cigarette at JACK*): He's got friends… connections.

JACK: Who are probably too scared to do anything right now.

CANDY: That's just it, "right now." And, why are you so late? The trial was over hours ago.

JACK: I was at the OTO. You know, Jane's group.

CANDY: I see.

JACK: Do you? I hope so, Candy. The occult fulfills a spiritual need in me. It's something that I have complete control over.

CANDY: I thought that science did that?

JACK: It does, but it's not enough; too many variables. And, Candy, put the cigarette out, please?

CANDY (*putting out her cigarette*): And, this mysticism has no variables? Come off it, Jack.

JACK: Jane and Grady are coming over. I invited them.

CANDY: To the lab?

JACK: I thought you liked them?

CANDY: I do. Grady's intelligent and nice and a little ambitious, I think. He'll be doing his Army service soon. I like Jane a lot.

JACK: Yes, Candy?

CANDY: Science is reliable. You control it. And, it's healthy for you.

JACK: Oh? Being blown up in the Arroyo is healthy, huh? Thanks a lot!

CANDY: You know what I mean. You can't serve two masters, especially two who oppose each other.

JACK: They compliment each other.

CANDY: They don't.

JACK: They do.

CANDY (*glancing out the window*): Here's Jane and Grady.

JACK: Let's get their opinions.

CANDY (*lighting another cigarette*): Oh, swell!. Grady's on the point of joining this OTO occult group founded by one Aleister Crowley and Jane's been a member for years having studied directly under Crowley. Real unbiased couple for you.

JACK: You see? Two intelligent people. Why don't you join? Put the cigarette out, please?

CANDY (*ignoring JACK'S request*): Have you, Jack? Level with me. Married people shouldn't keep secrets from each other. Not this kind, anyway.

JACK: I'm glad you caught yourself, baby. Are you keeping any secrets about a hidden past from your loving husband?

CANDY: I'm a scientist's wife, now, and I don't mind playing the part. But, Jack, I'm also an artist who feels things.

JACK: Yes? Tired of being the team photographer? You did volunteer for the job, you know.

CANDY: I'm not complaining.

JACK: But?

CANDY: Was I about to say something?

JACK: You were, Candy. Maybe, you're tired of being a scientist's wife or maybe you miss your old life as an unemployed artist.

CANDY: That's not fair. Being an artist is a tough life and there are no guarantees on the next day.

JACK: The same could be said of a scientist. I think I hear Jane and Grady. (*Enter JANE and GRADY from center stage.*)

GRADY (*waving his arms playfully about*): Candy? Jack? I sense tension in the air.

JANE: Everything okay here?

CANDY: No. Everything's not okay, Jane. Has Jack joined the OTO?

JANE: Yes.

JACK: Thanks, Jane.

GRADY: I haven't. Not yet.

CANDY: Why, Jack?

JACK: I need to account for myself?

CANDY: Yes! When it affects your work at the Arroyo and the lab. A lot of people are depending on you.

JACK: Like who, Candy?

CANDY: Ed. Your best and most loyal friend. You owe him a great deal, Jack. You need me to tell you this? Didn't he come to your defense at school when you were being beaten up? Don't you owe him for that?

JACK (*in a guilty and sobering voice*): My work at the Arroyo hasn't been affected...not really.

CANDY: Oh? You don't sound too convinced of that. You know it has affected your work. You're exhausted when you leave for work -- when you're able to go to work. Your mind isn't focused and razor sharp as it used to be. Everyone's noticed.

ED: Has Frank noticed?

CANDY: He's mentioned it. He's worried. You know how he feels about mysticism. He doesn't trust it.

JANE: Candy, Jack's occult work could very well advance what he's doing out there in the desert. Many men of science have practiced occultism.

CANDY: Maybe in the past, granted; but, not anymore.

JANE: Don't be too sure about that. Many don't admit to it, but it's still done.

CANDY: Jane, I like you a great deal, but I'm not buying that.

GRADY (*leaning against one of the window sills*): You don't know anything about it. No offense, but who are you to judge us?

CANDY: Shut up, Grady, and stick to your science fantasy clubs.

GRADY: Nobody tells me to shut up.

CANDY: I just did.

JANE (*getting between CANDY and GRADY*): Stop it -- both of you. It's Jack's decision, Candy, and no one else's. His vote is the only vote that counts.

CANDY: Swell.

JANE: Personal relationships are tenuous, at best.

CANDY: I think I've heard enough.

JANE: It's not Jack's occult work that's really bothering you, is it?

JACK (*lighting a cigarette and sitting on one of the lab tables*): Yes. I'm still here. No, Jane, it's not.

JANE: Is it the Benton trial? Isn't that just about over with?

JACK (*playing with a test tube*): Just about.

CANDY: No. It's not. Benton's a dangerous man. He has powerful allies in the police force and elsewhere. He's not a man to be trifled with.

JANE: He's headed for prison.

GRADY (*making the sign of the cross*): We hope.

CANDY: Exactly. We don't know that for sure.

JANE: Jack's testimony was pretty convincing. And, he wasn't the only expert witness for the D.A.

GRADY (*pushing himself off the window sill*): That mock-up bomb in court was a very nice touch. Those bits of debris and explosives at the scene, you identified 'em all, man.

CANDY: Grady, please. Even if Benton lands in jail, he'll get out some day.

GRADY: Some day.

CANDY: Yes! And, his type holds grudges.

JANE: Candy, Jack was called in as an expert witness in his field: an important witness to a horrific crime. He had to testify.

GRADY (*stopping near CANDY*): He's held in pretty high esteem. You should be proud of him. He's not afraid of Benton -- even if you are.

CANDY: Your breath smells.

JACK (*running interference before GRADY can respond*): I wanted to testify. The papers actually called me a Caltech man. I'll bet those snobs at Caltech choked on that one!

JANE (*leaning against the lab table that JACK is sitting on*): But, Candy's right, Jack. Be careful. I was at the court today. Yes, I was curious, Grady. Capt. Benton is pretty frightening and I didn't particularly care for the way he was staring at you. He's a low-life and revenge is right up his alley.

CANDY: Thank you, Jane. I'm feeling much better about things now. Thanks a lot!

JANE: I didn't mean to scare you, honey. Really. But, you're right. Jack, here, shouldn't be so cavalier about this.

JACK (*jumping down from the lab table*): Jack, here, has testified. Period. It's a fact and it's now recorded history. Yes. I wanted the publicity for myself and the team. You know, the Suicide Squad. Those bastards at Caltech snubbed me and Ed at their friggin' celebratory party. Us! Me and Ed! The ones responsible for everything: for sticking a match up people's backsides and telling them, "Yes! It can be done! If you use the word 'impossible' then turn in your God-damned, useless college degree!" (*He spits on the floor.*) I'm sorry, Candy, but this does lend some prestige to the name of Jack W. Parsons. Amen!

ACT TWO
Scene Three

Later that same year in the Visitor's Room at the county prison. RALPH BENTON is seated facing downstage. His VISITOR cannot be seen. There are three overhead lights giving off a hard, red glow.

BENTON (*facing the audience and not once looking at his visitor during the entire scene*): I want him killed.

VISITOR: Jack Parsons. The expert witness on explosives. Real hot shot or so he thinks.

BENTON: I want him to go out like those two other cops.

VISITOR: It won't look good. And, I'm not a practiced criminal.

BENTON: That's what they all say. And, I didn't say to pull the job right this minute. Wait. Let him sweat it out. I'll get you the help you need.

VISITOR: He does sweat a lot.

BENTON: Good. A test tube just might slip out of his hand some day. You know, a test tube with nitro in it.

VISITOR: He's not exactly stupid. But, he does tend to trust the wrong people.

BENTON: Then, he is stupid. But, we'll have to wait. I want that pig blown to fucking kingdom come. He married?

VISITOR: Yes. A redhead. She's very attractive, but she's independent and has more sense than he does.

BENTON: If she has any sense, she'll dump that loser.

VISITOR: He might be starting some government work soon. As a matter of fact, I'm sure he will

BENTON: What of it?

VISITOR: This "accident" won't be that simple to set up. The Feds will be keeping an eye on him and on everyone involved with him.

BENTON: You don't listen too good, do you? I told you: wait! I'll tell you when. He's got a high opinion of himself. I saw that in the courtroom. He's an explosives expert, huh? The real playboy type in his three piece suits and trimmed moustache.

VISITOR: That's a pathetic remnant from his family's more affluent days.

BENTON: What kind of government work is he doing? Something for the war effort? Must be.

VISITOR: Jet propelled airplanes.

BENTON: What the hell is that?

VISITOR: It's replacing propellers with rockets. They're faster on take-off.

BENTON: So, that's why he's not serving. Fair enough.

VISITOR: He's a loose cannon. He mixes business with mysticism. He's even the head of some kind of Lodge.

BENTON: And, the army puts up with that shit?

VISITOR: They put up with him. They don't like it and neither do some of his friends, if you get my drift.

BENTON: We'll wait; but keep me informed. A wife, huh? Hmm...maybe, we'll get her and a couple of his friends first. It'll soften the bastard up. He helped put me away. Me. Ralph Benton. (*The VISITOR exits.*) Do you know what evil is? If you do, you're one up on most of us, except me, of course. I'm evil, pal. Uncivilized. A Primitive. And, ya' spell that with a capital "P." We feed off of people. We're parasites. You're weak and too afraid to stand up to us. You're fools, and we hate you for it. Even our loyal followers, we despise them. That fool who just walked out of here? Watch out for him. He's a snake who knows how to smile while he's putting the knife in someone's back. My kind's easy to spot, his kind isn't. They're the weakest and most contemptible of all people. To gain a friendship, they think they have to despoil someone else's name. Even I can't stomach him. Now, Jack Parsons is a challenge. He's got convictions and can't be moved from them or so they say. He ignored me in court. Me. Captain Ralph Benton. I hate him. And, I will kill him. I have to because he's the type who can't be intimidated. You might scare him, but he'll never be a follower. He's an individual. But, to me, he's filth.

ACT THREE
Scene One

At the Arroyo Seco test site in 1941. The distant droning of jet engines can be heard as the remains of jet engine fumes disappear.

ED (*waving his right arm about*): We did it, Jack! The first jet airplane. This is history -- it's epic. We did it!

JACK: It's kind of primitive, but stable enough. We picked a good and "light" airplane to test them on.

CANDY: Let's not forget about the pilot, Mr. Homer Bushey.

ED: It took guts flying that plane as "light" as it was. Three cheers for Homer!

JACK: You're both right, baby. The JATOs work and the cylinders containing the fuel, we can improve on those -- and the fuel.

ED (*turning to face JACK*): But, it's the binder -- the asphalt. Your "Greek fire," man; that's what held the fuel together; that was the stabilizing force. It takes only a few minutes to pour it into a unit, and storage time in any weather is almost indefinite.

JACK (*half joking*): I just happened to be passing by a construction site and saw tar being poured on to the roadway. The connection with "Greek Fire" just clicked into place: tar… asphalt and no more cracked black powder. I was beginning to lose hope about solid fuel, but not anymore. We can use solid fuel and control it a lot better than liquid fuel.

CANDY: Gentlemen? Congratulations. I love the two of you.

ED: Careful, Jack might get jealous.

JACK: I'm not the jealous type.

FRANK: So, guys, the Air Force is going to be very happy. Jet assisted take-off will really help the war effort. Maybe, we should start cleaning up here?

VON KARMAN: It's marketable. We'll have to start filling orders soon. The Air Force will want hundreds more. We must get ourselves organized.

CANDY: The Professor's right, boys. The Galcit Project No. 1 has to be transformed into a private company.

AMO: You're right, Candy. But, I'm no businessman. How do we get started?

TSIEN: A factory must be set up for the manufacture of the JATOs, and we will need much guidance as to the ways of capitalism.

AMO: Agreed. Professor, do you have any ideas?

VON KARMAN: Our first orders will be from the Air Force. Jet propulsion is now a fact, at least on the terrestrial plane.

JACK: I'll say! But, I haven't forgotten that trip to the moon that I promised you, baby.

TSIEN: And, this epic day will make that possible.

JACK: But, business...I don't know.

CANDY: You and Ed will still be daredevil, hands-on experimenters: trail blazers...no...Skyblazers.

TSIEN: A very interesting term: skyblazers. Most apropos.

ED: I love it.

AMO: Hey, will that be the company's name?

VON KARMAN: No. I'm afraid not, Amo. It's just a little too...

CANDY: Ahead of its time, Professor?

VON KARMAN: If you like. I think a name like Aerojet would be more suitable.

AMO: The Air Force will like that. Nice sound to it.

CANDY: How about "Aerojet Engineering Corp.?"

VON KARMAN: That's it!

TSIEN: Very professional and serious: a sobering sort of a name.

FRANK: And, original. We've done it: the solid fuel, the binder with asphalt and the units. We've actually done it!

ED: Hey, Frank is letting his hair down. It's okay to be enthusiastic, man, and let loose. You need to.

CANDY: Ed's teasing you, Frank. I'm pretty excited myself. How fast will they reach, Jack; jet propulsion?

JACK: Propeller assisted air flight goes as fast as 400 mph. JATOs...a lot faster than that and, eventually, a lot higher in the atmosphere.

CANDY: All the way to the moon?

JACK: All the way to the stars.

AMO (*laughing*): Frank? Are you with us, man? You look like you've just taken off.

FRANK: Do you know what people are calling us?

ED: Yeah, I do. What of it?

FRANK: The Suicide Squad. Even with the JATOs, that name will stick.

ED: They're ignorant people. And, we take chances that they're afraid to take.

FRANK: Are they, Ed? Are they ignorant?

ED: And, you think they're not? You can't be serious. And, what's with the sudden change of moods, pal?

FRANK: We've going to get orders from the Air Force for JATOs that we can barely fill. The fuel's not yet perfected-

ED: It will be.

FRANK: -and the units-

ED: I'm perfecting 'em. You worry too much.

FRANK: Still planning on a trip to the moon, engineer?

ED (*placing his hands on his hips*): As a matter of fact, I am. The JATOs work. We just make 'em more powerful. Jack, here, will see to that.

FRANK: Will you, Jack? Will you be spending more time here, at the Arroyo, or at some occult ritual doing God-only-knows what. A waste of time, that. I thought you were a dedicated scientist.

JACK: You're wrong, Frank.

FRANK: No. I'm right. There's only one way to reach the stars.

JACK (*trying to be patient with FRANK*): Then, let's do it.

FRANK: Yes. Let's do it by putting in more time with your explosives. You're becoming unreliable.

JACK: We're ready for another test with a new mixture.

FRANK: Why wasn't I told about this? I've been here. You haven't. And, what's the hurry? We've just completed a successful test flight.

JACK (*losing his temper*): Hey, Frank, take it easy. I've been here, too, and I want another test done. We're just going to fire off one unit skyward and measure distance and velocity. Now, relax! God damn it!

CANDY (*annoyed with FRANK*): Frank, let Jack and Ed test the unit.

FRANK: Blind testing, again: that's why they call us the Suicide Squad. I want rocketry to be respectable and not a boy's game. Let's just revel in the success that we've had today.

JACK: Does that name affect any of us or what we do? It doesn't.

AMO: Jack's right. Let's just run the test. What say?

FRANK: Tsien? Professor?

TSIEN: Why not?

ED: Don't get too excited, man.

VON KARMAN: Let's go through with it. But this is improper and you both know this. First theory and, then, experimentation. How many times have I said this?

ED (*nodding his head up and down*): We know, Professor. We know.

VON KARMAN: Then, do it! Always the rebel, especially you, Mr. Parsons. You're the instigator. Ed will do whatever you tell him.

JACK: Guilty. But, we can't sit on our haunches. Today's flight was epic, but I'm still not entirely satisfied.

VON KARMAN: We'll have orders to fill and obligations to meet and a company to run.

JACK: Tell a rocket to stand still in mid-air. The JATOs work and, now, we have to make them even better.

VON KARMAN: And, I agree, Jack. But allow me and Frank to work out some equations first. It will not take long because now we're working from a solid foundation.

JACK: Just this one additional test, Professor.

VON KARMAN (*exasperated*): And, why not? What can happen? We'll all be blown to kingdom come!

TSIEN: I will see my revered ancestors sooner than I had planned.

AMO: That's the spirit, Tsien. Always looking on the bright side.

TSIEN: I was not joking, Amo. Science is respectable and not daredevil antics. We are all scientists here. You, as well, Candy. You are the sobering spirit for this group.

CANDY: Thanks, Tsien, really. Jack? Is the new explosive safe?

JACK (*smiling, but not with his eyes*): No explosive is safe, baby.

CANDY: Don't get smart.

JACK: It will work.

CANDY: It'll ignite?

JACK (*placing his arm on her shoulder*): Like a cocktail from Hell.

CANDY: Thanks a lot. Let's just get this over with, boys.

VON KARMAN: And, she encourages him!

AMO: Candy can handle Jack.

CANDY: You think so?

ED: She can even handle me.

FRANK: That calls for canonization.

ED: Just watch it, pal. I don't have your book learning or academic credentials, but I'm not your inferior. Savvy?

CANDY: Ed! Calm down! Frank was only joking. How many time have you joked with him? Too many, maybe. Don't mistake his sensitive nature for weakness.

ED: That's right. Take his side.

CANDY: I'm not taking his side. Without you, Ed, there'd be no unit to test. Now, the both of you shake hands. I mean it! Ed? Frank?

JACK: Candy's right: shake boys. Come on. Ed? Come on, engineer. Do it for Jack.

ED: Okay. (*He and FRANK shake hands.*)

TSIEN: Perhaps, I should leave. My doctorate thesis is taking up a great deal of my time.

CANDY: Please, Tsien, stay; at least until we run the test. Let's stick together for this one.

AMO (*annoyed*): Let's quit the arguing and just do it. All this talk is wasted on me. How about you, Professor?

VON KARMAN: Are you ready, gentlemen?

JACK: Just about. Ed?

ED: Okay.

VON KARMAN: Good. And, now we can proceed to meet Tsien's ancestors.

CANDY: Oh, God! Not you, too?

VON KARMAN: I'm sorry.

CANDY (*looking northward, beyond the area of the test site*): Professor- who was that?

JACK (*looking northward*): Somebody out there? There shouldn't be. This area's restricted.

CANDY: I saw a figure moving in the distance.

AMO: So did I.

JACK: Gone now. Did either of you recognize him?

CANDY: No. But, he was watching us; wasn't he, Amo?

AMO: It could have been somebody from the Air Force. But, this guy was watching us, all right.

CANDY: There was something almost menacing about that figure. He was up to no good. It gave me the willies.

TSIEN: A spy, do you think? It's not impossible. An industrial spy may be checking on our progress.

CANDY: You could be right, Tsien.

JACK: Industry doesn't take us seriously enough...at least, not yet. And, could he see all that much from that distance?

VON KARMAN: I doubt it. But-

CANDY: What is it, Professor?

VON KARMAN: We must be on our guard. Many people laugh at us: in that, you are quite correct, Frank, but most of these people are harmless...and others are not. There are people who hate progress and will do anything to stop it. And, of course, we'll probably soon be at war. We should notify the Air Force, at once about this.

FRANK: And, there's one more type, Professor vonKarman: those people who are on personal vendettas. Don't forget about them.

CANDY: What made you say that, Frank?

FRANK: Just giving voice to a thought. Nothing more. Why are you looking at me like that?

CANDY: The import of your words...it was a little more than a thought, wasn't it? Wasn't it?

FRANK: I don't know what you're talking about. (*All move toward the test site, except CANDY, who stares into the distance. JACK walks up to her and holds her by the waist.*)

JACK: I know what you're thinking.

CANDY: I wonder if you do. I don't trust him.

JACK: Who?

CANDY: Frank.

JACK: You're pulling my leg? Admittedly, he's a little to himself and maybe…

CANDY: Considers himself above the rest of us philistines?

JACK: You're wrong about him. I trust him.

CANDY: That's your trouble, Jack. You trust everyone and believe what they tell you. Don't.

JACK: I can't believe we're having this conversation. We're a team. We have to trust each other. We have to work with each other.

CANDY: Ed feels the same way.

JACK: Ed's jealous of my friendship with Frank. I'm very flattered, actually.

CANDY: It's more than just jealousy. Ed knows his way around. He goes with his gut reaction.

JACK: You're artist's imagination is getting the better of you. Don't speak against Frank.

CANDY: It's an opinion and-

JACK: And?

CANDY: Maybe…a warning.

JACK: And, maybe, you're wrong? How does Frank feel about you?

CANDY: It doesn't concern me.

JACK: I don't like this kind of talk, Candy. I know that things have been strained between us, but leave others out of our problems. Now, stop worrying. Tsien's probably right about it being an industrial spy. We're more respected than we think. Let's join the others. They're waiting for us. (*CANDY goes off with JACK while still glancing back.*)

ACT THREE
Scene Two

JANE'S apartment in Pasadena. The year is 1943 at around 11 P.M.. There's a wind storm raging outside. JANE'S apartment is sparsely furnished with only a loveseat, easy chair, and a second hand coffee table.

CANDY: Jane? I'm leaving Jack.

JANE (*sitting in the easy chair with her legs propped up on the coffee table*): Does he know?

CANDY: Yes. I told him today and I've been telling him nearly every day for the past few weeks. I've neglected my own work too long, Jane. I want to get back to my painting.

JANE: Pardon me if I don't believe you, honey. Have a seat.

CANDY (*sitting down on the love seat*): You're too perceptive. Maybe, there is something to all this occult ritual magic you practice.

JANE: Maybe there is. Just listen to that wind outside, will you. Must be one of those dust storms coming in from the desert.

CANDY: Jane, I'm worried about Jack.

JANE: You think that we're a bad influence on him? He's a big boy now.

CANDY: That's just it, he's not. He's too trusting. He's looking for s hero figure in his life that he never had; and he won't find it.

JANE: Heroes are pretty scarce.

CANDY: Try and keep an eye on him, will you?

JANE: You can do that a lot better than I can. Stay, Candy.

CANDY: I can't.

JANE: Oh?

CANDY: Look after him.

JANE: I'm not the maternal type. And, besides, Jack is no longer part of the Lodge.

CANDY: He told me that you accepted his resignation. Resignation! He wasn't a very good leader, was he? Don't answer that. He was in it over his head. I tried to warn him that he couldn't serve two masters. He just wouldn't listen.

JANE: What man does?

CANDY: True. Jane, a while back, at the first JATO launch, someone was spying on us. I saw him and so did Amo so it wasn't my imagination. It hasn't happened since, but-

JANE: You don't have to be defensive with me. I believe you. You thought it was that hood, Ralph Benton, right?

CANDY: You are psychic.

JANE: No. I just have this bit of common sense in me that I can't seem to shake. It's not my style at all.

CANDY: Do you think it was Benton?

JANE: He's still in the slammer as far as I know. But, at least you know he's an enemy.

CANDY: What do you mean by that?

JANE: Nothing…sort of.

CANDY: No. Tell me what you're hinting at. Why do I think I know. Tell me, Jane.

JANE: Hey, honey, I'm a natural born cynic. I don't really trust anyone.

CANDY: I wish you'd rub off on Jack. He could use some of your cynicism.

JANE: He's doing all right. Isn't he?

CANDY: That's a tough question to answer. But, let's get back to what you were hinting at.

JANE: I don't hint. I'm a bitch who just insults people to their face.

CANDY: You said that Benton was an obvious enemy. I think that's what you said.

JANE: Something like that. My short term memory isn't what it should be. They tell me that's a bad sign -- you know, senility setting in.

CANDY: You're far from senile. Now, what did you mean? Please tell me. I have to know.

JANE: To confirm your own suspicions?

CANDY: Yes! You're driving me mad, Jane!

JANE (*stands up and looks for the cigarette box*): Jack has friends, but I'm willing to wager that he's got a few enemies, too: bad ones: the jealous type, and they're the worst.

CANDY: Who? Do you know something? You do.

JANE (*shrugging and finding a cigarette, but not lighting it*): That's it, I don't. I just look at people and how they react with their eyes. Look at their eyes, Candy, and you'll know your enemy.

CANDY: Stop being so mysterious.

JANE: I'm giving you some sound, occult advice. Don't be so impatient. Cigarette?

CANDY: No, thanks.

JANE: Don't leave, Candy. Jack needs you and Ed. Now, that boy you can trust. I like him. In his own way, he's very sweet and he loves Jack.

CANDY: I'd trust Ed with my life. He'll take care of Jack.

JANE: You're really going, then?

CANDY: Who can't I trust? Tell me.

JANE: I don't even trust Grady. And, I should. I think he's harmless enough, but he's ambitious and I never trust that type.

CANDY: Oh, God! I said pretty much the same thing to Jack.

JANE: I didn't mean that Grady is untrustworthy; but he is studying directly under Mr. Crowley in London these days. And, as much as I admire the Grand Master, he does have his darker nature; but don't we all when it comes to that?

CANDY: Were you really talking about Grady before? I don't really think you were.

JANE (*at her most serious*): I wasn't. I don't like some of Jack's friends. They don't like me so I don't like them: that's very mature of me, isn't it?

CANDY: I don't trust some of them either. Some less than others.

JANE: Good for you. But, you want to know something? I think you'll be back. Go to Mexico for a few weeks, give me your address and phone -- if they have phones where you're staying -- and, I'll keep you posted on what this old girl knows. I am a busybody.

CANDY: Thanks, Jane. Listen to that wind outside!

JANE: I don't like wind. It serves no purpose.

CANDY (*getting ready to leave*): So Jack shouldn't trust his friends, huh? He'd never listen to that.

JANE: I know...and it may be his undoing.

ACT THREE
Scene Three

Early morning at the Caltech lab in 1943. JACK, ED, and FRANK are having a heated confrontation..

ED: You're just what I thought you were: a spineless cut-throat. Don't ever get yourself a conscience; it'll kill you.

JACK (*leaning against one of the lab tables*): Why, Frank? Because we're not Caltech men? Because we take chances? You might as well tell us now. Level with us, Frank. Now, we're the outsiders.

FRANK (*trying to keep his distance from ED*): It was part of the deal to keep Aerojet afloat. We couldn't do it by ourselves. We're not businessmen. We're scientists.

ED: No, pal, you're the bona-fide scientist in this group, Mr. Caltech man. Well, fuck you and the high horse you rode in on. Who are you to cut us adrift? Who are you to tell us we're not good enough?

FRANK: I never said that.

ED: You're real good at leaving things out. Liar! Fucking liar!

JACK: This has been our life and now we're tossed over. How do you expect us to feel? We sell our shares in our own company and-

FRANK: And, get a fair shake.

JACK: Maybe for now, Frank. But, Aerojet has a future-

FRANK: Now, it does.

ED: I love it! Without us, you mean.

JACK: Rocketry is on its way to becoming a respected science because of us. You didn't do it by yourself. No one did. And, it was Ed and I who got things started, or had you forgotten that?

FRANK: I'm not a businessman.

ED: You're not a friend, either. Never was. It's like I've been telling you, Jack, all along.

JACK: We shouldn't have sold our shares, at least not all of them. We were a couple of idiots. Did you sell your shares, Frank? Frank?

FRANK: I was in Europe. I didn't-

ED (*moving toward FRANK*): Didn't know what? That you agreed to have that lawyer con us?

FRANK (*backing off*): No one conned you. You were given a fair deal.

JACK (*getting between the two men*): No. We weren't. The takeover company didn't want Aerojet's name associated with its very founder. The attorney who sold General Tire on Aerojet's potential left us out of one of your equations. You knew this, Frank. You knew this and didn't tell us.

FRANK: That so called attorney saved our company.

ED: Not ours now, pal.

FRANK: Was it ever, Ed? You actually think of yourself as a businessman?

ED: Keep talking. I want to hear more.

JACK (*clenching his fist*): Ed's an engineer, Frank. The best engineer and my best friend, always. Okay, so we're not savvy businessmen, but we worked our butts off night and day to get a product: the JATOs. Or have you forgotten that, Frank? I also went cross country checking out possible competitors and making contacts. I didn't hear anyone complaining then. So others take over where we left off -- real easy pickings for them. I'm glad we found out about your backstabbing salesmanship. This takeover company didn't want a couple of "amateurs" or "crackpots!" associated with their new company: a company that we founded.

FRANK: It wasn't my idea.

ED: True.

FRANK: I didn't particularly like what was going on, but my hands were tied..

ED: Our attorney friend knew about it and a few of the other hoods that we've had to work with.

JACK: What about Amo and Tsien?

ED: They had to bail out before the company really had a chance to get started.

JACK: I wish they were here now.

ED: I don't. I think Tsien's having his own problems with the Feds: a security risk with this Communist witch hunt that's starting up.

JACK: What about Amo?

ED: Amo's found work with another engineering company, I think.

JACK (*turning back to FRANK*): But, why, Frank? Is it because Ed and I didn't fit in with the status quo? Real genius never does fit in -- it's individual and it has to be. Geniuses and daredevils don't punch a time clock. Is it because I was involved with an occult group? That's it, isn't it? Or is it something else you're not telling us about?

FRANK: Part of it, Jack. The raids by the cops on that occult group didn't help any, either. I was never keen on this mysticism stuff and neither were you, Ed. I tried to warn Jack, but he wouldn't listen. And, I haven't exactly gotten off unscathed. I was a card-carrying Communist, remember? The Feds are up my backside, as well.

ED: Good.

FRANK: I didn't deserve that, Ed. I'm leaving for Europe, again. I can't sweat this thing out here and in Europe, I can find work.

ED: Coward.

JACK: That's enough of that, Ed. What else are you keeping from us?

FRANK (*ignoring JACK'S question*): And, Jack, there's one more thing that you should know.

JACK: Do I want to hear this?

FRANK: Benton's about to be released.

ED: What are you telling us, man?

FRANK: Watch out for him. His kind doesn't change.

ED: They get worse.

JACK: That happened a long time ago.

FRANK (*putting on his hat*): And, he's had years in the slammer to brood about it. I'm sorry, Jack, truly. Maybe, you're right, Ed. Maybe, I am a snob. And, maybe, I should have been more up front with the sale of Aerojet. I'm sorry. But, please, be careful. Benton's a ruthless killer. Don't make the mistake of underestimating his hatred of you. And, he's had years to plot his revenge.

JACK: Good luck, Frank. And, thanks for the warning. But, I still get the feeling your not being square with us.

FRANK: Look after Jack, Ed.

JACK: Maybe our paths will cross again, one day. I don't know that they should.

ED: So long. I don't hold grudges for too long; but, I'm plenty steamed right now. I need time to cool off.

FRANK: I understand. I'll take my leave. (*Exits.*)

JACK: Say it. You're entitled to say it, Ed.

ED (*moving toward one of the lab's windows*): What do you mean?

JACK: That you never trusted Frank.

ED: Amen!

JACK: Well?

ED: And, he's still hiding something. I wish to hell I knew what it was. He's a liar.

JACK: What did he lie about? Lying is a distortion of reality, you know.

ED (*moving to where Jack is standing*): Yeah, I know. But, that bastard's hiding something...it's like he's resentful of you, Jack.

JACK: He's the academic. Not I.

ED: And, doesn't he know it, too. And, that's just it. He needs his textbooks and you don't. You've got an original mind and you're not afraid to take chances He's afraid.

JACK: Maybe. And, maybe you're a better judge of character than I am.

ED: Jack? He's gone so let's forget him.

JACK: I failed you, Ed. I failed.

ED: No, you didn't, man. We're still in the game. As long as we're breathing, we're still in the game. Don't you ever say that you failed me. Never say that!

JACK (*sitting up on one of the lab tables*): I don't know what we can do now.

ED: Just what we did before: hands-on testing with no Frank Malina looking over our shoulders. You'll make even better and more powerful explosives, and I'll fit them into better units. They'll come to us, Jack: the industrialists -- private enterprise.

JACK: Did I ever tell you, engineer, that you're the best friend I've ever had?

ED (*hoisting himself up next to JACK*): Every day. Every day. You're Jack Parsons and you're the best explosives expert on the whole fucking planet. And, we're gonna' blast off for the moon. Yes. I'm still a kid who loves to dream.

JACK: You're an engineer: the best there is. Okay. We're not licked, but it's not going to be easy, Ed.

ED: Good! We kind of thrive on challenges and hard times, don't we?

JACK: The rest of our team is gone-

ED: But, we're still here. We'll build another team -- a better one -- with skyblazers, like us.

JACK: Okay, let's get started. And, by the way, why didn't you bust Frank one?

ED: When I see him, again, I will.

ACT FOUR
Scene One

The Visitor's Room at the state prison in 1951. BENTON is and his VISITOR can barely be seen.

BENTON: So, Parsons' hit rock bottom? That's just great.

VISITOR: I thought you'd be pleased.

BENTON: Who says I'm not? I've been rotting in this cell… but not for much longer. I'm up for parole, son. You're talking to a model prisoner.

VISITOR: Perhaps, I should leave?

BENTON (*banging his fist on the table*): When I say you can leave. Remember: I'm getting out of here soon. Anyone is fair game for me. Remember.

VISITOR: I will. His wife left him, but I think she might be coming back.

BENTON: The witch? Candy's her name, right?

VISITOR: It's the one she goes by. Her real name's Marjorie.

BENTON: Candy sounds sweeter.

VISITOR: She's not so sweet. She sizes people up. She's pretty good at it, too.

BENTON: Let's hope she doesn't size you up, pal Then, you'd be in real trouble.

VISITOR: Parsons has financial troubles. He's even had to take a job at a gas station.

BENTON: How the mighty have fallen. But, he hasn't fallen far enough. He couldn't find work at a powder plant?

VISITOR: He has, but it's not enough. He still daydreams about going to the moon as if that were ever a possibility. He's been kicked out of that Lodge of his. Even the Master Crowley has turned against him. He was an incompetent leader and he's squandered most of his money. Some smooth talking navy vet conned him out of twenty grand. Parsons tracked him down to Miami and got some of it back, but not much.

BENTON: Keep talking.

VISITOR: He's trying to get his clearance from the government back, but I wouldn't count on that -- not with his track record.

BENTON: What about his best friend: Ed Forman?

VISITOR: He's nothing. A grease monkey who'll be lucky to get a job in a filling station. Without Parsons, he'll collapse.

BENTON: Don't make bet on that. Sometimes, people come through who you never thought could. I read that article about Parsons and Forman in that "Mechanics" magazine. Forman's no weakling. Watch your backside with him, son.

VISITOR: He's a cretin!

BENTON: Who can probably make mince meat out of you.

VISITOR: There is something that you should know. Parsons has been in touch with von Karman about work abroad. He's also contacted a few other people to help him find work with starting up an explosives firm. He just might pull it off if the Feds leave him alone.

BENTON: Make sure they don't leave him alone.

VISITOR: Me?

BENTON: You!

VISITOR: I have no influence there. None.

BENTON: Get to know people who have influence there.

VISITOR: You're asking the impossible. I've no way of doing that.

BENTON: I have a few connections in the Force. You're disappointing me, son. You just make sure that Parsons stays put where I can get to him.

VISITOR: How-

BENTON (*standing*): Just-do-it! And, don't ever say "no" to me, again. Now, get the hell out! Oh? And, one more thing... I've got my eye on you, son.

ACT FOUR
Scene Two

The year is 1952 and it's close to midnight. JANE is being confronted by BENTON, who's just been released from prison. GRADY was about to leave her apartment when the doorbell rang. They had just completed a ritual. She motions for him to go and hide in the kitchen.

JANE: You're Ralph Benton.

BENTON (*pushing his way in*): You recognized me, huh? You see my picture in the papers? Must have.

JANE: You're a man not easily forgotten, Mr. Benton. What the hell are you doing here?

BENTON: What do you care?

JANE: You're in my house; or haven't you noticed?

BENTON: I noticed.

JANE: What do you want here?

BENTON (*walking about the room and picking up objects at random*): Just having a look around. Your friend, Parsons, he's a member of...now what do you call it? Oh, yeah, the OTO... the Ordo Templi Orientis. He used to be head of this lodge, but your Master, Sir Aleister Crowley, gave him the brush off.

GRADY (*enters from the kitchen*): You're misinformed, Benton. Our Master hasn't been knighted, not yet.

BENTON: And, not likely to be, either, is he? He's got quite a reputation for himself: a real bad one. What's he called: the wickedest man in the world?

GRADY: Any worse than yours? He doesn't go around blowing up cars with people in them. He's not a cold blooded murderer like you. You killed your own fellow officers because they were about to turn honest -- and turn you in.

BENTON: Just watch it, punk. Watch what you say to me. And, for that matter, he does kill people. There was that ritual in Italy a few years back where a young boy died from eating dead animal remains.

GRADY: He had nothing-

BENTON: Nothing to do with it? Tell that to the boy's widow. Betty May's her name, isn't it? Her testimony almost put your Master in the slammer.

JANE: What do you want, Benton?

BENTON: Parson's been dethroned as head man, hasn't he? Couldn't bring your little group enough money and status, huh?

JANE: I'll ask one more time: what do you want?

BENTON (*moves towards JANE*): Nothing.

JANE (*backs away from BENTON*): Then, leave.

BENTON: You know who you're talkin' to, lady?

JANE: Who?

BENTON: An enemy.

JANE: You don't frighten me.

GRADY: Get out.

BENTON (*standing over JANE*): Make me.

JANE: Aren't you on parole? Shouldn't you be behaving yourself, Captain?

BENTON: None of your damned business.

JANE: We have nothing to tell you about Jack.

BENTON: Was I asking?

JANE: Yes.

GRADY: You want us to call the cops, Benton? We will.

BENTON: What's Parsons doing these days? Just curious.

JANE: I knew it! That's why you're here. You're a free man, Benton. Why don't you keep it that way

BENTON: Answer me.

JANE: No.

BENTON (*taking hold of a lighted candle*): Answer me.

GRADY: You heard the lady.

BENTON: I'm not talking to you, son.

JANE: Grady, call the cops. (*GRADY exits.*)

BENTON: Not smart. Is Parsons still with that red head -- that witch? I heard she ditched him and headed for Mexico. If she's smart, she'll stay there. Now, answer me!

JANE: Leave Candy alone! Leave them both alone. That decent people should have to breathe the same air- No!

BENTON (*waving a lighted candle in JANE'S face*): What do you think would happen if this candle were to drop hot, liquid wax in your eyes? Huh? It'd be the candle's fault...not mine.

JANE: Keep away! Grady!

GRADY (*rushing back in*): Rotten bastard! (He *leaps at BENTON and they both go down.*)

JANE (*grabs the candle and shoves it at the side of BENTON'S face*): There! That's what happens when hot liquid wax hits you! Bastard! Grady, get away from him!

BENTON (*getting to his feet and rubbing the side of his face*): He's still with that dame. Good. You told me what I wanted to know. Oh, and Priestess: leave town.

JANE: Get out!

BENTON: Call the friggin' cops. They've got a whole dossier on you perverts. (*Exits.*)

JANE (*frantic with worry*): Oh, God! We have to warn Jack and Candy.

GRADY: We've just been warned.

JANE: I know. But, he's right; the police won't believe us, not the L.A. police. They're as rotten as he is.

GRADY: What about the Pasadena cops?

JANE: We're talking different shades of corruption, Grady. Did you phone the police?

GRADY: No. And, he knew it.

JANE (*angry with GRADY*): Why not? He must be violating parole. This could land him right back in prison.

GRADY: The cops wouldn't have done anything.

JANE: You don't know that for sure. We could have threatened to go to the with this. The last thing the police want is more bad publicity.

GRADY: He beat it, didn't he?

JANE: I'd better call Candy. I think she and Jack are staying with his mom.

GRADY: And, call Ed Forman, too.

JANE (*looking at him askance as she hurries into the kitchen*): I will.

ACT FOUR
Scene Three

The date is June 17, 1952 and it's late afternoon at the Caltech lab. JACK and CANDY are discussing their upcoming trip to Mexico.

JACK: My mom loves having us at her place, Candy.

CANDY: And, I love her. She's very sweet and she lives for her son.

JACK: Glad we're still married?

CANDY: Yes.

JACK: So am I. We will get to the moon, you know.

CANDY: Ed wants to come with us.

JACK: He'll bring his new wife along.

CANDY: Are you glad I came back from Mexico?

JACK: I think so.

CANDY: The artist colony was fun.

JACK: And, living expenses pretty cheap. Why did you come back?

CANDY: Because the Feds were persecuting you. And, I don't like unfairness.

JACK: We're not going to split up, again, are we?

CANDY: We won't. We've got too many plans to keep us busy.

JACK: Is that the only reason?

CANDY: I just gave you a few reasons. The real reason is for kids to say.

JACK: I'm just a kid.

CANDY: Glad to hear you admit it. Yes. I love you.

JACK: You made me a happy little kid.

CANDY (*pulling a little away from JACK*): Jack, I'm worried. Benton's out of jail.

JACK: Don't worry. We're heading for Mexico, remember? Tomorrow, remember?

CANDY: Not soon enough for me.

JACK: We'll start a new company and once I get back my security clearance, we can really start-up. I'm serious about space flight. I'm not giving it up and neither is Ed.

CANDY: And, I'm not giving either one of you up. You'll conquer outer space. You've already conquered jet flight. The Feds have no right to keep you out.

JACK: I almost feel sorry for Frank, but I heard he hightailed it to Paris. He should've never hobnobbed with those Communist friends of his.

CANDY: Lucky you didn't join.

JACK: I'll say!

CANDY: And, don't feel too sorry for Frank. He has his academic credentials to fall back on. He'll find work. And, I'll be honest with you. I never trusted him. What about Tsien?

JACK: They won't let him become a U.S. citizen and they won't let him leave the country. They're fools. Do you know how much Tsien can contribute to space travel.

CANDY: I know. But, those idiots don't.

JACK: All packed?

CANDY: Just a few more supplies to get in. You finishing up here for that film company?

JACK: Another hour or so should do it. They want some special explosives for their new war movie. It's the latest fad.

CANDY: Don't take too long. Your mom's expecting us for dinner.

JACK: Then get moving. You can help me finish up when you get back.

CANDY: Jack, you're sweating too much and you're handling some pretty hot explosives. Take your time with this job.

JACK: I always sweat.

CANDY: Please, Jack -- and, about Benton-

JACK (a little annoyed): Forget about him, will you? You're getting to be obsessed with him. (*The phone rings.*)

CANDY: Hello? Jane? How are you? Yes. Yes. We know. He what? He came by and threatened you and Grady? Oh, God! He is out for revenge. I knew it. You're coming over? Okay. You've already phoned Ed. I'll tell Jack.

JACK: I heard. I can surmise Jane's end of the conversation. Why did Benton go there? What did he want with Jane and Grady? I'm an ex-member of bad standing -- a defunct occult leader.

CANDY: Benton's not a normal human being. He's sizing up your friends. I'll stay here with you-

JACK: No. Do your shopping and I'll finish up here.

CANDY: Just how did Benton find out about the OTO?

JACK: It's an open secret and the cops did raid the place a couple of times.

CANDY: Maybe. But, it sounds like someone's been keeping Capt. Benton pretty well informed.

JACK: There goes your artistic imagination, again. Come on, I'll walk you to the car.

CANDY: No, Jack, we should stay together. We can pick up the stuff tomorrow.

JACK: We can't. We're leaving at the crack of dawn. Come on. I'll walk you to the car and see you safely in.

CANDY: Don't make jokes.

JACK: I'm not making jokes. Let's go. You could've been there already. And, Ed's on his way and so is Jane and Grady.

CANDY: Lock up after I leave.

JACK: I will. I won't have you to protect me.

CANDY: Please, Jack.

JACK: I will baby. Promise. (*He and CANDY exit. A figure of a man sneaks in and lifts the floor boards and plants an explosive. He exits. JACK comes back in and starts working with his chemicals. He moves back and forth in the lab. He has a coffee can in his hand and he is sweating profusely. The can slips from his grasp and he stoops down to grab it. He steps back on to the booby-trapped floor boards and triggers off the first of two almost simultaneous explosions. CANDY and ED rush in. CANDY met ED as she was leaving.. She screams out JACK'S name and starts tossing aside debris looking for him. ED does the same, also calling out JACK'S name. They spot him pinned under a sink. ED moves it and they carefully turn JACK over. He's near death. His right arm has been blown off and his face is severely burned.)*

CANDY: Jack! Oh, God! Jack! Ed, he's breathing. He's still alive!

ED: Jack? Jack? Don't try and move.

CANDY: He's trying to say something.

ED: His face- dear, God! His face-

CANDY: Lie still, baby. Ed, go upstairs and-

ED: I'm not leaving him. Jack, man, don't die on me.

CANDY: Can he hear us?

ED: I think so. Jack, the police will be here-

CANDY: Ed, please, upstairs there's a phone. The one down here must be smashed to bits.

ED *(reluctantly)*: Okay.

CANDY *(gently stroking JACK'S hand)*: Jack? An ambulance will be here soon. Hold on. Try to hold on. Half the town must have heard that explosion. Listen. Just listen. We have a trip to take…not to Mexico, Jack…to the moon. Please..take me there. *(Blackout.)*

EPILOGUE

Dusk at the Arroyo Seco test site a few weeks later.

CANDY, ED, JANE, and GRADY are joined by VON KARMAN, AMO, and TSIEN. CANDY places JACK'S urn on to a JATO unit. Slowly, they look up at the stars, except CANDY. ED has his arm around her. A twilight and, then, a countdown: five, four, three, two, one, and lift-off. The Polaris rocket is seen breaking free of the atmosphere and streaking through the heavens.

End of play.

LEFT, RIGHT, AND NOWHERE

A Play in Two Acts

by

Gerard Denza

CHARACTERS

GLAUCUS, a mariner.
MORBIUS, more than a man: the last intellect.
LILLITH, a woman and a would-be goddess.
KRONOS, the last of the would-be sages.

PLACE
A spaceship is scraping against the outer boundaries of the universe.

TIME
The end of time.

SCENES

ACT ONE

Naked, GLAUCUS awakens in the cavernous chamber of a strange vehicle.

GLAUCUS: Where in God's name am I? What is this place? Am I in Heaven or in Hell eternal? *(His hand touches the chamber's metal floor. He sits up.)* What the- Have I died and been brought...where? What is this place?

MORBIUS *(turning his chair to face GLAUCUS)*: Put some clothes on, Glaucus. It's pretty cold in this ship. And, we don't want you to catch your death, if you'll pardon the rather tasteless expression.

GLAUCUS: Ship, you say? This is no sea vessel.

MORBIUS: Quite right. It's a space vessel.

GLAUCUS: A space vessel? What are you saying?

MORBIUS: Put your clothes on and we'll chat.

GLAUCUS *(noticing some clothes on the floor)*: Who are you? You sit upon a throne.

MORBIUS: No. Not a throne, dear boy, a pilot's seat. I'm neither a king nor a god.

GLAUCUS *(putting on the clothes)*: Then, what are you? Who are you? And, how did I come to be here in this metal craft?

MORBIUS: You're pretty direct, pal. I am the last intellect in a universe from which I seek safe passage from. You are in my escape vehicle, if you would. The last refuge.

GLAUCUS: What you say makes no sense to me. What are you escaping from?

MORBIUS: Funny, how you understood that part of the puzzle.

GLAUCUS: Then, answer my question.

MORBIUS: From destruction, you fool. But, you're really not a fool, are you? And, you look me in the eye. I admire that.

GLAUCUS (*walking toward MORBIUS*): What has been destroyed? A city? An empire?

MORBIUS: A universe.

GLAUCUS: Do you mean the stars and the planets are no more? Where have they gone to?

MORBIUS: Into the primeval thought. Some would call it the primordial egg or marble...some marble!

GLAUCUS: You're not making any sense.

MORBIUS: Everything has been sucked back in.

GLAUCUS: You haven't. Your ship hasn't. I haven't. Why not? Are there other survivors.

MORBIUS: Has no one lectured you in the fine art of conversation? You get to the point too quickly. Slow down, sailor.

GLAUCUS: Did you rescue me?

MORBIUS: Did I? Or did she? (*A beautiful woman enters the chamber from stage right.*)

GLAUCUS: Another survivor.

MORBIUS: It makes conversation more interesting. Well, let's hope it does.

GLAUCUS: Who are you?

LILLITH (*approaching GLAUCUS*): Perhaps, the one who rescued you from drowning?

MORBIUS: Don't lie to him, Lillith.

LILLITH (*turning to gaze at MORBIUS*): Was I lying? I was only putting forth a question. I didn't actually state that I saved him.

MORBIUS: You didn't.

LILLITH: Did you?

KRONOS (*entering the vast chamber*): Glaucus? I am Kronos and this woman calls herself Lillith. The man in the pilot's chair is Morbius. Don't trust them. Don't believe anything they tell you. He is steering this rather strange craft to God-only-knows where.

MORBIUS: Glaucus, I wouldn't trust him if I were you.

KRONOS (*touching GLAUCUS' sleeve*): Glaucus, I am one of the ancient seers of a near extinct universe. My life will soon end and you, my son, are to cast me into the dark abyss. Pray for me for we will meet, again, in another time and place.

MORBIUS: But, you've just met.

KRONOS (*approaching MORBIUS*): Silence!

MOBIUS: Make me.

KRONOS (*shaking his fist*): Child!

LILLITH (*walking over to KRONOS*): Why do you let him upset you so?

KRONOS: Evil is upsetting.

LILLITH: Evil is impotent. It feeds on your anger, Kronos. I shouldn't have to tell you this; even though you called me a liar, as well.

KRONOS (*ignoring LILLITH'S remark*): How goes the journey? Has the breach in the fabric of space and time been found? I can hear the ship scraping against the encasement of the now dead universe. Will the explosion be set off?

MORBIUS: You're getting ahead of the game, Kronos.

LILLITH: Take it easy. Don't excite yourself.

KRONOS: I was asking a question.

MORBIUS: Is that what you were doing? It sounded more like an inquisition.

KRONOS: If I were conducting an inquisition, you'd damned well know it.

LILLITH: The breach hasn't been found, but when it is, we'll be ready to act.

KRONOS: You hope.

GLAUCUS: What breach and what explosion?

LILLITH: Should I tell him?

MORBIUS: Would he understand?

KRONOS: Not yet, but soon. He must be prepared if he is to survive.

GLAUCUS: How was I brought to this vessel? How?

LILLITH: When your boat overturned, Glaucus, you were teleported into this spaceship. Your unconscious body was raised from the water and taken aboard.

GLAUCUS: That storm was unnatural. The whole planet seemed to be quivering. The sky was…horrible! (*He raises his hands to cover his face.*)

KRONOS: Cry, Glaucus, for all the good it will do.

MORBIUS: You mean for all the good it will not do.

KRONOS: Always the cynic. Why must we be burdened with you? What are you staring at?

MORBIUS: Just trying to see the other side of your face.

LILLITH: Kronos, you look tired. Why not rest for awhile?

KRONOS: You mean rest up for my own death? What irony that is!

LILLITH: You may not die. You may survive with the rest of us.

KRONOS: Small comfort that is! A megalomaniac and a new-

LILLITH: Stop. Don't say anymore. There may be other survivors lurking about in this ship.

KRONOS: You're quite right. I was being careless. Yes. I'll go and rest and you can throw me overboard later. (*Exits.*)

GLAUCUS (*staring up*): Am I in some kind of an airship?

MORBIUS: Let's say yes to that question.

GLAUCUS: Don't jest with me. I don't like it.

MORBIUS (*walking back to his pilot's chair*): Who does?

GLAUCUS: I'm warning you.

LILLITH: Ignore him. No one listens to him and he knows it. Don't' you?

MORBIUS: Careful, dear Lillith. My what an interesting name… It sounds so melodious and almost innocent. Are you innocent, my dear? Why don't you tell dear sailor boy how "innocent" you really are. That explanation should last until the next collapse.

LILLITH: Insults and innuendos don't offend me. They're pathetic defenses, really. Are you pathetic, Morbius?

MORBIUS: You avoided that question rather nicely.

LILLITH: What was the question?

MORBIUS (*shrugging his shoulders*): Are you a whore?

LILLITH: No. And, why I answered that, I don't know.

MORBIUS: I do. The truth is easy to remember, while a lie takes precision of memory and the faculty to carry it out into believability.

LILLITH: You oughta' know, pilot. (*Distracted.*) Does that scraping sound never stop? It's driving me mad!

GLAUCUS: What are we scraping against? The outer hull of another ship?

MORBIUS: The inner shell of the universe. I've said this already, must I repeat myself?

GLAUCUS: We are in the space of the stars? Are we in the heavens?

MORBIUS: There's nothing left of the heavens. You're catching on.

GLAUCUS: Who built this ship?

MORBIUS: I designed it and oversaw its completion.

GLAUCUS: You're a scientist.

MORBIUS: More than a scientist. I am looking for an exit back to my own time. I'm trying to remember why I came into your universe. The answer escapes me.

GLAUCUS: You were a stranger in our universe?

MORBIUS: Yes. Who came to be feared and worshipped as a god.

LILLITH: And, you reveled in it. How satisfying that must have been to your vanity.

MORBIUS: I did not dispute it. I took advantage of the willing slave labor. It gave them a reason to live. It gave them something to do.

LILLITH: I'll wager that it did.

MORBIUS: Do you question my motives? You shouldn't. My engineering feats have made your escape possible. You should be appropriately grateful.

LILLITH: If we ever find the breach in time…that crack in the shell which once contained our universe.

MORBIUS: You should have more confidence in my navigational arts.

GLAUCUS: I've navigated the seas of my world. How do you navigate your ship?

MORBIUS: Not by the stars. There aren't any more stars. The damned universe has collapsed in upon itself. We barely escaped the gravitational pull.

GLAUCUS: Why did you rescue me?

MORBIUS: You're handsome. You're strong. And, you have the makings of a so-called hero. And, this one craved the company.

LILLITH: I like you, Glaucus. I chose you to be with me.

MORBIUS: With us, my dear. Let's not upset the triangle. You need three points for solidity and balance. Without me, you're an infinite line that extends to nowhere. Of course, there is Kronos who would make it a cube and that's about as solid as you can get, if a trifle mundane.

GLAUCUS: What's he talking about?

LILLITH: He's showing off. Don't listen to him.

GLAUCUS: Why did you choose me, Lillith?

LILLITH: I-

MORBIUS: Because she likes pretty men to play with in gardens.

LILLITH: Shut your mouth! Just be careful of what you say to him. Yes. We need you, you bastard! Lucky us!

MORBIUS: Glad to hear you admit it. That admission hurt, didn't it?

GLAUCUS: When we find this breach, then what? Does the ship enter it?

MORBIUS: Oh, yes. And, with quite a bang. The likes of which you've never heard before.

GLAUCUS: What's he talking about?

LILLITH: I told you, don't listen to him. He's giving out too much information that you're not yet ready to hear.

MORBIUS: True. We've yet to plant the Tree of Knowledge alongside the Tree of Life. Do you like fruit, Glaucus? It could sicken as well as enlighten.

LILLITH: Morbius…

GLAUCUS: How big is this ship?

MORBIUS: Why not do some exploring? But, be on your guard against stowaways. And, try not to get lost. We don't know when penetration will occur…

LILLITH: You are lewd.

MORBIUS: What did I say? Go on, sailor, go and do your exploring. If we need you, we'll sound the alarm. Get moving.

GLAUCUS (to LILLITH): I won't be long. I just want a look around.

LILLITH: Bring Kronos back with you, if you can find him. We need him here, as well.

GLAUCUS: He went in that direction. I'll be back.

MORBIUS: Goodbye. (GLAUCUS exits.)

LILLITH (*turning on MORBIUS*): Why did you tell him all that for? It's too much for him. He doesn't need to know any of it. All he needs is his wits to survive.

MORBIUS (*getting up from his pilot's chair*): And, a certain amount of individuality. He must know who he is in order to discard the brute-like emotions of his race. Someone has to prepare him for the arts of identification. Glaucus must be ready.

LILLITH: For what? Annihilation or escape?

MORBIUS: My vote is for escape.

LILLITH: I don't like it. If we survive-

MORBIUS: I intend to survive.

LILLITH: As I was saying, if we survive, we'll have to start over. Will our memories be wiped out? Will there be enemies?

MORBIUS: Mine won't. Yours won't, either, I'll wager. But, what part will you play, Lillith? It may not be the part that you wanted. Glaucus may not be yours as you intended. Don't be too cavalier.

LILLITH: Then, whose?

MORBIUS: Another woman.

LILLITH (*a moment of intense silence, then speaking with a seething anger*): I'm the only woman on this voyage out.

MORBIUS: Another could be created easily enough from Glaucus, himself.

LILLITH: How? No. Don't tell me. I know. Not even you should entertain those thoughts, Morbius. That's dangerous and you know it.

MORBIUS: I like danger...and I like playing with it. Yes. The creation of a new race. To actually play the part of God.

LILLITH: Let nature take its course.

MORBIUS: Oh, you are becoming a bore. You used to be such fun. What's deadened your appetite?

LILLITH: Necessity. Leave Glaucus alone, Morbius. Let us alone. I'm warning you.

MORBIUS: Maybe Kronos can help you carry out your rather hollow threat. I need to steer this ship into the new void and, then, let all hell break loose. I find the prospect exhilarating.

LILLITH: Will Kronos survive? Will he last long enough?

MORBIUS: I've no idea. I wonder what he'll evolve into. He may be more disappointed than you. We know what our roles will be, but what's his? Snake? Devil? The sublime consciousness of mankind?

LILLITH: Stability? Perhaps, he'll be a sage amongst us all.

MORBIUS: Kronos is a loose cannon. He's- Yes! He's the severity of justice or the temptation of vice. How irksome. What's wrong? Do you hear something?

LILLITH (*looking about the ship's chamber, uneasily*): No. But, I feel as if I'm being watched.

MORBIUS: Paranoid, are we? But, you're right. There may really be other survivors aboard this ship.

LILLITH: That's impossible. How did they get here?

MORBIUS: Cunning are the desperate. If any more are here, they will be but slaves for the new universe, that is, when they take shape, again.

LILLITH: I wouldn't tell them that. You just might have an uprising on your hands.

MORBIUS: They should have died with the other unfortunate mortals.

LILLITH: Death would be preferable to slavery.

MORBIUS: You have it reversed. Everyone fears the great unknown. They seek solace in their religion. The more intelligent seek refuge in their theories and hypothesis even though they can't prove a damned thing.

LILLITH: What comes after death?

MORBIUS: Rephrase the question: what comes after life?

LILLITH: Well?

MORBIUS: I've no idea. I'll let you know when I drop dead.

LILLITH: I don't want to die.

MORBIUS: Good. You're a level-headed whore.

LILLITH: Why do you call me that? I was a priestess and soothsayer.

MORBIUS: And, I chose you amongst all women to be the progenitor of a new race. But, I-

LILLITH: Yes? You think someone or something might interfere with our plans? That's it, isn't, it?

MORBIUS: I do feel another's presence. It disturbs me. He is here and nowhere. I look to my left and right and see nothing.

LILLITH (*again, looking about the ship's chamber, uneasily*): You don't have to see him. He's standing with us now and we can't see him. Is he the all powerful God that religion speaks of?

MORBIUS: He's subtle like a sledgehammer.

LILLITH: Morbius, we're not alone in this damned spaceship. I know it!

MORBIUS: Easy, girl. I think I hear two people we can actually see coming down the corridor.

KRONOS (*entering the chamber, being supported by GLAUCUS.*): This young man insisted that I join the party.

GLAUCUS: I was told that you were needed here. I'll bring you back to your room, if you like.

KRONOS: That was the observation deck. Didn't you notice the porthole?

GLAUCUS: But, there was nothing to see.

KRONOS: Precisely. Haven't you been told? The universe has collapsed in upon itself: it is now the size of the primordial egg: whatever the hell that is.

GLAUCUS: We're looking for a new solar system?

KRONOS: If that were all!

LILLITH: Did you see anyone else in the corridors, Glaucus?

GLAUCUS: No. But, I did hear voices in other rooms, I think.

MORBIUS: Did you bother to open up a door or two?

GLAUCUS: No.

LILLITH: I wish you had. If there are others aboard, they could be of use.

MORBIUS (*walking back to his pilot's chair*): That's one way of putting it.

GLAUCUS: I could go back and have another look.

LILLITH (*taking GLAUCUS by the hand*): No. Don't do that. I find comfort in your presence. Stay here with us.

GLAUCUS: As you wish.

LILLITH: Do you wish it?

GLAUCUS (*placing his hand almost painfully to his forehead*): I keep seeing the sea...the sea where I lost my battle with the storm.

KRONOS: Tell us about it, young man.

MORBIUS: Must he?

KRONOS: Silence. Let the boy speak.

MORBIUS: You sound almost paternal.

GLAUCUS: The clouds had taken upon themselves a life of their own. They moved rapidly across the sky in an endless sea of blue and grey foam. It was as if they were descending to the ocean to touch the very ship I was navigating. I could feel the pressure and the rain as it descended upon me. I wanted to jump into the water for protection...the cold, blue water which bore my ship. I hesitated. But, then I heaved my body overboard and let the waves take me. I knew I would die, but the sky held even more terror than death. The water embraced my body. Cold. A coldness that was the harbinger of death... of the watery grave that I had chosen. And, yet, I did not die.

MORBIUS: No. You joined this quaint, little party of ours. Just as a footnote, I sent for you. Lillith, here, chose you; but, it was I who did the transportation trick.

GLAUCUS: But what is my destiny now?

MORBIUS: Ah! Good question, that. Lillith, care to enlighten the boy on his destiny…assuming that any of us has one.

LILLITH: Glaucus, when this spaceship passes through to another universe-

MORBIUS (*staring at his right hand*): You're telling it wrong. Strive for accuracy, my dear.

LILLITH (*glancing angrily at MORBIUS*): Pardon me! When this spaceship passes through the breach that leads to nowhere, a cataclysmic explosion will be triggered off.

KRONOS: Frightening.

LILLITH: And, a new universe will be created.

KRONOS (*starting toward the corridor at stage right*): Assuming that we're not all blown to kingdom come in the explosion.

MORBIUS: We won't. I guarantee you that.

KRONOS: You hope! There are no guarantees.

GLAUCUS: How can we survive? Who's going to trigger off this explosion?

MORBIUS: We'll trigger it off.

GLAUCUS: Like gun powder?

MORBIUS: Well, it's a little more sophisticated than that, but you've got the general idea.

GLAUCUS: And, how do we survive in this void?

MORBIUS: There is a brain in that head of yours.

GLAUCUS: Well? How do we survive in this void? How do we escape the explosion?

LILLITH: In an escape pod, Glaucus.

GLAUCUS: I don't know what that is.

LILLITH: It's a much smaller vessel than the one were standing in now. It's a sort of a lifeboat. The trick is to reach it in time and outrun the explosion.

GLAUCUS: Do we have a chance?

LILLITH (*almost too emphatically*): Yes.

MORBIUS: The thrust of the explosion should push us to relative safety. But-

KRONOS: Ah! A doubt in your cunning mind. I told you that there were no guarantees.

MORBIUS: If we don't survive, life could still…

KRONOS: Go on, I want to hear your theory.

MORBIUS: Life could still begin. That is why…

LILLITH: Oh, God! I see!

KRONOS: So do I. Your alternate plan is obscene…an obscenity! Human sacrifice!

MORBIUS: Have you a better one? No. You don't. If we all die, the chances are…eventually…life will commence, again.

KRONOS: I don't like it. I don't like any of this. Who are we to play the game of the gods?

MORBIUS: You're not expected to like it. But, your presence here tells me that your willing to give it a try.

LILLITH: Is there any other way, Morbius. No. I think I've just answered my own question. Damn it! Creators and murderers.

MORBIUS: Get used to it, dear. The name "Lillith" may not fare too well in the long run. You'll either be forgotten or you'll end up on the pages of infamy as a footnote of fiction.

LILLITH: How do you know that? How can you possibly know that? What are you keeping from me?

MORBIUS: Just a feeling.

LILLITH: Liar. You know something, don't you?

MORBIUS: Perhaps, I've read the Akashic records.

LILLITH: They don't exist, yet. Where do you come from, Morbius? Why don't you tell us that?

KRONOS: I'd like an answer to that question, as well.

MORBIUS: I didn't realize I was so popular.

LILLITH: Well? Well, we're listening.

KRONOS: And, none of your evasions.

MORBIUS: I come from another time and dimension.

KRONOS: The distant past or the future?

MORBIUS: You are a clever old cuss. From the universe before this one collapsed upon itself. I am that old. I am that wise.

LILLITH: How is it that you never die?

MORBIUS: Thought never dies; nor does substance, for that matter. I've conquered death and now I must build a new physical reality for myself.

GLAUCUS: Are you God?

MORBIUS (*in a cavalier manner*): Why not? It's as good a term as any for immortality.

KRONOS (*shrugging*): And, I thought I was old.

LILLITH: Morbius puts us all to shame. How did you manage it: immortality, that is?

MORBIUS: The manipulation of thought as applied to science and intent. A philosophy of the cosmos that I've perfected by gazing and studying the constellations of stars and galaxies. Look at them when they are once again reborn: the planets, the clusters of stars and the near infinity of galaxies. They, in their wisdom, do speak to mortal beings. They cast their ancient light upon the windows of the soul...let that light in and you will be as I.

LILLTIH (*running over to GLAUCUS*): I heard a voice just then, didn't you, Glaucus?

GLAUCUS: A woman's voice...a gasp...as if she'd been listening, but is afraid to come out. (*Shouting.*) Who is hiding in that corridor? No one here will hurt you.

MORBIUS: I'm not making any promises and neither should you, sailor. Lillith, here, can be quite vindictive.

LILLITH: Who's there? Come out! I order you to show yourself! (*A pronounced silence for a few moments.*)

KRONOS: No one. I thought so.

LILLITH: But, I did hear someone.

MORBIUS: A call from the distant future? It's a voice that you may not want to hear, again, Lillith. A woman's voice, you say? Perhaps, a creation of thought…to be made into the physical one day. Tempting! How would one go about it? A humanoid created from a humanoid. The primal man giving birth to the future progenitor of the human species.

KRONOS: You'd better erase such thoughts from that infernal head of yours, Morbius. Dangerous!

MORBIUS: Not if we succeed.

GLAUCUS: If there are others aboard, will they be saved, as well?

MORBIUS: Well…there substance certainly won't be lost. They'll be put to eventual use, my boy. (*A shudder is felt and everyone is thrown off their feet. The constant scraping noise has stopped, replaced by the ticking of a mechanism.*)

GLAUCUS (*helping LILLITH to her feet*): The ship hit something.

LILLITH: No. Just the opposite, Glaucus. We're entering the crack in the shell of the now dead universe.

GLAUCUS: Is anyone hurt?

KRONOS (*staggering to his feet with difficulty*): We must get to the observation deck and prepare to abandon ship. Hurry!

MORBIUS (*pulling himself up by means of his pilot's chair*): The ship may not be through just yet. If we detonate too soon it will be the end of all of us. We've not a moment to lose.

LILLITH (*screaming*): Dearest God! This is it…the beginning or the end of everything! (*Black out.*)

ACT TWO

A smaller chamber in the spaceship with a view toward infinity. On stage left, there is a metal hatchway which leads to the escape pod.

LILLITH: Glaucus, we're passing through the rift that connects the universes.

GLAUCUS: Like a tunnel? How long is this tunnel?

LILLITH: I don't know. I thought we'd just fall through and escape before the explosion.

GLAUCUS: Where are the others? I thought they were following us.

LILLITH: I don't know. Maybe-

GLAUCUS: Maybe, they're making good their escape? Are they trustworthy?

LILLITH: They need us. There's no future without us. We're to be the first man and woman. The prototypes for a new race.

GLAUCUS: But, there's nothing but emptiness out there: no planets, no stars…nothing except a terrible blackness.

LILLITH: There will be stars, once again and then-

GLAUCUS: And, then we do what?

LILLITH: Become man and woman and bear forth a new race upon a pristine planet.

GLAUCUS: But, that's millions of years into the future, Lillith. We'll be long dead.

LILLITH: No. We won't. Our escape vehicle will make a loop in the circular infinity of the new universe. We'll age but a moment. It'll be glorious!

GLAUCUS: I don't understand at all.

LILLITH: Time is to be used, Glaucus. We're not prisoners of it. It's malleable and quite irrelevant.

GLAUCUS (*laughing*): Now, I understand even less!

LILLITH: Don't laugh, darling. The others will soon be here; I don't know what's keeping them. But, Glaucus, Morbius mentioned something before about individuality. You'll have to think beyond brute force if your to match wits with him and Kronos.

GLAUCUS: A man's physical strength brings respect and power. It's always been that way with a man.

LILLITH: I'm a great admirer of a man's strength, but you must learn to conquer your emotions or else they'll blind you to reason.

GLAUCUS: You'll teach me this?

LILLITH: I won't have to, Glaucus. Just listen to your own thoughts, my love. I hear the others coming.

MORBIUS (*hurrying into the chamber with KRONOS*): We're passing through the rift. God knows how long this will take.

KRONOS: Not long, I fear. We'd better be ready, Morbius.

MORBIUS: The detonation is ready and so is the escape pod.

GLAUCUS: Where is this escape pod? Shouldn't we be in it?

MORBIUS: You are a survivor. Good. It's right through that door. Once we reach the new void, we'll enter the pod and this ship will self destruct. What a shame to lose such a vessel!

LILLITH: Oh, Glaucus, I gaze into your eyes and see the ocean that you love so. I see the cold and relentless waves pounding upon the shore of a deserted island. Your boat is gliding into the harbor and you're standing at the helm as a proud and courageous sailor. And, then, Glaucus, my vision shifts to a rock jutting from the sea. Another life and another place. You're a merman…a god of the sea and I an a sorceress who is madly in love with you. And…you'd better not reject me! I love you so. Hold me close, darling!

MORBIUS: As I was saying… What cost creation! This magnificent vessel must be sacrificed.

KRONOS: Many human lives have been sacrificed.

MORBIUS: What of it? All mortals die off eventually.

KRONOS: You're a cold-blooded bastard.

MORBIUS: Did you lock the door?

KRONOS: Yes.

MORBIUS: Good. You're not so warm-blooded yourself, Kronos. You call me a bastard, but I do what must be done. The four of us are not enough to begin a new race. No. We've got to help evolution along. No. There's no room in the escape pod for anyone else.

KRONOS: You're real broken up about that, huh?

MORBIUS: Frankly, no.

GLAUCUS: What are you two talking about?

MORBIUS: You wouldn't understand.

KRONOS: You're better off not knowing.

GLAUCUS: I'll be the judge of that.

LILLITH: It's too obscene.

GLAUCUS: Then, you tell me, Lillith. Don't treat me like a child. You said it was time for me to think more clearly.

MORBIUS: Oh, go ahead and tell the dear boy.

LILLITH: You can be quite hateful.

GLAUCUS: Tell me.

LILLITH: It's too difficult.

MORBIUS: Human sacrifice is never easy; essential, but never easy.

KRONOS: You don't seem to mind.

MORBIUS: Get off your sanctimonious high horse. You want to let the rabble in? Then, let them in and give up your place on the escape pod. Go ahead. I dare you! You'll experience the brutalities of the mob, first hand.

LILLITH: Glaucus, in the primal explosion all the elements of creation are needed.

MORBIUS: Continue, you're doing splendidly.

LILLITH: Shut up!

GLAUCUS: Go on. Don't listen to him.

LILLITH: A human gene pool is needed to reach all four corners of the newly created universe. Alone, we can't do it.

MORBIUS: Now, do you understand?

GLAUCUS: Yes. Human blood must be spread throughout the universe when this ship explodes.

MORBIUS: Crude, but accurate. The soul and essence of a man.

KRONOS: The boy does understand.

LILLITH: I didn't want to tell you any of this. You didn't have to know.

GLAUCUS: Why not? I should share in the burden…your burden is now mine, Lillith.

LILLITH: I think I love you for that.

MORBIUS: This is getting quite sickening. However, the two of you will need that love. You'd better not forget it.

GLAUCUS: We won't. How could we?

LILLITH: We couldn't forget, my love.

MORBIUS: Hold on to him, Lillith. Remember what I told you before about footnotes in history.

LILLITH: They're trying to force the door open, Morbius. It's horrible!

MORBIUS: The brute emotions of a mob. Never trust emotion, it will steer you wrong every time. I would speak to them, but there desperation wouldn't allow them to understand logic.

KRONOS: Some logic!

MORBIUS: You're beginning to annoy me. They will live again…perhaps, as they are now or, perhaps, as a newly reincarnated soul. It will happen. There will be no pain. They will cease to become aware for a moment and, then, reawaken to a new life. You imply that I'm a murderer. You're mistaken.

KRONOS (*looking toward the porthole*): I think we're almost through the rift. I see nothing but utter blackness ahead. It's almost time. The door, Morbius, they're breaking in!

MORBIUS: But, I thought you wanted them to break in?

KRONOS: Don't be an ass!

MORBIUS: So much for your humanitarianism. Survival will always win out. But, you're right…the door is beginning to give way. No matter. The blackness ahead tells me that we're almost through.

LILLITH: Listen! The triggering mechanism…it's growing louder and faster!

MORBIUS: It's set on automatic. As soon as the vessel emerges into the void, the blast will take place. We're almost there! Pray that I really know what the hell I'm doing!

KRONOS: It's a fine time to ask that.

MORBIUS: There! Into the escape pod! Now! (*He and KRONOS head toward stage left and an open hatchway.*)

LILLITH: Glaucus? What's wrong? We have to go now or it will be too late. Why are you hesitating?

GLAUCUS (*staring past LILLITH at the port hole*): Before I went to sea, a dear aunt took me to church. It was a beautiful church with steeples and a dome. The church was crowded and we had to stand in the aisle because there were no more seats. It felt good to be among strangers who all shared the same faith. They were good people, I think. I looked up at the dome and around it was a circular wall painted all blue and white and gold. I saw angels and clouds and, Lillith, I thought I saw Heaven. I really believed that I did. I thought that God must be wonderful and beautiful...and brilliant to gaze upon.

KRONOS (*shouting from the hatchway*): Your god stinks.

GLAUCUS (*coming out of his reverie*): Watch your mouth. I think you reveal yourself.

LILLITH: Don't let him provoke you. He's the last one to speak of God and anything holy and he knows it. (*To KRONOS.*) Morbius was right to look for the other side of your face, Kronos. You're a deceiver. (*Turning back to GLAUCUS.*) We have to go, Glaucus, or we'll be killed. We mustn't delay!

GLAUCUS: Maybe, we should have gone back into the light like all the other souls.

KRONOS: Regrets, boy? Too late for regrets.

MORBIUS (*standing impatiently in the hatchway*): Come on!

GLAUCUS: Maybe that light signaled our redemption into a better existence.

MORBIUS: Would anybody else care to join me?

KRONOS: Don't talk like a fool. The collapse signaled the end.

GLAUCUS: Why don't I believe that?

LILLITH: Glaucus, please!

MORBIUS: Oh, hi kids! I'm serving tea and scones. Let's go!

KRONOS: Enough of this prattle. Or do you prefer being blown to kingdom come?

GLAUCUS: Who are you?

KRONOS: The evil which feeds upon the good. Satisfied?

MORBIUS: Unfortunately, this vermin is needed...strictly for comparative standards. It makes us all look so much better. Now, please, join the party in this comfy cozy, little pod- What the-? Hurry! (*LILLITH and GLAUCUS run into the escape pod to join MORBIUS and KRONOS.. The spaceship begins to tremble violently. A black-out is followed by a blinding white light.*)

EPILOGUE

MORBIUS: Now, as I was saying….the Big Bang just occurred and the new universe is on its way to creation. Glaucus and Lillith will find themselves in the proverbial Garden and…. yes…the proverbial snake will be there with them. And, I? Well, I must build another vessel for the inevitable collapse. Or, maybe, this time I'll push myself into that infernal point of light. What's in it and who or what created it? It had to come from somewhere…or maybe from nowhere.

LILLITH: Morbius was right. I'm nothing more than a fictional footnote: a woman of notoriety who may or may not have existed. But, I still exist in the heart of every woman's sexual desire for her man. Nothing can ever erase that. What do I care for the Tree of Knowledge? The serpent didn't tempt me. I already knew who and what I was. I didn't have to eat some poisonous fruit for that. Eve was a fool and my Glaucus was deceived by a so-called innocent. Such innocence! A race of perfection was lost forever…but, perhaps, there is still hope. Perhaps, Morbius, was right after all. Adam and I were as one. Our children are the very Nephilim the Bible speaks of. When they return, the world will know it. Kronos, the snake, must be forever damned.

KRONOS: Yes. I'm the snake in the garden. What of it? It was almost too easy. Morbius' female creation failed the ultimate test. You should curse her and not me. Glaucus should have known better. He wasn't able to discern deceit from his companion. Lillith would have known better. I wouldn't have fooled that bitch. She probably would have trampled on me. No… Eve was the target. You were a fool Morbius to have created her. I tried to insinuate myself with Glaucus on the ship, but he only had eyes for Lillith.

GLAUCUS: Naked, I arose from the dust. My name is Adam…a name given to me by my creator. To rise up as a man and look to the heavens and the blue glazed sky is wondrous. All about me is the green lushness of life and vitality. My bare feet touch upon the soft earth and, suddenly, I behold the Tree of Life. It is magnificent. Its branches bear the golden fruit of eternal life and youth. I need not take of its fruit for my soul tells me that I am immortal. A gift bestowed upon me by my god…the god who created the white flash in the empty void. I recall that great white light and an explosion which never seemed to end. I was carried on the crest of this blinding white light. I don't remember anything else. And, yet…a woman was with me. She loved me and…and told me of a future life at sea as a mariner. And, then, of yet another life as one of the gods of the sea during a golden era of the rebirth of civilization. I would know her as a sorceress and she would love me and I must love her in return. I dare not refuse that love. Lillith. Her name was Lillith and I will love her one day when she comes to the rock which juts out of the water. I will raise my arms to her and we will embrace. My god-like form will not frighten her. Cursed be anyone who rejects me! Another woman's voice deceived me and blinded my soul's eyes. Lillith will restore my soul's vision and another race will be created…a godlike race that will last until this universe is once again a mere pinpoint of light.

VESTA

A Play in Four Acts

by

Gerard Denza

CHARACTERS

VESTA DAVIS, a woman who now believes in U.F.O.s..
KURT, Vesta's "boyfriend."
DETECTIVE DUNNSTON, a police investigator.
FRANCINE, Vesta's landlady and bakery owner.
JANIE, a young girl who works in Francine's bakery.
KIT, an old friend of Francine's.
THE ALIEN, a killer from another planet.

PLACE
The main action takes place in Vesta's ground floor apartment in a suburb in New York City.

TIME
The recent past.

SCENES

Act One
Vesta's apartment on a late night in August.

Act Two
Scene One: The following morning at Francine's bakery.
Scene Two: Early afternoon of the same day in the cellar.

Act Three
The same day, but later in the evening in Vesta's apartment.

Act Four
Early morning in the cellar.

ACT ONE

VESTA is a woman in her mid-thirties and an aspiring actress. She's tall and has platinum hair. Her apartment is a studio on the first floor of an old, four story apartment building. There is a sofa at center stage with a coffee table placed in front of it. On both sides of the sofa, there are two end tables with matching, small lamps. The small kitchen is off to stage left and upstage are two windows which face on to the street.

VESTA: Telling me that I'm insane doesn't make it go away.

KURT: You're not insane, Vesta.

VESTA: Those were pretty strong insinuations, then. Tell me, Kurt, what am I? And, what are you to me?

KURT: You've an overactive imagination. I'll have a look around.

VESTA: No. You won't find anything. I'm sure of that.

KURT: I might. You're not insane and you're not a liar.

VESTA: You haven't answered my question. What am I?

KURT: Insecure.

VESTA: I hate that term. I hate it! It says nothing.

KURT: Would you like me to leave?

VESTA: Not yet. Stay. Stay with me. Tell me that you love me. Tell me that you hate me. I'll accept either.

KURT: You'd willingly accept hatred, Vesta?

VESTA: Yes! It would mean that you actually feel something for me. Why must you be so dispassionate? I'm not.

KURT: I'd better leave now.

VESTA: I thought you wanted to have a look around.

KURT: You said-

VESTA: Never mind. I'll call Francine if anything should happen. If what I supposedly imagined should come back.

KURT: You're still frightened.

VESTA: Was I pretending not to be?

KURT: Were you?

VESTA: Please go, Kurt. I don't want you here. It's worse than having no one here. To you, I'm less than nothing.

KURT: That's not true. Call the police.

VESTA: I will. And, thanks. (*She closes the door and is about to get ready for bed when a knock on the door startles her.*) Yes?

FRANCINE: It's me, honey. Open the door. Are you okay?

VESTA (*annoyed, she lets her landlady in*): Francine, it's very late-

FRANCINE: All those lights and helicopters; what was it all about?

VESTA: I don't know. They seemed to be searching for something…or someone. It was confusing. I'm really not sure what was going on.

FRANCINE: You were shouting. I heard you.

VESTA: Yes?

FRANCINE: Why?

VESTA (*evading FRANCINE'S question*): I'd gone outside.

FRANCINE: I saw you from my window. My cat woke me up.

VESTA: I thought I saw something moving behind the parked cars across the street. I couldn't make it out, but there was something furtive about it…something sinister.

FRANCINE: I didn't see anything: just the helicopters overhead and the spotlights.

VESTA (*remembering*): Yes! That's it, Francine. One of the spotlights picked something out. It was the figure of a-

FRANCINE: Of what?

VESTA: Nothing. It was nothing.

FRANCINE: You seem awfully frightened by nothing.

VESTA: Maybe I am. You didn't see anything?

FRANCINE: A tenant coming into the building, that's all.

VESTA: Who was it? No one passed me. I would have seen someone.

FRANCINE: He came in through the side entrance.

VESTA: How do you know he was a tenant?

FRANCINE: He had a key.

VESTA (*doubtfully*): Then, I guess, it must have been a tenant.

FRANCINE: Of course, dear.

VESTA: Francine, would you have a look around with me, please?

FRANCINE: What's wrong?

VESTA: Just a feeling…which I'm ashamed to admit.

FRANCINE: Come on, let's have a look around. (*Carefully, the two women search the apartment.*)

VESTA: Thanks. I feel much better now. Thank you.

FRANCINE: If you need me for anything else, just bang on the wall. (She exits. A few minutes later, there is another knock on the door.)

VESTA: Who is it? Answer me, please.

DUNNSTON: The police.

VESTA (*not in the nicest tone of voice*): What is it?

DUNNSTON: May I come in?

VESTA: Come in.

DUNNSTON: Sorry to bother you at this late hour. Are you alone?

VESTA: What can I do for you, Detective? You are a detective.

DUNNSTON: There's been a disturbance in this area tonight. Perhaps, you're aware of it?

VESTA: What disturbance?

DUNNSTON: We've reason to believe a- a fugitive is on the loose: a very dangerous fugitive: a murderer.

VESTA: Were the helicopters looking for this man?

DUNNSTON: The Highway Patrol had no helicopters in operation.

VESTA: Oh? But, I thought-

DUNNSTON: Yes?

VESTA: It doesn't matter. You were saying?

DUNNSTON: Have you noticed anything out of the ordinary tonight? Anything that might have caught your attention?

VESTA: Yes. Those helicopters, Detective. They were searching all over the place. I'm not the only one who noticed this. My landlady, Francine-

DUNNSTON: I'd like to speak to Francine.

VESTA: She lives right next door. She probably hasn't gone to bed just yet. I'll get her for you. (*She goes to the wall and bangs on it. She turns back to DETECTIVE DUNNSTON.*) Francine will be right in. She notices everything. She owns a bakery around the corner. (*There's a knock on the door.*) Come in, Francine, there's a detective here who wants to ask us some pointed questions.

FRANCINE (*out of breath and clutching her robe about her*): Oh? I don't know what we can tell him.

DUNNSTON: Francine?

FRANCINE (*staying close to VESTA*): Yes, Detective? What can we do for you?

DUNNSTON: I'll ask you what I asked Miss-

VESTA: Davis. Vesta Davis. Yes. It's a stage name, Detective.

DUNNSTON: Francine, have you seen anything out of the ordinary tonight?

FRANCINE: Yes! Helicopters all over the place!

VESTA: The detective says that no helicopters were sent.

DUNNSTON: We're searching for a fugitive.

VESTA: A murderer, you said.

DUNNSTON: That's right, Miss Davis. Francine?

FRANCINE: Who was murdered? Who? Tell us!

DUNNSTON: A tenant of yours.

FRANCINE (*frightened and curious*): No! Who was it?

DUNNSTON: An artist by the name of Blake Hammond. His mutilated body was found not too far from your apartment house, Francine.

FRANCINE: When did this happen? Tonight? What time tonight?

DUNNSTON: No more than two hours ago. He was unrecognizable. He face had been eaten away as if by acid.

FRANCINE: Eaten away? What are you saying?

VESTA: How do you know who it was? He had I.D. on him?

DUNNSTON: Yes, Miss Davis. His wallet and personal possessions were found on the body as well as his artist supplies.

FRANCINE: Yes! He was going to the art store on 57th St. to purchase some new paint brushes today. He told me this!

DUNNSTON: When did he tell you this?

FRANCINE: It was about 5 o'clock this afternoon. He was going to meet some people at the Art Students League. He was taking classes in portraiture.

DUNNSTON: You seem to know a great deal about Mr. Hammond.

FRANCINE: I make it my business to know my tenants, Detective. I don't rent apartments to undesirables.

DUNNSTON: Good for you.

VESTA: Detective, just how did Mr. Hammond die?

DUNNSTON: It had the appearance of surgical amputation.

VESTA: Amputation?

FRANCINE: It's obscene!

VESTA: Was this amputation the actual cause of death?

DUNNSTON: Yes. A loss of blood is how he died. He was alive during the...process.

FRANCINE (*horrified*): No!

VESTA: What exactly do you want from us? How can we possibly help?

DUNNSTON: Did Mr. Hammond have any enemies?

FRANCINE: No.

VESTA: Everyone has enemies.

DUNNSTON (*impressed with VESTA'S rather cold-blooded attitude*): Do you, Miss Davis?

VESTA: I assume so. People who I've "rubbed" the wrong way or have taken an instant dislike to me. It does happen.

DUNNSTON: I'd have to agree with you on that.

FRANCINE: Mr. Hammond was a very quiet man who kept to himself. He often had coffee and a roll at my bakery on the corner. I still own the establishment, although I've hired a young girl to run it for me. I do quite a nice business there. Everything freshly baked-

DUNNSTON (*cutting FRANCINE off*): That murderer is on the loose. I want you both to stay locked up in your apartments tonight. Keep inside and if you should hear or see anything out of the ordinary, call the police. Don't do any investigating on your own.

FRANCINE: Of course!

VESTA: And, if we should see helicopters in the sky, Detective?

DUNNSTON: Call us. I mean it.

FRANCINE: We will, Detective.

VESTA: Wait a minute. Francine, didn't you say that you saw a tenant coming in before when I was outside sky gazing?

FRANCINE: Yes! Yes! I did, Detective. I thought-

DUNNSTON: Thought what, Francine?

FRANCINE: That it was a tenant. But, if Mr. Hammond was murdered....perhaps someone took his house keys? Oh, my God! Is the murderer in this building? We could all be killed in our beds!

DUNNSTON: I wish you'd told me this before. Miss Davis? May I use your telephone?

VESTA: It's right there on the coffee table. (*Taking a hold of FRANCINE.*) Francine, calm down. It just might have been a tenant you saw.

FRANCINE: I didn't see his face and…

VESTA: What? Tell us.

FRANCINE: I could be wrong. I do have an active imagination. But, I think we was wearing large sunglasses.

VESTA: Did you notice anything else about him? His height? What he was wearing?

FRANCINE: A trench coat…and he was tall and very thin. He had on gloves and a strange kind of a hat.

DUNNSTON (*putting the receiver back on the phone*): I heard all that. The police will be here soon and they'll conduct a search of your apartment building.

FRANCINE: Vesta, here, thought someone had gotten into her apartment tonight.

DUNNSTON: Is that correct, Miss Davis?

VESTA: It was only a feeling, but a pretty strong one. When I went outside to see the sky show, I very stupidly left my door open. But, we've searched the apartment and found nothing… or should I say no one?

DUNNSTON: Always lock your door, Miss Davis. Always.

VESTA: After tonight, I will.

DUNNSTON: I'm serious. We're dealing with a homicidal maniac. When I leave, lock your door.

FRANCINE: She will, Detective. (*DETECTIVE DUNNSTON exits. For a moment, the two women say nothing.*) I'm frightened.

VESTA: As long as we stay put like the Detective said, we should be all right.

FRANCINE: I don't like it. Why did he say that there were no helicopters out there? There were! We both saw them and they were looking for someone and probably this killer.

VESTA: That was strange, wasn't it? He had to be aware of it. But, Francine, did you notice something strange about those copters? They were very large and black and there were so many of them in a tight formation. It looked more like a military war game or whatever they call it.

FRANCINE: Yes. Yes. It was strange.

VESTA: What do you make of it? Don't hold out on me. I happen to know that you're a very learned woman who dabbles in the unusual.

FRANCINE: Yes! I do dabble! That's the reason I purchased this apartment building. It has a history to it, you know: a very strange and deadly history. I purchased it from a woman named Kit who is still a friend of mine. She owned a bookstore in Downtown Brooklyn, but has since left the city in fear. A pity! One cannot run away from fate.

VESTA: What do you make of those helicopters?

FRANCINE: They were frantic in their search. It was as if they were terrified of what they might find.

VESTA: Go on.

FRANCINE: I've read of these types of searches by the military. It's usually connected with an unusual incident. And, they usually deny their involvement afterwards.

VESTA: What kind of unusual incident?

FRANCINE: A reported U.F.O. sighting by a reliable source and it's usually a pilot.

VESTA: That doesn't make any sense. Why would they be hunting for something on the ground?

FRANCINE: Yes! Hunting! That is the word, Vesta. Hunting for someone or something!

VESTA: How did that Detective Dunnston come to knock on this particular apartment?

FRANCINE: This building has a history of murder and disappearance. I'm sure it's on the police files. But, Vesta, that man I saw enter the building…was he a tenant or-

VESTA: Or one of them?

ACT TWO
Scene One

FRANCINE'S bakery is just opening up for business. It is unseasonably chilly outside. VESTA walks in and sees FRANCINE talking with an attractive, blonde woman at one of the wrought iron tables.

FRANCINE: Vesta, dear, come over and join us. I'd like you to meet someone.

VESTA (*signaling to the girl behind the counter for coffee*): Hello, Francine. How are you today?

FRANCINE: Very chilly. I'd like you to meet a friend of mine, Miss Kit Mason. She's the former owner of the building we're living in. She's back in town for a visit.

VESTA: Miss Mason?

KIT: Call me Kit. Nice to meet you, Vesta. I love your sweater.

VESTA: Thank you. It came in handy, today. It feels more like November than August.

KIT: Doesn't it? But, it almost suits this offbeat neighborhood.

FRANCINE: Kit was never fond of this neighborhood. It used to put her on edge.

KIT (*trying to laugh*): Well…yes! Especially that old building you're living in now. You couldn't pay me to set foot in there, again. I don't mean to put you off, Vesta; but that house always gave me the creeps.

VESTA: Why exactly did you move out?

FRANCINE: You see, Kit? I told you she was very direct.

KIT: I like her. Well, Vesta, some very strange things happened there and to this day I'm not even sure I can explain them. My sister vanished years ago and she was last seen entering the building. Strange men have come in and out who you wouldn't want to meet in a dark alleyway. And, then, there was that terrible experience with Magdalena, my former business partner. If I told you about that, you'd really think I was off my rocker!

VESTA: I wouldn't. But if you don't want to talk about it, I understand. Up until last night, I had no feelings one way or the other about the building.

KIT: And, now?

VESTA: Now, I'm not so sure. Did Francine tell you about the murder last night?

KIT: Yes! How horrible! Be careful, the both of you. Francine says that the murderer hasn't been caught yet.

FRANCINE: It's no ordinary murderer, Kit. You tell her, Vesta.

VESTA (*lighting up a cigarette*): You'll think that I'm off my rocker.

KIT: Oh my God! I'll bet I know. It's that strange man come back, isn't it?

FRANCINE: I hadn't thought of that, but it could be. Yes! It could be!

VESTA: We think it might be an alien.

KIT (*laughing, but on edge*): An alien? Oh, you're kidding? Oh, Francine, that is wild.

FRANICNE: Is it, Kit? Is what happened to us that time-

KIT (*shaking her head*): You're right. You're right. I'm sorry. I didn't mean to laugh, but-

VESTA: What happened to you? Now, I'm intensely interested.

FRANCINE: Kit, you tell it. It'll take me all afternoon.

KIT: A few years ago, Francine, Magdalena, and I conducted a séance to find out what had happened to my sister. We made contact and it was rather unpleasant. Well…the next morning we awoke to find ourselves in some kind of alternate universe. Don't ask me how, I don't know. Maybe, it had to do with the séance.

FRANCINE: It did! I'm certain of it.

KIT: We met up with a stranger: a man. He was very charming and very enigmatic.

FRANCINE: He was very European.

KIT: Yes. Somehow, we managed to get back to the apartment building: to the basement. This man knew what to do. We touched the light bulb- Oh, it sounds so insane!

VESTA: It doesn't. Go on, Kit.

KIT: And, we were back in our own time and space. Magdalena was the last to join me and Francine. She was very frightened

and wouldn't talk about it. We never saw that man, again. And, I'm not sorry about that. I moved out of the house that same day and put it up for sale.

VESTA (*sipping her coffee*): What happened to Magdalena?

KIT: We were co-owners of a book shop. We sold it. Even that book shop had a taint of something unnatural about it. I don't know what's become of her.

VESTA: But, you came back here today. Why?

FRANCINE (*answering for KIT*): She felt compelled to come back: and today of all days! I don't believe in coincidence.

VESTA: It does happen. Are you here to visit Francine?

KIT (*laughing*): Honestly, no. No offense, Francine. I just had this urge to come to the bakery, today. I don't know why. Maybe, Francine is right. Maybe, there is a purpose to my being here.

VESTA: Where will you go from here, Kit?

KIT: Good question. I guess I'll head for home. Francine, you're right. My coming here makes no sense at all. I feel so cold! It's just like that time in that other world.

FRANCINE: Yes!

KIT: I'm frightened. Will you excuse me, Francine? Vesta, it was nice meeting you. But, be careful.

FRANCINE (*furtively*): Kit, have another cup of coffee. Someone just walked in... He looks like the man I saw enter the building last night.

VESTA (*giving an involuntary shudder*): It's how you described him to Detective Dunnston. (*Turning to THE STRANGER who is wearing a trench coat with the collar turned up.*) Would you close the door, please. You're letting all the cold air in.

THE STRANGER: Of course. Forgive me, I wasn't thinking. (*He closes the door.*)

VESTA: Thank you.

THE STRANGER (*walking over to the counter*): Coffee, please, black.

JANIE: You bet. Would you like to take it with you or will you have it here?

THE STRANGER: Here. If that is all right.

JANIE: Take that table right over there. It's so cold outside!

THE STRANGER: Yes. It is. Unusual for this time of year.

JANIE: Isn't it? I had to go back home for a sweater. Here's your coffee. I hope you enjoy it.

THE STRANGER: I'm sure that I will. You're a very pleasant young lady.

JANIE: It's my job.

THE STRANGER: No. Your pleasant demeanor is genuine. Never lose it.

JANIE: Thank you.

THE STRANGER: Excuse me. (*He goes to sit at a corner table.*)

FRANCINE: Janie, why don't you join us for a second.

JANIE: But, I've got so much to do. Here's another customer. May I help you?

KIT: I'm glad to see people coming in. That's a relief!

VESTA: Shouldn't people be coming in?

KIT: Yes. Absolutely.

FRANCINE (*addressing the man*): My name is Francine. I own the place.

THE STRANGER: Your coffee is quite good. Did the young lady brew it?

FRANCINE: I taught her.

THE STRANGER: She's learned her craft well.

FRANCINE: Have we met? Why not take off your sunglasses?

KIT: Francine! Really! That's none of your business.

THE STRANGER (*gulping down the hot coffee*): Your friend is correct. It is none of your business. Your rudeness disgusts me. (*He gets up and approaches FRANCINE.*) I will take my leave of your establishment. Perhaps, we will meet, again?

VESTA: Do you live in the neighborhood? You don't have to answer that.

THE STRANGER: Yes. I live very close to you. Good day. (*Exits.*)

KIT: What do you make of that?

FRANCINE: He frightened me! How pale his face was! And, did you notice that-

VESTA (*anticipating FRANCINE*): Yes. He covered his mouth with his coat collar the entire time.

KIT: And, those sunglasses...they were black. How in the world could he see anything?

VESTA: I'm not too sure I want to know.

KIT: You and me both!

JANIE (*walking over to the table*): What's going on? You gals are giving me the willies.

VESTA: That man seemed to like you.

JANIE: Oh, don't say that! He was just awful! That pasty white complexion and those dark glasses…

KIT: I don't like it. It's like something terrible is starting all over, again.

VESTA: Ladies? I don't mean to add to your worries, but the day has suddenly changed.

JANIE (*looking out the window*): It's getting cloudy. (*She places her fingertips on the glass.*) I think it's getting warmer, though. That's good. It should be warm in August.

FRANCINE: That cold was very unnatural. It was as if something interfered with the weather.

VESTA: Like what?

FRANCINE: The term alien was mentioned last night. There have been sightings…many sightings.

VESTA: You may have something there. I read somewhere that Air Force pilots have reported bogies.

FRANCINE: They've caused crashes: more than the authorities would like to admit.

JANIE: They haven't admitted to any! And, now that you bring it up, I did see fireballs in the sky last night.

KIT: So did I. It's funny how I seemed to forget about it. They were bright and unfocused and moving strangely.

JANIE: Oh, I know! It was after midnight. My boyfriend just dropped me off.

VESTA (*changing the subject, somewhat*): Does anyone know who Mr. Hammond was? I mean aside from his being an artist; does anyone really know anything about him?

KIT: The man who was killed? No. I'd never heard of him before today.

FRANCINE: He seemed very nice and respectful. I didn't sense anything strange about him.

KIT (*laughing*): And, if he were strange, you would have noticed!

FRANCINE: I have my instincts and I trust in them. It's the way he was killed that I find so disturbing.

VESTA: Amputation isn't pleasant.

JANIE: Oh, don't say that!

VESTA: Look how dark it's getting outside. I think we all better head for home or we might be stuck here indefinitely.

JANIE: Well, I have to stay. Don't all go, please! I'd like some company. Oh, I don't need this sweater anymore.

VESTA: The murderer must have stolen Mr. Hammond's keys. He was probably the man you saw, Francine, entering through the side door. But, that doesn't account for him knowing where Mr. Hammond lived and his knowing about the side entrance.

KIT: He probably went through the poor man's pants pockets. It's too awful to think about.

VESTA (*pensively*): Probably…but how did he know about the side entrance?

FRANCINE: I've been thinking about that, too. He probably saw you out front, Vesta, and hightailed it around to the side of the building and spotted the entrance from there.

VESTA: That does make sense.

FRANCINE: But, you don't think so?

VESTA: I don't know. It just doesn't add up. Didn't Detective Dunnston say that nothing was taken from Mr. Hammond?

FRANCINE: He did. I remember him saying that.

KIT: Maybe, he put the ID back in his wallet?

VESTA: If anything, he would have taken Mr. Hammond's ID or thrown it away.

JANIE: Do you think- I'm almost afraid to ask!

FRANCINE: Calm down, dear. Ask us what?

JANIE: That man who was just here…do you think he might be some kind of an alien?

VESTA: Yes.

ACT TWO
Scene Two

It's noon of the same day and VESTA, FRANCINE, and KIT are on the wooden cellar stairs examining a very curious light bulb. This light bulb is giving off a perfect arc of light, but the light is somehow "dirty."

KIT: Francine, I don't think we should have come down here. Why in the world did we?

FRANCINE: It's what lured you back here, Kit. You know it.

KIT: I really don't want to relive any of this. What's the point?

VESTA (*looking at the yellowish light bulb*): Is this the actual light?

KIT: Don't touch it, Vesta!

VESTA: And, this is what transported you into that other dimension?

FRANCINE: Yes!

KIT: It also got us out of that dead world. (*All three women start at the sound of approaching footsteps at the back of the cellar.*)

FRANCINE: Who is it?

KURT: It's Kurt. And, don't be afraid to touch that light bulb, Vesta. I have and I'm still here in the flesh.

VESTA: Why am I not surprised.

FRANCINE: You gave us quite a start, young man.

KIT: I'll say!

FRANCINE: What are you doing here? This is private property. We've met!

KURT: Yes. You very graciously showed me around the other day. I hope you don't mind my taking the liberty of coming back?

FRANCINE: I do. People don't usually come down here. I'll have to ask you to leave.

KURT: I'm Vesta's boyfriend.

VESTA: Since when, Kurt? I didn't figure you for a pragmatist.

KURT: Is that what I am, Vesta?

VESTA: Yes. And, I don't appreciate the condescending tone of voice.

KURT: This cellar has very dense walls: almost Roman concrete in texture; but stronger and harder than even that material. Who built this place?

FRANCINE: I've no idea. It pre-dates World War I.

KIT: I'll bet!

FRANCINE: It was and still is a working class neighborhood.

KURT: A good way to go unnoticed.

VESTA: What do you mean by that?

FRANCINE (*catching the drift of KURT'S comment*): You mean: hidden. Yes!

KIT: Francine, I think you've said enough.

VESTA: Why the interest, Kurt? You've seen all this before. Is an old cellar so fascinating to you?

KIT: Let's leave this place. It's really damp and musty down here. I don't like it at all.

KURT (*pointing to the light bulb*): This light has transportation qualities?

FRANCINE: Not of itself, young man, which is why nothing happened when you touched it. (*Her voice tinged with suspicion.*) Did something happen? Tell me!

KURT: I wish something had happened.

VESTA: I don't believe you.

KIT: Neither do I. Something did happen to you, didn't it? (*Not waiting for an answer.*) Ladies, I'll see you later. I'm getting out of here. (*Exits.*)

VESTA: Maybe, we should leave, too.

KURT: Nervous, Vesta?

VESTA: Go to hell.

KURT: Is that anger or fear that I hear in your voice?

VESTA: Impatience. Let's go.

KURT: I'll walk you to your door.

FRANCINE: And, I'll lock up. By the way, how did you get in?

KURT: I let myself in.

FRANCINE: I'll have to change all the locks.

KURT: It won't do you any good.

VESTA (*looking over her shoulder at KURT*): What do you mean by that?

KURT: I'll just let myself in, again.

ACT THREE

It's early evening of the same day at VESTA'S apartment. She's just come in and is carrying some books from the public library. She puts them down on to the coffee table. She puts on one of the lamps for some light. Through the windows, beams of spotlights can be seen getting closer to the apartment building.

VESTA: What in the world is going on out there? (*She walks over to the window and pulls up the Venetian blind, not noticing that the window is slightly open.*) What are they looking for? All those helicopters...am I the only one who's noticing all this? (*A knock on her door.*) Yes?

KURT: It's Kurt.

VESTA (*letting him in*): I'm glad you're here. Do you see what's going on outside?

KURT: A lot of helicopters flying around.

VESTA: But, for what? That's what I'd like to know. It was the same way last night.

KURT: Was it?

VESTA: Yes. And, I hear that doubt in your voice.

KURT: It was a question, Vesta. Why did you want me back here tonight?

VESTA: You're pretty direct. I'll tell you why: to witness this. (*She makes a sweeping gesture toward the window.*) You're a pretty cold-blooded and logical man who's not so prone to imagining things.

KURT: I assume that that was not a compliment.

VESTA: Kurt?

KURT: Yes?

VESTA: Well, what do you think is happening out there? I think it's very strange.

KURT: Unusual. Those are army copters and they're obviously bent on a search of some kind. What they're looking for, I don't know. It's really none of our business.

VESTA: I think it is. A detective came by last night and questioned me and Francine. Why would he do that Kurt?

KURT: Didn't you ask him? It's within your rights to.

VESTA: He was looking for a murderer. A tenant in this building had been killed...dissected like some kind of specimen.

KURT: This detective actually told you that?

VESTA: Yes. Why aren't you taking me seriously? I can see that you're not.

KURT (*spotting the library books and picking one of them up*): What's this? UFOs and ancient astronauts? Come on, Vesta, I gave you more credit than to fall for this nonsense.

VESTA (*taking the book from KURT*): What's going on outside is not nonsense.

KURT: No. You're right. It's concrete reality and I'm sure that there's a good reason behind it all.

VESTA (*walks over to her kitchenette to make some coffee*): The eternal cynic. You're tough to convince, aren't you? I should let you have a long talk with Francine.

KURT: Your landlady? We've met briefly. She's a busybody.

VESTA: She'd agree with you. Kurt, look at those spotlights, they're still playing on the front of the building. Why?

KURT: Vesta, I'll just come out and say it: was this some kind of a pretext to get me to come here tonight?

VESTA (*coming back into the main room*): A trick? A trick to get you here? You bastard. Bastard!

KURT: Don't get angry.

VESTA: I thought you'd be a reliable witness: someone who'd be devoid of any emotion. I was wrong. You could care less about anything. I think you'd just better leave.

KURT: Not like this. But-

VESTA: Yes, Kurt?

KURT (*turning to leave*): Don't waste my time, anymore.

VESTA: Is that what I'm doing? Wasting your time?

KURT: To see a helicopter display in the night sky? Yes.

VESTA: Yes. You only see what's in front of you, and that's a damned shame. We're through. (*She walks over to the coffee table and picks up one of the library books.*)

KURT: With what, Vesta?

VESTA (*flinging the library book at him*): With anything and everything we never had. And, I guess, we had nothing.

KURT (*bending down to pick up the book*): What did you want? My love?

VESTA (*snatching the book from his hand*): Your body would've done nicely. It is warm-blooded, I take it? It can be aroused; but, I guess it can't pretend. My God! I think I actually hate an automaton. Leave me alone, will you?

KURT: All right. But, if you need me for-

VESTA: I'll do my best not to call. Just leave. I have my books to keep me company. Do I have to ask you, again?

KURT: No. (*He exits as VESTA pointedly looks away. Slowly, she goes to the couch and sits down, staring at the library book in her hand. Behind her, one can see the figure of someone slip past her window. VESTA gets up and looks about but is too late to see the furtive figure. She lights a cigarette. Someone knocks on the door.*)

VESTA: Yes?

JANIE: It's me, Vesta. It's Janie. Please let me in.

VESTA: Janie?

JANIE: Yes! Please open up.

VESTA: Come in. Sit down. (*There is a movement from behind the drapes.*)

JANIE (*hysterical*): It was just so scary! I closed shop and started running!

VESTA (*coming around to the side of the couch*): What was scary, Janie? Did someone frighten you? (*Her mind went to KURT.*)

JANIE (*drawing in a deep breath*): Yes. Someone did. I think it was that man who came into the bakery this morning. I'm not sure.

VESTA: Take your time, Janie. You're safe here.

JANIE: I was closing up. It was really busy today and I didn't have time to think about anything, not really. It was time to close and a couple of last minute customers came in who wanted take-out coffees. It only took a second and they're good customers. So I went to lock up, kind of hoping that they'd still be there outside, but they were walking off in the other direction.

VESTA (*taking a drag on her cigarette*): Take it easy. Then, what happened?

JANIE: I locked the door and started to cross the street to get my bus. That's when I saw all the helicopters and the spotlights. It was so scary, Vesta: all that noise and light. Well, I crossed the street and coming up the block I saw this man. It must have been a man. He was staying close to the buildings, like he was hiding or something. It gave me the creeps! He ran past me and turned the corner.

VESTA: If he ran past you, why didn't you keep walking toward your bus stop? I don't understand.

JANIE: Another man was coming up and he was hugging the buildings, too! And, then, a spotlight hit him for a second. His face looked just awful. He looked straight at me...straight at me, Vesta! I screamed and just ran straight here. I knocked on Francine's door, but she didn't answer.

VESTA (*putting out her cigarette in the ashtray on the coffee table*): It's okay.

JANIE: I saw this other man leaving the building, but he looked normal enough and didn't seem to be in any big hurry.

VESTA: That must have been Kurt.

JANIE: Your boyfriend?

VESTA: A former acquaintance.

JANIE: That sounds like a boyfriend.

VESTA: Don't get any ideas about me and Kurt. He might be insulted that you called him normal.

JANIE: He looked kind of like a bookkeeper.

VESTA: He's an engineer.

JANIE: Is he any good at it?

VESTA: He's too good to say so.

JANIE: I don't think I understand that.

VESTA: A very bad joke. (*Abruptly changing the subject.*) Francine wasn't in? I wonder where she could be. She doesn't like going out nights.

JANIE: I know, that's why I'm surprised she wasn't in. Maybe, she's visiting a neighbor?

VESTA: That's probably it. She knows everybody in the building. She makes it her business to know everyone.

JANIE: A real busybody, but really nice and kind of interesting.

VESTA (*walking over to the window*): Did you see anyone in the hallway?

JANIE: No…but I heard the side door closing. I was too afraid to look.

VESTA (*turning about*): That was supposed to have been locked because of what happened last night. It forces us all to use the front entrance.

JANIE: I'm positive it was the side door. I've walked Francine home a few times and that's the entrance she always uses. That door makes a disgusting scraping sound.

VESTA: Do you think you'll be okay by yourself, Janie? I want to ask Francine about that door. That's very disturbing. That's how that fugitive might have gotten in last night.

JANIE (*standing up and leaning over the couch*): Oh, God, Vesta don't leave me alone! Can't you call her up?

VESTA: Good idea. Go in the kitchen and pour us some coffee. I could use a cup.

JANIE: Okay. (*VESTA picks up the phone's receiver and starts dialing. JANIE comes in from the kitchen.*) No answer?

VESTA: No. I'm not even getting a dial tone.

JANIE: Now, I'm worried. (*The lights flicker and go out.*) Oh God, Vesta! The lights just went.

VESTA (*putting down the phone*): Damn it! That's all we need. I'll get some candles. And, try not to worry, Francine's probably somewhere in the building.

JANIE: Why don't I believe that? Maybe-

VESTA (*crouching down*): What? Found them! (*She lights two candles on either side of the coffee table.*)

JANIE: Maybe, she's on the roof looking at those copters? She took me up there once to look for UFOs.

VESTA: You might have something there. (*There's a banging on the door.*)

JANIE: Oh, God!

FRANCINE: Let us in! Hurry! (*Runs in followed by KIT.*) Lock the door! Something terrible is going on outside. Lock the door! (*VESTA turns the dead bolt and slides the door chain into place.*) Kit and I were up on the roof-

JANIE: Told you.

FRANCINE: -to see what was going on. Helicopters circling all over the neighborhood looking for God-only-knows what.

KIT (*sitting down on the couch*): All those bright spotlights zigzagging all over the place. It was like some kind of a manhunt.

FRANCINE: We hope!

KIT: It must be that.

FRANCINE: My building seemed to be at the center of it all. I know these things. Whatever it is they're hunting for, it's in this building!

KIT: Then, maybe, we should get out of here. We can go to my place. If we can just make it to the bus, we'll be okay.

JANIE: I don't want to go outside. That thing- that alien may be out there. At least, we're safe in here.

VESTA: Are we, Janie? I'm not so sure. I'm going to call the police and try to get a hold of Detective Dunnston.

FRANCINE: If he can be trusted.

KIT: Oh, Francine, stop it, please!

JANIE: But, what can the police do? If those are military copters out there, what can anybody do?

FRANCINE: Precisely.

VESTA (*picking up the phone's receiver*): It's still dead. There's no buzz…nothing.

JANIE: Then, we're cut off from help.

KIT: Let's make a break for it. There are four of us and the bus stop is just a couple of blocks away.

VESTA: I don't like the idea of waiting for a bus in the dead of night. We'd be exposed.

JANIE: To what?

VESTA: Those spotlights. Who knows what those copters would do. I'm not going to risk my life out there. (*A knock on the door.*)

DUNNSTON: It's Detective Dunnston. Miss Davis, are you in there?

FRANCINE: Yes. We're in here.

VESTA (*unhooking the door's chain*): Detective, you're a welcome sight. Please, come in.

DUNNSTON: Thank you, Miss Davis. (*Catching sight of FRANCINE.*) Francine, I'm glad you're here, but you may not be too happy to see me.

FRANCINE: What's wrong? Has someone else been killed? Tell me.

DUNNSTON: There's been a break-in at your bakery.

FRANCINE (*putting her hands to her face*): A break-in? You mean a robbery?

DUNNSTON: The place was ransacked. It's as if somebody set off a bomb there.

FRANCINE (*quite beside herself*): No!

JANIE: Oh, God, Francine, I'm so sorry! I did lock up. I just know I did!

FRANCINE (*trying to compose herself*): I know you did, honey.

DUNNSTON: We need you to come down there. Now, if you can.

VESTA: Can't it wait until the morning, Detective?

FRANCINE: I don't want to go out there.

DUNNSTON: I'll be with you the entire time. And, I'll walk both of you back to your apartment building.

JANIE: Both of us?

DUNNSTON: Yes. You were the last one there before the break-in. We need your statement.

KIT: Detective, what's going on out there? A robbery and a murder and some kind of a fugitive: it sounds insane!

DUNNSTON: There's an investigation going on. It's a big city and crime is rampant. Unfortunately, it's hit this area pretty hard. A manhunt is on for a murderer so...when we leave ladies, please lock up.

VESTA: Will that help, Detective, if the murderer is in the building?

DUNNSTON (*staring pointedly at VESTA*): Is he, Miss Davis?

VESTA: I don't know; but, he might be. It's a possibility. That strange man coming in by the side door last night-

JANIE (*walking over to VESTA*): And, tonight, too! When I came in, I heard someone coming in through the side entrance.

KIT: Oh, no... Is any place safe? Can't we come with you, Detective? I think I'd feel a lot safer.

DUNNSTON: Why don't you keep Miss Davis, here, company? Lock up and you'll be safe enough. Francine? Janie? Are you ready?

JANIE (*doubtfully*): I guess. Francine? Are you really up to going?

FRANCINE (*in a pompous attempt to be valiant*): They say I'm a strong woman...well, let us see!

VESTA: We'll wait up for you.

KIT: That's for sure! Would you mind if I camped out here with you, Vesta?

VESTA: Not at all. I'll serve that coffee that's about a thousand years old by now. Hope you like it strong. And, Francine? When you and Janie come back, please knock on my door.

JANIE: We will. Promise! Let's just get this over with.

DUNNSTON (*opening the door for FRANCINE and JANIE*): Let's go ladies. (*All three exit.*)

VESTA: I'll get the coffee, Kit. Try and relax; and, if you can, you're better than I.

KIT: Relax? How? It's like living the nightmare all over, again.

VESTA: You mean what happened to your sister and that strange experience?

KIT: Oh, Vesta, you sound like you actually believe me. Thank you. It did happen, but it seems like it happened to another person and not me.

VESTA: I think I understand. Your sister was never found?

KIT: It's like she never existed…which would have been a blessing.

VESTA: Why do you say that?

KIT: She was a bitch. No one liked her. I didn't like her. (*Almost laughing.*) Maybe the police thought I killed her and hid the body.

VESTA (*looking shrewdly at KIT*): Did you?

KIT: Oh, God, no! I wouldn't want her blood on my hands. She wasn't worth a stretch in prison.

VESTA: Good for you. Here's your coffee.

KIT: Oh, thanks! (*Taking a sip.*) It's really strong!

VESTA: Kit?

KIT: Yes?

VESTA: Do you trust Detective Dunnston?

KIT: What do you mean? Shouldn't I?

VESTA: I don't know. He seems to know exactly where to find people.

KIT: Isn't that his job?

VESTA: I guess it is. But, aside from Detective Dunnston and those helicopters, I haven't seen anyone else.

KIT: Isn't that enough?

VESTA: I'm not sure that it is. I really don't know what I'm trying to get at.

KIT: Vesta, you've been in that cellar.

VESTA (*sitting down with her coffee*): You mean out little expedition there this afternoon?

KIT: That's where it all happened: that's where it all began. Don't ever go down there alone, Vesta. I think that's where my sister, Corinne, went and she never came out.

VESTA: But, you did and so did Francine and that woman-

KIT: Magdalena. Yes. We came out; but, we almost didn't. You should really get out of this building. It's not safe. (*Nerving up for her next question.*) Has anyone else gone down there?

VESTA: Only Kurt, as far as I know. He's been down there at least twice.

KIT: Your boyfriend?

VESTA (*angrily*): No!

KIT: And?

VESTA: And, nothing.

KIT: You think something might have happened to him that first time down there?

VESTA (*trying to remember the past few weeks*): I didn't see Kurt for a couple of weeks after. I didn't think too much of it, but-

KIT: I hope we don't have the same awful imagination.

VESTA: I can't really put my finger on it, but...there was a coldness about him...a coldness that I hadn't sensed before. I don't think it's my imagination. It was as if his outlook were different- no: indifferent! That's the word I've been looking for, Kit. He would show up because I asked him to or because he had a specific reason to. Not cold, but not so human anymore.

KIT: I think I've met someone like him.

VESTA: Oh?

KIT: That man in that other world: Mahler Peri- (*Two gunshots are heard.*) What was that? It sounded like gunshots.

VESTA (*putting down her coffee and going over to look out the window*): They were gunshots. I think they came from the direction of the bakery.

KIT: I knew they shouldn't have gone out there. Can you see anything?

VESTA: No. (*She looks in the other direction away from that of the bakery.*) Oh!

KIT: What is it?

VESTA: Someone just went into the alleyway. (*Both women are silent for a few moments until the creaking of a metal door can be heard. VESTA moves away from the window*) That was the side door...it was supposed to be locked. I forgot to tell Francine about it.

KIT (*trying not to scream*): Did you see who it was?

VESTA: Only an outline of a man, but he looked like the one I saw coming in last night.

KIT: No! You mean he could be the murderer?

VESTA: Yes. (*The drape where she is standing flutters. Neither woman notices as a shadow of a hand emerges from the side of the curtain near VESTA.*) I wish I knew what to do.

KIT: I feel more exposed here than out there.

VESTA: I know what you mean. And, those helicopters are back.

KIT: That's all we need. I wish they'd find whatever it is they're looking for. (*She crosses the room to where VESTA is standing.*) Maybe, we should go to the bakery?

VESTA: But, that's the direction the gun shots came from. What could we do?

KIT: Well, there's sure to be cops there.

VESTA: And, maybe a couple of desperate criminals, as well. No, thanks. I think Detective Dunnston knew what he was doing when he told us to stay inside.

KIT: I wish they'd hurry back.

VESTA: I don't- (*With a start, she sees the movement behind the curtain. She tries desperately not to scream, but KIT notices her abrupt change of manner.*)

KIT: Vesta? Are you okay?

VESTA (*staring out the window*): Just…worried. I'm not used to that. Kit?

KIT: What is it?

VESTA: Why don't you go to the bakery and find out what's keeping Francine and Janie?

KIT: By myself?

VESTA: No...I'll go with you.

KIT: What is it? You're really scaring me.

VESTA (*looking toward the door*): I just heard something in the hallway. Let's see what it is. (*She grabs KIT by the elbow and starts leading her away from the curtain.*)

KIT (*screaming*): Vesta-

VESTA: There it goes, again. Come on- (*A dark figure jumps out from behind the curtain and lunges toward the two women before VESTA can slip the chain off the door.*)

KIT: Oh, God, it's that murderer!

VESTA (*making it to the other side of the couch*): Kit! Over here! (*The figure of a man grabs KIT'S leg. VESTA looks around desperately for some kind of weapon to use. She slips off her shoe and throws it at the assailant hitting him square in the head. He lets go of KIT who rushes over to VESTA. The two women run back to the door and this time VESTA slips the chain off and unbolts the lock.*) Run! (*KIT runs out the door and into the hallway, but the assailant grabs VESTA by the hair before she can get out. He pulls her back in and kicks the door shut. VESTA kicks him and nearly falls on to the couch. She takes off her other shoe.*) Keep away!

THE ALIEN: I won't harm you.

VESTA: Then, get out of my way and let me go. Now! I mean it! My friend is on her way to the police right now. Get out!

THE ALIEN: I need to go back.

VESTA: Then, go! I'm not stopping you. No one is!

THE ALIEN: They're looking for me…and I…them.

VESTA: Who are you? Why are you hiding your face? You were the man in the bakery this morning.

THE ALIEN: Yes. That was I whom you spoke to. I should not have exposed myself that way, but I was desperate! I need to speak with Francine. It is she who has knowledge of hidden things. I am not from this world; that much you have surely surmised.

VESTA (*not quite believing what she's just heard*): Where are you from? What do you want? You murdered that man last night.

THE ALIEN: I have murdered no one. I swear this. More of us have crossed the infinite barrier which separates our universe from yours. We are immortals born of the great explosion…a similar event which took place in your own universe. We have migrated to this planet…we have aided your own civilization in countless ways. You should be grateful! You are our children! We are your creators!

VESTA: What are you saying? Look at yourself.

THE ALIEN: A remnant of myself. I have been too long exposed to the radiation which no longer affects you…Vesta. We are amongst you because you are in our image. I must return in order to be restored.

VESTA: I've already told you: go. I'm not keeping you here.

THE ALIEN: Those helicopters are preventing my rescue. The craft that is to rescue me cannot be exposed.

VESTA: Do you want to hide somewhere? Not here.

THE ALIEN: In your cellar…there is the portal to another universe…another creation of thought…but I need Francine to show me the way.

VESTA: You may be giving her too much credit.

THE ALIEN: No. With her aid, I can take refuge there until my companions are able to find me and, then, we will return to Cygnus.

VESTA: You mean that they'll actually land here? I can't believe any of this.

THE ALIEN: No. They will come for me and you will tell them where to find me and how they may reach me.

VESTA (*incredulous*): Is that all? And, what if I don't go for this?

THE ALIEN: You will.

VESTA: I can't help you. I don't know how.

THE ALIEN: You do. You were being confided in this morning by Francine and your friend who just fled the room.

VESTA (*trying to be evasive*): Francine spoke about a light bulb in the cellar; but I don't see how that-

THE ALIEN: Electricity…the current which contains light and energy…if placed in the proper conductor…this structure itself could be that conductor.

VESTA (*reacting to voices outside*): They're coming. You'd better go. I mean it. Go to the cellar; it's right across the main hallway. Go, now, before they cut you off. I don't even know why I'm telling you this.

THE ALIEN: Because you are an enlightened individual who knows the truth when she hears it. I will leave. (*He turns and flees into the hallway. VESTA hears the cellar door open and shut. Then, her apartment door bursts open and DETECTIVE DUNNSTON, KIT, FRANCINE, and JANIE rush in.*)

DUNNSTON: Miss Davis, are you all right?

VESTA (*lighting a cigarette*): I think so.

FRANCINE: Where is he? Where has he gone? He didn't come out the front door. He must have gone through the side door, again.

DUNNSTON: No. I have a man posted out there. Where is he Miss Davis? (*VESTA hesitates. She stares at her cigarette.*) Miss Davis?

FRANCINE: (*in a triumphal outburst*): The cellar! He's gone down to the cellar to escape.

DUNNSTON: Take me there. Now! (*He and JANIE hurry from the apartment with FRANCINE leading the way.*)

KIT: Is that where he's gone, Vesta?

VESTA: Yes.

KIT: Why didn't you want to tell Det. Dunnston?

VESTA: I'm not sure.

KIT: What did he say to you?

VESTA: That he's from another star system and had originally come from another universe.

KIT: And, you believed him? He could have been making all that up.

VESTA: I don't think so, Kit. He looked very pale but human enough. He said he didn't murder that man last night.

KIT: Did you expect him to admit it?

VESTA: No.

KIT: You believed him?

VESTA: Yes.

KIT: Then, who murdered that man last night? And, why is this alien still here.

VESTA: I don't know who killed that man. For a second, I got some crazy idea that Kurt was involved.

KIT: Your boyfriend?

VESTA (*angrily*): He's not my boyfriend! He's just been colder than usual, but he goes off on tangents a lot. It's not unlike him to be…well, uncivil.

KIT: You don't really think he's involved?

VESTA: No. I don't. I almost wish he were here. He's the cold and sober type.

KIT: I wish the lights would come back on. I hate it when the electricity goes out. You feel so helpless!

VESTA (*as if not having heard what KIT just said*): I told him about the cellar and the light bulb…but, if there's no electricity he won't be able to escape. (*She looks toward the window.*) Kit… the helicopters…they've gone. I don't hear them anymore.

KIT: Good! They made me nervous always hovering and flashing those blinding spotlights.

VESTA: I'm not so sorry to see them go either- (*Suddenly, a white light penetrates the room, blinding the two women. KIT screams. The light travel slowly upward, stops for a moment, and then vanishes. The electricity comes back on.*)

KIT: What in God's name was that?

VESTA: It couldn't be what I think it was. (*Noticing the lights.*) The lights are back on anyway. (*They hear footsteps coming toward them. The door opens and DETECITVE DUNNSTON, FRANCINE, and JANIE come in.*)

DUNNSTON: He's escaped. I thought I had him cornered, but all of sudden a blinding light hit us and he was gone.

FRANCINE: They took him back!

DUNNSTON: Who took him back?

FRANCINE: His alien race, of course. Isn't that right, Vesta?

JANIE: Oh, Vesta, you actually spoke to him? Weren't you scared?

VESTA: I think Francine's right. I don't think we'll see him, again.

DUNNSTON: You seem like a level-headed young woman, Miss Davis. Do you actually believe that this man was an alien from another world?

VESTA: Detective, two days ago I would have been as skeptical as you are. But early yesterday morning, I actually saw a UFO: a silver cylinder gliding just above the clouds. It had to be the length of a football field or even much longer. It was soundless...so quiet...there was almost a majestic quality about it. I even argued with my boy- Kurt about it. He was quite insistent that I hadn't seen anything. I can assure you Det. Dunnston that I did.

DUNNSTON: Miss Davis, I believe you. But this alien was a murderer.

VESTA: He said that he was innocent of that crime. And, if that's true-

DUNNSTON: We still have a murderer on our hands.

JANIE: Oh, Francine, can I stay with you tonight?

FRACINE (*putting an arm around JANIE'S shoulder*): Of course!

VESTA: Detective, will you be honest with us?

DUNNSTON: Try me.

VESTA: Those helicopters out there: were they looking for your murderer or for the alien.

DUNNSTON: Your alien, Miss Davis.

JANIE: So the government does know something!

DUNNSTON: I will deny what I've just said. I would advise you ladies to say nothing further on this matter. It can do no one any good.

VESTA: Detective, the alien said he didn't murder anyone.

DUNNSTON: Maybe, he didn't. Maybe, an associate of his did.

KIT: What are you trying to tell us.

DUNNSTON: You mean: do I have a hidden meaning?

KIT: Yes!

DUNNSTON: If what just escaped had told you he was, in fact, a murderer, how would you have reacted?

KIT: Don't ask!

VESTA: He needed an ally and that was me.

DUNNSTON: Yes, Miss Davis. He needed help...your help.

JANIE: Are we safe now?

DUNNSTON: I can't answer that question, Janie, but if you should see someone or something resembling our friend, don't take any chances. He's dangerous and we've reason to believe there are more of them amongst us. They're masters of assimilation.

ACT FOUR

Footsteps are heard coming down the flight of wooden stairs in the cellar.

VESTA: I know you're down here.

THE ALIEN: I had to remain. It wasn't yet my time to leave.

VESTA: In God's name, why?

THE ALIEN: That term means nothing to me.

VESTA: You sound almost human.

THE ALIEN: Your tone is of interest, as well.

VESTA: Are you a murderer?

THE ALIEN: Yes

VESTA: I see.

THE ALIEN: Takes your breath away, I dare say.

VESTA: Why did you lie to me?

THE ALIEN: Necessity and expediency. Forgive the subterfuge.

VESTA: Forgiven.

THE ALIEN: So easily does forgiveness come?

VESTA: Forgiveness implies sin or a crime: none have been committed, have they? I don't think so.

THE ALIEN: A strange interpretation…almost bordering on a philosophy. Are you a philosopher, Vesta?

VESTA: No. I am an alien.

THE ALIEN: I suspected, but was not certain. You play the charade admirably.

VESTA: You do not.

THE ALIEN: I was…injured. I will do better.

VESTA: We'll see. You can't remain here. There's much work to be done and you've become a liability. The end of days may be near, but we're not certain.

THE ALIEN: That light bulb…if I can trigger it-

VESTA: Yes?

THE ALIEN: I can slip into that other world for a time.

VESTA: You'd willingly take that risk?

THE ALIEN: Yes.

VESTA (*leaning forward*): Then, touch it, if you dare. The electricity is back on. Do it!

THE ALIEN: Your boyfriend attempted this.

VESTA: He's not my boyfriend! And, you're wasting time. Do it! (*THE ALIEN touches the bulb and there is a momentary black-out. And, then, she is standing by herself on the stairs.*) Well done. And, now I've an acting class to attend. And, I mustn't be late. (*She pulls the cord of the light bulb to switch it off. We, then, hear the door open and close shut.*)

End of play.

PRISON BOYS:

Patrick and Marco

A Play in Three Acts

by

Gerard Denza

Copyright 2014

CHARACTERS

PATRICK, an inmate of nineteen. His sentence: life.
MARCO, an inmate of twenty. His sentence: 25 years to life.
AUNT LORETTA, Patrick's rich great aunt.
NINA BRANDON, Patrick's mother.
STEVEN, Patrick's treacherous cousin.
NELLA, a sympathetic aunt.
PEGGY, Patrick's sister.
DORIS, nosey neighbor.

PLACE
State Prison and a suburb in the U.S.A.

TIME
Mid 1950's.

SCENES

Prison

Act One: The Birthday Cake

Prison

Act Two: The Fire Hydrant

Prison

Act Three: Garden of Eden

Prison

Act Four: Target Practice

Prison

PRISON

Inside a prison cell in a maximum security state penitentiary in upstate New York. A prisoner is writing in his journal after just coming in from the yard. His cellmate is watching him.

PATRICK: Why? When each day is like the rest of the fucking days in this cell. Why go on, but why not? How do I kill myself? Do I still want to? Don't know anything anymore. What the hell did I ever know? Nothing! Today...my birthday and I'm nineteen and I've got nothing! They say I'm a time bomb ready to go off, but they're wrong. I've gone off and it's like a chain reaction that's never gonna' stop. I don't want it to stop. If anyone cares, I'm innocent. I'm innocent, but I can't bust out of my skin. Why not? Why not! Hear me, God! Are you listening to this? Are you takin' this down? I hope so. I hope so! You failed me big time.

MARCO (*a young, Latin man who is extraordinarily handsome*): Hey, man? Shut the fuck up.

PATRICK: Make me. I'm losing it, Marco. I'm losing it, man. I can't go on with the games, man. Beating up guys doesn't help. I never get hurt, hardly.

MARCO: You still trying to kill yourself, man? Give it up. There are better ways. And, besides, maybe someday they'll find out you were framed.

PATRICK: It won't happen.

MARCO: It might. Capt. Flash thinks you're innocent. He likes you.

PATRICK: Don't say that.

MARCO (*laughing*): It's true. You know it's true. Maybe, you can work something out?

PATRICK: I'm glad you're laughing. I never hear you laugh.

MARCO: You hear it, now. You pummeled that guy good, today. You're the gladiator to beat. Your dad did good to send you to those karate classes. You should thank your old man.

PATRICK: I do.

MARCO: So they pinned a murder on you? That's what you say.

PATRICK: They pinned a lie on me. That's worse.

MARCO: What lie?

PATRICK: You don't care.

MARCO: I asked.

PATRICK: I never looked for trouble.

MARCO: Trouble finds you, man. Always.

PATRICK: You got some time on your hands, so I'll tell you something.

MARCO: I like a good story.

PATRICK: My great aunt was sick, but was expected to recover. She came to live with us. She wouldn't go into a hospital. She didn't trust them. She didn't' trust anybody.

MARCO: Who's us? You gotta' fill out the details, man.

PATRICK: My mother and my sister, Peggy. I knew something wasn't right. It just didn't make any sense.

MARCO: You're losing me. What didn't make any sense?

PATRICK: My great aunt hated me. She tolerated everyone else, but me, she hated.

MARCO: Hate me, don't tolerate me. Hate pumps me up and I'm ready for it. It's honest. So talk.

ACT ONE
The Birthday Cake

It's Friday evening on PATRICK'S birthday. The living room consists of a sofa and two armchairs. A coffee table is placed in front of the sofa with an elephant figurine set in the center. On stage right is a staircase and on stage left is a sliding glass door leading into NINA'S garden.

PATRICK: You could have waited.

AUNT LORETTA (*a very stately woman*): It wasn't my decision. I'm only an unwelcome guest in this house. Speak to your mother and not me.

PATRICK: I thought you had an opinon on everything.

AUNT LORETTA: Don't be impertinent, Patrick. Learn to value relatives even though you hate them.

PATRICK: You hate me.

AUNT LORETTA: Do I?

PATRICK: If it weren't true, you'd deny it. You haven't and that speaks volumes.

AUNT LORETTA: I play my cards with care. You're not well. You should get back into bed. Here's your mother.

NINA: What's wrong? Why are you out of bed?

PATRICK: I wasn't asleep. You brought out my birthday cake and served it up. Why? Why did you do that?

NINA: This is my house and since when do I answer to you?

PATRICK: That's how much you think of my birthday? That really tells me an awful lot.

AUNT LORETTA: About whom, Patrick?

PATRICK: Who else?

AUNT LORETTA: That's a very good answer: a very clever answer. Good. You need to be clever with others.

NINA: What are you talking about, Aunt Loretta?

AUNT LORETTA: About a trifle that means a very great deal to this emotional young man.

NINA: I see.

AUNT LORETTA: I doubt it. It's time I was back in my bed.

NINA: I'll take you there. It's time for your medicine.

AUNT LORETTA: I take too much medicine, but who cares at this point? I shouldn't, but I do. Life is still precious to me.

PATRICK: I'll get back to bed myself.

NINA: Have a slice of cake.

PATRICK: What's the point? I wasn't here when you cut it. Was that Aunt Nella I heard?

NINA: Yes. She said to wish you a happy birthday.

AUNT LORETTA: She wanted to wait for you before slicing the cake.

PATRICK: And, what about you, Aunt Loretta?

AUNT LORETTA: Do I matter? I said nothing.

PATRICK: Thanks.

NINA: Your cousin, Steven, is here. He had a slice.

PATRICK: Good. Maybe the pig will choke on it.

NINA: That's not very nice. (*STEVEN and NELLA enter from stage right.*)

STEVEN: What's not very nice?

NINA: My son objects to your having a piece of his birthday cake.

STEVEN: What were we supposed to do with it?

NELLA: Patrick? We should have waited for you. It's your birthday and you should have had your birthday wish.

STEVEN: This is really sickening. My cousin should really grow up.

NELLA: And, you should learn some manners, Steven.

STEVEN: Thank you very much. Did you have a nice conversation with your Aunt Loretta?

PATRICK: What makes you ask that?

STEVEN (*faking innocence*): I just wondered.

NELLA: Don't answer him, Patrick. I have to be going soon. (*Going over to kiss PATRICK.*) Happy birthday, baby.

PATRICK: Thanks, Aunt Nella.

NELLA: Aunt Loretta? Would you like me to help you upstairs?

AUNT LORETTA: No, thank you, Nella. I'll stay down here for a few more minutes. But, could I trouble you for a glass of water?

NELLA: Of course. I'll get it. (*Exits.*)

STEVEN: I'll leave with Aunt Nella.

NINA: Going so soon, Steven?

STEVEN: I don't think Patrick, here, likes my company.

PATRICK: No. He doesn't. Beat it.

NINA: This is my house, young man, and your cousin, Steven, is my guest.

PATRICK: In that case, I'll go back to my room.

NINA: Do that. (*NELLA enters from stage right holding a glass of water.*)

PATRICK: Aunt Nella, take care. Nice seeing you. (*Exits.*)

NELLA: Feel better, baby. Aunt Loretta, you feel better, too. Here's your water.

AUNT LORETTA: Thank you. I just feel a little strange, that's all.

STEVEN: I'll walk you home.

NELLA: I can manage on my own.

STEVEN: I'm going that way, anyway. Aunt Loretta? I'll call and we'll contiuue our conversation about you-know-who.

AUNT LORETTA: Goodbye. (*NELLA and STEVEN exit.*)

NINA: Shall I help you upstairs? Or would like some more cake?

AUNT LORETTA: Save that for Patrick: it is his birthday. You shouldn't have brought it out, Nina, that was very thoughtless of you.

NINA: Steven wanted a slice.

AUNT LORETTA: It was not Steven's birthday.

NINA: I think I'll go in the backyard and do some gardening. Just call me when you're ready to go upstairs.

AUNT LORETTA: I will. (*NINA exits.*) Dreadful woman. (*She is in her usual seat and for some reason she finds herself staring at the remains of PATRICK'S birthday cake. She hears noises coming from the backyard and movements upstairs. She is startled; although she recognizes them to be only the ordinary noises of a house. She tries to recover her composure, but is unable to. Her attention returns to the birthday cake.*) Why am I so afraid? Why? (*Another noise from above frightens her. She stifles a scream.*) It's only Patrick moving about. (*Again, her focus is on the birthday cake.*) Why do I keep staring at it so. I don't feel well. I don't feel well! (*With an effort, she calms herself.*) I must go upstaris and rest. And, I will not call for that woman to help me. (*Slowly, she gets up and walks toward the staircase. As she mounts the stairs, she glances back at the birthday cake.*)

PRISON

MARCO: She didn't hate you, man. You got it ass backwards. Your mother hated you. That's what I'm getting from this story.

PATRICK: And, I hated my mother, so that made us even.

MARCO: That's bad. Your great aunt knew something was up. She knew, and I think you did, too. Why didn't you do something about it? Was that cake poisoned? I'll bet it was.

PATRICK: It was just the beginning. It was just a feeling in the pit of your fuckin' stomach. What do you do about that? What can you do about that?

MARCO: You keep your guard up and kick ass. You let them fear you! Listen to what I'm telling you. You're doing that now, here, on the inside.

PATRICK: You're right, man.

MARCO: Go on with your story.

ACT TWO
The Fire Hydrant

PATRICK, PEGGY, AUNT LORETTA, and NELLA are having a discussion in the family living room. It's late afternoon.

PEGGY: Aunt Loretta doesn't hate you, Patrick. As a matter of fact, I think she's trying to help you. Mind you, she can be a bit brusque, at times.

PATRICK: Help me to do what?

PEGGY: To be more assertive and less emotional. You know that you are. Ya' gotta' speak up more, baby.

PATRICK: I didn't until now. What you just said kind of makes sense, Peggy.

PEGGY: You're not ticked off at me for saying it, are you?

PATRICK: No. I know you mean well by it.

PEGGY: You are a bit of a loose cannon, you know.

AUNT LORETTA: Be careful, or you'll backfire, young man. That's a poor analogy, but accurate.

PATRICK: I actually think I know what you mean, Aunt Loretta.

AUNT LORETTA: I still think that you harbor resentment toward me. Why?

PATRICK: You're Steven's champion. You fell victim to his so-called charms.

PEGGY: Charming like a snake!

PATRICK: You couldn't see that he's nothing but a fourteen karat phony. The way you always looked up to him! And, you're going to leave him everything in your will, aren't you?

AUNT LORETTA: Perhaps. But, that's none of your affair. Learn to mind your own business; and that's valuable advice that I'm giving you.

PEGGY: Tend to your own affairs, you mean? I think I know what you're getting at. Even a busybody like me. (*Laughing.*) Don't all disagree at once!

NELLA: How do you feel today, Aunt Loretta? You weren't feeling well the other day.

AUNT LORETTA: I'm better, but still upset.

NELLA: About what? Has someone upset you?

AUNT LORETTA: I want to say "yes" to that question; but I'm not sure who I could name.

PEGGY: Try to play the process of elimination game: it might just work, you know.

NELLA: That's not such a bad idea, Aunt Loretta. How's mom, Peggy?

PEGGY: You might ask her. She's out back as usual tending her garden. Really…

AUNT LORETTA: She spends a great deal of time out there. It's rather a shame that she hasn't more to show for her efforts.

PEGGY: Her garden does seem like a lost cause. It's like an overgrown jungle out there. It's a good place to hide in-

PATRICK: She oughta' leave it alone for awhile.

AUNT LORETTA: Yes. And, let nature do its work. What were you just going to say, Peggy?

NELLA (*looking toward stage left*): I don't see her out there now.

PEGGY: How could you? You'd need a machete to cut your way through the undergrowth. Maybe, she's given up and gone out front. Here she is. (*In an aside.*) Lucky us!

NINA (*Looking very cheerful, but a bit flushed*): I heard the mailman coming, so I went to intercept him. Here's a letter for you, Aunt Loretta. It looks legal. Yes. It's from your attorney.

AUNT LORETTA: I'll take it. Thank you. And, your might want to freshen up, Nina. You're looking quite disheveled. Nella, why don't you stay for some tea?

NELLA: I really can't.

AUNT LORETTA: Please. Humor an old woman.

NELLA: All right. But, just one cup.

PEGGY: I'll get it. It'll give me something to do.

NINA: I hate tea. Never could stand the taste of it. Except my own brand, of course. I'll think I'll go upstairs and lie down for awhile. Patrick, having tea with the ladies?

PATRICK: No. I'm going in the den to read. Don't leave without saying goodbye, Aunt Nella. (*NINA exits stage left.*)

NELLA: I won't. (*PATRICK exits stage right.*)

AUNT LORETTA: Good. We're by ourselves.

NELLA: I thought that's what you wanted. What do you want to talk about.

AUNT LORETTA: Hear me out before you label me a raving old fool.

NELLA: Promise.

AUNT LORETTA: Nella, I'm positive that someone is trying to murder me.

NELLA: What? Who would want such a thing? Oh, Aunt Loretta, you must be wrong. I'm sure you are.

AUNT LORETTA: I'm sure that I'm not.

NELLA: Then, who is trying to murder you?

AUNT LORETTA: I don't know. No. That's not entirely true. It's as if some inner and still voice in my head is telling me, but I'm afraid to actually hear the name.

NELLA: Then, it's someone you know.

AUNT LORETTA: Yes. I'm certain of that. And, Nella, some very strange things have been happening here, lately...strange and, yet, deceptively ordinary. Oh, I'm not making any sense!

NELLA: Aunt Loretta, you are making sense.

AUNT LORETTA: Then, you believe me?

NELLA: Yes. Lately...I've felt something sinister in this house.

AUNT LORETTA: Exactly! That's the word I would have used: sinister.

PEGGY (*carrying the tea tray*): What's sinister?

AUNT LORETTA: The atmosphere in this house, young lady.

PEGGY (*setting down the tray and pouring the tea*): I'd say downright bizarre...ever since summer started or didn't start, should I say?

NELLA (*helping herself to a cup of tea*): How's that, Peggy?

PEGGY (*handing AUNT LORETTA her tea*): Patrick's bank was broken into the other day.

AUNT LORETTA: I meant to bring that up, Nella. Yes. It's that red, plaster fire hydrant that he keeps all his spare change in.

NELLA: And, someone acutally stole it?

PEGGY: Well, they stole the money in it. Poor Jared!

NELLA: My God! That's terrible! I know Patrick was so proud of what he'd saved.

PEGGY: My little brother sure was. There must have been at least a hundred dollars stashed away in it. Someone actually carved out a hole in the bottom and just looted it. They left a nickel! Talk about insult to injury.

NELLA: That's despicable! Patrick must have been very upset.

AUNT LORETTA: He was, but he tried to conceal it. He'd been saving that money for months.

PEGGY: I really could have cried for him.

NELLA: But, who could have done it? And, why? I can't believe this. And-

AUNT LORETTA: Yes, Nella? You want to ask: what does this have to do with me?

NELLA: Well...yes!

AUNT LORETTA: There was something very vicious and vindictive about it. I am always in this house and I believe that Patrick suspected me of having done it.

NELLA: Oh, I don't believe that, Aunt Loretta. I'm sure he didn't.

AUNT LORETTA: It put doubt in his mind. It confused and upset him terribly. I believe that's why it was done...and as a means of getting at me.

NELLA: Who did it? Nina?

AUNT LORETTA: Peggy, what do you think?

PEGGY (*staring down at her tea cup*): I- I don't know.

AUNT LORETTA: You do know.

PEGGY: I don't. (*Shrugging.*) Well, my darling mother could have done it. All right. Yes. She's capable of it and a lot more.

NELLA: But, I still don't understand the connection to you, Aunt Loretta.

AUNT LORETTA: No. It's not obvious. I'll grant you that.

NELLA (*putting down her tea cup*): Good tea, Peggy. Well, ladies, I have to go. But, this is very upsetting.

AUNT LORETTA: Perhaps, I shouldn't have brought it up.

NELLA: No. If something is going on, I want to know about it. Patrick! I'm leaving. I'll see you soon. (*PATRICK'S voice from off stage.*)

PATRICK: Goodbye, Aunt Nella. Take care.

PEGGY: I'll clear these things away. (*She exits to the kitchen on stage right.*)

PATRICK (*entering from stage right*): Aunt Loretta, I overheard part of that conversation.

AUNT LORETTA: I thought you had. Did you want your Aunt Nella to know?

PATRICK: I did. I'm glad you told her; but, what good will it do?

AUNT LORETTA: Whoever is behind this will also know that I've told Nella. He or she will have to be more careful.

PATRICK: Aunt Loretta, that might be a bad thing.

AUNT LORETTA: Perhaps. But, I saw no other way.

PATRICK: I'd better get back to my books. (*Exits.*)

AUNT LORETTA: Peggy forgot a cup. I'd better bring it in. (*She hears a crash upstairs.*) What was that?

NINA (*from off stage*): Only me. I dropped an ash tray. Sorry.

AUNT LORETTA: I'll bring this cup in. (*The doorbell rings and she drops the china cup, breaking it.*) Drat! Who is it?

DORIS: It's Doris. May I come in?

AUNT LORETTA: That gossip! Of course. (*She stoops down to pick up the cup fragments.*) Come in, please!

DORIS: Is everything all right?

AUNT LORETTA: It's nothing. Only a smashed cup. Please, sit down.

DORIS: I can only stay for a minute. You seem upset.

AUNT LORETTA: Annoyed at my clumsiness.

DORIS: Was it a very expensive cup?

AUNT LORETTA: Not very, but it does ruin the set.

DORIS: Will Nina be very annoyed?

AUNT LORETTA: I don't think so. It was part of my tea set.

DORIS: I am sorry.

AUNT LORETTA: We've already spent too much time on it. What can I do for you?

DORIS: How is Patrick?

AUNT LORETTA (*quite surprised at the question*): He's fine. Why do you ask? Do you know each other?

DORIS: Oh, we've met.

AUNT LORETTA: I don't believe you. Why do you ask after my nephew? Tell me.

DORIS: I was only being neighborly.

AUNT LORETTA: Who put you up to this charade?

DORIS: Perhaps, I should leave?

AUNT LORETTA: Not until you've answered my questions. What's wrong? You certainly ask enough questions yourself.

DORIS: Is Nina at home?

AUNT LORETTA: Why do you ask after my nephew?

DORIS: I was told that he's a-

AUNT LORETTA: Say it, for heavens sake!

DORIS: Sensitive. Very sensitive.

AUNT LORETTA: What of it? Yes. He's a very sensitive, young man. If that's any of your affair. Now, who put you up to this?

DORIS: I should leave.

AUNT LORETTA: Good day. (*DORIS exits.*) Of all the impertinence! A bold faced liar is what that woman is. Something is going on here. But, is it me or Jared who- What was that? (*A knock on the glass patio door.*) Who's there? Answer me, please.

STEVEN: Only me, dearest Aunt.

AUNT LORETTA: You startled me. When did you arrive, Steven?

STEVEN (*laughing*): Just now. I found this in the backyard. Do you know what it is? (*He extends a fragment of a red piece of plaster.*)

AUNT LORETTA: What in the world? You found this in the backyard?

STEVEN: That's what I said. You seem jittery, Aunt Loretta.

AUNT LORETTA: Where in the backyard did you find this? It's part of Patrick's bank.

STEVEN: His what?

AUNT LORETTA: His piggy bank.

STEVEN: Isn't he a little too old for that?

AUNT LORETTA: Saving money is a very good habit.

STEVEN: Who broke into it?

AUNT LORETTA: We don't know. Have you any idea?

STEVEN: No.

AUNT LORETTA: What brought you here, today, Steven?

STEVEN: You did. I came for a visit. I hear you haven't been quite yourself.

AUNT LORETTA: And, from whom did you hear this?

STEVEN: It's bad form to mention names. You taught me that much, Aunt Loretta.

AUNT LORETTA: You don't like Patrick, do you? You're jealous of him.

STEVEN: You're joking? Jealous of what?

AUNT LORETTA: His intellect and his potential.

STEVEN: Wrong on both counts. He's a loser. And, I thought I was your favorite. Am I?

AUNT LORETTA: In the past few month, I've done a great deal of thinking.

STEVEN: Go on.

AUNT LORETTA: Don't take that arrogant tone with me, young man.

STEVEN: Is that what I am: arrogant?

AUNT LORETTA: You'd better watch that waistline.

STEVEN: I'm an arrogant young man with a growing waistline? My, how I've come down in the world!

AUNT LORETTA: That was rude of me. I apologize.

STEVEN: Accepted.

AUNT LORETTA: What were you doing in the back yard? That's Nina's sacred ground.

STEVEN: Just having a look around.

AUNT LORETTA (*not believing him*): I see.

STEVEN: You don't. But, then, arrogance answers to no one, does it?

AUNT LORETTA: Steven, what is going on? Your being here today and that snoopy neighbor-

STEVEN: What snoopy neighbor?

AUNT LORETTA (*looking at the plaster fragment*): You found this in Nina's garden? How very careless of her to leave it there.

STEVEN: It was under a bush.

AUNT LORETTA: Liar! I don't believe a word of what you're saying. What exactly is going on here?

STEVEN: You are upset…and frightened. The dowager of the family actually knows what fear is.

AUNT LORETTA: I think you'd better leave.

STEVEN: Am I being thrown out?

AUNT LORETTA: If you like. I don't appreciate being lied to. And, your condescending voice is quite annoying.

STEVEN: Is Patrick your favorite now? You can tell me.

AUNT LORETTA: Would you please leave, Steven. It's not nice to answer such a question.

STEVEN: I don't think I like you anymore. (*NINA enters from stage left.*)

AUNT LORETTA: Nina, you have a visitor.

STEVEN (*very sweetly*): But, I came to visit you, Aunt Loretta.

NINA (*laughing*): You two not getting along? But, Steven is your favorite, Aunt Loretta.

STEVEN: No. Patrick is.

NINA: Really?

AUNT LORETTA: I said no such thing.

STEVEN: Just as good. Aunt Nina, would you walk me to my car? My presence here is disturbing Aunt Loretta.

AUNT LORETTA: You needn't speak of me in the third person.

STEVEN: Goodbye, Aunt Loretta. Give my regards to dear Jared. (*He and NINA exit.*)

AUNT LORETTA: That young man is up to something. He came here today for a purpose. And, this...I don't believe he found it in the Nina's backyard. But, why bring it in? It makes no sense. (*She stares at the fragment for a moment and the sharp edge cuts into her hand. She drops it to the ground clutching at her hand. A car back firing outside startles her. Still clutching her hand, she goes to the front door. It opens suddenly and NINA walks in. Both women stare at each other saying nothing.*)

PRISON

MARCO: They were out to kill the old lady. You didn't know this? Shit!

PATRICK: And, pin it on me. And, they did. But, there's more to it. Aunt Loretta was right: it was a conspiracy and it'd been going on for months.

MARCO: That rat, Steven, stole your money. He did it to shake you down, man: to torment you. Fuck him! Now, keep talking to me. You got more to say. I like long stories. And, we got plenty of time to kill.

PATRICK: Funny you should use that word: kill.

MARCO: It fits.

ACT THREE
Garden of Eden

In the living room with AUNT LORETTA and PEGGY.

AUNT LORETTA: Peggy, I've been so preoccupied with Patrick that I've neglected you. How are things with you?

PEGGY: Well, Auntie, that's a tough one. It's been a lousy summer so far and I don't think things are going to pick up any.

AUNT LORETTA: You used to love the warm weather. You always looked forward to it: counting the weeks off on the calendar.

PEGGY: I still do, but there's nothing to do and I can't explain it. It all started-

AUNT LORETTA: Yes?

PEGGY: Around the end of May; and, that's when things should have been nice, like they always were. The end of school was just around the corner and…it's so darned hard to explain.

AUNT LORETTA: Try. I need you to.

PEGGY: We had a really rough winter and not once did I catch so much as a sniffle. And, then, when the warm weather finally decides to get here, I come down with this god awful cold!

AUNT LORETTA: Yes. I remember that.

PEGGY: I was over at Jenny's house in her backyard for a swimming pool party. Everyone was in their bathing suits and there I was shivering in a bulky sweater. I mean really...

AUNT LORETTA: But, you got over your cold.

PEGGY: It took a while, actually. And, then, the summer turned so flat...almost grey even when it was sunny. And, I know that makes no sense. And, I'm still not completely over that darned cold.

AUNT LORETTA: Nothing makes sense in this house. You and Jared always ill.

PEGGY: And, you're always feeling so weak which is not like you at all.

AUNT LORETTA: And your mother always in that garden of hers.

PEGGY: You mean the "Garden of Eden?" Yes. Always there doing her "gardening."

AUNT LORETTA: You suspect something? Tell me what it is.

PEGGY: I threw all my mother's tea out the other day and she had a fit! It was old and smelled bad- no...it had the smell of something rotted. That's when I bought good ole' Lipton tea bags.

AUNT LORETTA: You did right to throw that horrible stuff out.

PEGGY: I think it was making us all sick. And, I told her that.

AUNT LORETTA: Good. It'll teach her that she's not above criticism. What else did she say?

PEGGY: Not much. What could she say? Oh! And, Steven walked in. So, what else is new?

AUNT LORETTA: He's a regular visitor in this house.

PEGGY: You could say that, I suppose.

AUNT LORETTA: What are you hinting at? Or do I already suspect?

PEGGY: Steven and mother have always been awfully close: a little too close if you catch my drift.

AUNT LORETTA: What are you saying?

PEGGY: I think they're lovers. I know they're lovers. Have been for quite a while; ever since father died and maybe even before that.

AUNT LORETTA: Good gracious! I'd have never- No. That's not true. Yes. You're right, Peggy. And how they have flaunted it right before our eyes! It's obscene! And, to subject a young girl of sixteen to this depravity...

PEGGY: I caught them once in mother's garden. They didn't see me. Not a pretty sight!

AUNT LORETTA: Disgraceful! You should have told me this, Peggy. Why didn't you?

PEGGY: Because you always seemed blind to Steven's faults. I didn't think you'd believe me.

AUNT LORETTA: Does Patrick know?

PEGGY: I think he's guessed. I haven't told him anything. I didn't want to upset him.

AUNT LORETTA: You should have told us both, young lady! He needs to know that his mother is a viper! You should both leave this house. And, you actually saw them-

PEGGY: I caught them in the act, Auntie, and not the kissing act, either.

AUNT LORETTA: Out in the open, where anyone could witness this?

PEGGY: Yes. In the actual sex act; if you can imagine it! And, in mother's home made "Garden of Eden." Really, I can understand her taking a lover, but her own nephew? It's almost laughable.

AUNT LORETTA: It is not in the least funny, my dear. I've heard enough. I'll speak to Nella at once. I want you and Patrick to leave this house.

PEGGY: She won't go for it.

AUNT LORETTA: We'll just see about that. If they want my money, they'll have to do as I say.

PEGGY: And, go where?

AUNT LORETTA: Nella will take you in. You're graduating next year. Patrick will be of age. I- I don't know what to say. Evil. They are evil. What in the world is next?

PEGGY: Patrick's new suit.

AUNT LORETTA: What? His new suit? What do you mean?

PEGGY: My darling mother thought it was time he got a new suit and she deliberately had the pants taken out to make him look like a fool.

AUNT LORETTA: Why?

PEGGY: She doesn't like Patrick. Never has. Don't ask me why. She tolerates me because I don't bruise so easily.

AUNT LORETTA: Your mother and Steven have long range plans. They seem very patient and cunning.

PEGGY: You mean to say: sly. They're too stupid to be cunning.

AUNT LORETTA: They're not that stupid. They're arrogant.

PEGGY: He's cold-blooded. I don't want to think what he's really capable of.

AUNT LORETTA: Of great cruelty. Yes. He and Nina are after my money and jewels.

PEGGY: Tell me something I don't know, Aunt Loretta.

AUNT LORETTA: They want money the easy way.

PEGGY: And, Aunt Loretta, you're their meal ticket.

AUNT LORETTA: I've received a letter from my attorney the other day. It was mislaid.

PEGGY: Mislaid?

AUNT LORETTA: Stolen. It doesn't matter, though. It was simply a verification of the contents of my Last Will.

PEGGY: Aunt Loretta, I think it really does matter. Whoever got their hands on that letter now knows all about your personal business. My darling mother took it.

AUNT LORETTA: I'm going to die soon, Peggy. It doesn't matter.

PEGGY: Don't talk like that. You're not going to die. Let me get you some tea, Lipton, Auntie. Perfectly legit. (*Exits*.)

AUNT LORETTA: Yes. I'm going to die. I'm going to be murdered.

PRISON

MARCO: So, what happened? She was killed. Was that tea of your mom's poisoned, too? I'll bet she got it from that garden of hers. I've heard of people doing that.

PATRICK: Aunt Loretta was murdered. He did it.

MARCO: Who? That piece of crap, Steven? You should've killed him, man. Some people deserve to diie. He did. You gotta' know when to kill the right person. That's important.

PATRICK: There's not much left to tell.

MARCO: So, tell it to me. In the end, there's a lot to tell.

PATRICK: Listen.

MARCO: That's what I've been doing. We both been in solitary; and, you're a pretty good storyteller. Solitary. Fuck! Looking through a slot and seeing nothing! Nothing! Just guards pacing up and down and, then, they come for you. They shackle your wrists and your feet and lead you out. And, to fucking where? Nowhere! (*Putting a hand on PATRICK'S shoulder.*) Now, tell me the rest.

ACT FOUR
Target Practice

Afternoon at PATRICK'S home.

AUNT LORETTA: Patrick? Steven? Stop this bickering at once.

PATRICK: Tell that to your favorite nephew. You know, the nephew who can do no wrong.

STEVEN: Do you hear this sensitive little boy? His feelings are hurt…as usual.

AUNT LORETTA: Patrick, you have always been too sensitive for your own good.

PATRICK: Interesting. When I defend myself, I'm being too sensitive. When I say nothing, I don't speak out. It's lose and lose.

STEVEN: You're a loser. Face it.

AUNT LORETTA: That remark was uncalled for.

STEVEN: Ah, but listen, Patrick, carefully. It was uncalled for, but not inaccurate. She's really not defending you, you know.

PATRICK: I heard.

STEVEN: Oh, and now you're really hurt. Too bad.

PATRICK: You're a rotten bastard.

STEVEN (*going to the bureau and taking out a small handgun*): Here. Shoot me. It's loaded. Shoot, you coward. Nina keeps this in the house for protection

PATRICK: Why do you hate me?

AUNT LORETTA (*getting to her feet*): He's jealous of you. Haven't you guessed.?

STEVEN: Jealous of what, for God's sake?

AUNT LORETTA: He's good and you are evil. Look at yourself, Steven. You're even starting to turn to fat and you're still a young man. You don't have Jared's intellect or his integrity.

STEVEN (*in a rage*): You rotten, stinking old bitch! You see this gun? I think I'll use you as target practice. (*PATRICK lunges for the gun and the two men fall to the floor. AUNT LORETTA tries to break up the fight and the gun goes off. She staggers back and collapses to the floor. She is dead: shot through the heart. The two men get to their feet. STEVEN wipes his fingerprints off the gun and, then, shoves it into the stunned PATRICK'S hand.*)

PEGGY (*running into the room*): What on earth happened? Aunt Loretta! (*Runs over to her aunt to feel for any pulse; finding none, she looks up at PATRICK.*) Patrick, are you all right?

STEVEN: He's got a gun in his hand. I'd say he's doing better than the woman he just murdered.

PEGGY: What are you saying? Patrick, speak to me. Please!

PATRICK: The gun went off. He was aiming it at Aunt Loretta and I went to grab it from him. We both fell to the floor and and it went off.

STEVEN (*in a sneering voice*): At least he can think on his feet.

PEGGY: Shut the hell up, Steven! I believe every word Patrick just said. What were you trying to do?

STEVEN: Since when do I take orders from you?

PATRICK: We'd better call the police.

STEVEN: I will. They'll want to hear the truth.

PEGGY: I'll call them.

NINA (*coming in from her garden*): Steven are you hurt? I heard a gun shot.

PEGGY: Aunt Loretta's been shot.

NINA: Has she?

PEGGY (*taken aback by her mother's callous attitude*): I think she's dead. Do you hear me?

NINA (*touching Steven's arm*): Yes. Steven? Are you all right?

STEVEN: I will be as soon as we get this murderer behind bars.

NINA: I'll use the phone upstairs. Be careful, he's still holding the gun.

PEGGY: I can't believe what I'm hearing. You're condemning your own son on this bastard's word? That's awful!

NINA: My son is a murderer.

PEGGY: Says Steven, your lover! Don't think I don't know what's been going on between the two of you. (*Turning to PATRICK.*) Patrick, you call the police.

STEVEN: I'll do that.

PEGGY: And, I'll bet you'll just love doing it! Pompous ass! Go ahead and call them. It's your word against my brother's. (*Turning to PATRICK.*) And, you'd better stick up for yourself. (*DORIS walks in unannounced.*) What are you doing here? How dare you just walk in? We have a tragedy to cope with.

DORIS (*looking at PATRICK and not the body*): Yes. I know. Are you all right, Nina? Has your son finally broken down?

PEGGY (*incredulous*): Are you serious? And, what the hell are you talking about? My aunt is dead and the police are on their way and you're asking after her health and accusing my brother of God-only-knows what?

DORIS: She's upset.

PEGGY: You could've fooled me.

NINA: They're coming for Patrick.

DORIS: Of course. He'll be looked after.

PEGGY: Get out! Get the hell out before I throw you out. Are you part of this conspiracy- Yes! That's what it is, Patrick: a conspiracy. Aunt Loretta was right. Patrick? Patrick? (*PATRICK is now leaning against the wall in a daze. He drops the gun to the carpet. She goes over to him and shakes him.*) Don't leave us. We're with you. I'll call Aunt Nella and she'll help. But, you've got to help yourself. Please, Patrick, don't leave us!

PRISON

MARCO: They pinned your aunt's murder on you.

PATRICK: They tried to, but the charge wouldn't stick. It was termed "accidental homicide." Peggy was a good character witness and my mother's testimony fell apart in court. No one believed her or that bastard.

MARCO: Then, what are you doing here, man? You're in for life. You lying to me?

PATRICK: No. I went back and killed them.

MARCO (*leaning against the bars*): What are you telling me, man? Why did you do that? You were cleared.

PATRICK: Because Steven and that woman would have killed me and my sister and I couldn't let them do that. They were evil and they ended up dead. What couldn't be said, had to be done. It was a conspiracy: the two of them had found out that Aunt Loretta had left everything to Peggy. They were to get me out of the way and, then, they'd deal with her

MARCO: And, you did it and ended up here. Was it worth it to you? What's your sister doing, now?

PATRICK: Peggy is safe. It was worth it. The sister I love is still alive.

MARCO: I hear what you're saying, man. It's a steep price. You could've been a lot more clever, man.

PATRICK: Maybe.

MARCO: You're gonna' be hurting your sister and aunt. They love you. I know. They visit you and send you stuff. Try an appeal on insanity.

PATRICK (*turning to face MARCO*): Thanks for listening, Marco. Just for once, I felt like talking. Maybe, you're right, man. Maybe, you're right.

MARCO: I still see the hurt in your eyes. It goes deep. You should have been smarter, Patrick. Look what they did to you.

PATRICK: It can't be undone.

MARCO: Your sister, Peggy, is good. She won't let you rot in here. And, your Aunt Nella, man, I'll bet she's working to get you out. You go for insanity. You get yourself a retrial. It's been done.

PATRICK: OK, Marco, I'll try. Maybe…just maybe, I was out of my mind

MARCO (*moving closer to PATRICK and whispering in a conspiratorial tone of voice*): You were. You just keep telling yourself that, Patrick, and you'll believe it and they'll believe you. You keep telling yourself that. Don't stop. Just keep repeating it over and over in your head. Do it, man. You do it. You're insane, man. You listening to Marco? Your mother was a fucking pervert who lied…she lied under oath. Steven picked a fight and shot the old lady…he pulled the trigger. And, you cracked because of what they were doing to you. Right? Say it. Tell it to Marco. Say it.

PATRICK (*in an almost a trance-like state*): Yes, Marco. You're right. I believe you.

MARCO: That's it. Say it, again and again. It sounds good 'cause it's right. Don't stop. Don't' stop. Do it, Patrick. Do it… (*Fade out with MARCO still stage whispering in PATRICK'S ear.*)

End of play.

ELLIPSIS

A Play in Four Acts

by

Gerard Denza

THE TIME TRAVELLERS

BAYLA ORTIZ, a high priestess and manipulator.
DAMIEN WILHELM, a vampire and real estate broker.
CORNFIELD, a Magus.
COLETTE, a Frenchwoman and disciple of Cornfield's.
CONSTANCE, a middle-aged and desperate social climber.
ROSE, Constance's sister and an alcoholic.
HARRY LU, a con artist.
MARLENA LAKE, a master criminal.
LEIGH DUAN, a stockbroker.
THOMAS GENTRY, a lost time traveler and stockbroker.
FATHER XAVIER CHENG, a tormented Jesuit priest.

PLACE
New York City.

TIME
2059 and 1947.

SCENES

Prologue One

Prologue Two

Act One
Scene One: In Cornfield's apartment.
Scene Two: In Connie's run down apartment.
Scene Three: In Marlena's upper east side town house.
Scene Four: In Leigh Duan's apartment.
Scene Five: In Father Cheng's rectory.

Act Two
The next evening in Damien's skyscraper penthouse.

Act Three
Scene One: At a bar and grill in 1947.
Scene Two: At a bar and grill in 1947.

Act Four
At an amusement park in Brooklyn in the Hall of Mirrors.

PROLOGUE ONE

BAYLA: There is a need in my life which must be met; but, I am at a loss to the remedy. Revenge? Murder? Not satisfactory. Those weapons are banal. The art of subterfuge is what the ancients excelled at. The manipulation of others is a very potent weapon: a fine art, really. I've procured Damien's guest list and, quite frankly, I'm unable to make any sense of it. The names of enemies. A religious name. There may be a peculiar logic in that. Revenge and torture, respectively. I approve because that is Damien's nature. But, there are several pedestrian names on his guest list. Why? And, the date and time of this gathering are unsettling: the Autumnal equinox and atop that rather garish glass tower. I'm tempted not to go. But, Damien knows that I will be there. It's as good a place as any to usher in the end of the world. The anticipated and dreaded apocalypse may be ready to descend upon us. No one can stop it. The thermo-nuclear holocaust that will destroy us all. Or will it? I think that I'll have a stab at changing destiny. If a mortal is a terrestrial god, then I think it can be done. If God can create and destroy, then, why can't I?

PROLOGUE TWO

DAMIEN: I'm Damien Wilhelm: vampire. I've lived a great many years, if you could call my existence a life. I see myself as a self created god who now dwells within this magnificent glass skyscraper. I like that word: skyscraper. It denotes a defiance of heaven. Lucifer rising from the terrestrial to reclaim his throne and spit in the face of the Creator. (*Slowly walking about his penthouse.*) I became a vampire through an unholy ritual and the dark power of dreams: a deliberate attempt to be an immortal killer. (*He glances out the large window to take in the breathtaking vista.*) Nice view, huh? New York City is still rather magnificent from a distant height. Artificial light inserted into the many glass and stone skyscrapers: civilization at its technological best. And, how people sneer at it; that is, until the lights go out. And, the lights will go out very soon, which is why I'm having my party tomorrow night. It will be a gathering of allies and enemies. The last feast before the end. Not the Last Supper, mind you, that meant only the end of my enemy's son's life…and he reversed the cycle of death and life. Bully for Him! (*Walking closer to the audience.*) No. This will be the last supper: the last morsel of life.

ACT ONE
Scene One

The stage is bare except for an armchair. It is the same for all scenes in Act One.

COLETTE (*agitated*): I cannot believe that you actually accepted such an invitation. Mon Dieu! In the name of Heaven, why, Cornfield?

CORNFIELD (*sitting in an armchair*): Curiosity?

COLETTE: Can be quite deadly. Damien is a murderer: a fiend! He killed one of your disciples-

CORNFIELD: Antonia was a traitor.

COLETTE: - and he attempted to kill me, as well.

CORNFIELD: I wonder if Bayla will be there?

COLETTE: Do you doubt it? That bitch and he were lovers. If you can imagine such a thing!

CORNFIELD: A rather unholy alliance, granted. But, I feel that our vampire friend has broken away from my former pupil.

COLETTE: He was her slave.

CORNFIELD: Don't underestimate Damien, Colette.

COLETTE: I do not. And, that is why we should not attend this Last Supper. Last Supper! The double entendre does not escape me..

CORNFIELD: Vampires can die, too, you know.

COLETTE: This one has managed quite well to elude death. He's learned his craft from Bayla. How I hate her name!

CORNFIELD: You hate her as do I. But, she is talented in her black arts.

COLETTE: And, she revels in it. Always the enigmatic one: appears and then vanishes as she pleases.

CORNFIELD: You once admired her.

COLETTE: I did. I will not deny it. And, so did you until she left your Order.

CORNFIELD: I wonder if she put Damien up to this?

COLETTE: I don't think so.

CORNFIELD: Nor do I. It's just not her style. She keeps away from people.

COLETTE: I've noticed that, as well. And, she never removes the veil from her hat.

CORNFIELD: Vanity.

COLETTE: She is not vain, but…

CORNFIELD: Go on.

COLETTE: Her eyes have a strange focus to them as of late.

CORNFIELD: You've spoken to her recently? When?

COLETTE: It was before the Summer Equinox and quite by accident. I was purchasing some jewels and quite unexpectedly she was standing next to me.

CORNFIELD: What did you make of her? I'm intensely interested.

COLETTE: The figure was still intact and her clothes were quite nice. But, her eyes seemed veiled behind the actual veil of the hat.

CORNFIELD: What civilities were exchanged?

COLETTE: I merely uttered her name. She smiled and, then, nodded to the young man beside her and left.

CORNFIELD:: Who was this young man?

COLETTE: A stranger to me. What do you make of it, Cornfield?

CORNFIELD: Your presence told Bayla that I am here in New York City. Maybe...just maybe, mind you, she did put Damien up to his Last Supper.

ACT ONE
Scene Two

CONSTANCE (*leaning over the back of the armchair and smoking a cigarette*): Dear, sweet Rose, whatever is the matter? We've been invited to a party! Surely, you have something to wear? And, not that dreadful pull-out print, please.

ROSE (*a woman who is comical without trying to be*): I could wear my black dress and borrow your pearls.

CONSTANCE: It's a party, sister, not a funeral. And, you cannot borrow my pearls.

ROSE: That's what I thought! I'll wear my mannish suit and "bob" my hair.

CONSTANCE: Do that. Make an idiot of yourself.

ROSE: Done!

CONSTANCE: I mean it, Rose. I will not have you embarrass me tomorrow night. Damien Wilhelm is a very important man.

ROSE: Is he?

CONSTANCE: Yes. I've met him only once or twice, mind you-

ROSE: And, he was impressed by your beauty and charm, no doubt?

CONSTANCE: Thanks for the sarcasm.

ROSE: Don't mention it.

CONSTANCE: He owns a great deal of real estate in the city.

ROSE: This Damien Wilhelm?

CONSTANCE: No. Our dead mother!

ROSE: Well, pardon me! And, where exactly is this party? No. The Last Supper. What in hell does that mean?

CONSTANCE: A play on words, dear.

ROSE: I don't like it. And, just where is this party?

CONSTANCE: In his penthouse.

ROSE: Forget it! You're not getting me up there to the 200th floor!

CONSTANCE (*sitting down in the armchair*): The 186th floor. You see? It's closer to the ground than you think.

ROSE: Not close enough! And, there's only that one glass elevator that goes there. Shit!

CONSTANCE: You can close your eyes as we're going up. This invitation included you -- God only knows why! -- and Damien Wilhelm is my ticket into real estate.

ROSE: Aren't we the social climber.

CONSTANCE: What of it?

ROSE: All right, you talked me into it. We'll go!

CONSTANCE: And, you'll behave yourself?

ROSE: Of course! I'll sit quietly in a corner and get plastered.

CONSTANCE: You are impossible!

ACT ONE
Scene Three

HARRY: Marlena?

MARLENA (*sitting in the armchair, she exudes self confidence*): Yes? What is it?

HARRY: Have you finished reading your Bible verse? Have you said your final Hail Mary?

MARLENA (*putting down the Bible*): You'd do well to read the Bible, Harry. You'd learn about all manner of people.

HARRY (*pointing upward*): And, what about Him?

MARLENA: You'd learn of His origin; and the origin of the human race.

HARRY: No, thanks, Marlena. I'm interested in people: present tense and their potential market value.

MARLENA (*pulling out an invitation from her overstuffed purse*): I'm not axquainted with this Damien Wilhelm; but, I seem to recall his name mentioned to me.

HARRY: In one of your inner circles?

MARLENA: Yes. I was- it was during a business transaction of sorts. I was in Paris and dealing with quite an interesting woman. The transaction did not go well. She was difficult and quite unyielding. We did not part friends.

HARRY: You don't have many friends, do you?

MARLENA: I collect people and file them away for future use. I've made your reacquaintance, haven't I?

HARRY: Am I supposed to be flattered by that remark?

MARLENA: Not if you have any self respect.

HARRY: Don't laugh at me, Marlena.

MARLENA: I've scattered men into the dust. I fear no one: not a blackmailer like yourself or anyone: not even our vampire host, Mr Wilhelm.

HARRY: A vampire? Is that what this guy is? I think your occult antics are getting to you.

MARLENA: You've just insulted me, Harry.

HARRY (*a little nervous*): Not my intention, honest.

MARLENA: I accept your apology. And, now, the question is: why? How does Damien Wilhelm know of me?

HARRY: Well, you're pretty well known in those inner circles of yours.

MARLENA: True.

HARRY: And, you're pretty resourceful in your own way.

MARLENA: Yes, Harry. One day, I must tell you of an event: an unknown war where-in the human race was saved.

HARRY: And, were you the savior, Marlena?

MARLENA: Yes. I was.

ACT ONE
Scene Four

LEIGH: Who are you?

THOMAS: You went through my wallet. You tell me.

LEIGH: Mr. Thomas Gentry, stockbroker. You live on Staten Island which is not very convenient.

THOMAS: I guess not, Miss?

LEIGH: Leigh Duan. I'm a stockbroker, as well, Thomas.

THOMAS: Who picks up amnesiac victims.

LEIGH: You looked lost in that bar. And, your dress and manner seemed so mid-twentieth century: and, that's a compliment.

THOMAS: I take it that this is not the twentieth century?

LEIGH: Leigh. No. It's not, Thomas. The year is 2059.

THOMAS: My God! It's happened-

LEIGH: Say it.

THOMAS: It's as if I've lived in other times. As if my existence were fragmented.

LEIGH: What was your last memory before the bar? Think carefully, it could be important.

THOMAS: I was in Egypt on a plain near the great Pyramid. A war had been waged...a war had been won.

LEIGH: What war? What year was it?

THOMAS: The year was 1947.

LEIGH: That can't be right. You must mean 2047: that would make perfect sense.

THOMAS (*reaching into his trouser pocket*): Here. Take a look at these coins.

LEIGH (*examining the coins*): 1920's coins. 1930's coins. 1940's coins. It still doesn't prove anything. You could be a coin collector.

THOMAS: I don't think so, Leigh. You looked at my billfold.

LEIGH: Yes. The bills weren't current. But, I can't believe some science fiction story.

THOMAS: You mean that I may have traveled through time and space? It is incredible, I'll grant you that.

LEIGH: How did you travel through time, then? You must have some idea. Yes. I'm humoring you. I'll play along.

THOMAS: I didn't belong in 1947. That's not where it started.

LEIGH: Where what started?

THOMAS: My origin.

LEIGH: You're either being very mysterious or evasive.

THOMAS: I don't mean to be. I was with a pretty interesting group of people in a downtown bar in Manhattan and the sun-

LEIGH: Go on.

THOMAS: The sun never rose in the sky. It was daylight, but there was no sun.

LEIGH: Are you sure you didn't dream this? You might have, you know.

THOMAS: It seems like a dream, but I don't think it was.

LEIGH: In any event, are you up to a party tomorrow night?

THOMAS: I don't know. I'm still pretty disoriented. I should head for home: assuming I still have a place to go home to.

LEIGH: I think you do. I'll tell you what, Thomas. I'll give you cab fare and you can shower and change clothes for tomorrow nignt. Be at the Glass Tower at seven. How deos that sound?

THOMAS: The Glass Tower?

LEIGH: You are disoriented. It's within walking distance of the Staten Island ferry. You can't miss it: it's a solid red glass skyscraper close to 200 stories tall.

THOMAS (*shaking his head*): I don't know, Leigh.

LEIGH: On second thought, stay here with me. We'll send your clothes out to the cleaners and I'll cook dinner for us.

THOMAS (*getting up from the armchair*): That sounds perfect. I'll undress.

ACT ONE
Scene Five

FATHER CHENG: Yes. The Catholic church has been singled out for repeated criticism. And, by whom? The media and by you. There is a distinct lack of respect toward Caholicism. You cannot deny it. Hatred masquerading as opinion: a platform in which to vent one's bigotry. Quite disgusting. Myself? I'm a Jesuit and a persecutor. My kind has much to answer for. The entire history of Catholicism is fraught with redemption and persecution, but so is all religion. Religion is a primitive form of philosophy: a philosophy which has barely staggered past its infancy. Why? The fear of death and reprisal by a Supreme Being? The answer is pathetic: yes. Perhaps, I can raise these questions at Mr. Wilhelm's party tomorrow night? Perhaps, Mr Wilhelm's venue may not be appropriate for religious discussion? He might object to the subjective nature of it. If he's an intelligent man, he will object to it.

ACT TWO

The sun is just setting as a red glow envelopes DAMIEN'S penthouse. The main room contains an austere living room and a bar area. The few articles of furniture are masculine to the extreme. The lighting is subtle with electric tubular candles placed at strategic points. No music is playing, but one can almost detect an ever present vibration in the air.

CONSTANCE: Oh, I do hope we're not the first to arrive.

ROSE: Looks like we're the first arrivals. Where's your boyfriend?

CONSTANCE: I've no idea. I'm sure he'll be along soon.

ROSE: Good. I need a drink. There's the bar, let's help ourselves.

CONSTANCE: Behave yourself!

ROSE: I'm a Philistine, what can I tell you?

CONSTANCE: Dear Rose, why don't you make yourself comfortable in that nice chair over there in the far corner?

ROSE: Trying to get rid of me, huh?

DAMIEN (*walking in from stage left*): Constance! Welcome to my primeval den suspended in mid-air.

CONSTANCE (*flushed*): Mr. Wilhelm-

DAMIEN: Damien. And, this must be your sister, Rose.

ROSE: Pleased to meet you. I almost passed out on the way up!

DAMIEN: The ascent is quite dramatic. I'll fix you ladies a drink.

ROSE: Scotch, straight.

CONSTANCE: Champagne cocktail, Damien.

ROSE: Get a load of her!

CONSTANCE: Rose, dear, be quiet.

ROSE: My sister, here, tells me you're quite the real estate magnet. You own this tower, handsome?

DAMIEN: Sections of it, including the foundation.

ROSE: I don't get you.

DAMIEN: Drinks, ladies?

CONSTANCE: Damien owns quite a bit of real estate in Manhattan.

DAMIEN: Not enough. I'd like to own all of this splendid island. It would be like owning a kingdom.

ROSE: And, you'd be King, huh?

DAMIEN: Head lawgiver.

ROSE: The ambitious type!

CONSTANCE: There's no other way to be is there, Damien?

DAMIEN: None that I'd care to know of. (*Catching sight of the elevator's light beam on stage right.*) Ah! Other guests are arriving. Constance? Rose? My bar is yours, so make yourselves at home. Polish off that Scotch, Rose, pour yourself a double.

CONSTANCE: Don't encourage her.

ROSE: I think me and handsome, here, speak the same language. (*THOMAS and LEIGH step out of the elevator.*)

DAMIEN: Leigh, so glad you could come to the Last Supper.

LEIGH: Wouldn't have missed it for anything. I brought a friend of mine with me: Mr. Thomas Gentry. He's a fellow stockbroker with an interesting past.

THOMAS: With no past. Glad to meet you, Mr. Wilhelm.

DAMIEN: Damien. Are you a lost soul, Thomas? So am I. Actually, I collect souls.

THOMAS: How's that, Damien?

DAMIEN: Upon the end of this life, the soul is released. I try to persuade it to stay. I even succeed at times.

LEIGH: Dare I ask how?

DAMIEN: A murdered soul wants revenge: it'll stick around for that.

THOMAS: That would explain hauntings.

DAMIEN: It would. And, I'd be responsible for some of them.

LEIGH: You're being morbid, Damien. And, I don't believe you.

THOMAS: I think I'll join the ladies at the bar. Can I get you a drink, Leigh? How about you, Damien?

DAMIEN: I don't drink any liquor.

LEIGH: A Manhattan for me, Thomas. Thanks. (*THOMAS goes over to the bar and introduces himself to CONSTANCE and ROSE.*)

DAMIEN: What did you mean when you said he's a lost soul?

LEIGH: You said he's a lost soul. He's an amnesiac. He doesn't recall his past. No. That's not right. He remembers fragments of different past lives

DAMIEN: A time traveler? Fascinating. Where did you find him or did Thomas find you?

LEIGH: At a bar last night. What do you mean that he found me?

DAMIEN: Just wondering about coincidence. Does he recall any specifics: like dates and places and events?

LEIGH: He remembers being in Egypt in 1947.

DAMIEN: Indeed. A friend of mine, whom you'll meet later, once mentioned that date to me. It does have import, but I can't seem to recall in what context. I must speak with Thomas later. He seems to be amusing himself with Rose and Constance. (*He catches a glimpse of the elevator doors opening.*) Uh-oh. The religious sect has arrived. Introduce yourself to the ladies at the bar, Leigh. They're amusing enough. (*FATHER CHENG approaches him.*) Father Cheng, welcome to the Last Supper.

FATHER CHENG: I couldn't resist such an invitation, Mr. Wilhelm. Are you being amusing, ironic or blasphemous?

DAMIEN: Never blasphemous, Father. I'm a very holy man, in my own way. I've taken vows of a sort.

FATHER CHENG: And, what are those, Mr. Wilhelm?

DAMIEN: Vows that are not easily broken on this plane.

FATHER CHENG: An evasive, but interesting answer.

DAMIEN: It was a precise answer, Father.

FATHER CHENG: I stand corrected.

DAMIEN: Father Cheng, I'd like you to meet my stockbroker, Leigh Duan: the attractive blonde at the bar. She'll pour you a glass of wine.

FATHER CHENG: I could do with a glass of red wine. Excuse me.

DAMIEN (*indicating the bar*): Please help yourself. I see that my elevator is on the ascent. Pardon me, please. (*To the audience.*) Enemies approach. I know this because I have the blood instincts of an animal. Cornfield is on his way up. Colette is clinging to him. Cornfield is a Magus who is not to be trifled with. Even I fear him. Tonight's confrontation was inevitable. Witnesses were needed for not everyone will leave here alive. At least, I hope not. I'm thirsty for some blood. (*The elevator doors open and four people emerge: CORNFIELD, COLETTE, MARLENA, and HARRY.*) Good evening.

MARLENA: Good evening, Mr. Wilhelm. Marlena Lake.

DAMIEN: I know. And, your escort?

MARLENA: Mr. Harry Lu. We met in Hong Kong.

HARRY: Pleased to make your acquaintance. Your penthouse is pretty impressive, Mr. Wilhelm.

DAMIEN: Thank you. Pardon me, please. (*He moves toward CORNFIELD and COLETTE.*) Colette! Dear, sweet Colette! You've come after all.

COLETTE: Not entirely by choice.

DAMIEN: Through curiosity, perhaps?

CORNFIELD: Through my influence, Damien.

DAMIEN: Cornfield! You're looking well. Still trying to arrange your own death and rebirth?

CORNFIELD: It's been known to be done. A Master seeking to replicate the Master.

DAMIEN: You should saunter over to the bar and have a long talk with Father Cheng. He's busy sipping some red wine.

COLETTE: Oh? Was it transformed from tap water by you, Damien?

DAMIEN: I am not a magician, Madame. I am a vampire.

CORNFIELD: I've noticed the lack of mirrors.

DAMIEN: I was never vain as a mortal or as a vampire.

CORNFIELD: I think I will speak to Father Cheng. This party does have possibilities.

COLETTE: Damien, who was that very interesting woman who came up with us? Somehow, she is familiar to me.

DAMIEN: Marlena Lake. You two should have much to talk about, Colette.

COLETTE: I know that name.

DAMIEN: Her notoriety precedes her.

COLETTE: A good friend of yours?

DAMIEN: She'd be far more interesting as an enemy.

COLETTE: Am I your enemy, Damien?

DAMIEN: You were my first enemy. Pardon me, please. (*To the audience.*) Dear Colette will never learn her lesson. Anyway, the Last Supper participants are here. Now, the drama will unfold, but the conversations should be of interest. I'll eavesdrop and participate. I can't completely relax because Bayla is not yet here. Her entrance should be magnificent. She'll be admired and resented. In the interim, I must attend to my guests and even throw out some hints as to why they've really been invited. Come.

MARLENA: I have a respectful interest in your religion, as I do most religions.

FATHER CHENG: Are you a Catholic, Miss Lake?

MARLENA: No. My husband was a Rabbi. Are you aware that religion was the first philosophy?

FATHER CHENG: There is only one true religion.

MARLENA: I disagree. There are many which have points of validity.

FATHER CHENG: Were you converted to Judaism?

MARLENA: No. I was not.

FATHER CHENG: And, your husband didn't object?

MARLENA: He did, but to no avail.

LEIGH: I have no religion.

FATHER CHENG: To have no religion, Miss Duan, is to have no philosophy.

LEIGH: I'm not buying that.

FATHER CHENG: How do you manage to function in life?

LEIGH: Quite well, thank you.

FATHER CHENG: Are you an atheist?

LEIGH: No. I wouldn't say that. I simply don't dwell on the premise of God.

FATHER CHENG: That would be considered a healthy outlook by some.

LEIGH: How do you see it?

FATHER CHENG: I, myself, have an intellectual belief in God.

LEIGH: Just how intellectual is it? I'm interested.

FATHER CHENG: God can be measured within the parameters of the physical universe: an abstraction which can be reduced to a formula or to a mortal man.

HARRY: Aren't we in His image, Father?

FATHER CHENG: A key component to be taken in the literal sense.

CONSTANCE: Should one discuss religion? Shouldn't it be avoided like one's politics?

THOMAS: Agreed, Constance. Religion is a topic that I almost fear.

CONSTANCE (*flirting with THOMAS*): For Heaven's sake, why, Thomas?

THOMAS: Doesn't it contain the mysteries of creation and the Creator?

CONSTANCE: You are a deep thinker. Let's have dear Rose pour us another drink. Rose? Dear?

HARRY: Marlena seems to be having a good time.

CORNFIELD: She hasn't taken her eyes off Thomas. He's a time traveler, I hear.

HARRY: A what? He actually travels through time? Neat trick. Maybe, he'll teach it to me. I'd like to take a Steve Brody now and then.

CORNFIELD: Would your creditors appreciate that?

HARRY: You're sharp.

CORNFIELD: I judge character.

HARRY: How do you rate our host over there?

CORNFIELD: He's a cold-blooded killer.

HARRY: You don't mince words. You're like me.

CORNFIELD: Look. Marlena is approaching Thomas. She's drawing him into a most intimate conversation.

HARRY: What's your interest?

CORNFIELD: Like yourself, I would like to travel through time.

MARLENA: This meeting was inevitable.

THOMAS: I know you.

MARLENA: You do. Together, we battled an old enemy of mine and won.

THOMAS: In Egypt.

MARLENA: You've traveled through time once again, Thomas.

THOMAS: But, so have you. You're the same as you were a hundred years ago.

MARLENA:. No. I have slowed the process of age.

THOMAS: That's no mean feat, Marlena.

MARLENA: You disappeared from the battlefield in Egypt. I was quite distraught. Why?

THOMAS: I wish to God I knew. I honestly don't.

MARLENA: My daughter, Susan, was very upset. She liked you.

THOMAS: How is she? Is she well?

MARLENA: She's dead.

THOMAS: I'm so sorry, Marlena. Truly.

MARLENA: She was a dear, plain girl. She missed you. She was in love with you.

THOMAS: I don't know what to say.

MARLENA: You came with that Asian businesswoman?

THOMAS: Leigh Duan. Yes.

MARLENA: When did you make your appearance in this era? I must know.

THOMAS: As far as I can recollect, it was late yesterday afternoon.

MARLENA: And just prior to that?

THOMAS: Same old, demanding Marlena. I was with you on the plain before the Great Pyramid.

MARLENA: You're here for a purpose and tonight's party is that purpose.

THOMAS: Care to share that purpose with an old friend?

MARLENA: An event is about to occur and our host needs witnesses.

THOMAS: Why so mnay? And, what's the event?

MARLENA: It must be epic in proportion, Thomas. It leaves one unsettled.

THOMAS: What is it, Marlena?

MARLENA: Are you up on your current events? No. Of course you're not.

LEIGH: I am.

MARLENA: Miss Duan, what is your theory? You have been listening.

LEIGH: I have. The threat of nuclear war has been making headlines, but that's nothing new.

MARLENA: I believe war to be iminent, Miss Duan. I take those headlines seriously.

LEIGH: Then, what are we doing in a mile high glass tower? Shouldn't we be running to the nearest fall-out shelter?

MARLENA: A complete waste of time: delaying the inevitable by seconds, if that.

FATHER CHENG: I agree, Miss Lake. Better to got out with the first blast: much quicker and almost a mercy.

COLETTE: But is death a mercy, Father?

FATHER CHENG: If one one dies free of sin and restriction, yes.

HARRY (*laughing*): Then, I'd say we're all doomed!

ROSE: Speak for yourself, bud.

CONSTANCE: Let's not talk about death. It's so depressing! (*A blinding white light appears for an instant.*) What in the world was that? Did anyone see that?

LEIGH (*looking toward the western window*): I did. Was it a lightning flash? We're up high enough.

FATHER CHENG: It didn't look like lightning.

MARLENA: No. It didn't. What do you make of it, Cornfield?

CORNFIELD: I'm not sure. It was more like a light pulse: a burst of energy, perhaps.

COLETTE: It was disturbing. I don't like it.

ROSE: Scared the crap out of me!

CORNFIELD (*turning to face DAMIEN*): Damien, tell us why we've been invited here tonight. (*Before DAMIEN can answer, the elevator doors open and BAYLA emerges.*)

DAMIEN: Bayla! At last, the party can really begin.

COLETTE: I was under the impression it already had.

DAMIEN: Bayla? A few words for our guests? They might be of use.

FATHER CHENG: I don't like the way you said that.

DAMIEN: Too bad. Silence! All of you! Bayla?

BAYLA: Damien, my love, this will be our last meeting before the end of the world.

FATHER CHENG: Would you explain that, please?

DAMIEN: Shut up.

BAYLA: The end of one epoch and the beginning of another. But, the sacrifice must be offered. No?

FATHER CHENG (*understanding the import of her words*): And, who is to die, Miss Ortiz? Does that flash of light we just witnessed have anything to do with this?

BAYLA: You are a magician, Father. Good. I respect you.

ROSE (*quite plastered*): What in hell is going on here?

LEIGH: Thomas, you know, don't you? I trust you. I don't trust her.

BAYLA: I've taken the liberty of disconnecting the elevator.

FATHER CHENG: You don't have that right.

ROSE: That you can say again, Father. Shit!

HARRY: Get that elevator back up here, lady. If we're gonna' die -- and I think that's what you mean -- I'll pick the time and place of my death.

BAYLA: You are required to stay.

HARRY: Get it back!

BAYLA: Look out the window to the east. It hovers.

CONSTANCE: What is she talking about? Does anybody know?

ROSE: Beats the hell out of me.

COLETTE: Always so mysterious. A straight forward answer is beyond her powers. Bitch!

CORNFIELD: What is "hovering," Bayla? (*His gaze turns toward where BAYLA is pointing.*) My God!

DAMIEN: It looks like a bi-plane.

BAYLA: It is. You disappoint me, Damien.

LEIGH: It's going to crash into the building!

ROSE: We've had it!

BAYLA: It's not going to "crash," Miss Duan.

FATHER CHENG (*moving quickly to the other side of the penthouse*): Look out over here: this window in the western sky. What black magic is this?

DAMIEN: You should know, Father.

FATHER CHENG: Go to hell!

THOMAS: I think we have.

LEIGH: Thomas, what's going on?

FATHER CHENG: That other glass tower is shattering. I see the people within- look! We're in that other building!

MARLENA: Glass shattering- horrible! It's being destroyed by a thermo-nuclear blast. We must be caught between the pulses of time itself.

BAYLA: My congratulations, Miss Lake, on your deduction.

MARLENA: But, to what end, Miss Ortiz? Yes. I've been informed of your various intrigues.

BAYLA: I like your question. Matters must be attended to and rather quickly.

MARLENA: How? And, don't mince words.

BAYLA: We'll need help and do not resist when it arrives. My purpose is to prevent the destruction of civilization.

HARRY: The elevator's coming up. I'm getting on it.

ROSE: I'm with you, Harry. Let's get the hell out of here.

FATHER CHENG: The doors are opening.

LEIGH: I see people inside.

CONSTANCE: So do I. I don't like it. (*Figures emerge from the elevator.*)

THOMAS: Marlena, who are they?

MARLENA: I'd only be guessing.

THOMAS: Then, guess for God's sake!

MARLENA: Guides, Miss Ortiz? Or executioners? (*The men approach each individual and takes each by the wrist toward the elevator.*)

FATHER CHENG (*struggling to free himself*): What is this? I demand an explanation!

DAMIEN: Shut the hell up.

BAYLA: I told you not to resist. We've one chance to avert what you see toward the west. Even I am being led.

FATHER CHENG: Toward what, Miss Ortiz?

BAYLA: To circumvent God. And, you'd better pray that we're successful.

ACT THREE
Scene One

The place is a mid-town bar and grill. Our protagonists are sitting at a table in the rear: some are smoking and some are drinking.

FATHER CHENG: How on earth did we get here?

DAMIEN: Not enjoying yourself, Father?

FATHER CHENG: I am, actually. The meal was simple, but quite good. I'm a man of simple needs.

DAMIEN: And, the company, Father?

ROSE: Don't let him bait you.

CONSTANCE: Dear Rose, it was a simple question.

FATHER CHENG: The company was quite convivial, Damien.

COLETTE: Bayla, you still drink absinthe.

BAYLA: It's my only addiction.

CORNFIELD: Mine is power.

ROSE: What kind of power, baby?

CORNFIELD: The ultimate power of life and death.

FATHER CHENG: But, how would you attain such power?

BAYLA: You may be sorry you asked that question.

CORNFIELD: Through trickery, manipulation, and the black magic of the ancients.

FATHER CHENG: Terrible.

BAYLA: I did warn you, Father.

FATHER CHENG: Do you actually practice the Black Mass?

CORNFIELD: It is the centerpiece of my philosophy.

CONSTANCE: Could I trouble someone for a light? Thank you, Damien.

DAMIEN: Quite welcome.

ROSE: Well, as long as I've got my drink in hand, what in hell are we doing here? How did we get here and where are we? Shit!

DAMIEN: That's an awful lot of questions, Rose.

FATHER CHENG: They're good questions. Miss Ortiz, do you have the answers for us?

BAYLA: We are in a mid-town bar and grill in Manhattan and the year is 1947.

CONSTANCE: 1947? Someone mentioned that year at Damien's party. Who was it?

DAMIEN: Thomas. Thomas Gentry, our time traveler.

BAYLA: We were brought here by Time Guardians, if you will.

COLETTE: Slaves of yours, Bayla?

BAYLA: Servants who I was fortunate enough to make contact with. They do not follow a specific time sequence.

ROSE: So, what are we doing here, lady? You've got all the answers.

BAYLA: Not all of them.

CONSTANCE: I saw a mirror image of Damien's skyscraper in the process of being shattered by what looked like a nuclear blast.

BAYLA: Please, continue.

CONSTANCE: Are we here to prevent that little occurrence?

ROSE: That's what I'd like to know.

DAMIEN: That's a question that needs answering, Bayla.

BAYLA: The moment I entered the penthouse is when the blast occurred. I was not destined to be there. My presence upset the liner time frame. We could no longer remain in that time and survive. We are a split second ahead of the destruction. Time in 2059 A.D. is now at a standstill.

ROSE: I need a refill. Pardon me.

DAMIEN: Why, Bayla? Why did you save us?

BAYLA: I wouldn't have put it that way.

COLETTE: Yes. Saving people is not your style at all, is it? Cornfield, what do you think?

CORNFIELD: What do you hope to gain, Bayla? You don't give a damn about us.

BAYLA: There are certain guests in the party who interest me.

COLETTE: How very flattering.

CORNFIELD: And, just who are the lucky people?

BAYLA: Don't turn your back on cheating death, Cornfield.

CORNFIELD: I'm not. Who is of interest to you?

BAYLA: Would you believe me if I said you are amongst them?

CORNFIELD: No. Try, again.

CONSTANCE (*gesturing with her cigarette for effect*): I don't mean to interrupt this little tete-a-tete, but how can we save ourselves? Isn't that the pertinent question?

FATHER CHENG: I agree with Constance. Can't we simply remain here or can destiny be changed?

BAYLA: Our respite is only temporary. We would be drawn back to the fatal moment.

CORNFIELD: You mean that we would, not you, Bayla. It's becoming clear to me.

COLETTE: Tell us, Cornfield, do we have a chance? She talks in riddles.

CORNFIELD: You put Damien up to that skyscraper party. It was bait to lure us all there. You knew of the impending destruction and so lured us back through time. Why? A direct answer, please.

BAYLA: I despise direct answers.

CORNFIELD: Give it a try.

COLETTE: A direct answer is an honest one, and this witch is incapable of honesty.

ROSE (*coming back from the bar*): Well, how do we stand?

DAMIEN: How do we save ourselves, Bayla? Tell us.

BAYLA: There's a Hall of Mirrors. We must go there.

CONSTANCE: Why?

COLETTE: Why not bring us there to begin with? So much simpler, no? So much more expedient.

BAYLA: Preparation was needed.

CORNFIELD: A Hall of Mirrors in order to obliterate our images.

BAYLA: The image of future time will be shattered. When one looks into the mirror, one sees an instant into the future. We'll each have a weapon, of course.

ROSE: You mean target practice? And, that's all we have to do?

BAYLA: Simplicity itself, my dear.

FATHER CHENG: We destroy our future image in these mirrors and, then, what?

CONSTANCE: We can stay here? I might like it here.

CORNFIELD: Let's get to this Hall of Mirrors. I'd like a good look at myself. (*Laughing.*) Damien? I'd like to see your reflection in a mirror!

ACT THREE
Scene Two

The time frame is two hours prior to the previous scene. It's the same bar and grill and the protagonists are sitting at the same table.

THOMAS: We've been in this restaurant before, Marlena.

MARLENA: We met here. You were with a young woman, Yolanda, at the time. (*Turning to BAYLA.*) What year is this, Miss Ortiz?

BAYLA: 1947.

MARLENA: Impossible. Would I actually encounter myself? You're lying.

BAYLA: We won't be here very long, Miss Lake.

THOMAS: I was here in April of 1947.

BAYLA: It's late September of that year.

LEIGH: Why are we here?

THOMAS: I was just about to ask that question.

LEIGH: I saved you the trouble, Thomas.

BAYLA: We are here to divert a nuclear holocaust.

LEIGH: That's pretty ambitious stuff. Do we have any chance of actually doing it?

HARRY: Miss Ortiz brought us here: I'd say that's pretty ambitious!

MARLENA: How did you manage it, Miss Ortiz?

BAYLA: We're wasting time.

HARRY: But, you control time, lady, don't you? So, why don't we just stay put and live out our lives here? I'm willing to give it a shot.

BAYLA: That is not possible.

MARLENA: We'd be thrown out, so so speak, of this self-made time pocket?

BAYLA: Possibly, Miss Lake.

THOMAS: Then, that's why I never seem to stay put in one time frame, I guess.

MARLENA: Is he right?

BAYLA: He could be, but his seems to be a special case.

LEIGH: Miss Ortiz, why are we here? How do we avoid being blasted to kindgom come?

THOMAS: You've just answered your own question, Leigh. Are we here to avoid being killed: yes or no?

BAYLA: Yes.

HARRY: Liar.

THOMAS: Your eyes tell a different story.

BAYLA: Oh? And, what story is that?

THOMAS: Deceit. Marlena, what's your opinion?

HARRY: So, how do we avoid annihilation? By sitting here in a Bar and Grill? That'd by my way out. Cheers!

MARLENA: The surroundings do seem rather incongruous, Miss Ortiz.

LEIGH: Damn it! What is our next move? If we can't stay put in 1947, then what?

BAYLA: The Hall of Mirrors.

LEIGH: I've heard of that, actually. That used to be an amusement park attraction., wasn't it?

MARLENA: My father spoke of it. It was in Brooklyn, I believe. Why there?

BAYLA: A glimpse into the future. Find the mirror and shatter it.

HARRY: Like in Damien's skyscraper? You ain't leveling with us lady, And, I don't like it. You hear what I'm telling you? I don't have an education. And, I don't have friggin' patience with a double-dealing bitch like you. I don't have your guile or your gall. And, I don't have your put-on mannerisms. But, I got a brain in this head and I know a set-up when I hear one. You want us to do your dirty work for you. Shut up! I'm still talkin'. Well, find yourself another patsy. I'm staying right here 'cause I can make myself pretty comfortable in any place and in any time. What do I give a crap what year it is? I've got my wits and I'm not so proud that I can't take up manual work. Thanks for the meal. I think I'll head for a park bench or the nearest flop house or subway car. I know my way around.

LEIGH: Harry, don't go. We should stick together.

MARLENA: She's right. You'd better stay.

HARRY: I'm not gonna' run into myself, Marlena. And, besides, how can I die if I haven't even been born yet? Maybe, that'll shake things up.

LEIGH: Harry might just have a point. I could make myself a very wealthy woman if I stayed in 1947. I'm willing to give it a try. Thomas, how about you?

MARLENA: We're losing the thread of all this. We're here to avert disaster.

THOMAS: If Miss Ortiz is telling us the truth.

MARLENA: We were witnesses to this disaster. But, was it on a worldwide scale? If that's the case, then we might not succeed. But, I'd still like to see this Hall of Mirrors.

BAYLA: Then, we should leave at once.

THOMAS: Marlena, these mirrors might be actual fractures in the time continuum or port holes to God-only-knows where. I'm not sure how I know this, but it could mean our salvation or destruction. It seems almost haphazard.

MARLENA: Is it?

HARRY: Yeah, Miss Ortiz, level with us.

BAYLA: It's a gamble worth taking. Harry? Maybe, you should stay. It might "shake things up" as you say.

HARRY: I intend to stay. But, I'll come along for the fun. I always did like amusement parks.

MARLENA: Thomas, what about you?

THOMAS: Maybe, I'll find my way back into my own time. I really don't have anything to lose, least of all an identity.

LEIGH: I'm game. But, I'm with Harry. I might just stay here.

MARLENA: Then, we'd better be off. But, I still feel that you're keeping things from us, Miss Ortiz. Are you?

BAYLA: You'll just have to find out for yourselves, Miss Lake. Shall we leave?

ACT FOUR

The Hall of Mirrors. The backdrop has segments of mirrors and on stage left and stage right, as well. The effect is disconcerting as the audience can see endless images of themselves.

COLETTE: Cornfield, I don't trust her.

CORNFIELD: And, you think that I do?

COLETTE: So, what is your plan? Look at all these mirrors! And, yet, they're strange...almost-

CORNFIELD: As if the very reflections were alive. I noticed. Be prepared to run for your life. We may have to remain in this time frame after all.

COLETTE: Would that be so dreadful?

CORNFIELD: It would be rather interesting. The ramifications could be profound.

COLETTE: Or less than insignificant. I don't like any of this. Bayla is up to something and it's sure to benefit her.

CONRFIELD: I was certain of that much quite a while ago.

COLETTE: And, yet, you walk into her trap? Why, Cornfield? We should leave now before the others arrive.

CORNFIELD: And, miss all the fun? No. Bayla is treacherous, but she's also over confident, and that will be her undoing.

DAMIEN: A little strategy talk going on here?

CORNFIELD: Yes, Damien.

COLETTE: Damien, what is Bayla's objective? Surely, you must know, cherie.

DAMIEN: I've no idea. Truly. She's up to something fairly elaborate from the looks of it. Excuse me, please, the others are arriving and I still feel as if I'm the host.

COLETTE: Oh? I thought the party was quite over?

DAMIEN: It looks like the parlor games are just beginning. Again, dear Colette, pardon me?

COLETTE: Of course.

ROSE (*taking a good look around*): Get a load of all these mirrors, will you? And, I hate looking at myself in a mirror. Shit!

CONSTANCE: Dear Rose, do behave yourself.

ROSE: Why should I? Don't we get to break a few of these mirrors anyway?

CONSTANCE: Damien, what is our next move?

DAMIEN: Beats me. But, I wouldn't break any mirrors just yet.

ROSE: I guess that bitch, Bayla's, calling the shots.

DAMIEN: You might say that.

CONSTANCE: But, Damien, you seem so removed from the general fear of our little party.

DAMIEN: I'm immune to chills and most mass hysteria. More people just walked in. I think we're all here now, except for Bayla. She'll make her usual late entrance.

CONSTANCE: I'm sure. Who exactly is she?

DAMIEN: A magician. A priestess. A murderer.

LEIGH: And, a manipulator. She does that quite well, I've noticed.

CONSTANCE: I've noticed that, too.

HARRY: Hey, Damien, where are the sledgehammers?

DAMIEN: I don't think sledgehammers is what Bayla had in mind.

MARLENA: She mentioned weapons.

THOMAS: I thought you always carried a gun in your purse, Marlena.

MARLENA: I have it with me now. And, I'm ready to use it.

HARRY: I'll bet! I like you, Marlena. You're a tough broad. I'd put you up against Bayla any day.

MARLENA: Why thank you, Harry.

HARRY: Don't mention it.

MARLENA: Father Cheng, are you here to administer our last rites or, perhaps, to adminsiter grace?

FATHER CHENG: Sarcasm, Miss Lake?

MARLENA: A question, Father Cheng.

FATHER CHENG: I'm a mere participant like yourself.

MARLENA: I take charge of situations, priest. And, don't forget that!

FATHER CHENG: Temper. Temper, Miss Lake. Emotions can be an impediment to a self-made villain.

MARLENA: Just stay out of my way or else.

FATHER CHENG: Or else what?

THOMAS (*stepping between the two combatants*): Let's not fight amongst ourselves.

MARLENA: Quite right, Thomas.

FATHER CHENG: But where is Miss Ortiz? Curious how the instigator of all this is the last to arrive.

COLETTE: It's quite typical of her, Father.

FATHER CHENG: You're formerly acquainted with our hostess, then?

COLETTE: Intimately. We have been enemies for many years.

THOMAS: Shouldn't we get on with this?

MARLENA: Patience, Thomas. We've all the time in the world.

HARRY: I thought we had just the opposite, Marlena? What makes you so special, huh?

MARLENA: I'm no one's pawn and we've yet to play the game.

LEIGH: I'm with Thomas. Anyone care to smash a mirror?

MARLENA: I wouldn't if I were you, Miss Duan. Magical apparati are not to be trifled with.

LEIGH: Let's give it a try. I'll just jostle one- Oh! (*The entire chamber vibrates.*)

MARLENA: I warned you, you little fool!

LEIGH (*carefully taking her hand away from the mirror*): You did, Miss Lake. I'm suitably admonished.

MARLENA: You're a gracious little thing.

CONSTANCE: I think we should all leave and take up residence in 1947. Who's to stop us?

ROSE: Bayla?

CONSTANCE: How could she?

ROSE: I wouldn't play footsey with that one, Connie. I mean it.

CONSTANCE: You do sound rather serious, dear Rose.

DAMIEN: Don't look now, but I think I hear her coming.

CONSTANCE (*in a petulant tone of voice*): But, why can't we stay here?

CORNFIELD: It would mean dying before our intended birth. We could be caught in an endless time continuum.

DAMIEN: Cornfield might be right. We really can't stay here. Hello! Here's Bayla.

BAYLA (making her entrance from stage right): Sorry for the delay. I had to procure these pistols. Each of you take one. We've no time to lose. There is one bullet in each pistol Select a mirror and take dead aim at the center.

ROSE: Suppose we miss, honey, then what?

BAYLA: Try not to find out.

HARRY: Don't you ever answer a question, lady?

BAYLA: Never. (*Handing HARRY a pistol.*) Your pistol, Harry?

HARRY (*checking out the gun*): Suppose I shoot you?

BAYLA: You may try.

DAMIEN: Get in front of a mirror, pal.

HARRY: Make me.

COLETTE: Don't antagonize him, cherie. He'll kill you. Come. Stand next to me.

HARRY: I don't back down.

DAMIEN: You should.

HARRY: Make me.

DAMIEN: Sorry to spoil your arrangements, Bayla, but I've been challenged. (*He grabs HARRY by the neck and sinks his fangs into him. HARRY collapses to the floor.*)

FATHER CHENG: My God! He is a vampire! Is Harry dead?

CORNFIELD: If he is, it could ruin everything.

DAMIEN (*straightening up*): He's dead.

FATHER CHENG: But, this is cold-blooded murder.

BAYLA: Silence! If he's dead, then he's dead.

CONSTANCE: A rather cavalier attitude, dear.

LEIGH: Look. His body is disappearing. It's gone. What happened to it.

THOMAS: Pushed forward into his own time, I'll bet.

ROSE: Can we please get on with this?

CORNFIELD: An excellent idea, Rose. (*Turning to BAYLA.*) Bayla? We each have our weapon, shall we take aim?

BAYLA: Please.

CORNFIELD (*taking aim at a mirror*): Here goes nothing.

COLETTE: Be careful, Cornfield. (*CORNFIELD fires dead center at his image setting off a bright flash. The bullet goes through the mirror and shatters it.*)

BAYLA: Step through it.

CORNFIELD: Very well. (*He steps on the shattered glass and disappears into what appears to be a glass tunnel.*)

COLETTE: Where has he gone? Tell me, please.

BAYLA: For the moment, he walks toward the future.

COLETTE: And? There is more. Tell me!

BAYLA: He knows of events to occur and can now freely alter his decisions. The power of free will will be taken to its highest and intended level. Follow him, Colette. We can now change the future.

COLETTE: To what year?

ROSE: That's what I'd like to know.

FATHER CHENG: Not back to the skyscraper, surely, for that would mean certain death.

BAYLA: We must follow him. Our combined knowledge will alter everything. Hurry! (*Each person takes aim and fires as glass shatters everywhere. Each person walks on the shards of glass and vanishes into tunnels of glass, except for DAMIEN, BAYLA, THOMAS, and MARLENA.*)

DAMIEN: As a vampire, I have difficulty with mirrors. You know this Bayla.

BAYLA: I do. Marlena? Thomas?

THOMAS: As a time traveler, lost, I have no reflection either.

DAMIEN: What about you, Marlena?

MARLENA: I don't play parlor games.

BAYLA: The maneuvers of life are games.

MARLENA: What's your game, Miss Ortiz?

DAMIEN: Come on, Bayla, tell us the why to all of this.

BAYLA: Haven't you guessed, Damien? I thought I'd sharpened your wits.

DAMIEN: My claws for the kill, yes. Out with it.

THOMAS: You intend to stay here, Miss Ortiz, in this time?

BAYLA: Yes. That was always my intention. (*She throws her pistol to the floor.*)

DAMIEN: I thought we couldn't stay here?

BAYLA: I lied. Nothing can stop the so-called holocaust.

DAMIEN: You lost me.

MARLENA: So you decided to save your own neck.

BAYLA: In a manner of speaking, Miss Lake. And, I also saved your neck, as well, and anyone else who was clever enough to see through my deception. Let's not forget that.

MARLENA: Is that a compliment, Miss Ortiz?

BAYLA: It is. You're not only cunning, but astute, as well.

THOMAS: So, we stay put in 1947?

CORNFIELD (*appearing from behind a broken mirror*): Yes. You see, Bayla, I was not taken in, either. Trust you? Never. My shot went just wide enough and I willed myself to vanish from your miserable sight. Colette? Come out, my dear.

COLETTE (*emerging from the glass tunnel*): You've still much to learn from the Master, Bayla. How very dreadful for you.

THOMAS: Is anyone else hiding? (*No response.*)

BAYLA: Life begets sacrifice and death. It was necessary. Your presence, Cornfield, does lend some drama.

CORNFIELD: Colette, let's remove ourselves from this fun house. We've much to do. We must assimilate ourselves into this new era. Good day.

COLETTE (*glancing over her shoulder*): Be seeing you, Bayla. (*She and CORNFIELD exit.*)

MARLENA: Now what?

BAYLA: I suggest you go home to your town house, Miss Lake. Don't worry, you won't meet yourself. When your entered this time frame an instantaneous merger occurred. Leave us, now.

MARLENA: Thomas, you coming? We'll have a late night repast and you and my daughter, Susan, can become re-acquainted. The dear girl will be delighted.

THOMAS: You look exhilarated, Marlena.

MARLENA: I am. Armed with foreknowledge there isn't much that I can't do. Come, dear boy, we've plans to make. Goodbye, Miss Ortiz. (*She and THOMAS exit.*)

DAMIEN: Once again, Bayla, that leaves just us. How about a full explanation?

BAYLA: I like you, Damien. And, let me say this: the future has been changed.

DAMIEN: But, if I stay here-

BAYLA: You will. You have given your skyscraper party, but the disaster never actually occurred. How could it? When it was I who staged it?

DAMIEN (*raising his arms toward the ceiling*): What a fool I was not to have guessed! But, why lure us back here to 1947?

BAYLA: Marlena and Cornfield stated it best: power and foreknowledge. The two of them were worthy opponents and will keep me quite alert and that is to the good. Things as they stood in the future were at a stalemate: a new beginning was necessary. I learned of the significance of 1947 through Marlena's inner circle of friends. I knew of Thomas and his recent sojourn into that- this year.

DAMIEN: And, Cornfield never suspected?

BAYLA (*lighting a cigarette*): He did. But, he couldn't see through the initial illusion, although he distrusted it.

DAMIEN: So the battle lines are drawn once again. But, Bayla, Marlena is damned clever.

BAYLA: She's arrogant. And, besides, Thomas is unstable and not at all inclined to evil.

DAMIEN: Where does he fit in: this lost time traveler?

BAYLA: A mystery man. I'll have to acquaint myself better with that young man. I want to know of his origin. And, Damien, now your free to settle scores with Colette.

DAMIEN: She's become rather a bore: always clinging to Cornfield. (*Touching his mouth.*) Bayla, I suddenly feel a thirst coming on. I'll meet up with you later.

BAYLA: Of course. Good hunting. (*DAMIEN exits.*) And, for now, the charade is at an end.: a thrust back into the past has been successful. I'm now in a position to correct all my past mistakes: mistakes that will never be made. How very sweet and convenient. The illusion of death is a very powerful stimulant. All of Damien's guests are quite safe back in their own time, except for that fool, Harry. He's dead. And, what of me? I gazed directly into the mirror at my own illusion of nuclear war. My aim was off. I must assume that. I don't know. Perhaps, you could tell me for I am now blind. It was necessary. The vision had to be removed for my prayer to be answered. Perhaps, in time, I will recapture that vision. Pray for me. But, I played the masquerade well. Did you guess my secret? Damien, my vampire, didn't. And, if I could deceive him and my old nemesis, Cornfield, I can deceive God, Himself.

End of play.

I, SYBIL SCHMIDLAP-SCHWAB

A Play in Three Acts

by

Gerard Denza

CHARACTERS

SYBIL SCHMIDLAP-SCHWAB, author and housewife.
SAM SCHWAB, Sybil's husband and troublemaker.
SOLOMON SCHWAB, Sybil's pampered, neurotic son.
SAMANTHA SCHWAB, Sybil's repressed daughter.
GRANDPA SCHWAB, Sam's irascible father.
GRANDMA SCHWAB, Sam's doting mother.
HAZEL SEED, Sybil's back stabbing friend.
MR. AZIZ, Sybil's would-be lover and kidnapper.

PLACE
The main action takes place in the Schwab's living room and
Queen Nefertiti's palace.

TIME
Present.

SCENES

Act One
A rainy afternoon in December in the Schwab's living room.

Act Two
The next day at Mr. Aziz's house at the edge of the airport.

Act Three
The following evening in a temple in Egypt,

Act Four
The next day back in Piscataway, New Jersey.

ACT ONE

In the SCHWAB household in Piscataway, New Jersey. It's early evening in December.

SYBIL (*gazing into a vanity mirror*): La Presidente? No Too ethnic. Mrs. President? No. Too throwback. President Sybil Schmidlap-Schwab? No. Too familiar. Madame President? Yes! Of course! As befits my station in life. A title I was born to have. A role I was meant to play. Just think of all the laws I can enact and break. It's just too delicious. A world famous author and President with all expenses paid, of course. Yes. Madame President. And, now I can truly conquer the world! To rule with an iron fist. To crush those who oppose me. I'll need allies, of course…allies who I can eventually turn on at my slightest whim. But, whom can one trust? People are so dishonest. It's just awful! (*She bursts into tears, but quickly recovers as her husband SAM and her daughter, SAMANTHA, come into the room.*)

SAM (*wearing an artist smock and beret*): Something wrong, Sybil?

SYBIL: Oh, it's you. Why no. What makes you ask? I'm in perfect health and spirits.

SAM: We heard you bursting into tears just now. We were deeply concerned. We love you so.

SYBIL: I'll bet.

SAMANTHA (*wearing an old fashioned navy suit*): Yes, mother, your health means a great deal to us.

SAM: After all, you are our meal ticket.

SYBIL: You have some gall.

SAMANTHA: I'm sure father means it as a compliment, don't you, father?

SAM: Of course.

SAMANTHA: I hear Solomon coming up the stairs. I thought you'd given him a sedative, father.

SAM: I did. We'll have to get him a stronger prescription. He's still a tad unstable.

SAMANTHA: Mother, how is your campaign going?

SAM: Yes, your grass roots party was a bit sparse.

SOLOMON: No one showed up. I was looking through the key hole. I was keeping an eye on mother. I believe she hates me. She's cut me out of her will, again. Mommy doesn't love Solly anymore!

SYBIL: How did you find out about that- I mean that's not true, Solomon. Why would mother cut you out of her will? How could you doubt my love?

SOLOMON (*pointing at SAM*): That's what father told me; didn't you, father?.

SYBIL: Did you tell him that? Answer me.

SAM: I may have let a few facts slip. But, Sybil, dear, your campaign party-

SYBIL: Never mind about my campaign party. I want to know how you found out about my will. Did you bribe my attorney, again?

SAM: I cannot tell a lie.

SAMANTHA: Mother, you seem distressed. Is it your campaign?

SAM: Yes. Has it gone awry?

SYBIL: I've nothing to worry about. Nothing.

SAM: Money worries, dear?

SYBIL: What makes you ask that? Never mind. I have some errands for you all to run. Samantha? Solomon? I need you to go to Herr Kraut's Bakery and pick up some French pastries. I crave them so! Sam? Go to the cleaners and pick up my evening attire. Now, you all have your little errands to do, so run along.

SAM: Trying to get rid of us?

SYBIL: Yes.

SAM: Well!

SAMANTHA: Mother, you do seem troubled. Is something preying on your mind? You can tell us.

SOLOMON: Yes, mother, you can tell Solly: in spite of the fact that you had me committed. I'm still fifty-five percent behind you.

SYBIL: What the hell does that mean?

SOLOMON: I was only joking, mother. We are bonded: never forget that. Never.

SYBIL (*nervously*): No. Why, of course not, Solomon. Bonded, you say? Yes.

SAMANTHA: I feel we're straying from the topic.

SAM: Yes. We are. Here come Grandpa and Gramdma Schwab. Perhaps, they can cast some light on Sybil's dilemma.

SYBIL: Just what are you up to?

SAM: Not a thing. Not a thing... I'm simply concerned for my darling wife's financial welfare.

SYBIL: That I believe!

GRANDPA: What's going on here? How's the presidential candidate?

GRANDMA: She'd better lose some weight.

GRANDPA: Hey, Syb, can you spare a couple of bucks? Grandma, here, won't give me a cent and I've got a sure winner in today's race. (*Scrutinizing SYBIL.*) Have you been putting on more weight.

GRANDMA: You're loaded, Sybil. Give your father-in-law some money.

SYBIL: Not one cent. And, I'm not gaining weight! I'm losing weight.

SAM: Oh, up a hundred pounds and down two.

SYBIL: You're walking a thin line...

SAM: "Thin" did you say?

GRANDMA: Can't you blackmail her?

GRANDPA: I'm working on it, but these things take time.

GRANDMA: Well, hurry it up. I've got some Christmas shopping to do. You are cheap, Sybil.

SAM: Ah! That brings us back to the main topic: Sybil's troubles.

SYBIL: What do you know of my troubles?

SAM: So you do admit that you have troubles? I knew it.

SAMANTHA: So did I, father. What are you keeping from us, mother.

SOLOMON: Yes, mother, we have a right to know. We demand an explanation.

GRANDMA: What are you all talking about?

SYBIL: Ignore them.

GRANDPA: If it's money troubles, I demand an answer.

SYBIL: Demand? Demand, did you say, you old leech? You can go to hell in a handbag. And, I'll kick you down there myself. What is this: a cross examination?

SAM: Oh, you could say that. Tell us, dear, are you broke?

SYBIL (*taken aback*): Why, of course not. Whatever gave you that idea? Why I'm a world famous authoress.

SAM: But, you have been making those investments.

SYBIL: And, just what do you know about those?

SAMANTHA: We know all about your stock investments, mother. "Queen of the Eternal Nile Perfume?"

GRANDMA: Sounds like a waste of money to me.

GRANDPA: Never heard of it.

SOLOMON: Is it a good investment?

SAMANTHA: Will it sell?

SAM: How much money did you throw away on it?

GRANDPA: Where the hell is this company? In somebody's basement?

GRANDMA: Does the perfume stink? You're not wearing it now, are you?

SYBIL: Enough! Yes. I am wearing it.

SOLOMON: You smell wonderful, mother.

SAM: Well, it is a bit of an unusual scent. One can't quite seem to place it.

SAMANTHA: Mother, what is troubling you?

SAM (*sniffing the air around SYBIL*): Company gone bankrupt? What is this perfume made of?

SYBIL: Oh...a few exotic herbs and spices...found only in Egypt, mind you, and along the Yucatan peninsula.

SAM: Where? In a swamp zone?

SOLOMON: How much does this parfum cost to make, mother?

SAM: Good question, Solomon.

SAMANTHA: Yes, mother, what is the cost per bottle?

GRANDPA: Out with it, Syb.

GRANDMA: Yeah, tell us.

SYBIL: Out! All of you! I must commune with my thoughts and my financial advisor. Out! I mean it. Sam? Samantha? Solomon? You all have errands to do: do them! Snap to it!

SAM: We'll get it out of her later.

SAMANTHA: Yes, father, I believe we will. We'll be back soon, mother.

SYBIL: Goodbye. Grandpa Schwab? Grandma Schwab? Why don't you accompany your grandson? He's still a bit wary about going out alone.

GRANDPA: Well-

SYBIL: Get out! *(Everyone exits. The phone rings.)*

SAM *(sneaking back in.)*: Sybil?

SYBIL: Get out!

SAM: Money troubles. I knew it.

SYBIL: You know nothing. The phone's ringing.

SAM: Who's more important: your husband or a mere phone ringing off the hook?

SYBIL *(smiling)*: Guess.

SAM: You're broke. Destitute. Tell Sam-Sam all about it.

SYBIL *(phone stops ringing)*: Now look what you've done.

SAM: They'll call back. Now, are you completely broke or do you still have a few crumbs you can toss my way?

SYBIL: I'm simply short on liquid assets.

SAM: That's not good, Sybil. Oh no...that's not good at all. We need cash. I have bills to pay and people to bribe.

SYBIL: And, I have a husband I have to kick out! I'm meeting tomorrow with my financial advisor.

SAM: And whom might that be?

SYBIL: How dare you? That's none of your damned business.

SAM: I'll make a suggestion.

SYBIL: No.

SAM (*ignoring SYBIL*): I'll be your business advisor. I'll take charge of your investments and your credit cards and any other odds and ends that I might see fit to take over. There. That's settled.

SYBIL: Are you insane?

SAM: Where are your credit cards? I'll take one with me now.

SYBIL: You'll take my shoe in your backside if you don't get out of here now. I mean it, Sam. (*The phone starts ringing, again.*) There's the phone. Out!

SAM: I'll be back. Just hand me your purse-

SYBIL: Out! (*SAM runs out the door. She answers the phone.*) Hello? Who is this? (*She tries popping a chocolate bon-bon in her mouth and almost chokes on it.*) Yes? Oh! Hazel? Hazel Seed? Why it's been so long, dear. What are you up to? How long can you talk? Oh? Oh, really? You're a Jehovah's witness, are you? How fascinating. I couldn't be happier for you. What? You'd like to come over? Well, I'm afraid that's impossible. I'm terribly busy and up to my neck in- Yes. No, I'm not trying to put you off dear, but I really am- No. Of course, I don't mind. When would you like to visit? Now? (*Horrified at the thought.*) What's the rush. You want to guide me? Guide me where? Oh…there. But, I was just stepping out and I'm sure that

you're miles away- Oh? You're right down the block. Well...
if you insist, dear. Hello? (*The phone clicks off and she slams it
down.*) That's all I need is some religious fanatic coming over.
Maybe, if I make a run for it, I can- (*The doorbell rings.*) It can't
be. (*She goes to open the door. HAZEL is standing there, smiling,
with a prayer book in her hand.*) Why, Hazel, dear, how on
earth did you get here so quickly?

HAZEL: With God's speed all things are possible.

SYBIL: Oh, that would explain it. Please come in, dear, and
make yourself...well, not too comfortable. I must be going
soon.

HAZEL: Have you no time for God and prayer? Shame on
you, Sybil.

SYBIL: Hazel, what can I do for you?

HAZEL: I want you to come with me to Kingdom Come Hall.

SYBIL: Why?

HAZEL: You know why.

SYBIL: I'm afraid I do. Hazel, I'm really not at all religious;
although, I do respect your beliefs. I'm afraid that mine are a
bit more bohemian.

HAZEL: You mean sinful. Solomon has leaned in God's
direction.

SYBIL: Has he? Well, he hasn't told his mother. Hmm. I must
speak with him about this. You know his mental health is very
fragile. He could shatter at any moment. He upsets very easily.

HAZEL: God will light his way.

SYBIL: Hazel-

HAZEL: I've come for money. You must make restitution for your sins.

SYBIL: Sins? Who the- Ah! Solomon has been talking about his mother.

HAZEL: Yes. He's spilled the proverbial beans. Your soul needs cleansing and twenty percent of all your earnings should disinfect quite nicely.

SYBIL: Go to hell, lady.

HAZEL: Shocking!

SYBIL: Isn't it? I'll light your way to the door. And, I'd like to know who put you up to this. It doesn't sound quite like Solomon. Hmm... (*The doorbell rings.*) Who in the world could this be? Hazel?

HAZEL: I'll remain.

SYBIL: Get out! (*The doorbell keeps ringing.*)

HAZEL: You're keeping visitors waiting, Sybil. Answer the door, I won't mind.

SYBIL (*walks over to open the door*): Yes?

MR. AZIZ: Sybil Schmidlap-Schwab?

SYBIL: Yes.

MR. AZIZ: Allow me to present my humble self to your greatness. I am Mr. Aziz.

SYBIL: Yes, Mr. Aziz?

MR. AZIZ: May I come in Mrs. Schwab?

SYBIL: Why, yes…why not? I am a bohemian, am I not? You can sit on the sofa next to Hazel. Mr. Aziz? Miss Hazel Seed. Hazel? Mr. Aziz.

HAZEL: Are you a Jehovah's Witness?

MR. AZIZ: What do you say? A Jehovah's Witness? You must be insane.

SYBIL (*sitting down in her favorite armchair*): Mr. Aziz, what can I do for you?

MR. AZIZ: I have come to your greatness to do something for you.

SYBIL: Oh?

MR. AZIZ: There will be a party tomorrow night in my house and you and your family are most cordially invited.

SYBIL: Well, that's very nice of you, Mr. Aziz; but, I really can't-

MR. AZIZ: I insist. I will not accept no for an answer. It will be a very special party commemorating your Presidential campign. I know you plan to run.

SYBIL: Well…it may be fun at that. Where do you live?

HAZEL: In a God fearing neighborhood, one would hope

MR. AZIZ: Is she insane?

SYBIL: Ignore her.

MR. AZIZ: My house is on the very perimeter of the airport. I feel safe when the jets fly overhead. The noise is most comforting. The vibrations are so soothing to one's nerves.

SYBIL: What time tomorrow night?

MR. AZIZ: Midnight.

SYBIL: Isn't that rather late for a party?

MR. AZIZ: But, we are bohemians, are we not? But, if midnight is too late for your family, you will surely come alone.

HAZEL: She will certainly not. It's scandalous. We'll all be there.

SYBIL: "We?"

HAZEL: I assumed I was being asked, as well.

MR. AZIZ: I've no objection to a religious fanatic being present.

HAZEL: I don't particularly care for that statement, Mr. Aziz.

MR. AZIZ: You are religious, no?

HAZEL: I believe in God and the power of righteousness and the glory and the king-

MR. AZIZ: And, you are most obviously a fanatic. I find it amusing.

HAZEL: And, what exactly is your religion? Heathen! Blasphemer!

MR. AZIZ: She is very amusing, Mrs. Schwab. It will be nice to poke fun of her tomorrow night. I look forward to it.

HAZEL: I won't come.

MR. AZIZ: My reverse psychology worked.

HAZEL: I will be getting on. And, Sybil, there is that contribution to Kingdom Come Hall; please, don't forget. That is, if you can afford it.

SYBIL: Leaving so soon, Hazel?

HAZEL: Well-

SYBIL: Goodbye, dear. I'll see you to the door. Goodbye. (*She slams the door after HAZEL.*) Good riddance!

MR. AZIZ: I'm glad she is gone, Sybil. I invite you to my house not to raise funds for your campaign, but to lure you to my home in Egypt.

SYBIL: Why, Mr. Aziz, I don't know what to say.

MR. AZIZ: You can write your next novel in the great pyramid with me at your feet. You are the reincarnation of the great Nefertiti. The resemblance is uncanny.

SYBIL: I've been told that I'm the reincarnation of Cleopatra. She was the most beautiful woman in the world, you know.

MR. AZIZ: She was a bum. Unfit to wear the crown. Her tawdry love affair with those two Roman hoods was a disgrace. The snake that bit her? I say good for the snake. No. You are Queen Nefertiti. Once in Egypt, we can overthrow the government and establish the old dynastic order. You will rule not as a mere American President, but as a most royal Queen: a goddess!

SYBIL: But, Mr. Aziz, are you quite sure? I do have my writing to keep me busy.

MR. AZIZ: I happen to know that you are quite desperate for money. Whatever you have left will be used for our first class plane fare and five star hotel accommodations. We must travel in style. And, I insist you be there tomorrow night or we will come for you.

SYBIL: Come for me? What the hell does that mean?

MR. AZIZ: I love your spirit. It means come to my place tomorrow at midnight or else...

SYBIL: Or else?

MR. AZIZ: Or else. And, now I leave you to think things over and pack a suitcase for tomorrow night's journey. Sybil?

SYBIL: What?

MR. AZIZ: Do not disappoint me for you cannot escape me. You are mine! You are my Queen. You are my goddess! You are so gloriously fat! (*He recovers himself.*) Bring your family, if you like, they'll be left behind in any event (*Exits.*)

SYBIL: What the hell was that all about? How did he know I was broke? I'd better go to that party of his and find out. Something's not right here. And, how dare he threaten me?

SOLOMON (*walking in with SAM and SAMANTHA*): Mother, who was that man who just left?

SAMANTHA: Yes, mother, he smiled at me. Did you notice that father?

SAM: I don't trust people who smile. Who was he Sybil?

SYBIL: Oh, just a fan.

SOLOMON: Not another admirer? Haven't we had enough of those?

SAM: Yes. We have. The last one ended up dead.

SAMANTHA: Mother, you seem agitated. Did he upset you. And, what is his name?

SAM: The man who you thought smiled at you?

SAMANTHA: Don't be cruel, father. He did smile at me. He did.

SOLOMON: Mother? You're not answering us.

SYBIL: He called himself, Mr. Aziz.

SAMANTHA: An Egyptian? How terribly romantic!

SAM: Reminded me of a cobra oil salesman.

SAMANTHA: How very unkind, father. After all-

SAM: Yes. He smiled at you. What did he want: this smiling Egyptian?

SYBIL: We're all invited to a party at his place tomorrow night.

SAM: The occasion?

SYBIL: Oh…frivolity.

SOLOMON: I am against frivolity. It sows the seeds of depravity.

SAMANTHA: Oh, you are a bore. What time tomorrow night, mother? I'll have to wear my new party dress.

SYBIL: Midnight.

SAM: Midnight at the oasis?

SAMANTHA: Oh, it does sound terribly romantic. We are going, aren't we? I'll wear my new orange polka-dot dress.

SAM: Can we afford not to go?

SYBIL: What made you say that? Do you know something? Are you up to your old tricks?

SAM: Amon-Ra forbid.

SYBIL: Well, if you must know, I felt threatened! Solomon, you must protect mother.

SOLOMON: Of course. Solly is always here for mother. And, you really should divorce your husband. He's no good and he's still after your money.

SYBIL: Tell me something I don't know.

SOLOMON: We should go this depraved party and expose this Mr. Aziz. Any idea what he's up to?

SYBIL: He wants to carry mother off to Egypt. He said that I resembled Queen Nefertiti.

SAM: Good God! Yes! I can see the resemblance: especially in profile!

SAMANTHA: Really mother… And, you believed him?

SYBIL: I humored him. I want to know what he's up to and how he knows about my finances.

SAM: Ah ha! Then, you are broke!

SYBIL: Temporarily cash poor. But, my next bestseller will solve that.

SAM: You hope.

SYBIL: It will. I know it. I feel it! And, I'm worried about this Mr. Aziz. He frightened me for some reason.

SAM: Well, that was quite a lie he told: about wanting to carry you.

SYBIL: I feel he's sly…cunning…fanatical. I think he plans to kidnap me!

SAM: So, why are you frightened?

SYBIL: Go to hell!

GRANDMA (*walking in with GRANDPA*): Who was the man who just left?

GRANDPA: We were in the bushes spying on you, Syb. Out with it: is he one of your creditors?

GRANDMA: We hear your flat broke. Where does that leave us?

SYBIL: Oh…out in the street, perhaps.

GRANDPA: When's your new book coming out? We need the money. (*A knock on the door.*)

SYBIL: Who is it? (*No answer.*)

GRANDPA: I'll get it. (*He goes to open the door. There's a package on the doorstep and a ticking sound can be heard.*)

SYBIL (*hears the ticking*): Don't bring it in! Slam the door shut!

GRANDPA (*picking up the brown paper package*): Sounds like an alarm clock, Syb. Here. You open it up, Syb. Might be a big surprise.

SYBIL (*screaming*): Everybody run for your life! It's a bomb! (*Everyone scrambles behind the sofa and even GRANDPA finally catches on as he hurls the package across the room. Black out. A very strange explosion is heard.*)

ACT TWO

In the foyer of MR. AZIZ'S house.

SYBIL: This must be Mr. Aziz's house.

SAM: This is a house?

SYBIL: Don't be cruel. I'll knock.

GRANDPA: I hope the house doesn't fall down. Hey, Syb, slip me a few bucks, will you?

SYBIL: I told you that your blackmailing days are over. Too bad.

GRANDMA: I thought you had something on her.

GRANDPA: I'm working on it. (*The door opens and HAZEL is standing there.*)

SYIBL: Why, Hazel, what on earth are you doing here? And, where is Mr. Aziz?

HAZEL: I took the liberty of coming in my attempt to convert Mr. Aziz. Did you know that he's a heathen?

SYBIL: Oh, really? Perhaps, Mr. Aziz considers you a heathen?

HAZEL: That's blasphemous! How dare you? I'm a God fearing woman who hates sinners. Are you sinner?

SAM: I'm thirsty. I could stand a drink.

HAZEL: Liquor? Did you say liquor? The devil speaks through liquor. He speaks smut!

GRANDMA: Just get the hell out of our way. I'm a God fearing woman, too: and pious. I'm very pious. Now, where's the booze? (*The SCHWAB family enters the main room of Mr. Aziz's house. There is a cardboard pyramid in the center of the room.*)

SOLOMON: I'm not sure that I like this place. I think Miss Seed is right. It's a den for sinners.

SAMANTHA: I think it's very romantic. But, where is Mr. Aziz?

SOLOMON: Yes. It's not polite to keep guests waiting.

SAM: No. It's not.

SYBIL: I'm still wondering who sent that trick package.

SAM: I've no idea.

SYBIL: I'll bet. Was it you?

SAM: Heaven forbid. Do you think me capable of such a dastardly thing?

SYBIL: Yes.

SAM: Well!

SYBIL: And, another thing: how is it that everyone knows I'm broke.

SAM: I didn't tell anyone. Honest.

SYBIL: Liar. You probably told everyone.

SAM: What about your financial advisor?

SYBIL: What about her?

SAM: It is a she. I knew it.

SYBIL: What of it?

SAM: Does "she" have a name.

SYBIL: Why, yes, of course.

SAM: What is her name? You can tell us.

SAMANTHA: Yes, mother, we are your family.

SOLOMON: If you are truly broke, mother, that means that I stand to inherit nothing

SAM: Except her outstanding debts.

SOLOMON: As I was saying before father interrupted: if you are truly broke, mother, how sound can her advice be? What is it based on?

GRANDPA: Yeah, Syb, out with her name.

GRANDMA: Must be some crackpot.

SYBIL: I will not be badgered by my own family.

SAM: It's too late for that. So, what's her name.

SYBIL: I'm not telling!

SAM: Oh, come on.

SYBIL: No. And, you can't make me!

GRANDPA: Out with it, Syb.

SOLOMON: Mother, simply say her name.

SAMANTHA: What is the fuss about?

SYBIL: Her name is Madame-

HAZEL: Madame? Not that kind of Madame of ill repute? How dreadful.

SYBIL: You know, lady, for someone so religious, you've got a filthy mind. Madame Piles is a star gazer and-

SAM: Ah ha! Madame Piles.

SYBIL: You got that out of me.

SAM: I did, didn't I?

SAMANTHA (*trying not to laugh*): Really, mother…Madame Piles? Even for you that's eccentric.

SOLOMON: I must agree with Samantha. Mother…an astrologer for a financial advisor?

GRANDPA: No wonder she's flat broke.

SYBIL: But, the stars are beginning to shift in my favor.

GRANDMA: Says who? Madame Piles? Oh, this is too much! Wait'll I tell the girls at the beauty parlor.

SAM: It just might make headlines.

HAZEL: Really, Sybil, to associate with a heathen? God is punishing you.

MR. AZIZ (*making his appearance*): Sybil, dear, forgive me for keeping you waiting, but I was attending to our travel arrangements. Come. I must speak to you in private. Everyone, please help yourselves to drinks. My liquor is your liquor.

SYBIL: Mr. Aziz, why are we all here?

MR. AZIZ: To prepare for our flight to Egypt. The plane leaves within the hour.

SYBIL: Within the hour? Isn't that cutting it rather short, assuming that I agree to come?

MR. AZIZ: Fate commands you to come. The gods of Egypt command you to come. I command you to come!

GRANDMA (*listening in*): Sounds dirty to me.

SAM: What sounds dirty?

SYBIL: Would you please leave us alone?

GRANDPA: Better not. I think Syb is up to no good.

SAMANTHA: What are you up to, mother? You really should communicate more with your family.

SAM: Yes. It would save me- us a lot of trouble.

SYBIL: I'm sure.

MR. AZIZ: We plan on running away to Egypt. There. It has been said. It will be done. Are you packed?

SYBIL: Well, no, I-

MR. AZIZ: No problem. You will romp through the pyramid naked.

HAZEL: Horrors!

SAM: I'll say!

SOLOMON: This is smut! I feel a nervous breakdown coming on.

SAMANTHA: Oh, get a grip, Solomon. She hasn't left yet. Have you, mother?

SYBIL: I really can't, Mr. Aziz.

HAZEL: Sybil, the stars cast a dim outlook on you traveling anywhere. I strongly advise against this lascivious trip. On the other hand, I could take your place-

SYBIL: Mr. Aziz, I think I just might go on that pyramid trip. I'll absorb some of the local color for my next book: "A Palm Tree Grows in Egypt." Oh, I like it!

MR. AZIZ: Music to my ears. And, after we cash your forthcoming advance, money will be of no object.

SAM: He's on to her advance.

SAMANTHA: Father, what will we do? We can't let her get on that plane. You know how easily she's influenced: especially by mysterious men who are obviously up to no good.

SAM: We'll have to gang up on her and trick her into coming home.

SAMANTHA: But, how? Look how she's starting to melt under his charm. It's quite disgusting, really.

SAM: We may have an ally.

SAMANTHA: Who?

SAM: Hazel.

SAMANTHA: Miss Seed? But, she's mother's friend.

SAM: Oh, I've met Miss Seed on business.

SAMANTHA: On business? What kind of business, father? You don't mean to say that you and Miss Seed have-

SAM: Perish the thought. I'm loyal to Sybil and her money. No. Miss Seed and I have been business associates.

SAMANTHA: You lost me.

SAM (*whispering*): Lend me your ear.

SOLOMON: Mother, you cannot go on any plane with this man. Take me along, instead.

MR. AZIZ: Is this boy mad? Go home, little one.

SOLOMON: I an not your little one. I am my mother's son. We're bonded.

MR. AZIZ: Ah! I know of this kind of bonding. It's-

SAM: Unnatural is the word you're looking for.

SYBIL: Just shut your mouth, you insect. Solly is mommy's little man. There is nothing unnatural about our relationship. He's mommy's little boy.

GRANDPA: Not unnatural, huh?

GRANDMA: You belong here with your family.

SAM: As dysfunctional as we are.

SAMANTHA: Exactly. Well put, father.

SAM: Why thank you.

HAZEL (*leading SOLOMON away from the group*): Young man, we must stop this at once. Your mother, quite frankly, is our meal ticket.

SOLOMON: A crude way of putting it. However, Miss Seed, you are quite right. What do you suggest?

HAZEL: Warn her about her money.

SOLOMON: But, that will only put her back up.

HAZEL: Not if it's done right and coming from someone she trusts.

SOLOMON: When it comes to money, mother trusts no one.

HAZEL: What about this financial advisor who's advised her into destitution?

SOLOMON: But, why would she trust Madame Piles?

HAZEL (*whispering*): Come closer, dear.

GRANDMA: Look, Sebastian, over there. Solomon and that Hazel Seed -- what a name! -- are in cahoots about something.

GRANDPA: Be grateful he's with a woman.

GRANDMA: Whatever are your talking about?

GRANDPA: Don't ask.

GRANDMA: I think I understand. Never mind. We've more important things to attend to and quickly! Sybil mustn't get on that plane! If she gets on that plane, her book advance goes with her and that Aziz character. I wouldn't trust him from here to the door.

GRANDPA: If she's made up her mind to go, then what the hell can we do about it? You know how Syb is. Her mind made up is like Roman concrete.

GRANDMA: Look. Over there. Sam and Samantha are talking. I'll bet Sam's up to something. If I know my son, he has an ace in the hole somewhere. He'll stop his would-be philandering wife.

GRANDPA: Especially if there's money in it. Let's go over and have a talk with our darling boy.

SYBIL: Oh, Hazel, dear? I'd like a word with you if I may?

MR. AZIZ: Make it quick, Sybil, we have a plane to catch.

SYBIL: Hazel?

HAZEL: What is it, Sybil? I hope you're not too angry at me for volunteering to take your place on this illicit love tryst.

SYBIL: Well, quite frankly, I was a little taken aback on your eagerness. But, never mind that: I've something else to ask you.

HAZEL (*feeling uneasy*): Can't it wait?

SYBIL: No.

HAZEL: But, Sybil, Mr. Aziz is getting very impatient.

SYBIL: Let him wait. You mentioned something about the stars being unfavorable before.

HAZEL: A vagrant comment, dear.

SYBIL: Since when is a Jehovah's Witness interested in astrology? And, just how did you know I was broke? Out with it!

HAZEL: Here comes Sam.

SYBIL: I should have guessed. I knew you'd be in on this.

SAM: In on what?

SYBIL: How did you know about Madame Piles?

SAM: I'm innocent.

SYBIL: That'll be the day. (*Turning to HAZEL.*) Are you Madame Piles?

SAM: Well…

HAZEL: We did it for your own good.

SYBIL: Just tell me how much of my money you two have embezzled.

HAZEL: That's a very dirty word.

SYBIL: We live in a very dirty world. How much?

SAM: We lost it all. It was Hazel's fault. (*Conspiratorially to SYBIL.*) She gambles, you know.

HAZEL: You little liar. I made a few bad investments. They were about to discover an underground ocean in Nevada and build resorts all around it. If it had only been true!

SYBIL: I'm surrounded by thieves! How could I have trusted someone by the name of Madame Piles? It sounded fake so I thought it had to be legit.

MR. AZIZ: Place yourself -- and your money, of course -- in my hands and we will rule Egypt. Come, let's be off.

SYBIL: No. I'm afraid not. I've things to attend to here: like putting my no good husband and Miss Seed, here, in the slammer!

SAMANTHA: Mother, I'm sure father has not left any paper trail; have you, father?

SAM: No. As a matter of fact, I haven't.

SYBIL: Mr. Aziz, let's fly to Egypt!

GRANDPA: Did I just hear something outside?

GRANDMA: Probably one of those jets flying overhead.

SOLOMON: No. I heard it, too, Grandma Schwab. (*Black out. Everyone gasps and screams as a hail of a hundred bullets descends upon them.*)

ACT THREE

In the palace of Queen Nefertiti in Egypt.

SAM: It's amazing how no one was hurt with all that gun fire.

SAMANTHA: It is rather strange, father. It does make one wonder.

SAM: If they were hired assassins, I'd fire them.

SAMANTHA: They were quite incompetent.

SYBIL: You wanted them to kill us?

SAMANTHA: Of course not, mother; but as hired assassins, they did fall short of the mark. I just made a very clever joke, father, didn't I?

SAM: Yes. You did.

HAZEL: But, who could have hired those dreadful men?

SOLOMON: We never actually saw anyone. It could have been anyone.

SAM: Or, perhaps, no one...

SAMANTHA: Father, you know something, don't you. You are very clever.

SYBIL: Conniving is more like it. It was strange how no one was hit.

SAM: Wasn't it?

SYBIL: What did you have to do with that shooting? Out with it!

GRANDPA: Hey, Syb, shouldn't we be trying to get ourselves out of this palace? We've been kidnapped.

SYBIL: No one was holding a gun to your head.

SOLOMON: Yes, Grandpa Schwab, you weren't pushed into the plane as mother was. Did you hurt yourself, mother? I almost cried for you.

SYBIL: Of course not, dear. Mother is fine. Where is your grandmother?

GRANDMA: Over here, gazing at your former splendor.

SYBIL (*walking over to her*): Why it's Queen Nefertiti carved in stone. There is a likeness.

SAM: Yes. But, you'd need three statues lined up to see it.

SYBIL: Go-to-hell.

GRANDPA: Is that anyway for a Queen to talk? Hey, Syb, can you spare a couple of bucks.

SAM: I'm afraid the Queen is flat broke.

HAZEL: Where is Mr. Aziz?

SOLOMON: I saw him disappear around that column.

SYBIL: Why don't we break up into groups and have a look around? We may find a way out.

SAM: Or even some priceless jewels.

SAMANTHA: Yes, father, the palace must be simply loaded with priceless antiques.

SAM: Let's go!

SAMANTHA: I'm with you.

SOLOMON: I think I'll tag along to keep an eye on father.

SYBIL: Good idea, Solomon. Don't take your eyes off him and report back to me.

SOLOMON: Solly won't fail you.

SYBIL: Such a dear boy. Be careful! (*SAM, SAMANTHA, and SOLOMON exit, but come back and hide behind a column on stage right.*)

GRANDPA: Let's you and me hightail it to that end of the palace. We might find a mummy or something.

GRAMDMA: Oh, but there always so dusty and dirty. And, one of them might come to life.

GRANDPA: You've seen too many Hollywood movies. Come on.

GRANDMA: If we run into one, I'm getting the hell out of here. Where's the light switch. (*She and GRANDPA exit, but come back and hide behind a column upstage.*)

SYBIL: Well, Madame Piles, that leaves you and me.

HAZEL: I'm a little ashamed of my deception. Can you forgive me, Sybil?

SYBIL: Hmm. If I didn't need your help, I wouldn't let you in on my little secret.

HAZEL: Oh, you can tell me anything, Sybil. You know how trustworthy and religious I am.

SYBIL: Do I?

HAZEL: You know how devoutly self righteous I can be. I'd sooner die than be anything but truthful.

SYBIL: Oh, really?

HAZEL: You sound very cynical and that's not nice.

SYBIL: Oh, brother! Why don't you follow Sam and the others? I think they may be on to something.

HAZEL: And, what about you? I can't leave you here by yourself.

SYBIL: I'll wait for Mr. Aziz's return. Now, go on. Hurry along before you lose them. Hurry! (*Reluctantly, HAZEL exits and hides behind the same column as SAM, SAMANTHA, and SOLOMON.*) Finally! Mr. Aziz, you may come out now.

MR. AZIZ (*coming out of hiding*): I thought they'd never leave.

SYBIL: It took some doing, but I knew I could get rid of them. And, now, Mr. Aziz?

MR. AZIZ: Yes, my dear?

SYBIL: You were very naughty pushing me into that airplane. I almost tripped and hurt myself.

MR. AZIZ: Your Highness, forgive me!

SYBIL: In due time. Don't you have something for me? Something that you promised your Queen during our very long flight here. Come now, Mr. Aziz, must I insist?

MR. AZIZ: A thousand pardons.

SYBIL: I want the Queen's jewels. You can keep your thousand pardons. And, what a flight it was! My leach of a family somehow managed to get on board and make the entire trip miserable! I suspect my husband was behind it.

MR. AZIZ: You must divorce him.

SYBIL: The jewels, please? I'm waiting. Get 'em!

MR. AZIZ (*runs around a column and brings out a chest*): Here. As promised.

SYBIL: Please, open it. It looks so terribly dirty. Oh! A spider!

MR. AZIZ (*ignoring SYBIL'S outburst*): Let your eyes behold your treasure.

SYBIL: They are stunning, rather. Oh, and this necklace! I think Joan Collins wore something like it in one of her movies.

MR. AZIZ: It is all yours, my dear. Look…a ruby as big as a vulture's egg.

SYBIL: My…what a poetic analogy.

GRANDPA (*appearing from around a far column with GRANDMA*): It looks like you laid it, Sybil.

GRANDMA (*spotting the spider on the floor*): I got ya'! I got ya'! I got ya'! (*Triumphantly, she steps on it.*)

MR. AZIZ: This is sacrilege. Blasphemer.

GRAMDMA: I am a religious woman and so very, very pious.

GRANDPA: Forget about the pious bit, let's see those jewels. Looks like Syb, here, hit the jackpot.

HAZEL (*comes out of hiding with SAM, SAMANTHA, and SOLOMON*): Sybil, you lied to me. You deliberately tried to get rid of me so you could have a clandestine meeting with Mr. Aziz. Shame on you.

SYBIL: Screw you, lady. And, don't even think of putting your grubby little hands on my jewels.

SAM (*peeking around a column*): Jewels, did one say?

SAMANTHA: Oh, mother, do show us. That's very selfish of you to keep them all to yourself. I could do with a new bracelet.

SOLOMON: Filthy lucre from a heathen's treasure trove.

MR. AZIZ: Is the boy insane? You really should have him committed.

SAM: When we get back to Jersey. In the meantime... Samantha, start stuffing your pockets! We're filthy rich!

HAZEL: I agree with Solomon.

SAM: Good. Then, we'll take your share off your hands.

GRANDMA: That's telling him, son. You make a mother proud.

SAM: Thank you, mommy.

GRANDMA (*stuffing her pocketbook with jewels*): Such a good boy. When we get back home, you can divorce that cow and we can buy our own little mother and son house and live happily ever after.

GRANDPA: Where do I fit in?

SAM: Oh, you can visit once in a long while. And, don't forget to bring those French pastries from Herr Kraut's with you. You know I have a weakness for them.

MR. AZIZ: Sybil, we must stop them. They cannot be allowed to leave here alive.

SYBIL: What do you suggest?

MR. AZIZ: Death by a thousand cuts.

SYBIL: Why don't you be a lamb and run along and get the sword? I'll keep these Philistines busy.

MR. AZIZ: Wonderful idea. I won't be a moment. I'm a little out of practice, but I'm sure I can manage to murder them all.

SYBIL: Of course. Now, off you go! Hurry! (*MR. AZIZ exits.*)

SAM: Where's lover boy gone off to?

SYBIL: Never mind that, we've got to get the hell out of here. He plans to kill you and keep me here forever! Can you imagine such a thing: imprisoned like some slave girl?

SAM: No!

SYBIL: I should leave you here.

SOLOMON: Mother, how do we get out? (*A red, blinking EXIT sign can be seen on stage left.*)

HAZEL: I don't remember how we got in. All those passageways and blind alleys.

SAMANTHA: It was very confusing, but I think we're not too far from the entrance. Mr. Aziz was leading us around in circles.

HAZEL: What a smart girl you are.

SYBIL: But, her mother is smarter. I marked the way with my new lip balm lipstick. The color is luscious lime: it's quite flattering.

SAMANTHA: I think I hear Mr. Aziz coming back. What will we do?

GRANDPA: That's easy. It's six against one. You'll gang up on him.

SOLOMON: And, what about you Grandpa Schwab? Conveniently leaving yourself out of the fray?

HAZEL: You should be ashamed of yourself Mr. Schwab. Shame on you.

GRANDPA: You're taking my place, lady Lay one on him.

HAZEL: I think you're horrid!

GRANDPA: What of it?

HAZEL: Oh!

SAM: Here he comes. Look. Here's a scepter. Sybil, bang him on the head with it. He won't expect it coming from you.

SYBIL: My hero!

SAMANTHA: Too late. Mr. Aziz!

MR. AZIZ: Plotting against me. Yes. I know. I am all to familiar with court intrigue. Sybil, leave us. I do not want your eyes to feast on so much bloodshed. Your delicate nerves could not stand such a sight.

SAM: Neither can mine. I'll leave with you.

MR. AZIZ: Coward. A divorce will not be necessary. You will be the first, Mr. Schwab.

GRANDMA: You're not laying a hand on my son! (*She hits MR. AZIZ on the head with her pocket book and knocks him out.*)

SYIBL: Everyone, run for your life!

SAMANTHA: But, no one really knows the way out.

SYBIL (*going over to the now prostrate MR. AZIZ*): Mr. Aziz? This is your Queen speaking. How the hell do we get out of this dump?

MR. AZIZ: And, you will stay with me forever and sign over your book advance to me? Swear this for I am quite desperate for money.

SYBIL: Why you dirty, little- Why, of course, I will. Promise.

MR. AZIZ: Touch the base of the column over there where there is a stain of cat urine.

SYBIL: You can't be serious.

MR. AZIZ: I am. Touch it. The cat was a holy cat.

SYBIL: Was he indeed?

MR. AZIZ: By all that is holy, touch it.

SAM: Go ahead, Sybil, touch it.

SYBIL: I'll settle with you later. (*She goes over to the column and touches the spot. Nothing happens.*)

MR. AZIZ (*laughing hysterically*): Fooled you! Fooled you!

SYBIL: How about I step on you, pal? Rotten, little bastard!

SAMANTHA: No, mother! We still need Mr. Aziz's help.

SAM: Sybil, I have an idea.

SYBIL: And, I should trust you?

SOLOMON: He's as bad as Mr. Aziz, mother. I say divorce him on grounds of mental cruelty and gross incompatibility. I'll be your witness.

GRANDMA: Mamma's boy!

SAM: Listen, before Mr. Aziz becomes too coherent, play along with his own gag.

SYBIL: What do you mean? And, this better not be one of your tricks.

SAM: Pretend to be Queen Nefertiti.

SYBIL: That's not a bad idea. I'll do it. Now, just sit back and watch. (*Going over to MR. AZIZ who is struggling to his feet.*) Yes! I feel it! I! I am Queen Nefertiti! I command you, peasant! Tell me the way out or I will place my frightful curse upon you: the curse of endless diarrhea!

MR. AZIZ: Huh?

SYBIL: Listen, lest I smite thee within an inch of your miserable life. Open the damned door!

MR. AZIZ: Here. (*He pulls a lever and the door swings open.*) Get out. But, I wouldn't take those jewels if I were you, "Queen Nefertiti." Bitch!

SYBIL: Ha! Peasant! (*She sees the open doorway.*) Look! There! The door was right there! It's opening! I knew it all the time. (*Sunlight spills into the temple as the SCHWABS and HAZEL run for the entrance.*) Follow me! I shall lead the way to safety: I, Sybil Schmidlap- Schwab!

ACT FOUR

Back home in the Schwab household. It's just past midnight.

SAM: Home at last!

SYBIL: I'm quite ravenous. Samantha, would you go into the kitchen and fix mother a hero sandwich: anything will do, but go easy on the salad dressing. I'm dieting.

GRANDMA: It's about time.

SOLOMON: My mother's figure is perfection.

SAM: Yes. A perfect sphere.

HAZEL: Well, I really should be off. It is late and I've a sermon to give tomorrow on the perils of temptation.

SYBIL: Do that, Madame Piles.

SAM: And, don't forget my horoscope chart. You promised.

HAZEL: I'll send my bill along with it.

SAM: Of course. Make it out to Sybil.

HAZEL: Well, adios! (*Exits.*)

GRANDMA: Good riddance to the bitch.

GRANDPA: Don't be cruel to that phony.

SAM: Grandpa Schwab is right. She may be a fraud, but she's fun.

SYBIL: True. Hazel does have her good points.

SAM: Now, Sybil, what did you manage to smuggle into the country?

SYIBL: Why, I don't know what you mean, Sam. Smuggle, you say? Why, it was highly insulting that they took all our souvenirs away from us at the airport and, then, have the gall to insist that we never enter the country again.

SAM: Now, Sybil, let's have it. Show Sam what's in your tapestry bag.

GRANDPA: Out with it, Syb. I saw the way that airport cop was looking at you.

GRANDMA: Don't be greedy, daughter-in-law.

SAMANTHA (*entering with a tray of food*): Yes, mother, you did smuggle something in.

SYBIL: I did not!

SOLOMON: You all leave my mother alone. If she tells anyone, it will be her Solly.

SAMANTHA: It was in your girdle and, then, you had to switch it to your tapestry bag when we landed.

SAM (*laughing*): Your lopsided walk was quite a sight! It just might have given you away when you kept taking a hitch on your girdle..

SYBIL: Such an observant family... (*Trying to change the subject.*) Why can't you find yourself a man, Samantha?

SAMANTHA: Mr. Aziz did smile at me.

SYBIL: Good God!

GRANDPA: Come on, Syb.

SAM: Yes. Whatever it is, it will hold us all over until your book advance arrives.

SYBIL: Oh, how I wish I still carried my hammer around with me.

SOLOMON (*snuggling up to SYBIL*): Mother, just show us and put an end to this very tasteless inquisition.

SYBIL: Very well. (*HAZEL bursts in.*)

GRANDPA: Well, look who's back. What's up, Seed?

GRANDMA: Lucky us.

HAZEL: I forgot my purse.

SAMANTHA: How convenient, Miss Seed.

HAZEL: Am I intruding? I was only gone for a few minutes.

SAM: Yes. We know. Sybil, here, was about to make an unveiling.

HAZEL: Sounds positively lurid. What is it, Sybil?

SYBIL: Enough! Here. (*She takes out a rather gaudy necklace.*)

SAM: Wasn't that the necklace Joan Collins wore in that Egyptian movie? Oh, you know, the one where they bury her alive?

SYBIL (*handing the necklace to SAM*): Here. You take it.

SAM: Not me! You put it on.

SAMANTHA: That's what frightened the airport security man. I do believe he was ready to pass out.

GRANDPA: He did seem kind of pale, Syb.

GRANDMA: It's a death necklace.

GRANDPA: Syb, try it on.

SAM: Here, I'll help you. Hold still... Stop struggling.... There! The clasp is good and tight.

GRANDMA: Nice going, son.

SAM: Thank you.

HAZEL: Well, Sybil how does it feel to be wearing a Queen's necklace? (*SYBIL mumbles something which no one can understand.*)

SAM: If it's good enough for Joan Collins then it's certainly good enough for you to be buried alive in. (*SYBIL again mumbles something.*)

GRANDPA: Speak up, Syb. We can't understand a word you're saying.

SAMANTHA: Yes, mother, you pride yourself on being such a grammarian; although, at times, your syntax is rather garbled.

SOLOMON: Mother, are you trying to tell us something? (*Again, SYBIL mumbles something while pointing to the necklace which she is desperately trying to take off.*)

SAM: If you don't speak up, Sybil, we'll have to start calling you Queen Mumbles.

SAMANTHA: Father, how very clever.

HAZEL: I do believe something is terribly wrong with her. Sybil, speak up, you're beginning to annoy me.

GRANDMA: We'll have to have that necklace appraised.

GRANDPA: I know a man in the Diamond District. Very discreet. Very honest.

SAM: How much can he get on the black market for it.

GRANDPA: I'll ask. (*SYBIL is now standing in the middle of the room struggling with the clasp. She's pointing at SAM to help her.*)

SAMANTHA: Father, I do believe mother is in need of your assistance.

GRANDMA: And high time, too.

SAM: I'm on my way. You want me to take the necklace off? (*SYBIL mumbles something quite loud.*)

SAM: Is the necklace choking you, dear?

HAZEL: I'll try it on.

SOLOMON: It's too loose to be choking mother. Whatever is wrong? Mother? Mother? Try to enunciate your syllables. It will help your diction tremendously. (*SYBIL rantings come out as mumbles. She's now frantically waving her arms about.*)

SAMANTHA: Perhaps, if I prepared a sedative for mother? It might do a world of good. Mother? Just nod if you agree. (*SYBIL glares angrily at her...and mumbles something.*)

HAZEL: I have it! It's Sybil's desperate desire to be the center of attention. (*SYBIL lunges at HAZEL who narrowly escapes. SAM is still trying to unhook the necklace.*)

SAM: Ah ha! I've figured it out through the process of reasonable deduction. Mind you, one has to think like Sherlock Holmes.

SAMANTHA (*eating SYBIL'S hero sandwich*): Oh, do tell us father. I'll save you some of mother's sandwich. I put lots of anchovies in it.

SAM: It's the necklace! It's cursed!

SOLOMON: I believe that father may actually be right.

SAMANTHA: Of course he's right. Well done, father.

SAM: The clasp is caught on her dress. Hold still, dear, we'll have this off in no time and Grandpa will have it on the black market before you can mumble one-more-word! Here! We'll try it from this angle. (*He reverses the necklace and SYBIL starts speaking backwards.*) I don't think that helped. Just one more second… Got it! (*SYBIL collapses on to a chair as he holds up the necklace in a triumphant gesture.*)

HAZEL: Oh, let me have it, Sam.

SAM: I wouldn't put it on if I were you.

HAZEL: Heavens, no. This certainly didn't happen to Joan Collins. The idea!

SOLOMON: Mother are you all right. Are you quite recovered? And will you speak or will you mumble?

SAM: Yes. To mumble or not to mumble: that is the question.

SAMANTHA: Oh, father, how very Shakespearean.

SYBIL (*clearing her throat*): Oh, I can speak all right. That thing is dangerous! No wonder airport security let it through.

SAMANTHA: Perhaps, they were trying to punish you, mother, for attempting to steal it. I hear that the Egyptian authorities are very strict when it comes to artifacts.

SYBIL: Well, they can have this one back. (*And, with a vicious smile.*) Hazel, put it on.

SAM: We'll just leave this in Grandpa's greedy care.

GRANDPA (*snatching it from HAZEL*): Give it here, Seed. I'll take charge of it.

GRANDMA: And, get all you can for it.

SAMANTHA: Do be clever, Grandpa Schwab.

SAM: We need the money. And, by the way, Syb, how much is this book advance amounting to?

SYBIL: Oh...a goodly amount. (*Turning to GRANDPA.*) Get all you can for that necklace. I'm desperate, rather.

SAM: That bad, huh?

SYBIL: Well...not as much as one could hope for.

HAZEL (*snatching up her handbag*): It's obvious Sybil's still broke. I'm off! (*Exits.*)

SYBIL: What happened to my sandwich? Samantha, have you and my husband devoured it?

SAMANTHA: Well, you were rather indisposed, mother.

SAM: It was quite delicious, in fact. I thought of saving you a morsel.

SYBIL: Quickly, make me another! I may starve to death.

SAMANTHA: Very well, mother. (*Exits.*)

SAM: Hurry! Before she starves to death!

GRANDPA: I'm headed for bed. Goodnight. And, I'll just wear this beauty to sleep. What do I give a crap if I mumble. (*He puts on the necklace and mumbles "goodnight."*)

GRANDMA: I think I'll join mumbles. Goodnight. (*Exits.*)

SYBIL: If we're lucky, he'll never take it off.

SAM: So true.

SOLOMON: Goodnight. I'm quite exhausted. I must write about our trip to the land of Egypt. Perhaps, I can get it published and be an authoress like mother.

SYBIL: Maybe... Goodnight, dear.

SAM: Goodnight. (*SOLOMON exits to the basement.*)

SYBIL: I wonder how much your father can get for the necklace? He won't run off with the money will he?

SAM: I'll send Grandma along with him.

SYBIL: Good idea. Where is Samantha with my food?

SAM: Is there a book advance coming?

SYBIL: A very tiny one, I'm afraid. They're not too crazy about my new book: Suicidal Sweets. It is rather depressing.

SAM: Still running for President?

SYBIL: Oh, that! It was just a publicity campaign for my new book.

SAM: Thought so.

SYBIL: Well, I shall have my midnight snack and retire for the evening. I've plans to make.

SAM: Oh? What plans?

SYBIL: Well, now that we know where the buried treasure of Nefertiti is, what's to stop us from going back?

SAM: Oh…the Egyptian police who'll probably give us ten life sentences each!

SYBIL: You may be right. Yes. One must work for one's bread.

SAM: Mustn't one.

SYBIL: And, how would you know?

SAM: It's not easy being a sponge.

SYBIL (*patting SAM affectionately on the shoulder*): Your words, not mine.

SAM: I think I'll also retire for the night. I'll see what's keeping Samantha.

SYBIL: Do. (*SAM exits.*) Well, all alone and broke. But, what can one get for a cursed necklace? I just may base my next book on it. Yes! A splendid idea! Now, what will I call it? Yes! "Mumbled Magic." Goodnight, all!

End of play.

DEATHDREAMER CAFÉ

A One Act Play

by

Gerard Denza

THE PATRONS

DANIELLE, a young woman with a desperate wish.
HECTOR, an ex-con and a ladies man.
EMILE, a fair-minded cop.
GERARD, a young and disillusioned male prostitute.
MARCEL, Gerard's possessive pimp.
TIGER, a mean, old bartender and ex-con.
GUY, an American who's down on his luck.

PLACE
A café in a suburb of Paris.

TIME
The present.

ACT ONE

In a café just on the outskirts of Paris. It is early morning and the coolness of the night is beginning to wear off. The café is small with room for only six tables with the bar off to stage left. The bartender, TIGER, is serving drinks and listening to the various conversations going on. Several men are at the bar, but one man is standing alone by the doorway. Throughout the play, a blue spotlight is focused on the various protagonists at the moment of conversation while the rest of the café and its patrons are in a muted, green/grey light.

(Blue spotlight on DANIELLE and HECTOR.)

DANIELLE: Gerard will protect his cousin.

HECTOR: You think so? He's a prostitute. You must know this.

DANIELLE: Don't underestimate him.

HECTOR: I don't. That would be a mistake: and I don't make mistakes. *(Laughing.)* Just one: getting caught with the blade in my hand. Now, let me touch you.

DANIELLE: No.

HECTOR: It won't hurt. I'll grease it up for you.

DANIELLE: No. Mother wouldn't approve.

HECTOR: Whose mother, cherie?

DANIELLE: Mine. You don't have any.

HECTOR: Watch what you say to me. My mother lives and she is a good woman.

DANIELLE: Then, I apologize.

HECTOR: Touch it.

DANIELLE: How about a nice and hard slap in the face?

HECTOR: Give me your hand.

DANIELLE: I should have brought my girlfriend with me. You'd have no trouble with her.

HECTOR: Bring her here, then. (*Looking over his shoulder.*) Who are you staring at? The boy? You like him.

DANIELLE (*staring past HECTOR*): Gerard? What is he up to over there?

HECTOR: Emile, the cop, is buying him a drink. He wants your cousin, Danielle. I want you. And, you cousin had better watch it. Emile might be setting him up.

DANIELLE: I don't like this Emile.

HECTOR: What about me, cherie?

DANIELLE: Do you see that man over there; the stocky one by the door?

HECTOR (*not bothering to look*): What about him.

DANIELLE: That's Marcel. He's led Gerard into the street life. I hate him for that.

HECTOR: You didn't answer my question. You like Hector? Better say "yes."

DANIELLE: Such male pride.

HECTOR: So?

DANIELLE: You'll do.

HECTOR: Let's go in the backroom. I won't hurt you.

DANIELLE: Later…maybe. And, you might prefer Justine. I'm sure of it.

HECTOR: I will decide that.

DANIELLE: I may want you to do me a favor, Hector.

HECTOR: Anything.

DANIELLE: I need to go to the W.C. Look out for Gerard. You might be right about Emile.

HECTOR: Emile's looking out for your cousin.

DANIELLE: Will you do it? It's not much of a favor. I won't be five minutes.

HECTOR: Then you owe me a favor.

DANIELLE: I'll be right back.

HECTOR: I'll keep an eye on the boy.

(*Blue spotlight on EMILE and GERARD.*)

EMILE: So, tell me about yourself.

GERARD: You know what I am.

EMILE: A young and confused boy.

GERARD: What more do you want to know?

EMILE: Are you married?

GERARD: You're joking, for sure? My kind doesn't get married.

EMILE: Don't say that, Gerard.

GERARD: I didn't tell you my name. Where did you hear it? And, thanks for the drink. I have no money.

EMILE: You know that I am a cop.

GERARD: Yes. What of it?

EMILE: I want to be up front with you.

GERARD: Doesn't matter. Not much does. What will this drink buy me?

EMILE: A good way of phrasing it.

GERARD: You want me pretty bad. I can see it in your eyes.

EMILE: Emile.

GERARD: Emile. You'd like me to kiss you. In the courtyard, you can even caress me. I kiss you deep and hard. (*Glancing over his shoulder.*) Who is that man by the door? No. Not Marcel. Him, I know quite well. The tall one who is smoking and deep in thought. I haven't seen him here before.

EMILE: I don't know. Why don't you ask him?

GERARD: I'm with you.

EMILE: But, you notice other men.

GERARD: Part of my trade. Always looking for the next hit.

EMILE: How, Gerard? How did this happen to you? You're not a thug. I can see this. Let me help you.

GERARD: I have Marcel to help me. He does pretty good.

MARCEL (*walking over to them and standing next to GERARD*): My name was mentioned? I like that.

EMILE: I know you, Marcel.

MARCEL: I know that you do. You've put bracelets on me a couple of times. Not very flattering.

EMILE: We've quite a dossier on you.

MARCEL: Now that is flattering. I must read it sometime.

GERARD: Danielle. (*She walks over to them having just come out of the W.C.*) Maybe, Emile, here, will buy you a drink. Ask him.

DANIELLE: I don't want any. I want to talk to you.

GERARD: Not now. I'm busy.

DAMIELLE: Busy at what?

MARCEL: Leave the boy alone. Let him enjoy his drink and his new friend.

DANIELLE: Some friend!

MARCEL: He's a cop. And, I might have something on him. He'd better watch his step.

DANIELLE: And, what about you, Marcel?

MARCEL: Your hatred is too obvious.

DANIELLE: Hatred is always obvious even when you choose not to see it.

MARCEL: You hate me, but not Gerard.

DANIELLE: I love Gerard. You've corrupted him and for that I hate you. See how simple it is?

MARCEL: You're a fool, Danielle. You play your cards for everyone to see. You're a rotten gambler.

GERARD: (*turning away from EMILE to face MARCEL and DANIELLE*): Stop it, you two. All this heated talk and for nothing.

MARCEL: Your cousin thinks I've corrupted you, Gerard. Have I?

GERARD: The day I was born is when the corruption began. My father took me by the hand. Together, we walked down the boulevard waving goodbye to Mama. A sunny morning that one wants to hold forever…and in a moment, it is gone… and that is forever. My father struck down by a car and killed in the prime of his manhood. It should have been me, the son, who met death that day. Nothing was ever the same. Nothing.

MARCEL: And, still you grieve him. The moment is over. Leave it in the past. Bury it, mon ami.

DANIELLE: And, how does one go about burying a memory, Marcel? Eh? You ask the impossible.

MARCEL: You feed the boy's grief and you are wrong to do that, Danielle.

DANIELLE (*turning her back to MARCEL as HECTOR walks up to her*): And, you have contaminated him.

MARCEL: I oughta' strike you good for that.

TIGER: None of that in here.

EMILE: Another cognac, please?

HECTOR: Why didn't you come back to the table?

DANIELLE: I would have, in a moment.

HECTOR: Don't forget that favor you owe me.

DANIELLE: Oh? You don't waste any time collecting debts, do you?

HECTOR: I wasted too many years in prison.

DANIELLE: What did they get you for? You mentioned something about a blade. Who did you kill? A wife? A lover?

HECTOR: Maybe, myself more than anyone.

DANIELLE: Now, you're being evasive.

HECTOR: Killing a body is easy, nothing to it. To kill the soul takes a lifetime...maybe several.

DANIELLE: Let's go back to the table. You interest me.

(*Blue spotlight on TIGER and GUY.*)

GUY: Bartender? Beer, please?

TIGER: Coming up.

GUY: Thanks.

TIGER: You an American?

GUY: Yes.

TIGER: A tourist?

GUY: No.

TIGER: What, then? Here on business? You don't look like a businessman.

GUY: I'm not.

TIGER: So, what are you? Here's your beer.

GUY: Thanks.

TIGER: So?

GUY: For now, I'm living in Paris.

TIGER: What do you do for a living?

GUY: Long haul trucker.

TIGER: Why here?

GUY: I don't know. It's really none of your business.

TIGER: You came here not knowing? Makes no sense.

GUY: Not even to me.

TIGER: Don't believe you. Sure you're not a crook?

GUY: I'm sure. What about you, pal?

TIGER: Go fuck yourself. And, for a crook, you're pretty stupid. (*Indicating EMILE.*) Don't know a cop when you see one?

GUY: The gendarme?

TIGER: That's what we call them.

GUY: You don't like cops.

TIGER: No.

GUY: Not many people do, until they need them.

TIGER: I should ever have such a need.

GUY (*nodding toward GERARD*): Who's that over there?

TIGER (*smiling slyly*): You like boys?

GUY: Well?

TIGER: Gerard Driest. A loose cannon, that one.

GUY: He looks angry. He's too young to be so angry.

TIGER: Maybe, you soften him up. (*Looking toward the window.*) Look. The sun's coming up. We'll be closing soon. You work on Sundays?

GUY: Sometimes.

TIGER: Me, too. I do it because I hate God.

GUY: The French cop wants another drink.

TIGER: Fuck him and all his kind. (*Turning to EMILE.*) What?

(*Blue spotlight on TIGER and EMILE.*)

EMILE: Another cognac, please.

TIGER: That's your third.

EMILE: I've paid for them.

TIGER: Now, pay for this one, cop.

EMILE: You don't like me.

TIGER: Yes.

EMILE: My father was a cop, too. You hate him, as well?

TIGER: I hate him, too.

EMILE: What's your problem, ex-con?

TIGER: How you know that?

EMILE: You wear it on your face. How long have you been out?

TIGER: Long enough to own this bar and take your money.

EMILE: What were you in for?

TIGER: For wanting to kill coppers. It's too bad. The cop I wanted to kill was already dead when I got out. Too bad for me.

EMILE: Who was he? Maybe, I know him.

TIGER: Why should I tell you? He's dead and not by my hand, but by God's.

EMILE: You believe in God?

TIGER: From time to time.

EMILE: When it suits you?

TIGER: I believe in retribution, too. My crime wasn't serious, but my punishment was.

EMILE: Nice talking to you, cop hater.

(*Blue spotlight on GERARD and MARCEL.*)

GERARD: He wants me -- the cop over there who's talking to Emile. That's his third drink. I think he's working up his nerve.

MARCEL: Watch your step with him. Don't let him entrap you. You know what to do.

GERARD: I'm not sure why he's here.

MARCEL: For a pick-up, what else?

GERARD: He's not the type. When he walked in, he was deep in thought...almost distracted.

MARCEL Until he saw you, my beauty.

GERARD: I don't flatter myself. Something's preying on his mind. I think he's a death dreamer.

MARCEL: What do you say? "Death dreamer?" What's that?

GERARD: He wants to kill someone.

MARCEL (*laughing*): Is that what you call them? Who does he want to kill?

GERARD: Male prostitutes, maybe? Me?

MARCEL: Now, you talk nonsense. But, be careful, mon ami.

GERARD: It's starting to get warm. The sun's coming up.

MARCEL: What's wrong?

GERARD: Just a feeling, Marcel, that someone's gonna' die in this dive.

MARCEL: Go back to your cop. And, remember…be careful.

GERARD (*not moving*): I wonder what Danielle is saying to Hector? You know that he just got out of prison.

MARCEL: Tell me something I don't know. He's trouble and your cousin is in cahoots with him.

GERARD: Danielle?

MARCEL: No, me! Who else?

GERARD: You don't like her.

MARCEL: Your cousin hates me. No. Despises me. Maybe, she's plotting to have me killed. I wouldn't put it past her.

GERARD: She might do that.

MARCEL: You admit it. Good. You're growing up and because of me.

GERARD: I grew up when I was fifteen. I was laying naked beside you.

MARCEL: The first step in your education, that was. (*Smiling, lighting a cigarette, and blowing the smoke in GERARD'S face.*) I have fond memories of it.

(*Blue spotlight on DANIELLE and HECTOR.*)

DANIELLE: Will you do it?

HECTOR: No.

DANIELLE: Then, the favor I owe you is paid. Leave me.

HECTOR: The favor has not been repaid. I watch your cousin for a few moments and you expect me to kill a man? You're crazy. You want Marcel dead? Kill him yourself.

DANIELLE: You would send a woman to do a man's job?

HECTOR: It's time I went back to my wife.

DANIELLE: She can have you. You have children?

HECTOR: A son and a daughter. Why do you ask?

DANIELLE: Send your son to me. He'll do what his father failed to do. Coward.

HECTOR: Maybe, I kill you. Stinking bitch! Leave my family out of this. Your plan for revenge doesn't interest me.

DANIELLE: Then, leave my table. Leave!

(*Blue spotlight on GUY and GERARD.*)

GUY: Hello.

GERARD: You're an American. I heard you talking to Tiger. Where in America do you come from?

GUY: New York City.

GERARD: I've never even left Paris.

GUY: Do you want to?

GERARD: I live from day to day.

GUY: Why, Gerard?

GERARD: I've no trade and my Catholic education is useless to me.

GUY: I don't have much education, but I earn an honest living.

GERARD: I don't. You know this.

GUY: Is that young lady over there your cousin?

GERARD: Yes. And, she loves me very much. She tries to help.

GUY: Then, let her.

GERARD: And, leave Marcel? Is that what you mean? I cannot.

GUY: Just turn your back on him. You might be surprised just how easy it is.

GERARD: You ask too much of me. And, who are you to ask it? Danielle may have that right, but not you.

GUY: Friends have to assume certain rights.

GERARD: When did we become friends? You jump to many fences for that.

GUY: I don't mean to be presumptuous, Gerard. Sorry.

GERARD: You were being kind. But, even kindness can be a base insult. It borders on pity.

GUY: I'm sorry. I don't pity you. But, I don't want to see you waste your life.

GERARD: Each to his own fate.

GUY: How old are you?

GERARD: I just became nineteen. I'll leave you now.

(*Blue spotlight on HECTOR and MARCEL.*)

HECTOR (*walking over to MARCEL*): Hey, Marcel? Watch your back with that woman.

MARCEL: She wanted you to kill me. You're not the first one she's asked.

HECTOR: She's beautiful. Some fool will take her up on it some day.

MARCEL: Thanks for the tip-off. You going back to your wife?

HECTOR: Not yet. Danielle still owes me a favor.

MARCEL: I wouldn't count on collecting it.

HECTOR: That American is getting pretty friendly with your boy.

MARCEL: I'd like to know what he's up to.

HECTOR: His game? He looks lost to me.

MARCEL: You don't come to the Dream Café for nothing. You have to qualify as scum.

HECTOR: Is that what we are? Maybe, you're right at that.

MARCEL: All of humanity is scum. I meant no insult by it.

HECTOR: Insults don't hurt. Knives hurt.

MARCEL: You carry a blade?

HECTOR: Always.

MARCEL: If you intend to use it, step out into the courtyard.

HECTOR: I've no reason to use it. I don't kill for the sake of killing. I'm not as heartless as that.

(*Blue spotlight on TIGER and EMILE.*)

TIGER: So, your father was a copper, too?

EMILE: A very good one.

TIGER: And, his son? Is he a good one, too?

EMILE: He was better. He lived for his job and took pride in it.

TIGER: And, you? Not so prideful?

EMILE: I- I lost my way. In a way, revenge took hold of me.

TIGER: Now, you begin to interest Tiger. Who are you after?

EMILE: The man who killed my father.

TIGER: Oh? And, what will you do to this man? Kill him? Arrest him? Tell Tiger.

EMILE: I will cut his nose from his face. And, then, slit the pig's throat.

TIGER: And, you, a cop talk in such a way.

EMILE: I'm no longer a cop.

TIGER: So, you can go around killing people and picking up young boys?

EMILE: You're quite right. I know that now. Now…that I look into my father's murderer's face.

TIGER: What are you saying? You talk to me-

EMILE: I talk to a pig! A cretin! It was your kind who killed him.

TIGER: I never killed anyone. And, don't call me a pig. Get out! (*Pointing to the empty glass on the bar.*) And, pay for that drink.

EMILE (*flinging coins in TIGER'S face*): Take it!

TIGER: If I'd known your sacred father, I'd have killed him. You suffer? Good. Here! Suffer this! (*He sets fire to a dish rag and pours cognac over it.*)

EMILE: You fool! Someone help me put this out!

HECTOR (*running over to the bar*): This spray bottle should do it. (*He sees GERARD trying to pat down the small blaze with his bare hand.*) Gerard! Watch your hand! (*The fire is quickly put out as TIGER pours himself a drink.*)

MARCEL (*massaging GERARD'S hand*): You trying to burn the place down? Do it when I'm not here, please. The boy burned himself. Idiot!

TIGER (*gulping down his drink*): Drop dead.

MARCEL: Not yet, my friend. Gerard, let's go. I'll take care of that at home. This place smells of more than smoke.

GUY (*to GERARD*): Talk to me, first.

GERARD: We've talked. I can't afford to talk.

DANIELLE (*seizing the opportunity, she goes over to the two men and places herself between GERARD and MARCEL*): Talk to this man, Gerard. I like him.

MARCEL: The boy comes with me.

DANIELLE: Let him decide that.

MARCEL: It is for me to decide, bitch.

GERARD: Marcel-

MARCEL: Shut up. We're going.

DANIELLE: Don't listen to him.

GUY: I'll buy you a beer.

MARCEL: He doesn't need your handouts.

HECTOR: What's the trouble here?

MARCEL: An American who doesn't know how to mind his own business.

EMILE: Let the boy decide for himself.

MARCEL (*turning to GERARD*) Well, decide.

GERARD: I want to stay for a while, Marcel.

MARCEL: So be it. We're finished. You're on your own and good luck. Ingrate! (*He storms out of the café, but can be seen lurking outside.*)

DANIELLE (*kissing GERARD*) Well done, cousin! Now, let this nice man buy you that beer. I'll be over there with Hector. (*To EMILE.*) Keep away from him.

EMILE: The boy's hand is burned. Let me take a look at it.

DANIELLE: Are you hurt, cherie?

HECTOR: It doesn't look too bad.

GERARD: A beer will help. (*DANIELLE and HECTOR go back to their table.*)

GUY: So, talk to me.

GERARD (*sitting down next to GUY*): Tiger, a beer, please.

TIGER: Sorry about that fire. This copper got me all riled up.

EMILE: Oh? It thought you did a pretty good job of that yourself? Make an account to the boy, not me.

GUY: Simmer down, the two of you. It's past.

EMILE: You're quite correct. Gerard, how's your hand?

GERARD: It's fine.

(*Blue spotlight on GUY and GERARD.*)

GUY: Where do you go from here?

GERARD: I thought you would tell me, monsieur.

GUY: I'll put you up for a few days.

GERARD: And, then, what? Back in the streets?

GUY: I'll help you get a job. Would you mind manual labor?

GERARD: I'm not above it. But, I've never held a job.

GUY: So, now you will.

GERARD: I'm not so sure.

GUY: Why? You afraid?

GERARD: No. I can get used to it. (*Looking out the window.*) Marcel's out front.

GUY: I'm not surprised.

GERARD: I should talk to him.

GUY: Don't. It's just what he wants. Don't look at him. Remember what I told you: just turn your back on him.

GERARD: That's not so easy.

GUY: It is.

(*Blue spotlight on HECTOR and DANIELLE.*)

HECTOR: So, you invite me back to your table, cherie.

DANIELLE: I'm in a good mood.

HECTOR: So, put me in a good mood.

DANIELLE: Buy me a drink.

HECTOR: How many does it take?

DANIELLE: Only one.

HECTOR: You like it sober? Good. Me, too. The pleasure lasts longer.

DANIELLE: Marcel is still outside.

HECTOR: You didn't expect him to go away so easy, did you?

DANIELLE: No.

HECTOR (*leaning closer to DANIELLE*): Who are you, cherie?

DANIELLE: A woman quite desperate for someone. I'm lonely, Hector. (*Smiling.*) Didn't expect that, did you?

HECTOR: It pleases me.

DANIELLE: A pity you're married.

HECTOR: Be my mistress. I could use one.

DANIELLE: Not good enough.

HECTOR: I'll love you more than my wife.

DANIELLE (*raising an eyebrow*): Will you?

HECTOR: Of course. But, that goes without saying.

DANIELLE: No.

HECTOR: Again! You say "no" too often. Look! Marcel is now pacing. He looks plenty mad. Don't laugh. His type is dangerous.

DANIELLE: Let him fume. As long as he stays outside, he's harmless.

HECTOR: He might come back in.

DANIELLE: Let him.

HECTOR: Don't be so cavalier. I have to leave soon.

DANIELLE: To go back to your wife?

HECTOR: It can't be helped.

DANIELLE: Bastard.

HECTOR: Can I get you one more?

DANIELLE: No.

HECTOR: Again...that answer. You know, for a beautiful woman, you can be a bore.

DANIELLE: I thought you were leaving?

HECTOR: So long, bitch. Better look out for that one.

DANIELLE: Marcel?

HECTOR: No. Your cousin. (*He goes over to the bar, pays for his drinks, and leaves.*)

(*Blue spotlight on TIGER and EMILE.*)

TIGER: The fire has left me.

EMILE: Good. A fourth and last cognac, please. Then, I'll be on my way and we won't have to look into each other's eyes.

TIGER: Here. Drink up.

EMILE: To you, Tiger.

TIGER: You still want the boy?

EMILE: No. Never did.

TIGER: Thought so. Why you come here?

EMILE: To have it out with you. It was my father who eventually died of wounds inflicted by you.

TIGER: A lie-

EMILE: No. His life had been shattered in the crash and this led to complications.

TIGER: He knew the risks.

EMILE: The bitterness is still here. (Pounding his chest.) But, my reason has returned.

TIGER: A good thing. Don't lose it, again.

EMILE: And, you mon ami?

TIGER: Bitter to the core. Maybe in my grave, I'll mellow. Probably not. Bitter and lonely. Come back for a drink, copper, and keep an old enemy company.

EMILE: Maybe, one day, we'll kill each other. Could still happen, you know.

TIGER: We'll see who pulls out the blade first. I look forward to it.

(*Blue spotlight on GERARD and GUY.*)

GERARD: I miss my papa. He was killed.

GUY: You have Danielle.

GERARD: I am very fortunate to have her. But, the pain is no less.

GUY: Let me be your friend.

GERARD: But, why? You don't know me.

GUY: We've entered each other's awareness and you can't undo that. In the short time we've known each other, we've shared a couple of pretty intense experiences. Friends share these kinds of things.

GERARD. You talk like a philosopher. We have many in France.

GUY: You're in pain, Gerard. I see it in you eyes and in your face.

GERARD: You see anger, too. I have plenty of that.

GUY: Who are you angry at?

GERARD: At my own deficiencies. I want to help Danielle and I can't. My father was killed by a motorist. He left me alone and I needed him. Still, I want to be with him. I want to be that small boy, again. The boy who was happy.

GUY: You can't go back in time.

GERARD: Okay, philosopher, then what do I do? How do I help that beautiful girl over there?

GUY: By helping yourself, pal. We'll find you a job: an honest job.

GERARD: It can't be done.

GUY: We'll get it done.

GERARD: Maybe, I don't want your honest job?

GUY: I don't believe that.

GERARD: Where is Danielle?

DANIELLE (*walking up to the bar*): Here, cherie. Drink your beer and listen to this good man.

GERARD: Where's Hector?

DANIELLE: Gone back to his wife.

GERARD: He wants to get me a job.

DANIELLE: Do you want one?

GERARD: As what? It wouldn't work.

DANIELLE: You don't know that. (*To GUY.*) Can you find him work?

GUY: Absolutely.

DANIELLE: Then, you must do it.

GUY: I can't force it on the boy.

DANIELLE: He'll listen to me. Gerard?

GERARD: Yes? Marcel's coming back in.

DANIELLE: I was afraid of that. (*Touching GUY'S elbow.*) He'll cause trouble. He has influence over my cousin.

GUY: I'll handle him. (*MARCEL and he confront each other.*) Get lost, pal. You're not wanted here.

MARCEL: Go fuck yourself.

GUY: And, you go to hell. Leave the boy alone.

MARCEL: You gonna' make me?

GUY: As a matter of fact, I am. (*He punches MARCEL in the eye. MARCEL staggers back and, then, lunges at GUY knocking him off balance. GUY hit's the opposite wall, but comes back at MARCEL with clenched fists.*)

DANELLE: Say nothing, Gerard. Let the men settle it. Maybe, Guy will get lucky and kill him.

GERARD: Don't say that, Danielle.

DANIELLE: You should say it. Look, Guy is the better fighter. He fights like a man: with his fists.

GERARD: He might kill Marcel.

DANIELLE: He'll teach him a lesson. Guy's not the type to kill. (*The two men continue to brawl. For a moment, EMILE looks like he's going to step in, but decides not to. MARCEL tries tripping up GUY, but GUY is ready for him with a right upper-cut. MARCEL staggers under the blow, but gets up, grabs a bottle from the bar, smashes it and lunges at GUY.*) You fight dirty, Marcel!

MARCEL: Go to hell. (*This distracts MARCEL'S attention toward GERARD. He plunges the jagged glass into GERARD'S neck, mortally wounding him.*)

DANIELLE (*standing up and screaming*): What have you done?

MARCEL (*dropping the bottle and placing his bloodied hands to cover his face*): I have killed my son!

DANIELLE: Gerard-

EMILE (*running over*): Let me have a look. He's punctured the artery. He's bleeding like a pig. I can't stop the bleeding!

DANIELLE: Help him. (*A few tortuous moments pass as EMILE desperately tries to save GERARD.*)

EMILE (*getting to his feet and looking at his blood stained hands*): It's too late.

TIGER (*shouting from the bar*): I'll call the medics! Maybe, they can-

EMILE (*shaking his head*): It's too late.

DANIELLE (*sobbing*): It can't be.

GUY (*standing over the prostrate MARCEL*): Get. Up. (*To TIGER.*) You got a back room?

TIGER: I'll help you with the boy.

GUY: Let's carry him inside. (*Black out.*)

(*Blue spotlight on DANIELLE and GUY.*)

DANIELLE: I have no one to look after now.

GUY: Will you be all right?

DANIELLE: No. Do you really care?

GUY: I'll take you home, if you like.

DANIELLE: I'm not going home. Leave me to my existence.

GUY: Marcel...he said he'd just killed his son.

DANIELLE: I heard that, too.

GUY: What did he mean by that?

DANIELLE: I would know? One would think that, wouldn't one? Please, I don't want to talk anymore.

GUY: I'm sorry.

DANIELLE: Will you go back to America? I would.

GUY: Maybe...in time.

DANIELLE (*staring vacantly into space*): If I satisfy your curiosity, will you go? Marcel and Gerard were related, but not in the way that you think. I helped support them. My living is an honest one at the dressmaker's. (*Looking directly at GUY.*) Surprised? And, maybe it's good that he's dead.

GUY: Don't say that.

DANIELLE: My cousin was too sensitive for this world. His pain is ended. Marcel's is just beginning and mine will never end. A father has killed his son...if only that were true. Now, go. I have my liquor and you have your freedom. Don't waste it on what you cannot change or understand. Leave me alone, Guy. (*GUY quietly gets up and walks over to the bar for another beer.*)

EMILE: Go back to her, mon ami.

TIGER: Mind your own damned business.

EMILE: Don't listen to this one. Go to her. (*TIGER makes to speak, but EMILE warns him with his fist not to say anything more. At first, GUY hesitates. Slowly, he walks back to DANIELLE'S table and sits down. The blue spotlight slowly fades as DANIELLE looks up and extends her hand to GUY.*)

End of play.

TWO VAMPIRES

A One Act Play

by

Gerard Denza

CHARACTERS

FERNANDO MONTEZ, vampire.
DR. RAYMOND, a physician of questionable ethics.
ACHILLEUS CARMINO, a magus.

PLACE
In a dark and abandoned room on the outskirts of Mexico City.

TIME
The present.

ACT ONE

Past midnight in an abandoned building. The room that the two men are in is bare except for a few articles of old furniture. The night is warm, but the sky is overcast.

MONTEZ: You have a cure? Liar. I don't believe you, Doctor.

DR. RAYMOND: Would I lie to you, vampire? The truth, I do not distort.

MONTEZ: What do you say is truth?

DR. RAYMOND: The unrelenting hardness of reality.

MONTEZ: That's real interesting. What do you mean by it?

DR. RAYMOND: I can cure you, vampire.

MONTEZ: The name is Fernando Montez. Remember it.

DR. RAYMOND: I shall, Montez.

MONTEZ: Tell me about the cure.

DR. RAYMOND: It contains fire.

MONTEZ: I knew it! You speak of death, Doctor. I will not die by my own hand or by yours. I don't like your cure. Want me to cure you?

DR. RAYMOND: When you arose from your coffin, Montez -- the first time -- the very first time…tell me the details and the emotions.

MONTEZ: Of my death-

DR. RAMYOND: And, resurrection. As He was once resurrected.

MONTEZ: I wasn't aware of a similarity.

DR. RAYMOND: But, the thought intrigues you, Montez. Tell me of the illness and the death and the crossover to immortality. Begin, if you would.

MONTEZ: I was bitten by another vampire.

DR. RAYMOND: There are others, then?

MONTEZ: Many.

DR. RAYMOND: Go on. I'll try not to interrupt you, again. (*At this point, he recedes into the background of the room; although, he can still be seen listening and watching intently.*)

MONTEZ: I had welcomed a guest into my home that evening. A man. His name was Achilleus Carmino. His appearance was mesmerizing and every subtle gesture and nuance had a hypnotic effect. The eyes were dark and smoldering. His hair was cut very short and was almost like a helmet upon his head. The black suit was of an expensive cut and make. I offered him more coffee.

CARMINO: Then, I must go. Tell me, Mr. Montez, do you find life interesting?

MONTEZ (*bringing his guest another cup of coffee*): At the moment, it's picked up, actually.

CARMINO: Therefore, I can offer you no assistance.

MONTEZ (*sitting back down and facing his guest*): Assistance is always welcome. My future is by no means set.

CARMINO: No one's future is "set." However, the path which we follow is certainly pre-ordained.

MONTEZ: Is it? I wasn't aware of that.

CARMINO: Then, you should be.

MONTEZ: Why?

CARMINO: So, that you may alter it. Is that your wish?

MONTEZ: I don't know.

CARMINO: Your answer?

MONTEZ: Yes.

CARMINO: If your life is to change, Mr. Montez, then you must change your self and your circumstances. Are you willing to do that?

MONTEZ (*standing up*): Again, yes. But, why me?

CARMINO: Why not? It involves the vague and often tangled concepts of reincarnation. Are you troubled, young man?

MONTEZ: You're too perceptive, Mr. Carmino.

CARMINO: An impertinent question, no?

MONTEZ: I'm listening.

CARMINO: You've not long to live. I can see that in the shadow that you cast. If you want to live, you must agree to an alteration.

MONTEZ (*leaning on the back of his armchair*): Start from the beginning, please.

CARMINO: You will soon be murdered for knowledge that you do not possess, young man: a case of mistaken identity. You've been followed recently.

MONTEZ (*coming around to the front of the armchair*): Yes. I have...by some van-

CARMINO: I know of this vehicle. It's a sign that your death warrant has been issued.

MONTEZ: What are you telling me? Please, explain all this.

CARMINO: Sit down, please. I'll be staying in the city. Visit me tomorrow night. Be warned: if you come to me, it will mean that change has been affected and there will be no turning back. And, you may one day wish for death and that wish will be denied by you, Mr. Montez. But, your life will be very interesting.

MONTEZ (*sitting down on the edge of the armchair*): You talk in riddles; but, I think I know your meaning. Am I going to become a vampire?

CARMINO (*placing his cup of coffee on to the coffee table*): Yes. We need a young vampire to help us. Someone who can disappear into the fabric of a wall. Someone who can walk into a room full of people unnoticed and, yet, kill anyone there of his choosing.

MONTEZ: Why do you want me?

CARMINO: Your beauty should not end in death. There are many lifetimes, Mr. Montez, but this lifetime is the most important for it may be your last.

MONTEZ: Reincarnation offers hope.

CARMINO: Reincarnation is an act of courage, but it can also be a very dangerous and futile act. (*Changing the subject, abruptly.*) What is your profession?

MONTEZ: I have none. I write some poetry-

CARMINO: Do you come from wealth? You don't.

MONTEZ: I come from poverty.

CARMINO: Good. You're honest. You'll need money. We can help you. When you have the means, then you can indulge yourself in writing your poetry. However, until that time, you must focus on the more practical.

MONTEZ: I don't know what you mean by that.

CARMINO (*impatiently*): It can't be explained to you in a sentence. It must be worked out on paper in pen. You don't understand. I'm talking about contracts and vows of allegiance. Is that clear enough for you?

MONTEZ: I've nothing to lose. When you have nothing, you lose nothing. And, I'm not afraid to die.

CARMINO: You can have one last incarnation as a vampire.

MONTEZ: An immortal? Eternal youth? I'd like that well enough because it's an impossibility.

CARMINO: It can be done, Mr. Montez, but immortality is a heavy burden. Your soul would be forever trapped in your flesh. It could not renew itself. You must be told of the burden, for there is one.

MONTEZ: Who cares?

CARMINO (*slamming his right fist into the palm of his left hand*): You should care! The soul needs to be released so that an overview of one's life may be attained. A life must be viewed without the cloud of emotion.

MONTEZ: I'm willing to try. What's the process of making me immortal? Pain...will there be pain?

CARMINO: More than you can imagine. Don't be so foolhardy as to make the decision tonight.

MONTEZ: Are you a vampire, Mr. Carmino?

CARMINO (*not comfortable with MONTEZ'S question*): Some would call me a psychic vampire. And, perhaps, they would be correct to use that term.

MONTEZ: Then, I accept your offer of vampirism.

CARMINO: I've misjudged you, Mr. Montez. And, if your answer is "yes," then I must accept it. Are you that dissatisfied with your lot?

MONTEZ: I hate it.

CARMINO: And, the degenerate life of a vampire is preferable to you?

MONTEZ: Yes.

CARMINO: So firm with your answer.

MONTEZ: How is it done?

CARMINO: In the traditional manner. The mark will be placed upon your neck and on the third night, you will die. (*Hesitates.*) And, on the fourth night-

MONTEZ: Yes?

CARMINO: You arise.

MONTEZ (*once again, he is addressing DR. RAYMOND as CARMINO leaves the room*): During the next four days, I suffered the torments of the dying and faced the darkness of the bottomless chasm to face the awakening shadow life of the vampire. I felt the hot breath of the vampire. The fangs were at my throat piercing the tender skin. I cried out. Again. And, again. I screamed to God almighty, but He was gone. The vampire was now my master and new god. Again, he kissed me hard on the neck. My strength was gone and would not return until I arose. The transformation from a human being to a vampire had begun.

DR. RAYMOND: Tell me about your new god.

MONTEZ: I never saw him. He was only a specter hovering next to me.

DR. RAYMOND: Continue.

MONTEZ: The fever grew worse. My vision was hazy. It felt as if I were lying on my back in a pit with voices and images distorted. I tasted the blood in my mouth. Was I drunk? I felt so off balance as if one side of the room were coming up at me to slap me in the face. Everything was so dark. Voices called to me from within my soul that I couldn't recognize. My death was slow in the sense of realizing that I was actually no longer living. As they carried out my body, I had the sensation of crossing a bridge. I could hear the waves splashing against the columns of the structure but could not see anything...not really. I got up to walk across the bridge. My feet made soft echoing sounds that mingled into the mist and the darkness. How strange. No other sounds could be heard except my footsteps and the rhythmic splashing of the water below. Why was I here? To recollect myself and bring that soul back into the recesses of the corpse which was being put to rest in the ground? Would I awake to forgetfulness? Was I to be my own creator? How very bitter!

DR. RAYMOND: But the awakening…how did you manage it?

MONTEZ: Every vital organ in my body felt as if it were embraced by searing hot barbed wires. Yet, I felt coldly objective toward it. I tried to move my hand in order to brush aside a tear trickling down my cheek. I couldn't move my hand. They had placed my body into the confinement of a coffin. I was buried in the cold and barren earth. I pushed my hands against the barrier that separated me from my new depraved existence. The coffin was sealed with a waxed lining. It cracked under the pressure of my hands and the dirt came rushing in. It soiled my clothes. The pine started to crack, but by no means must I damage it! (*He collapses to his knees as if actually reliving the moment.*) I was seized with panic. Bloody sweat covered my face…my body was drenched with it. And, at last, I could wipe away that tear from my cheek. I dug my way through the dirt like some animal who had been trapped by some loathsome hunter. My hands knew what to do. Faster and faster they dug through the loosening dirt. I lifted my body up and through the barrier not by mere strength but by will of the mind. My body began to "slip" through the ground until, at last, my hand reached into the night air and I was free! The night air was cold and moist as I stood upon the open grave.

DR. RAYMOND: You told it well, Montez.

MONTEZ: You want to cure me, Doctor?

DR. RAYMOND: You misunderstood me. I want to cure you of any relapse.

MONTEZ: Relapse? I don't follow you.

DR. RAYMOND: You spoke of a vampire who had bitten you.

MONTEZ: Yes?

DR. RAYMOND: And, you didn't actually see this apparition?

MONTEZ: No. It wasn't necessary to see it. I told you…it was a cold and dark specter.

DR. RAYMOND: You are, therefore, not acquainted with the catalyst of your vampirism?

MONTEZ: No. Why do you ask, Doctor?

DR. RAYMOND: You wish to be made human, again? Or is it death that you wish for?

MONTEZ: What are you asking me?

DR. RAYMOND: I am inquiring into the doubts of your own mind. These doubts and second thoughts must be erased if you are to be of use to us.

MONTEZ: Who are you?

DR. RAYMOND: I? I am the vampire who made you what you are. Come closer, Montez. Now. It would appear that another inoculation is advisable. Another bite on the neck is needed. Your conscience is far too human. Come. (*MONTEZ walks over to him. DR. RAYMOND rips off MONTEZ'S collar and sinks his fangs into his neck.*)

End of play.

SELECTED MONOLOGUES

ICARUS: It is once again occurring. Dearest gods in the heavens, have pity on your son who calls out to you. Hear one who once stood in your presence in the great Hall of Truth and Light. Hear the disobedient son! (*Facing the audience.*) Why have I come to be in this forsaken place? Have I fallen into the vestibule of the lower world where there lies only the feeble hope and malice of faith and the evils of forgiveness? The light? Where has it gone? How long have I been here and toward what end does it signify? I need to take possession of my soul once more to form my being as a man, as a god, as a soul of creation…as an Atlas of the gods.

From ICARUS,
Act One

THE PRIEST: Everyone's desolation is fed unto me. And, I, in turn, unleash it back upon them so as to fulfill their most dread hope of seeing it. I dare not even hope for any challenge, but a mere silence would do. A silence before my horse tramples upon the half-wit. A silence before my scimitar detaches the empty head from its pathetic body. Acknowledgement? Is there a glimmer of it here? Dare I hope to find the man who stands on his own? A worthy opponent whom I may respect with my pure hatred? I? Mere repetition. And, still more repetition. The simplicity of folly and so simple-mindedly predictable. The hollow mind that is incapable of thought: my feeding ground, actually. A hunger that is never quite satisfied.

From ICARUS,
Act One

ICARUS: The stars appeared. The beautiful constellations of the night glittered like brilliant gem stones...so soft...and, yet, bright. But, how could I perceive this? The stars seemed to spread out before me as if reaching into the black velvet sky beyond infinity's edge. Did I glimpse what a mortal could not...but, no longer was I a mortal. My flight through the heavens brought me to where a mortal should not trespass. The sky hovered over me as I swept through it like an eagle on a glorious flight. It was a moment of supreme triumph! A moment not to be held, for what is a moment? What is time, itself, but the thread to be cut by Death? Upon my wings were the specters of death...the heat and, then, the flame that robbed me of my wings. The moment was lost. I held it no longer! The radiant god driving his chariot of golden flame over the sacred pathway would not allow me entrance into his kingdom. And, then, I saw within the eternity of a moment, the shimmering blue glass of the water as it caught the reflection of the fire of heaven. The fiery pinpoints of light were caught upon the waves and hurled toward the shore. All of this wonder as my body was flung earthward.

From ICARUS,
Act One

THE STRANGER: I will begin. A man is altered by darkness. One feels darkness, but does not actually see it manifesting within himself and turning his soul into blackness. A man must change himself from the primeval essence that is undeniably his starting point and begin the metamorphosis into his role of a civilized man, a human being, if you would. When a civilized man finds himself in the midst of a savage landscape, he cannot help but become affected. He knows that his countenance can be shattered. He realizes that he is not a being who is at the apex of human evolution. He discovers that the primeval instincts are still within him.

From MAHLER, The Man Who Was Never Born,
Act One, Scene One

DAMIEN: I am alone. There is no God in this place. Have I found my spirit? Does even that remnant of myself still exist? I fear not. I have been dreaming for a long time, but I have now awakened from my dream. A dream has a memory of its own and this memory is independent of the dreamer for it has a life and a place and a framework in the scheme of one's life. It is a fragile reminder of the impermanence of creation. A dream is created and destroyed for it must be destroyed if one is to awaken. It has power and death. Death. A word that I have come to embrace and to feel sublimely comfortable with and to long for. (*He hugs his arms about his torso as if he feels a coldness.*) It's still dark outside, but there is light in the room. I lift my arm to place my hand in front of my eyes and the light vanishes completely and the room becomes a pitch-black void of nonexistence. The terror that I feel takes a grip on my body, and every muscle shudders as a cold spasm sweeps through me. I try to cry out. Did I moan in agony or in ecstasy? Or was it just my imagination? (*He gets up and pulls his pants on. He places his hand to his mouth while suppressing the urge to laugh hysterically.*) I've bitten myself, again. (*He turns about and circles the stage in the opposite direction, occasionally glancing at the audience.*) When I was a small boy, I would receive communion. The little, blessed wafer: the body and the blood of the Christ: a holy ritual of magic is what it was and remains. It was my favorite part of the Mass, kneeling before the priest and feeling the cold marble beneath my knees. Everyone would be looking at you. You were holy and they were not. (*Staring incredulously at the audience.*) Was that when my life began to be cursed? a jealous onlooker? a darkness that had entered the receptacle of the church…a darkness that had been allowed inside? Yes. The blasphemers within would permit such a thing. A darkness that would crawl along the tiled floor and wind its way down the central aisle…only the central aisle…neither to the right nor to the left. Coiling its way and alerting any sensitive person to its presence. It coiled its way down looking for me. It saw me and struck at me when I was kneeling. The wafer fell to the ground and the snake lodged itself in my throat. The priest looked at me with contempt and moved on to the next little boy. Didn't he see what had just happened? Was he not a magician? A sage? A sinner? He would admit to nothing. The fool. Fool!

From THE DYING GOD: A Vampire's Tale,
Act One, Scene One

DAMIEN: I feel myself weakening: a sign that I am beginning to lose control. I am becoming a vampire, but not in the conventional sense of that term. I have transformed myself into a predatory thing, but it is not complete. It needs the consecration of murder. For most of my life, I have been involved with the occult arts and with its dangers and promises and many misleading paths. If I could love a thing, it is this thing that would claim a love. It was during one, dark occult ceremony that I made my usual prayer, request if you would, of immortality. Not so much of eternal youth, but to see the world die about me and for myself to remain unchanged. It was a long ceremony with Colette and Antonia present to give it its needed momentum and female sustenance. We erected an unholy cross of supplication...yes...supplication to the gods of darkness who granted favors but not forgiveness... never forgiveness...never that. I placed myself upon this cross and prayed to be given immortality at any cost. An unholy messenger answered my plea. When the ceremony had ended, I arose naked from the cross. Colette and Antonia were exhilarated. And I? I felt nothing but coldness and, yet, my body was bathed in sweat...that had the odor of death about it. I touched my chest with my fingertips. Hard. Too hard. Something in me had changed. I knew that my prayers had been answered. A vampire who may dwell in the shadow of daylight and prey upon the living in the sanctuary of the night.

From THE DYING GOD, A Vampire's Tale,
Act One, Scene One

DAMIEN: It felt heavy on my shoulder. Was it the weight of the body or was the sin pressing itself upon me? The sun had not yet risen, but I could see as if it were merely dusk. I could see all those uneventful things that no ordinary person could. I did not feel privileged or even exhilarated. I was strong and immortal, but the vitality of life had gone from me.

From THE DYING GOD: A Vampire's Tale,
Act One, Scene Four

DAMIEN Light a match and see the fire burn white and orange and blue all suspended on a little stick of paper whose life is being burned away. But, the stick of paper doesn't mind, because for a moment, it is a glorious and wonderful glaring point of light and heat. It is transformed from compressed paper and just a bit of sulfur into a fabulous living and dying creature and, then, into a charcoal blackness like a dead star of the sky. Before that final moment, I place the burning star next to the end of the cigarette and puff. With the tips of my fingers, I extinguish the match and crush it into the street pavement. It's good to be smoking, again. I've always enjoyed the taste of tobacco and there's no longer any reason to give them up. Do I offend anyone? Too bad.

From THE DYING GOD: A Vampire's Tale,
Act One, Scene Five

DAMIEN: An Earth shift. The planet is going to roll over on its damned axis. (*Looking heavenward.*) On that day, it was as if the sun had never set. The air was stagnant. There were no waves upon the shore. The Earth had stopped moving or so it seemed. For a moment, there was that blind panic that feeds itself to the primitive emotions of terror. Anything that had been in motion now seemed to quiver and want to topple over. The axis began to shift. The planet was balancing itself to a new position in its never ceasing orbit. The oceans began to render their destruction: first along the sea coasts and, then, stretching into the interior of the continents. Landslides, volcanic eruptions, and earthquakes rocked the globe as continental plates shifted and pressed against each other pushing to make room for their own land mass. The Earth was cleansing itself.

From THE DYING GOD: A Vampire's Tale,
Act Three, Scene One

BAYLA: He is going to die, but it will be no ordinary death. Before his last breath, he will leave his body and with the aid of the magic triangle he shall be brought to the astral plane with consciousness and identity. He will re-enter the physical plane in like manner. I must stop him. It has come down to this. He wants me to attempt to thwart his final plan. It would be a glorious moment for him, truly: to defeat me and to cross over with my aid. He would have it no other way. The thorn in his side would be finally removed and he will come back to settle scores with me. I accept the challenge. It could mean my own death, but what of it? (*She drains the last of her absinthe.*)

From THE DYING GOD: A Vampire's Tale,
Act Three, Scene One

DAMIEN: And, what of me? My claws and my cunning have been sharpened by experience and the necessity of the kill. I enjoy myself, but not wholeheartedly for there is a futility to it all. One cannot gloat over a corpse. It is a pleasure that is denied to the killer who possesses an intellect. I am immortal, but I can choose to die. When will that day be? I don't know. And there-in lies the filthy rub. One gets used to the physical life and one gets attached to it. Dangerous! The desire to rip the soul from the body diminishes and one loses the thought of even attempting it. And, Bayla, what of her? Who is this woman who seeks to hold me? Hold me? (*He throws his head back and laughs.*) No. That will not do. That will not do at all.

From THE DYING GOD: A Vampire's Tale,
Epilogue

MALKIN: Fun? I do not believe in "fun." No. There is no "fun" at a party that I herald. Here! This drink is not to herald "fun.." (*He takes his glass and raises it to eye level.*) Interesting substance, eh? A beautiful liquid that redefines one's sense of proportion and sobriety. It penetrates the air that hovers just above its tiny ripples of intoxication. One cherishes its impact upon the senses even before the first swallow. It touches one's lips like a stinging and breathless kiss of abandon. It hurts the mouth. It should hurt for it is penetrating. And in its penetration, it enfolds the body and mind and heart and...the emotions. That beautiful liquid with a kick that can stain one's virtue or liberate it. Cheers!

From SHADOWS BEHIND THE FOOTLIGHTS,
Act One, Scene Three

FRANK: And an alcoholic. Let's not leave that out of the equation. Yes. A writer who is making a feeble attempt at playing detective. You know exactly nothing. But, here, I'll freshen your drink for you. Here. I'll start to pour. But, when should I stop? Huh? I could pour the whole bottle down your throat and it wouldn't be enough. Look...liquor! Come on! It's good stuff! Down the hatch! I insist. You stole that cigarette case. You invited Miss Chen here, tonight, to quiz her on... me! You ask too many questions for your own damned good and find out nothing. Always alert. Always posturing. Too bad it doesn't translate into anything useful. When I came here, tonight, I was undecided: terrify her, threaten her, steal back what she stole, or kill her? Drink up, it'll help deaden the nerve. You see, I'm not unlike yourself. Our futures are decided. The fateful third sister is about to cut the dreaded thread on both of us. You suffer. I suffer. I walk the streets at night: a long and lonely dreadful affair. It is preferable to your flop house or train station or a park bench. Address: unknown but malleable. Identity: uncertain. Past: nonexistent. Present: classified. Future: cement slab in the city morgue. I want company on that slab! (*He smashes the bottle and holds the jagged edge toward her.*) Keep me company?

From SHADOWS BEHIND THE FOOTLIGHTS,
Act Two, Scene Two

EDMUND: It's a hard life. Every dime I make from modeling and coaching goes back into body building: gym membership, good food, and all the work-out gear: the gym gear, the posing trunks, body lotion, travel expenses, decent clothes. I have one suit, one pair of sneakers, and a pair of wing-tips that I picked up at a thrift shop. I've got one white shirt to go with the suit and a borrowed tie from my uncle: his only tie. Any book that I happen to read comes from the Public Library. The muscle magazines, I buy. They're like reference books for me: textbooks. I live in my uncle's spare bedroom in a working class neighborhood in Brooklyn; but, it's clean and it's right across the Williamsburg Bridge. Travel time is short and the subway fare is cheap. I happen to think it's worth it.

From EDMUND: The Likely,
Act Two, Scene One

BENTON: Do you know what evil is? If you do, you're one up on most of us, except me, of course. I'm evil, pal. Uncivilized. A Primitive. And, ya' spell that with a capital "P." We feed off of people. We're parasites. You're weak and too afraid to stand up to us. You're fools, and we hate you for it. Even our loyal followers, we despise them. That fool who just walked out of here? Watch out for him. He's a snake who knows how to smile while he's putting the knife in someone's back. My kind's easy to spot, his kind isn't. They're the weakest and most contemptible of all people. To gain a friendship they think they have to despoil someone else's name. Even I can't stomach him. Now, Jack Parsons is a challenge. He's got convictions and can't be moved from them or so they say. He ignored me in court. Me. Capt. Ralph Benton. I hate him. And, I will kill him. I have to because he's the type who can't be intimidated. You might scare him, but he'll never be a follower. He's an individual. But, to me, he's filth.

From SKYBLAZERS,
Act Two, Scene Three

GLAUCUS: The clouds had taken upon themselves a life of their own. They moved rapidly across the sky in an endless sea of blue and grey foam. It was as if they were descending to the ocean to touch the very ship I was navigating. I could feel the pressure and the rain as it descended upon me. I wanted to jump into the water for protection...the cold, blue water which bore my ship. I hesitated. But, then I heaved my body overboard and let the waves take me. I knew I would die, but the sky held even more terror than death. The water embraced my body. Cold. A coldness that was the harbinger of death… of the watery grave that I had chosen. And, yet, I did not die.

From LEFT, RIGHT, and NOWHERE,
Act One

MORBIUS: The manipulation of thought as applied to science and intent. A philosophy of the cosmos that I've perfected by gazing and studying the constellations of stars and galaxies. Look at them when they are once again reborn: the planets, the clusters of stars and the near infinity of galaxies. They, in their wisdom, do speak to mortal beings. They cast their ancient light upon the windows of the soul…let that light in and you will be as I.

From LEFT, RIGHT, and NOWHERE,
Act One

LILLITH: Morbius was right. I'm nothing more than a fictional footnote: a woman of notoriety who may or may not have existed. But, I still exist in the heart of every woman's sexual desire for her man. Nothing can ever erase that. What do I care for the Tree of Knowledge? The serpent didn't tempt me. I already knew who and what I was. I didn't have to eat some poisonous fruit for that. Eve was a fool and my Glaucus was deceived by a so-called innocent. Such innocence! A race of perfection was lost forever…but, perhaps, there is still hope. Perhaps, Morbius, was right after all. Adam and I were as one. Our children are the very Nephilim the Bible speaks of. When they return, the world will know it. Kronos, the snake, must be forever damned!

From LEFT, RIGHT, and NOWHERE,
Epilogue

GLAUCUS: Naked, I arose from the dust. My name is Adam…a name given to me by my creator. To rise up as a man and look to the heavens and the blue glazed sky is wondrous. All about me is the green lushness of life and vitality. My bare feet touch upon the soft earth and, suddenly, I behold the Tree of Life. It is magnificent. Its branches bear the golden fruit of eternal life and youth. I need not take of its fruit for my soul tells me that I am immortal. A gift bestowed upon me by my god…the god who created the white flash in the empty void. I recall that great white light and an explosion which never seemed to end. I was carried on the crest of this blinding white light. I don't remember anything else. And, yet…a woman was with me. She loved me and…and told me of a future life at sea as a mariner. And, then, of yet another life as one of the gods of the sea during a golden era of the rebirth of civilization. I would know her as a sorceress and she would love me and I must love her in return. I dare not refuse that love. Lillith. Her name was Lillith and I will love her one day when she comes to the rock which juts out of the water. I will raise my arms to her and we will embrace. My god-like form will not frighten her. Cursed be anyone who rejects me! Another woman's voice deceived me and blinded my soul's eyes. Lillith will restore my soul's vision and another race will be created…a godlike race that will last until this universe is once again a mere pinpoint of light.

From LEFT, RIGHT, and NOWHERE,

Epilogue

PATRICK: Why? When each day is like the rest of the fucking days in this cell. Why go on, but why not? How do I kill myself? Do I still want to? Don't know anything anymore. What the hell did I ever know? Nothing! Today…my birthday and I'm nineteen and I've got nothing! They say I'm a time bomb ready to go off, but they're wrong. I've gone off and it's like a chain reaction that's never gonna' stop. I don't want it to stop. If anyone cares, I'm innocent. I'm innocent, but I can't bust out of my skin. Why not? Why not! Hear me, God! Are you listening to this? Are you takin' this down? I hope so. I hope so! You failed me big time.

From PRISON BOYS: Patrick and Marco

BAYLA: There is a need in my life which must be met; but, I am at a loss to the remedy. Revenge? Murder? Not satisfactory. Those weapons are banal. The art of subterfuge is what the ancients excelled at. The manipulation of others is a very potent weapon: a fine art, really. I've procured Damien's guest list and, quite frankly, I'm unable to make any sense of it. The names of enemies. A religious name. There may be a peculiar logic in that. Revenge and torture, respectively. I approve because that is Damien's nature. But, there are several pedestrian names on his guest list. Why? And, the date and time of this gathering are unsettling: the Autumnal equinox and atop that rather garish glass tower. I'm tempted not to go. But, Damien knows that I will be there. It's as good a place as any to usher in the end of the world. The anticipated and dreaded apocalypse may be ready to descend upon us. No one can stop it. The thermo-nuclear holocaust that will destroy us all. Or will it? I think that I'll have a stab at changing destiny. If a mortal is a terrestrial god, then I think it can be done. If God can create and destroy, then, why can't I?

From ELLIPSIS,
Prologue One

DAMIEN: I'm Damien Wilhelm: vampire. I've lived a great many years, if you could call my existence a life. I see myself as a self created god who now dwells within this magnificent glass skyscraper. I like that word: skyscraper. It denotes a defiance of heaven. Lucifer rising from the terrestrial to reclaim his throne and spit in the face of the Creator. I became a vampire through an unholy ritual and the dark power of dreams: a deliberate attempt to be an immortal killer. (*He glances out the large window to take in the breathtaking vista below.*) Nice view, huh? New York City is still rather magnificent from a distant height. Artificial light inserted into the many glass and stone skyscrapers: civilization at its technological best. And, how people sneer at it; that is, until the lights go out. And, the lights will go out very soon, which is why I'm having my party tomorrow night. It will be a gathering of allies and enemies. The last feast before the end. Not the Last Supper, mind you, that meant only the end of my enemy's son's life...and he reversed the cycle of death and life. Bully for Him! No. This will be the last supper: the last morsel of life.

From ELLIPSIS,
Prologue Two

HARRY: You ain't leveling with us lady, And, I don't like it. You hear what I'm telling you? I don't have an education. And, I don't have friggin' patience with a double-dealing bitch like you. I don't have your guile or your gall. And, I don't have your put-on mannerisms. But, I got a brain in this head and I know a set-up when I hear one. You want us to do your dirty work for you. Shut up! I'm still talkin'. Well, find yourself another patsy. I'm staying right here 'cause I can make myself pretty comfortable in any place and in any time. What do I give a crap what year it is? I've got my wits and I'm not so proud that I can't take up manual work. Thanks for the meal. I think I'll head for a park bench or the nearest flop house or subway car. I know my way around.

From ELLIPSIS,
Act Three, Scene Two

BAYLA: And, for now, the charade is at an end.: a thrust back into the past has been successful. I'm now in a position to correct all my past mistakes: mistakes that will never be made. How very sweet and convenient. The illusion of death is a very powerful stimulant. All of Damien's guests are quite safe back in their own time, except for that fool, Harry. He's dead. And, what of me? I gazed directly into the mirror at my own illusion of nuclear war. My aim was off. I must assume that. I don't know. Perhaps, you could tell me for I am now blind. It was necessary. The vision had to be removed for my prayer to be answered. Perhaps, in time, I will recapture that vision. Pray for me. But, I played the masquerade well. Did you guess my secret? Damien, my vampire, didn't. And, if I could deceive him and my old nemesis, Cornfield, I can deceive God, Himself.

From ELLIPSIS,
Act Four

SYBIL: La Presidente? No Too ethnic. Mrs. President? No. Too throwback. President Sybil Schmidlap-Schwab? No. Too familiar. Madame President? Yes! Of course! As befits my station in life. A title I was born to have. A role I was meant to play. Just think of all the laws I can enact and break. It's just too delicious. A world famous author and President with all expenses paid, of course. Yes. Madame President. And, now I can truly conquer the world! To rule with an iron fist. To crush those who oppose me. I'll need allies, of course…allies who I can eventually turn on at my slightest whim. But, whom can one trust? People are so dishonest. It's just awful!

From I, SYBIL SCHMIDLAP-SCHWAB,
Act One

GERARD: The day I was born is when the corruption began. My father took me by the hand. Together, we walked down the boulevard waving goodbye to Mama. A sunny morning that one wants to hold forever…and in a moment, it is gone… and that is forever. My father struck down by a car and killed in the prime of his manhood. It should have been me, the son, who met death that day. Nothing was ever the same. Nothing.

From DEATHDREAMER CAFE

MONTEZ: During the next four days, I suffered the torments of the dying and faced the darkness of the bottomless chasm to face the awakening shadow life of the vampire. I felt the hot breath of the vampire. The fangs were at my throat piercing the tender skin. I cried out. Again. And, again. I screamed to God almighty, but He was gone. The vampire was now my master and new god. Again, he kissed me hard on the neck. My strength was gone and would not return until I arose. The transformation from a human being to a vampire had begun. The fever grew worse. My vision was hazy. It felt as if I were lying on my back in a pit with voices and images distorted. I tasted the blood in my mouth. Was I drunk? I felt so off balance as if one side of the room were coming up at me to slap me in the face. Everything was so dark. Voices called to me from within my soul that I couldn't recognize. My death was slow in the sense of realizing that I was actually no longer living. As they carried out my body, I had the sensation of crossing a bridge. I could hear the waves splashing against the columns of the structure but could not see anything…not really. I got up to walk across the bridge. My feet made soft echoing sounds that mingled into the mist and the darkness. How strange. No other sounds could be heard except my footsteps and the rhythmic splashing of the water below. Why was I here? To recollect myself and bring that soul back into the recesses of the corpse which was being put to rest in the ground? Would I awake to forgetfulness? Was I to be my own creator? How very bitter! Every vital organ in my body felt as if it were embraced by searing hot barbed wires. Yet, I felt coldly objective toward it. I tried to move my hand in order to brush aside a tear trickling down my cheek. I couldn't move my hand. They had placed my body into the confinement of a coffin. I was buried in the cold and barren earth. I pushed my hands against the barrier that separated me from my new depraved existence. The coffin was sealed with a waxed lining. It cracked under the pressure of my hands and the dirt came rushing in. It soiled my clothes. The pine started to crack, but by no means must I damage it! (*He collapses to his knees as if actually reliving the moment.*) I was seized with panic. Bloody sweat covered my face…my body was drenched with it. And, at last, I could wipe away that tear from my cheek. I dug my way through the dirt like some animal who had been trapped by some loathsome hunter. My hands knew what to do. Faster and faster they dug through the loosening dirt. I lifted my body up and through the barrier not by mere strength but by will of the mind. My body began to "slip" through the ground until, at last, my hand reached into the night air and I was free! The night air was cold and moist as I stood upon the open grave.

From TWO VAMPIRES

GUY: Nice night outside: a full moon and stars all over the sky. Very still. Very peaceful. I'm here in this café in the middle of nowhere. I'm lost. I'm a truck driver who's lost his way. I was headed cross country on a run to Santa Ana. I'd never been to California before or even the west coast, for that matter. All my life, I've lived in New York City. It used to be a fine town… used to be. You were free to do pretty much what you wanted as long as you stayed within the law. And, now? I can't even smoke in my own truck. I have to watch every word I say lest it offends someone. I can't even state a god-damned opinion without being called on it. Whatever happened to everyone's living without whining about life? You had to earn a living and you did just that. You did what you had to do. I've been alone all my life. I go home and there's no one there. It's a one room walk up in the back of a building. I've got a nice view of the back alleyway, which is just fine by me. I kind of keep waiting for something unexpected to happen. It never does. I've got my cat…my little tabby cat, Tommy. He died last week. I'm still crying. I loved that little guy. He was old and he died peacefully in my arms and I'm grateful for that. It doesn't ease the pain. I had to leave my apartment after I buried Tommy and put him to rest. He'll always be with me. Always. Nice night outside.

THE VERY LAST STOP

Printed in the United States
By Bookmasters